CRITICAL TERMS *for* THE STUDY OF AFRICA

CRITICAL TERMS *for* THE STUDY OF AFRICA

Edited by

GAURAV DESAI
ADELINE MASQUELIER

THE UNIVERSITY OF CHICAGO PRESS
Chicago and London

The University of Chicago Press, Chicago 60637
The University of Chicago Press, Ltd., London

Published 2018
Printed in the United States of America

27 26 25 24 23 22 21 20 19 18 1 2 3 4 5

ISBN-13: 978-0-226-54883-8 (cloth)
ISBN-13: 978-0-226-54897-5 (paper)
ISBN-13: 978-0-226-54902-6 (e-book)
DOI: https://doi.org/10.7208/chicago/9780226549026.001.0001

Library of Congress Cataloging-in-Publication Data

Names: Desai, Gaurav Gajanan, editor. | Masquelier, Adeline Marie, 1960– editor.
Title: Critical terms for the study of Africa / edited by Gaurav Desai and Adeline Masquelier.
Description: Chicago : The University of Chicago Press, 2018. | Includes index.
Identifiers: LCCN 2018019723 | ISBN 9780226548838 (cloth : alk. paper) | ISBN 9780226548975 (pbk. : alk. paper) | ISBN 9780226549026 (e-book)
Subjects: LCSH: Africa.
Classification: LCC DT3 .C75 2018 | DDC 960—dc23
LC record available at https://lccn.loc.gov/2018019723

♾ This paper meets the requirements of ANSI/NISO Z39.48–1992 (Permanence of Paper).

Contents

Introduction

Adeline Masquelier and Gaurav Desai

Africa has long been represented as a featureless void—a mysterious place about which little is known but much is speculated. From the "Dark Continent" of nineteenth-century European explorers to the informational "black hole" of late-twentieth-century social theorists, outsiders have envisioned the continent as an empty landscape without people and history—a "blank" space that could be populated with all kinds of creatures dreamed up in European imaginations. Indeed, from time to time these perceptions have found quite literal expression. The eighteenth-century French mapmaker Jean Baptiste Bourguignon d'Anville, for example, inserted blank spaces on his maps to represent regions about which nothing was known. Other cartographers filled unknown regions with animals, mountains, or flamboyant lettering.

To be sure, mapmakers everywhere have depicted the world not as it is but rather as they have seen it. Maps are social constructions, and, as such, they can shed light on their makers' conscious (or unconscious) manipulation of the world while also revealing something of the political context in which they were created.

The cartographic history of the Kong Mountains—a fictitious mountain chain featured on most maps of Africa in the nineteenth century—is a case in point. The mountains first appeared on two maps drawn for Scottish explorer Mungo Park's account of his celebrated voyage to the Niger River in 1795–97. Subsequent generations of writers, including the famed British explorer Richard Burton, perpetuated the fiction of the Kong Mountains in their travelogues. Needless to say, the reports they produced were based on hearsay. While traveling in the region in 1886, the Lt. Governor of Senegal and Dependencies thus claimed to have gathered "reliable" information indicating that crossing the Kong Mountains might not be as arduous as was previously assumed. He went so far as to suggest that ostriches be used as pack animals during part of the crossing. All this might seem strange in an age of detailed satellite imagery, but it points to the long-standing persuasiveness of maps and their power to authorize particular imaginings of space—even when those imaginings are purely fanciful.

In the nineteenth century the massive expansion in cartographic production allowed a broader European public to gaze at Africa "from above." By then maps had earned a scientific respectability that made them largely impervious to criticism. The "reality" they summoned in two-dimensional form shaped the conceptual geographies of their readers. Although experts differed sometimes as to the geomorphology of the Kong Mountains, they did not question their very existence. Indeed, the mythical mountain range soon loomed large in the popular imagination as the El Dorado of West Africa. Lending credibility to these outlandish tales of hidden wealth was the unique authority of the map as a scientific device assumed to be inherently factual, accurate, and reliable. The use of precise descriptors ("blue," "snow covered," "gold rich," and so on) to describe the mountain range further consolidated the public's mental images of the Kong Mountains. So powerful was cartography's perceived hold on truth that, despite the emergence of new evidence that cast serious doubt on the existence of the Kong Mountains, for decades maps went on to depict West Africa as significantly mountainous. It was not until the end of the nineteenth century that maps of West Africa stopped featuring the mountain range. By then the colonial conquest of Africa had fully begun, facilitated by various technologies, including improved cartography. Indeed, as geographers Thomas Bassett and Philip Porter note, the disappearance of the Kong Mountains from maps boosted the progression of empire building by eliminating what Europeans had previously seen as a significant geographical impediment to trade between the Guinea coast and its hinterland.

Today, we may be tempted to chuckle at such episodes. But we should remember that we too bring our own assumptions to bear on the map of Africa. Save for a narrow strip of land in the northeast that connects the continent to Asia, Africa is surrounded by bodies of water. Yet it is routinely (and problematically) divided into North Africa and sub-Saharan Africa. According to this geographical convention, the former is seen as an extension of the Middle East on the basis of shared environmental, linguistic, and cultural characteristics, while the latter is identified as the "true" Africa. Thus, while Egypt is in the Mediterranean zone, Ethiopia belongs to sub-Saharan Africa. Such a division has important implications for the way that knowledge of the continent is mapped into distinct, area specific fields of study. Whereas scholars of Ethiopia are considered Africanists, Egypt specialists are folded into Middle Eastern studies.

The conflation of sub-Saharan Africa with "Africa proper" can be traced to the rise of modern Europe and concomitant efforts by Europeans to map race onto geography. The images of Africans that circulated in twentieth-century Europe still drew on the language of primordialism. They offered a racialized view of Africa that justified excising Northern Africa and Egypt from the rest of the continent. Racial mapping of this sort became so common that even highly regarded scholars like Fernand Braudel could assert a strong distinction between "Black Africa" and "White Africa," where Islam was the dominant tradition. The creation of "area studies" in the US in the 1950s further solidified the division between Northern and sub-Saharan Africa by overemphasizing cultural and historical differences between the two zones while downplaying their commonalities.

The exclusion of North Africa—also called the "Maghreb"—hinged on the assumption that the Sahara is a clear line that separates the region that lies north of it (North Africa) from the region that lies south of it (sub-Saharan Africa). This is another cartographic fiction. The Sahara is a vast territory that encompasses countries from both zones and, as such, it cannot be said to delimit precisely any space. Yet, it has often been conceptualized as a natural boundary between distinct territories. In the heydays of the Roman Empire, the Sahara desert was seen as forming a natural divide between Roman Africa and the mysterious hinterland beyond. To this day it continues to be popularly referred to as a "sea of sand."

In recent years, scholars have adopted a more critical approach to borders as spaces of flow. Some reject the Sahara boundary altogether. Political scientist Ali Mazrui, for example, campaigned for the rejection of the concept of sub-Saharan Africa. He insisted that the Arabian peninsula should be included as part of Africa on the basis that the divide between the two regions was a product of Western engineering (through the creation of the Suez canal) and Western monopoly over world cartography. The creation of the Organization of African Unity (later known as the African Union) in 1963 was another attempt to disrupt dominant imaginings of Africa and conceptualize it as a cohesive cartographic unit.

The study of Africa as a geographically bounded but culturally diverse entity cannot be disassociated from Europe's imperialist designs on Africa. Geography played a major role in the exploration of the continent by

European powers. Though ostensibly motivated by a quest for knowledge, those who sought to discover the Nile River's source or follow the Niger River to its outlet were acting on behalf of European commercial interests during the period when Europe was united by the desire to gain commercial access to Africa, not direct control of its territory. The subsequent carving out of the continent by rival European nations and the implementation of colonial rule impacted greatly the maps and surveys of the continent that were produced thereafter. For many the image that best sums up the late nineteenth-century scramble for Africa is that of European diplomats at the Berlin conference of 1884–85 clustered around a map of the continent as they drew the borders of the territories they claimed for their respective countries.

Africans did not wait for the arrival of Europeans on their shores to map their world. Muslims, for instance, had likely been mapping out trade routes for centuries. The geographic imagination of Africans also found expression in a multiplicity of visual patterns and processes, but since these did not fit the narrow definition of what a "map" was, they have largely been ignored by scholars (when they were not altogether displaced by European mapping technologies).

Seeking to redress this imbalance, a new crop of studies has drawn attention to the ways that Africans have graphically represented their world through mnemonic maps, body art, the layout of villages, the design of buildings, and sacred topographies. Additional efforts to trace the contested genealogy of cartographic imaginations have also produced novel understandings of how Africans have used spatial strategies to counter the power of the state, redefine community and belonging, and remap civic pluralism through appeals to locality rather than ancestry. Understanding how African people have used cartography as a form of power has necessitated a fundamental shift in the topographical imagination, a shift that could help scholars see beyond the dictates of cartographic scale and the "truth" of colonial surveys.

The logical outcome of this critique is that Africa does not exist in a vacuum. Africa has always been a part of a complex, globalized world, even if the density and spread of the networks it is enmeshed in have increased in the last several decades. To be sure, such claims are far from new. As early as 1946 W. E. B. Du Bois insisted that Africa should be seen not as a neatly bounded entity but as part of the world and the product of long-term interactions between unequal polities.

With the end of the Cold War, many wondered about the fate of African studies given that area studies was often seen to be no more than a product of the postwar US-Soviet rivalry. Following the fall of the Berlin Wall, the new mantra in the academy was to call for the end of area studies in a world which had declared, with popular historian Francis Fukuyama, the "End of History" and the ascendance of democratic governance, market economics, and neoliberalism. Certainly, Africanist and non-Africanist scholars had much to gain by forging new cross-area and trans-regional conversations. In the context of African studies in particular, the study of the Black Atlantic reopened long-standing conversations with diasporic communities and scholars. On the other side of the continent, the growing interest in the Indian Ocean and connections between Africa and the East likewise fostered tremendously rich research and ways of thinking about African peoples and spaces as part of a long history of exchange. And yet, for all these developments, the relevance and importance of area-specific knowledge never went away. As we hope will be clear to readers of this volume, the ways in which we now conceive of area studies in general, and of African studies in particular, have certainly shifted—in our estimation, in fruitful and productive ways—but giving up on the project of coming to terms with local African knowledges, interests, and priorities in the name of something called the "global" has never seemed to be a satisfactory alternative.

Furthermore, research today may be no less implicated in statist and capitalist desires than in earlier periods even though geopolitical priorities have shifted. Today the so-called war on terror, African migration "crises" in Europe, or the competition with China and India over African markets are more likely to spur extra-academic attention to Africa. But the attention, it seems, is here to stay. Regardless of where individual scholars place themselves in relation to such interests, it is imperative, we think, for Africanists—and particularly younger scholars coming into the field—to be critically engaged with both the historical trajectories of African studies as they have been practiced and the demands and pulls made on them as scholars, citizens, and activists committed to the study of a historically much abused and maligned continent.

In 1979 Australian Stuart McArthur published what he titled the Universal Corrective Map of the World—an "upside down" view of the world that challenged many people's perspective of the globe. By upending cartographic "commonsense," he made plain the profound arbitrariness of current conventions. Why, the McArthur model asked, should the Northern Hemisphere always be placed in the top half of world maps? There is nothing natural about the Northern Hemisphere always dominating the South. That convention began with Flemish cartographer Gerardus Mercator's 1569 model of the world and was reproduced throughout the centuries despite the fact that it significantly inflates North America and Europe and diminishes Africa. The fact that cartographic conventions locate Africa at the bottom tells us something about how mapmakers use the persuasive power of what J. B. Harley has called "subliminal geometry" to shape people's knowledge of the world.

Conceptually, this collection of essays is animated by the same spirit that inspired McArthur's map. Scholars have started to reflect on what it might mean to write from the Global South and to turn conventional models upside down. The contributors to our volume cover thematic territory previously charted by other scholars but with an eye to finding ways to shift the center of gravity of previous analyses. Our collective interest has been to make a case for the ways in which an engagement with Africa has allowed us to sharpen, rethink, modulate, and sometimes jettison the conceptual frames with which we have studied Africa's pasts, presents, and futures.

The terms we have collected in this volume are meant to both reflect the current state of African studies and to push the field in new directions. Our choice of terms in this volume is not meant to be comprehensive. Rather, we find that the terms we have chosen, some expected—such as "colonialism," "labor," and "narrative"—and others less so—such as "bondage," "evidence," and "design"—are good for Africanists "to think with." Any such lists are ultimately subject to ongoing debate, and what we have chosen not to include will potentially raise as many eyebrows as what we have included. So, for instance, some might be surprised not to find the term "history" on the list; we have chosen instead to go with the term "evidence" since we think it has both a broader as well as more focused reach in terms of coming to terms with "what happened." As Luise White shows, a focus on "evidence" allows for a wonderfully fruitful meditation on how material and social facts become evidence and how archaeological, oral, and archival sources can be brought together to narrate meaningful histories. Likewise, we have preferred to include the term "bondage" as opposed to "slavery" since as Gwyn Campbell's chapter argues, it allows for a more capacious grasp of various kinds of unfree labor—serfdom, indenture, slavery—than a conventional accounting of slavery might. By bringing in the historical circumstances of Indian Ocean Africa, and by also insisting on more contemporary forms of bondage and human trafficking, the chapter allows us to both check in place a long-standing Atlanticist emphasis on African studies as well as a tendency to think of bondage solely as a thing of the past. After much debate and deliberation, we have chosen to include the term "witchcraft." We are mindful of the debates that surround this term, but we hope that our inclusion of this term will allow for the debate to be staged in the classroom.

The choice of a term like "design" has the virtue of allowing for a discussion of multiple material forms (textiles, sculpture, architecture, tyre marks, fractals) which may not have been easily brought together under an alternate term. Likewise, rather than a chapter on a specific genre of performance such as music or theater, we have chosen to include a chapter on "performance" as a practice and as a process. This allows, as Tsitsi Jaji shows us, a discussion not only of an event such as the 1966 First World Festival of Black Arts in Dakar, but also of the performance of gender and the performance of the state. Some might find it objectionable that we have no dedicated chapter here on film and the study of media. Yet media analysis plays an important role in many of the chapters, most notably in Stephanie Newell's reading of the narrative of cyberspace and internet scammers but also in Francis B. Nyamnjoh's critical reading of an ad campaign by the South African restaurant chain Nandos. We should admit that part of what has made the process of selecting the terms not only intellectually exciting but also pleasurable has been the debate that we have had with each other and in many ways with the contributors who have written for the volume. As readers will note, some contributors fully embrace the term they write on, others are more circumspect in their relation with the term—offering other corollary or competing terms as possibilities in their stead, and a couple stage a covert insurrection against the term! As editors, we have not only allowed for this range of authorial positioning, but actively encouraged it. Our project is ultimately not wedded to the terms themselves but rather to the energies and debates they inspire and generate.

Rather than provide an outline of each chapter here, we want instead to notice some general patterns and tendencies. Almost all the chapters in the volume consider the long legacies of non-African discursive and representational practices that have engaged with the African continent. If "representation" itself is not a critical term we engage (as do several other volumes in this series) it is because issues of the representation of Africa, as Jemima Pierre's opening chapter on the racialization of "Africa/African" shows, are all pervasive in discussions of the continent. The role of outsiders in both describing and prescribing African practices whether of cosmology and religion, "customary" laws, state governance, citizenship, gender and sexual identities, or vernacular orthographies has been a major factor in the continent's history and it continues to make its mark on both academic and extra-academic accounts of the subject. Another point of connection between many of the chapters is their emphasis on the contradictions of the respective term as it was thought of and applied in African contexts. So, for instance, John L. and Jean Comaroff point to the contradictions of the colonial project which was intended to help Africans modernize but did so by reifying traditions and customs that were often quite dynamic; or, for instance, Simon Gikandi points out how the project of modernity in Africa relied not on the Enlightenment idea of a secular, post-religious rationality but rather on Christian missionary practice. The chapter on governance by Brenda Chalfin and Omolade Adunbi shows how the pursuit of good governance and the structural adjustment programs associated with it actually resulted in rather bad forms of governance and economic depravity. Rogaia Mustafa Abusharaf likewise points to the contradictions of humanitarian projects which in the urge to "save" Africans often pit them against one another and rely on the same civilizational tropes associated with the project of colonialism. And finally, by the end of his chapter on spirit, Matthew Engelke invites us to consider whether the term ought to be jettisoned altogether.

An emphasis on the quotidian aspects of African lives as opposed to the larger structural institutions in which they participate is shared by many of the contributors here. Thus, for instance, in his chapter on gender and sexuality, Marc Epprecht foregrounds the flexible manner in which Africans have negotiated gender norms and the strictures on heteronormativity. Deborah Durham discusses how "youth" gets defined in contingent and relative ways by members of a community even as the state might define "youth" in more stringent ways. Peter Geschiere shares Francis B. Nyamnjoh's advocacy of flexible citizenship and asks how and why discussions of belonging seem to have shifted in the 1980s from earlier, more open forms of identification to narrower considerations of autochthony.

And in her chapter on health, Susan Reynolds Whyte foregrounds how, by negotiating their understanding of accountability, connections, and care, Africans engage in efforts to overcome disease and strive for general well-being even when the government's health care system fails them.

In her chapter on liberation, Elisabeth McMahon insists that even while it was taken up by various actors in Africa and its diaspora, in so far as it was rooted in the Western idea of individual liberty, the concept, for all the work that it has done, nevertheless retains a Eurocentric legacy. As such, she includes in her chapter a discussion not only of liberation movements such as the abolition of slavery and the independence movements on the continent but also a discussion of epistemological liberation as advocated by the Kenyan writer Ngũgĩ wa Thiong'o. Even before embarking on this project of putting together a volume of critical terms for African studies, we have been humbled by the limitations of our project. For all the talk of the need for Africa-centered scholarship, perspectives, and epistemologies, it is sobering that the critical debates that continue to take place, at least in the circles of the academy if not in the streets of Nairobi or Dakar, are in the ex-colonial—though now, in many cases, Africanized—European languages. As a thought experiment we have often wondered—what might a volume such as this look like, what different directions and turns would it take, if the critical terms assembled were drawn from African languages? While we pose this as a challenge and a call to others more competent than ourselves in assembling such a project, we are encouraged that more than one of our contributors engages in a discussion of relevant terms in African languages and what they might have to offer in terms of a critique, juxtaposition, or enhancement of the English terms we employ here. So, for instance, Jane I. Guyer brings in Shona terms via the work of Clapperton Mavhunga, Suzanne Preston Blier refers to Yoruba and Zulu terms related to design, Simon Gikandi refers to Julius Nyerere's preference of the Kiswahili term *Maendeleo* for development, and Derek R. Peterson discusses the term for "culture" in Kikuyu and Yoruba.

Besides such noticeable connections among the chapters, we have found in our classroom discussions of the chapters with our students that students are quick to make connections between groups or pairs of chapters collected here. Many of our students found it useful to discuss Patrick Manning's chapter on mobility, which debunks still circulated notions of a static Africa by historicizing African mobility across time, along with the chapters on belonging and citizenship. Others found Kamari M. Clarke's discussion of structural violence, the violence of the "normal," and more recent legal norms to establish individual accountability to war criminals and dictatorial leaders to be a provocative companion piece to Adam Ashforth's chapter on discussions of violence and accusations of witchcraft. Yet others found it useful to read and think through Joseph Slaughter and Jennifer Wenzel's discussion of the Hegelian negation of Africa and their own critical questioning of what *counts* as theory in the first place with Jemima Pierre's history of the boundary disputes within African studies. Students found that the chapter on value coauthored by Leonard Wantchekon and Paul-Aarons Ngomo and the chapter on environment by Maano Ramutsindela both addressed important elements of social justice in the economic and environmental spheres. But perhaps the most memorable and interventionist response was when our students, on the one hand rightly disturbed by the colonialist representational politics of humanitarianism as outlined by Rogaia Mustafa Abusharaf, but on the other hand unwilling to let go of the impulse to help others who might well need the help, insisted that we go back to the drawing board and recast the chapter on humanitarianism as a chapter on reparations. Their logic was that if it is true that many of the crises that now call for humanitarian interventions in Africa were rooted in the structures and practices of colonialism, then contemporary efforts to solve them must be seen not as acts of charity toward helpless victims but rather as reparations to societies that had been destroyed by the colonizers in the first place.

Whatever one finally makes of our students' proposition, it should be clear that the chapters in this volume have proven to engage them and hopefully make them more critically aware of the ways in which Africa and Africans have been, and continue to be, represented both in scholarly studies and the world at large. And so, while we anticipate debates on the inclusions and exclusions in this volume, we hope that, collectively, the twenty-five terms that we have gathered here will give readers a sufficiently diverse picture of the current state of African studies, the key concepts that drive it, and the potential for more engagement with their interstices.

Acknowledgment: We would like to thank Elisabeth McMahon for her comments on an earlier draft of this chapter.

Suggested Readings

Alpers, Edward A., and Allen F. Roberts. 2002. "What Is African Studies? Some Reflections." *African Issues* 30 (2): 11–18.

Bassett, Thomas J., and Philip W. Porter. 1991. "From the Best Authorities: The Mountains of Kong in the Cartography of West Africa." *Journal of African History* 32(3): 367–413.

Bates, Robert H., V. Y. Mudimbe, and Jean O'Barr, eds. 1993. *Africa and the Disciplines: The Contributions of Research in Africa to the Social Sciences and Humanities*. Chicago: University of Chicago Press.

Brantlinger, Patrick. 1985. "Victorians and Africans: The Genealogy of the Myth of the Dark Continent." *Critical Inquiry* 12 (1): 166–203.

Comaroff, Jean, and John L. Comaroff. 2012. *Theory from the South: Or, How Euro-America Is Evolving Toward Africa*. New York: Routledge.

Fabian, Johannes. 2000. *Out of Our Minds: Reason and Madness in the Exploration of Central Africa*. Berkeley: University of California Press.

Mazrui, Ali A. 1980. *The African Condition: A Political Diagnosis*. Cambridge: Cambridge University Press.

Mbembe, Achille, and Sarah Nuttall. 2004. "Writing the World from an African Metropolis." *Public Culture* 16 (3): 347–72.

Mudimbe, V. Y. 1988. *The Invention of Africa: Gnosis, Philosophy, and the Order of Knowledge*. Bloomington: Indiana University Press.

Said, Edward. 1979. *Orientalism*. New York: Vintage.

Tilley, Helen. 2011. *Africa as a Living Laboratory: Empire, Development, and the Problem of Scientific Knowledge, 1870–1950*. Chicago: University of Chicago Press.

1 AFRICA/AFRICAN

Jemima Pierre

When Africa is mentioned in the public sphere, it is often either described as in "crisis" or "rising." Most often it is a combination of the two: Africa has the *potential* to rise if it can ever get itself out of crisis. These seemingly contradictory narratives are not new or surprising; they are part of a long history, intellectual and popular, of confirming the alterity of Africa.

The Africa in crisis narrative is currently ubiquitous. War. Poverty. Failed states. Corruption. Genocide. Terrorism. Disease. The unending circulation of tales of crisis in Africa is fueled as much by actual events as by the world's predictable and prejudiced response to phenomena on the continent. Thus, at the height of the global panic over the recent Ebola outbreak in Liberia, Sierra Leone, and Guinea in the fall of 2014, the US magazine *Newsweek* ran a lead story with the following headline: "A Back Door for Ebola: Smuggled Bushmeat Could Spark a U.S. Epidemic," with a cover photo of a large chimpanzee. The authors used pseudoscientific theories to accentuate this moment of African "crisis" by claiming that Ebola was at the door of the US. Doing so required them to implicate the African continent as a place of endemic and contagious disease (and Africans as disease carriers) and to also affirm the centuries-old stereotypes of Africans' unique link to primates.

This trope is not new, of course. Primates, in general, are the stand in, variously, for Africa, its people, and its people's presumed natural savagery/nobility. As Winthrop Jordan demonstrates, late eighteenth-century English writings easily drew direct connections between apes and Africans, a connection no doubt aided by the relentless literary imagery of "beastlike men of Africa." At the height of the transatlantic slave trade and African enslavement, there was the need for Europeans to point to natural and "*sexual* association of apes with Negroes" in order to further separate Africans from themselves and, ultimately, humanity.

The *Newsweek* story articulated what had been clear in the global and local medical response to the Ebola crisis: the established inferior position of African life—that is *Black* African life. Accordingly, the other less prominent response to the medical crisis was the simultaneous valuation of non-African life (that is, white and Western life) and devaluation of African life. Indeed, by the time of the *Newsweek* story, Ebola had already arrived in the US as two white missionaries infected in Liberia were given an experimental drug and flown to the US for treatment. Another white American was flown to Nebraska. By then, the disease was already ravaging the West African country, having infected thousands of Liberians, including health workers, and by late July, killing scores. As African medical workers died, including several prominent physicians (such as Drs. Olivet Buck and Sheik Umar Khan), many recognized and decried the racial disparity in the treatment of African doctors and health care workers, compared to non-Black missionaries and health workers (Giorgis 2014).

The Ebola story is a useful synecdoche for the long-standing historical, popular, and even academic construction of Africa. It is also one for understanding the significance of Africa's Blackness. The crisis-ridden continent both cannot help itself in promulgating crisis, nor can it save itself. In come Africa's numerous "saviors." Such "saviors" have to be non-African, usually white, and their participation in "saving" the African continent depends directly on the trope of (Black) Africa in crisis. Novelist Teju Cole (2014), who coined the term "White Savior Industrial Complex," notes in this regard: "Africa serves as a backdrop for white fantasies of conquest and heroism. From the colonial project to *Out of Africa* to *The Constant Gardener* and Kony 2012, Africa has to provide a space onto which white egos can conveniently be projected."

Alongside numerous forecasts of Africa as ongoing disaster, we also have another narrative from some corners of the Western economic and political world that Africa is "rising." This is epitomized most fervently by the recent headline from the conservative *Economist* magazine: "Africa Rising: The Hopeful Continent." But it was the same magazine whose May 13, 2000, issue had a solid black cover with an outline of the map of Africa inside of which was a young man holding a large weapon with the screaming headline, "The Hopeless Continent." Although the accompanying article was focused on Sierra Leone, it equated that country with the entire continent while arguing that Africans are "buried in their cultures" and, therefore, exceptional violence such as "rape, cannibalism and amputation have been common" (2000). The "hopeful" take on the African continent does not deviate much from established orthodoxy, as we are reminded, "optimism about Africa has to be taken in small doses . . . [as] corruption, strife will not disappear overnight" (2011). Nevertheless, the "Africa rising" narrative is primarily for the benefit of the Western business elite and governments whose control of and investments in Africa's resources need the occasional justification. (One may note that this "Africa Rising" narrative is distinct from the "African renaissance" one espoused by former South African president Thabo Mbeki. Mbeki's call for recognizing this African renaissance came in the triumphant post-Apartheid moment and the consequent triumphant calls for African self-determination.)

It is significant that those engaged in teaching and writing about the African continent often begin with a refutation of "myths and stereotypes" about the African continent. But to what avail if the discussion does not take into account what Michel-Rolph Trouillot calls the "enunciative context" of these representations and narratives? For Africa, the context is a violent colonial encounter and its aftermath. It is a long history of enslavement and conquest and the establishment of sets of racial hierarchies that depended upon the debasement of the continent's peoples. The enunciative context of enslavement and colonialism is a physical, structural, and epistemological violence. This context has created the material conditions that shape Africa's political, social, and economic positioning within the world. It has also created forms of knowledge production, archives, and ideologies that, in turn, naturalize this historical and material condition into imperial stereotypes that serve as its justification. The resulting understanding of Africa—and the idea of Africans—is one that reinforces the racial and cultural logic of the imperial context. Race and racialization—specifically, the construction and maintenance of Africa's "Blackness" (and, importantly, Europe's "whiteness")—then, are key determinants in understanding the meaning of Africa and "Africans."

What Is Africa? Who Is an African?

The racialization of the continent has often involved a geographical split. As Amadou-Mahtar M'Bow pointed out in introducing UNESCO's *General History of Africa*, historically, "emphasis was laid on everything likely to lend credence to the idea that a split had existed, from time immemorial, between a 'white Africa' and a 'black Africa'" (1981, xvii). While the explicit racial discourse surrounding this geographical-cum-racial division of the African continent is not as prevalent today, the distinction remains a central and persistent aspect of contemporary thinking, research, writing, and politics about Africa. Academic scholarship continues to maintain, for example, the divergent focus on "MENA" (Middle East and North African) studies as often contrasted to—or indifferent to—African studies. A cursory review of recent political events clearly reveals this point. Thus, in both the mass media and academic discussions around the 2011 Arab Spring, there was hardly any mention of the African continent—even as these uprisings occurred in Tunisia, Egypt, and Libya, respectively.

Historian Ghislaine Lydon points out that it took a long time for scholars and colonists to erect the Saharan divide and fabricate the idea of two "Africas." But even before scholars took up this project, religious leaders had already laid the foundations. Both the Arab and the European conquerors of Africa were first influenced by, and in turn helped sediment, the "Negro-Hamitic" hypothesis. This hypothesis stems from the biblical story of Noah's curse of his son, Ham, with servitude. While the original sources of this tale did not generally reference race, later interpretations of the curse presented Ham as "Black," linking the idea of blackness to servitude and to a racial hierarchy. The Hamitic hypothesis was disseminated through the three main external religious traditions that have impacted the African continent—Judaism, Christianity, and Islam (El Hamel 2014).

The link of a presumed inferiority to racial Blackness served to not only erect a geo-racial barrier on the African continent, but to also justify the already established trans-Saharan slave trade and the beginnings of European conquest of the African continent. By the fourteenth century, "racial stereotypes of black Africans were conspicuous in Arabic sources" (El Hamel 2014, 72). They were conspicuous in European "classical" texts as well. By the time of the Arab invasions and occupation of the northern part of the continent in the seventh century, ideas about racial Blackness contributed to the erection of the Saharan desert as an ideological, civilizational, cultural, religious, and racial barrier. It must be noted that a few Islamic scholars disputed the Judeo-Christian—and by now Islamic—view about Blackness and the curse of Ham. The Maghrebi fourteenth-century scholar, Ibn Khaldūn, for example, argued that it was hot climate and not a religious curse that caused the "Black" skin of Africans. Yet he also concurred with other Islamic writers that Western Africa, Sudan (the *Bilād al-Sūdān*), and the geographical area south of the Sahara was the "land of Blacks." After the spread of Islam in the northern part of Africa, certain

Arab Muslim scholars began demarcating the African continent into distinct zones that had explicit racial inferences. Some of these Arab Muslim communities over time "came to label themselves as 'whites' (*bidān*), and began writing about theirs as 'a territory of the whites' '(*trāb al-bidān*)'" (Lydon 2015, 8).

But as Paul Zeleza notes, the North African/sub-Saharan split "got its epistemic and ideological imprimatur with the emergence of Eurocentricism following the rise of modern Europe" through the transatlantic slave trade and, later, the conquest of the African continent. While many point to anthropologist C. G. Seligman's *Races of Africa* as the key text for establishing this racialized distinction (his thesis: "the Hamites—who are 'Europeans'—belong to the same great branch of mankind as the 'Whites'"), the first edition of that text was not published until 1930 (Harris 1987, 24). Others point to the French scholar, Émile-Félix Gautier whose 1939 book, *l'Afrique blanche* "equated the Sahara to an 'ethnic partition' (*cloison ethnique*) separating the black African from the white African, and . . . [assimilating] the latter to the 'White Mediterranean'" (Lydon 2015, 10). These works, however, only articulated the shift that had occurred in Europe's engagement with the African continent—and the Negro-Hamite hypothesis alongside the consolidation of European whiteness.

By the early 1900s, the Hamitic Hypothesis had taken a unique turn from its original conception of Ham as cursed with racial blackness and servitude. Hamites were now European, and white, and the sole carriers of civilization and culture to the African continent. This sharp shift in thinking occurred through an accumulated set of historical, political, and intellectual developments. The expansion of the transatlantic trade in Africans, the entrenchment of slavery in the New World, and the struggle among European nations for global hegemony that would eventually lead to formal colonial control of the African continent (as well as Asia), all worked to further sediment racist attitudes toward Africans. At the same time the emergence and consolidation of racial science worked to justify the exploitation and dehumanization of Africans, on the continent and abroad. But it was not until Napoleon Bonaparte's invasion of Egypt in 1798, however, that we see intensification of European intellectual investment in the racial division of the continent. Napoleon traveled to Egypt with a large number of archaeologists, engineers, and other scientists to study Egyptian history and culture. This scientific expedition yielded numerous studies and publications covering every aspect of Egyptian culture and its people. Not only was Egypt's civilization said to be much older than

European scientists had assumed, but the foundation of Western civilization was to be found there as well. But because Egypt was in Africa, the land of the "inferior" Negroes, and because Negro-Hamites were thought to be Egyptian (a fact which many of the early French scholars ironically affirmed), this new knowledge meant a renewed effort to construct Egypt as white (Diop 1974).

In the context of the transatlantic slave trade and European empire making, the quick ascent of French—and later, European—Egyptology was the "attempt to prove in some way that the Egyptians were not Negroes" (Sanders 1969, 525). Thus, the insistence that Egyptians were white and "Caucasoid"—or just not Black or Negro—served as the basis for the new Hamitic hypothesis which argued either that both ancient and modern Egyptians were Hamites, or that white Hamitic outsiders brought civilization to the African continent. The new Hamitic hypothesis had a double function. On the one hand, it further racialized the idea of civilization as "white" (and European). On the other hand, it racialized "Africanness" as "Blackness" and therefore as lacking civilization and history. As Kamugisha contends, "The status and nature of 'blackness' here are important, as this is little more than another way of saying that ancient Egypt is not an African civilization, despite its location in Africa" (2003, 42). Thus, the point was not only to demonstrate that Egypt was not "Black" but also to show that it was not "African." For, to be "Negro" (or "Black") was to be "African," and to be "African" was to be "Negro" (or "Black"). Such tautology not only had the effect of removing Egypt from Africa, it also insisted on the racial/biological and cultural unity of the rest of non-Hamite or "Black Africa."

Immanuel Wallerstein reminds us that it would not matter who the Egyptians were had it not been such an obsession during the period of European colonialism. Egypt was the key site for the "invention of 'white Africa'" (Lydon 2015, 8) and the enduring racial separation of the African continent. This developed throughout various European schools of thought and was entrenched in European epistemologies, particularly the French and British, whose colonial ventures on the northern part of the African continent depended on it. The French, for example, deployed this "white Africa" formulation in the administration of its colonies. While France lost Egypt to the British, it managed to take over Algeria by 1830 (and by 1885, a group of Western European nations met at the Berlin Conference to carve up the rest of the African continent). But even as France sought to build an African empire, this empire depended upon the racial distinction between the "north" and the rest of Africa. Thus, Algeria, and later Morocco and Tunisia, were part of "white Africa" and designated as the extension of France, despite their large Muslim populations, long Arab legacy, and the presence of indigenous Black populations. This did not mean, of course, that North Africans did not also suffer dehumanizing racialization. Rather, this was a distinct process of racialization inasmuch as colonies in the north were considered—and constructed as—non-Black (ostensibly erasing the history and presence of the indigenous Black population of North Africa). A clear example of this is the way that French colonial rule distinguished between Arabs and "Blacks" (or "Africans") through both its political and juridical practices. French colonial authorities passed a decree in 1911 to prohibit spoken Arabic throughout their administration in "black" Africa, starting in courthouses (Lydon 2015, 11). In its intense fixation on Islamic resistance to its rule (and presumed Islamic radicalism), French politicians and scholars also measured degree of radicalization based on race, and particular constructions of Blackness ("Sudanese Islam . . . has the advantage of tending to lose its fanatical character in measure of the increase in the black color"). Colonial authorities and scholars inevitably distinguished between "Arab Islam" and "Black Islam" (or "African Islam," depending on context). Black or African Islam was deemed inferior to Arab Islam, and while Islamic culture, and its Arab practitioners, were considered to lag behind Western (white) civilization, they were seen to be more advanced than "fetishistic" Black African ones (Triaud 2000). African Islam was "ethnicized" and "tribalized," and ceased to "be a historic agent while waiting for its final assimilation to civilization" (174).

This production of African Blackness is fundamental to colonial ideology and practice and it has a long reach, as we see in the ways that scholars continue to lament ongoing racist representations of Africa and Africans. It is also a production that has been consistently violent—physically, culturally, politically, and epistemologically—and has depended on a near complete dehumanization of the racialized-as-Black African subject/object. Thus, just as French colonial policy and practice distinguished between Black/African and Arab Islam, and therefore between its colonies in the north and Western Africa, British African colonial policy also depended on constructions of racial difference. Under indirect rule, Britain deployed legal justification to consolidate the various ethno-cultural groupings as racialized "Natives" as distinct from (racialized-as-white) "European," and established practices, from residential racial segregation to the demotion of African elites from their professional jobs/positions to the aiding of business monopolies that actively displaced local entrepreneurs in favor of European and Levantine companies, among other practices. However inchoate European colonial power may have been, it nevertheless erected a solid racial edifice for the construction of "African Blackness" to justify the large-scale atrocities committed against the continent's populations. Forced labor, concentration camps, segregation, land theft, torture, genocide—all that depended upon not only the need to pacify subject populations, but also to uphold the belief in the inferiority of Blacks. Thus, the violent experiences of Southern Africa's Saartjie Baartman—a young Khoikhoi woman exhibited in European "human zoos" and whose body was dissected and analyzed and helped shape European racial science—the brutalization and murder of ten million Congolese by King Leopold's Belgian agents, the genocide of the Herero and Nama by Germany, the violent British repression against the Kikuyu resistance (known derisively as "Mau Mau"), Portuguese forced labor and torture in Angola and Mozambique; all are but articulations of these racialist interpretations of Africans.

The North-sub-Saharan African divide was never accidental, but constitutive of the racialized historical, philosophical, anthropological, cultural and political rendering of the African continent. The eruption of renewed debates about Egypt and its racial origins in the 1980s and 1990s only confirms this reality. Martin Bernal's publication of the three-volume *Black Athena*, which argued for the need to rethink Greek civilization as directly influenced by Egyptian and Phoenician societies and, more controversially, that Egypt was African (and undeniably "Black"), created a firestorm of protest from the US academy, in particular. Bernal's publication, which also complemented the rise of what would be known as "Afrocentrism," received much condemnation for its claims about the "Africanness" of Egypt. Yet, Bernal only reaffirmed the scholarship of African scholars such as Cheikh Anta Diop and Theophile Obenga, which dates back to the 1960s and 1970s and asserted Africanness of Egypt and the Egyptian influence on other African civilizations. And Diop's work is also part of an even longer tradition of "vindicationist" scholarship by Africans and people of African descent, such as Edward Blyden, Amy Jacques and Marcus Garvey, W. E. B. Du Bois, and Carter G. Woodson, among others, who sought to valorize the African past against white supremacist constructions of Africa and Africans. Diop, whose work was completely ignored by the Western academy, roundly critiqued the ongoing need for some Western scholars to separate Egypt from the rest of Africa and to "try in vain to find a White origin for Egyptian civilization" (1974, 45). But beyond the critique was

Diop's significant contribution to challenging the underpinning of racialization of Africans. It seems that Diop understood "that not all Africans are alike, while remaining African rather than members of another 'race' or a 'mixture' of races" (Kamugisha 2003, 34). Thus, the backlash leveled at both Diop (along with Diop's students) and Bernal seemed to suggest that it was the "Blackness" of Egyptians that offended scholars the most. Indeed, for many of Bernal and Diop's opponents, "it seems enough to cast doubt on the 'blackness' of the Egyptians, in order circuitously to call into question whether they were indeed 'African'" (Kamugisha 2003, 45–46).

Here, then, is the predicament of understanding "Africa." It would not be an exaggeration to say that the "Africa" we know does not exist outside the legacies of slavery and imperialism, Arab and European white supremacy, racialization, and, most importantly, Blackness. It is this reality that drives the "highly racialized" nature of *how* Africa is studied, what scholar Mahmood Mamdani decries as "Bantu Studies": "The meaning of Africa would change with the beginning of white control. Africa would cease to be the entire continent. North Africa would become part of the Middle East, considered civilized, even if just barely. White-controlled Africa in the south would be considered an exception. . . . Africa . . . would refer geographically to equatorial Africa, and socially to Black Africa, or Bantu Africa, or Negro Africa" (1998).

African Studies

Given that the modern study of Africa and of Africans developed outside of Africa through imperial structures, frictions, and contradictions, it is necessary to interrogate not a real or material "Africa," but the uses to which "Africa" has been put. In the introduction to their 1999 edited volume, *Out of One, Many Africas*, editors William G. Martin and Michael O. West explore three distinct traditions of African studies: "Africanist," "continental," and "transcontinental." The "Africanist" tradition brings together the European and North American studies of Africa that begin with European colonial rule of the continent and expand in the post–World War II period with the elevation of North American Africanists. Martin and West argue, however, that this tradition supplanted, indeed marginalized, the much older, yet often unacknowledged, "transcontinental" one. This marginalization is linked to what is seemingly a general racial division of labor that structured the rise of US African studies (Armory 1997). The transcontinental tradition of the study of Africa emerged in the African diaspora and can be traced to the end of the nineteenth and beginning of the twentieth century, through the work of scholars of African descent in the Americas. Indeed, historically black colleges and universities (HBCUs) were the first US institutions of higher learning to introduce African studies into the curriculum—with an explicit goal of "vindicating" Africa and its people from their inferior status as "savage" and "uncivilized." Within this tradition, "Africa" also extends to the diaspora, as the histories of enslavement and racial terror similarly position communities of African descent in the global world order. Meanwhile, the "continental tradition"—which is made up of African scholars on the continent—does not emerge until the post-independence period. Martin and West contend that this tradition is concerned with the "promotion of indigenous paradigms and intellectual networks, a rejection of Africanist generalizations, and an immersion in the concrete problems and conditions of the continent" (1999, 16).

This configuration of the landscape of African studies is not universal among those who study Africa, and that has much to do with the cultural politics of knowledge making within unequal global contexts and relations. For the British and French in particular, colonialism structured the study—and epistemic construction—of Africa and Africans. And while the French had already established the study of Egypt and a presumed non-Black Northern Africa at the close of the nineteenth century, it had a *Société des Africanistes* by 1930 and a "French Africanist" school by the 1950s (Coquery-Vidrovitch 1999, 40–41). The role of anthropology, criticized as a handmaiden to colonialism, must be pointed out here as the discipline's development depended directly on its theories culled from research for colonial rule. As the early "science of race," anthropology was particularly responsible for giving "scientific" credence to racial theories of white superiority and Black (and nonwhite) inferiority. The US "Africanist" study of Africa, on the other hand, emerges out of Cold War politics and the establishment of area studies. Significantly, the Title VI (initially known as "Title VI of the National Defense Education Act" to fund stronger language capacity and area studies) grants and foundation support have greatly impacted the study of Africa in the US. The consequence of this impact continues to be debated, but some of this tradition's clear epistemic distinctions are: specific focus on "Africa south of the Sahara;" investment in a wide variety of analytical and theoretical approaches where the goal is to "fill the map" with basic knowledge about Africa (Robinson 2004, 140); and a general convergence of intellectual production and Western (the US, in particular) political goals.

For many, US Africanist studies begins with the work of anthropologist Melville Herskovits. Herskovits conceptualized a "Black Africa" (and, in particular, West Africa), with a cultural influence extending to formerly enslaved communities of African descendants—the African diaspora. He and his students traced the degrees of "Africanisms" in the diaspora as Africa and African descendants in the New World. The Herskovitsian influence remains prevalent in some circles of African studies and African diaspora studies, even while current popular trends in African diaspora studies argue against the idea of Africanisms as racial essentialism and instead advocate a *delinking* of the continent from the diaspora as remedy. What has emerged within a particular postmodernist trend in African diaspora studies since the early 1990s and the publication of Paul Gilroy's *The Black Atlantic* is a focus on "Black identity formation" that seeks to move beyond presumed cultural and racial affinities to the African continent. Instead, the idea is that such Black—rather than "African"—identity is always already constructed, forged though the experiences of slavery and racial terror (in the Western Hemisphere, and not in Africa, ironically). What has driven this trend is a critique of a strand of "Afrocentrism" that emerged in the 1980s with the prominence of African American scholar Molefi Asante. It is a critique that reveals the struggle over the meaning of Africa—Asante's brand of Afrocentrism makes the claim to an "African Cultural System," as what links Africa and its communities of descendants abroad. This African Cultural System, which implies that all "Africans" (at home and abroad) have the "same cosmological sensibilities," actually recalls Herskovits's African cultural continuities formulation. The more prominent responses to this understanding of Afrocentrism have led many who conduct research on the African diaspora to, however unwittingly, move away from any engagement with the African continent, historical or otherwise.

African Diaspora studies has other enduring trends, those that Martin and West refer to as the (often marginalized) "transcontinental tradition." Here we must turn to the claim of anthropologist St. Clair Drake that African diaspora studies was an aspect of Pan-Africanism. Both a political and intellectual project, Pan-Africanism sought to expose the similar conditions of Black communities throughout the world. Invoked at the beginning of the twentieth century by a group of intellectuals, professionals, and politicians from the Caribbean, North America, and the African continent, Pan-Africanism was dedicated to the liberation of worldwide Black populations, calling for the end of racism in the post-emancipation communities of the Americas, and colonialism and imperialism on the African continent. After World War II, the center of the movement shifted to the African continent, as it struggled for independence from colonialism. For many, this led to a shift in political strategy, a "continental" Pan-Africanism, that was focused more on continental unity and less on global (racial) "Black" emancipation (Drake 1982). Yet, even this focus on continental unity did not stop the calls for global Black emancipation. Along with its complement, the francophone African-led Négritude movement, Pan-Africanism inspired the first and second World Black Festival of Arts and Culture (Dakar 1966 and Nigeria 1977), which celebrated "Black and African" culture and civilization and advocated self-determination.

It is important to note, nevertheless, that despite this seeming shift to the African continent, groups of African diaspora scholars continue this trend of detailing the "African presence" far and wide. And while African diaspora studies focuses primarily on African-descended populations in the Americas, a number of other studies expand this geography, exploring the "African" communities in Asia and the Indian World (Harris 2003), in the Mediterranean (Hunwick and Powell 2002); and more recently, in terms of postcolonial African migrants to Eurocapitalist centers. (The relatively new field of trans-Saharan studies is also engaged in the ongoing work of redefining the meaning of Africa through the excavation, and reconstruction, of unknown histories. Unfortunately, much of this work rarely engages, much less cites, the African scholars and scholars of African descent who made similar claims much earlier, or the contemporary scholarship produced by a new generation of African academics.)

Conclusion

The invention of Africa, the idea of Africa, the definition of Africa, the study of Africa—all depend on a particular trajectory of power and knowledge production, one that also demands the denial of agency of so-called Africans to define themselves. While there have always been movements emerging from within the African continent as well as communities of African descent abroad (all contested and varied) it is also not lost on most that, in the context of a racialized and unequal global order, "counter-narrative is the only weapon they have" (Adesanmi 2013). Indeed, without its "colonial conditions of possibility," the epistemological and political project that is Africa "would hardly exist in its current form" (Desai 2001, 98). To understand the meaning of Africa—and to know what it means to be "African"—is to recognize this sobering reality.

Suggested Readings

Amadiume, Ifi. 1997. *Re-Inventing Africa: Matriarchy, Religion, Culture*. New York: Zed.

Davidson, Basil. 1995. *Africa in History*. New York: Touchstone Books.

Dubois, W. E. B. 1965. *The World and Africa: An Inquiry into the Part which Africa Has Played in World History*. New York: International Publishers, Co., Inc.

Emeagwali, Gloria. 2002. *Africa and the Academy: Challenging Hegemonic Discourses on Africa*. Trenton, NJ: Africa World Press.

Esedebe, P. Olisanwuche. 1994. *Pan-Africanism: The Idea and Movement, 1776–1963*. Washington, DC: Howard University Press.

Grovogui, Siba. 1997. *Sovereigns, Quasi-Sovereigns, and Africans: Race and Self-Determination in International Law*. Minneapolis: University of Minnesota Press.

Harris, Joseph, ed. 1982. *Global Dimensions of the African Diaspora*. Washington, DC: Howard University Press.

Imam, Ayesha, Anima Mama, and Fatou Sow, eds. 2000. *Engendering African Social Sciences*. Dakar: CODESRIA.

James, C. L.R. 1995. *A History of Pan-African Revolt*. Introduction by Robin D. G. Kelley. Chicago: C. H. Kerr, 1995. Originally published in 1938 as *A History of Negro Revolt*.

Mazrui, Ali. 1986. *The Africans: A Triple Heritage*. New York: Little Brown & Co.

Ntarangwi, Mwenda, David Mills, and Mustafa Babiker. 2006. *African Anthropologies: History, Critique and Practice*. Dakar: CODESRIA.

Rodney, Walter. 1972. *How Europe Underdeveloped Africa*. London: Bogle L'Ouverture.

References

ABC News/AP. 2014. http://wjla.com/news/nation-world/two-americans-with-ebola-to-be-flown-back-to-u-s-105639.

Adesanmi, Pius. 2013 "Dowry: Managing Africa's Many Lovers" *Ikhide*. February 18, 2013. http://xokigbo.com/2013/02/18/guest-blog-post-professor-pius-adesanmi-dowry-managing-africas-many-lovers/

"Africa Rising: The Hopeful Continent." 2011. *The Economist*, December 3.

Armory, Deborah. 1997. "African Studies as American Institution." In *Anthropological Locations: Boundaries and Grounds of a Field Science*, edited by Akhil Gupta and James Ferguson, 102–16. Berkeley: University of California Press.

Asante, Molefi. 1988. *Afrocentricity*. Trenton, NJ: Africa World Press.

BBC News. 2015. "Ebola: Mapping the Outbreak," June 19. http://www.bbc.com/news/world-africa-28755033.

Bernal, Martin. 1987. *The Fabrication of Ancient Greece 1785–1985*. Vol. 1 of *Black Athena: The Afroasiatic Roots of Classical Civilization*. Rutgers, NJ: Rutgers University Press.

———. 1991. *The Archaeological and Documentary Evidence*. Vol. 2 of *Black Athena: The Afroasiatic Roots of Classical Civilization*. Rutgers, NJ: Rutgers University Press.

———. 2006. *The Linguistic Evidence*. Vol. 3 of *Black Athena: The Afroasiatic Roots of Classical Civilization*. Rutgers, NJ: Rutgers University Press.

Blyden, Edward. 1887. *Christianity, Islam and the Negro Race*. London: W. B. Whittingham & Co.

Cole, Teju. 2012. "The White Savior Industrial Complex." *The Atlantic*, March 21. http://www.theatlantic.com/international/archive/2012/03/the-white-savior-industrial-complex/254843/. Accessed March 21, 2014.

Coquery-Vidrovitch, Catherine. 1999. "The Rise of Francophone African Social Science: From Colonial Knowledge to Knowledge of Africa." In *Out of One, Many Africas: Reconstructing the Study and Meaning of Africa*, edited by William G. Martin and Michael O. West, 39–53. Urbana: University of Illinois Press.

Desai, Gaurav. 2001. *Subject to Colonialism: African Self-Fashioning and the Colonial Library*. Durham, NC: Duke University Press.

Diop, Cheikh Anta. 1974. *The African Origin of Civilization: Myth or Reality*. Chicago: Lawrence Hill.

Drake, St. Clair. 1982. "Diaspora Studies and Pan-Africanism." In *Global Dimensions of the African Diaspora*, edited by Joseph E. Harris. Washington, DC: Howard University Press.

El Hamel, Chouki. 2014. *Black Morocco: A History of Slavery, Race, and Islam*. Cambridge: Cambridge University Press.

Flynn, Gerard, and Susan Scutti. 2014. "Smuggled Bushmeat Is Ebola's Back Door to America." *Newsweek*, August 21. http://www.newsweek.com/2014/08/29/smuggled-bushmeat-ebolas-back-door-america-265668.html. Accessed September 14, 2014.

Gilroy, Paul. 1993. *The Black Atlantic: Modernity and Double Consciousness*. Cambridge, MA: Harvard University Press.

Giorgis, Hannah. 2014. "The Problem with the West's Ebola Response Is Still Fear of a Black Patient." *The Guardian* (UK), October 16, 2014. http://www.theguardian.com/commentisfree/2014/oct/16/west-ebola-response-black-patient. Accessed January 20, 2015.

Harris, Joseph. 1987. *Africans and Their History*. New York: New American Library.

———. 2003. "Expanding the Scope of African Diaspora Studies: The Middle East and India, a Research Agenda." *Radical History Review* 87: 157–68.

Herskovits, Melville. 1941. *The Myth of the Negro Past*. Boston: Beacon.

"Hopeless Africa." 2000. *The Economist*, May 13–19.

Hunwick, John O., and Eve Troutt Powell, eds. 2002. *The African Diaspora in the Mediterranean Lands of Islam*. Princeton, NJ: Markus Weiner.

Kamugisha, Aaron. 2003. "Finally in Africa? Egypt, from Diop to Celenko." *Race and Class* 45 (1): 31–60.

Jordan, Winthrop D. 1968. *White over Black: American Attitudes toward the Negro, 1550—1812*. Chapel Hill: University of North Carolina Press.

Lydon, Ghislaine. 2015. "Saharan Oceans and Bridges, Barriers and Divides in Africa's Historical Landscape." *Journal of African History* 56 (1): 3–22.

Mamdani, Mahmood. 1998. "Is African Studies at UCT a New Home for Bantu Education?" http://ccs.ukzn.ac.za/files/mamdani.pdf. Accessed May 28, 2015.

Martin, William G., and Michael O. West. 1999. Introduction to *Out of One, Many Africas: Reconstructing the Study and Meaning of Africa*, edited by William G. Martin and Micheal O. West, 1–38. Urbana: University of Illinois Press.

M'Bow, Amadou-Mahtar. 1981. Preface to *UNESCO General History of Africa, Volume 1: Methodology and African Prehistory*, edited by Joseph Ki-Zerbo. Berkeley: University of California Press.

Obenga, Théophile. 1978. "The Genetic Linguistic Relationship between Egyptian (Ancient Egyptian and Coptic) and Modern Negro-African Languages." In *The Peopling of Ancient Egypt and the Deciphering of the Meroitic Script: Proceedings of the Symposium, Held in Cairo from 28 January to 3 February 1974*, 65–71. Paris: UNESCO.

Pierre, Jemima. 2012. *The Predicament of Blackness: Postcolonial Ghana and the Politics of Race*. Chicago: University of Chicago Press.

Robinson, Pearl T. 2004. "Area Studies in Search of Africa." In *The Politics of Knowledge: Area Studies and the Disciplines*, edited by David Szanton, 119–83. Berkeley: University of California Press.

Sanders, Edith R. 1969. "The Hamitic Hypothesis: Its Origins and Functions in Time Perspective." *Journal of African History* 10 (4): 521–32.

Seligman, C. G. 1930. *Races of Africa*. London: Thornton Butterworth, Ltd.

Triaud, Jean-Louis. 2000. "Islam in Africa under French Colonial Rule." In *The History of Islam in Africa*, edited by Nehemia Levtzion and Randall Pouwels, 169–88. Athens: Ohio University Press.

Trouillot, Michel-Rolph. 1991. "Anthropology and the Savage Slot: The Poetics and Politics of Otherness." In *Recapturing Anthropology: Working in the Present*, edited by Richard Fox, 17–44. Santa Fe: School of American Research Press.

Wallerstein, Immanuel. 2005. *Africa: The Politics of Independence and Unity*. Lincoln: University of Nebraska Press.

Woodson, Carter G. 1936. *The African Background Outlined: Or, Handbook for the Study of the Negro*. Washington, DC: Association for the Study of Negro Life and History, Inc.

Zeleza, Paul. 2005. "Africa, Idea of." *New Dictionary of the History of Ideas. Encyclopedia.com*. http://www.encyclopedia.com/doc/1G2-3424300018.html. Accessed August 5, 2015.

2 BELONGING

Peter Geschiere

The English word "belonging" raises intriguing questions. Why has it such a strong emotional appeal? And why is it quite difficult to translate into many other languages? For instance, French or German equivalents are flat and lack the emotional (nostalgic?) ring that makes the English word such a powerful slogan, not only in Africa (and not only among Anglophones) but in the rest of the world as well. Two aspects of the English word may explain its appeal. First, most dictionaries emphasize its localizing connotations: of course, one can belong in different ways—religiously, professionally, or locally. But the last sense of belonging seems to be the most obvious one, giving the term a deep, chthonic meaning. Second, the word combines "being" and "longing" (its origin would be a composition of "be" and the archaic verb "long," to yearn). This link with "longing" seems to give the English word a special appeal.

This may also explain the term's inclusion in this collection. "Belonging" seems to be a relative newcomer as a critical term in African studies; after all, it sits uneasily with the celebration of mobility, more often seen as characteristic for African societies. The term's insertion in the list for this collection is clearly related to developments over the last few decades—the explosion of fierce conflicts between people who claim to belong to an area, and those who came later. It is in such contexts that belonging—and exclusion as its inevitable counterpart—became a critical issue. How can we explain this recent intensification? The notorious example of the havoc raised in Côte d'Ivoire by the country's new President Laurent Gbagbo, when he announced in 2002 his plan for a National Operation of Identification, might give some hints.

The plan—announced in the context of a bloody civil war—was to oblige all persons in the country to return to their "village of origin" in order to prove their citizenship. A certain Mr. Wayoro, "director of identification" for this operation, explained that to be Ivorian necessarily meant having a village and that those who had forgotten the name of their village or could not show that they belonged to one are people "without bearing and so dangerous" that they must report where they come from. Gbagbo had won the elections as a champion defending the *autochtons* (locals) from the South against *allogènes* ("strangers") from the North—both from northern Côte d'Ivoire and from neighboring countries like Mali and Burkina Faso (formerly Upper-Volta). The concept of national operation of identification he promoted (which was never put into practice but constantly referred to by his supporters) was an extreme elaboration of the idea of autochthony ("from the soil itself") that in the 1990s suddenly acquired new vigor. As d'Ivorians and their neighbors experienced ever-increasing forms of mobility, suspicion and exclusion of "strangers" was underwritten by localist calls of belonging.

Such a recent intensification of struggles over belonging in Africa is certainly not exceptional. The end of the Cold War—or what Charles Piot has called the post–Cold War moment—has inaugurated "a global conjuncture of belonging": a proliferation of communal conflicts and an obsession with cultural differences that are quite striking for a world that thinks it is globalizing. But this "global conjuncture" has acquired special implications in African contexts because there the growing concern with local belonging has to be articulated with great and even increasing mobility, often of an informal and shifting character. In this sense the examples below may also be of interest outside the field of African studies, since they highlight alternative and often paradoxical ways of combining mobility and belonging. A view from Africa can, for instance, serve to bring out the hidden tension, often overlooked, in one of the most pregnant and aggressive formulations of ideas about belonging that the modern world has produced: *Blut und Boden*. The combination of "blood and soil" is threatening because the two concepts appear to fortify each other. However, many of the African examples cited below point to an inevitable strain between "blood" and "soil." While belonging to the soil presupposes being always on the same spot (which is, of course, an illusion since history is always about movement), blood relations require at least some mixing: because of the need for exogamy (marrying outside) they always open up the local community to a broader network of relations. This articulation of closure and opening is at the heart of the dynamics of social formations in Africa—maybe in a more manifest way than elsewhere but expressing a tension that is universal. Even the Nazis found that raising *Blut und Boden* as a self-evident ideological unit necessitated in practice all sorts of subterfuges and artifices.

From "Wealth in People" to Belonging and the Exclusion of "Strangers"

To understand the specific twists of notions of belonging in Africa, it might be helpful to consider traits that are often seen as particular to African social formations. A recurrent one is the emphasis on "wealth in people" rather than—but in constant interaction with—"wealth in things." One of the milestones in the crystallization of this line of thought was Jack Goody's famous contrast between the prevalence of dowry (the bride taking her part of the heritage with her into marriage) in Eurasia, and of bridewealth (goods mainly circulating in the opposite direction, from the elders of the groom to those of the bride's group) in Africa. Of course, it soon became clear that this contrast had to be nuanced, with goods circulating in both directions. Yet, Goody connected this contrast meaningfully to other variables, notably important differences in the relation between humans and natural resources. In the seminomadic forms of agriculture dominating in Africa, it was not land but control over labor that was the crucial variable. So-called slash-and-burn agriculture required constantly that new plots be opened up when the production cycle had exhausted earlier plots. This was sustainable for as long as land remained an open resource. In contrast to many parts of Eurasia, no landed gentry emerged in Africa. There, accumulation of riches depended on control over people (labor), rather than over land. Again, this contrast is much too general. North Africa and Ethiopia are certainly an exception: agriculture via plough and animal traction rather than hoe allowed long-term land use and promoted landlordism. Moreover, even south of the Sahara some areas have a long history of very intensive and permanent land use—as in irrigated zones along the Sahel rivers or the wet rice cultures in southern Senegal and western Guinea. Thus, for as long as we can go back in time, African forms of "wealth in people" existed in constant articulation with the accumulation of things.

Yet, Goody's all-too-general schema highlights certain resilient traits of African formations that can be helpful for understanding particular trajectories of notions of belonging, also in interaction with modern changes.

A dominant trait was no doubt the emphasis on inclusion as expressed by all sorts of arrangements that allowed for the mobility of people: the prevalence of adoption, systems of slavery that in practice were—at least in some contexts—oriented toward inclusion of new people in the group, but most of all the very open terminology of kinship that allowed (and still allows) for including ever more persons in one's group. "The African family is very, very large," as my informants in the forest area of Cameroon used to tell me mockingly when once again I was puzzled by the complex equivocations by which they managed to forge a kinship link between two people who until then had clearly been strangers to each other.

It is against this background that the current emphasis on belonging and exclusion of "strangers" stands out. There is now an overall tendency toward closure of the local group and exclusion of newcomers, while in many cases in a not-too-distant past there was rather an emphasis on openness and inclusion. To mention just one example: the bitter civil war that rocked Côte d'Ivoire over the last two decades was about excluding migrants from the North as "strangers," while only one or two generations ago the latter had been welcomed as clients to reinforce the labor force under "traditional" arrangements of "tutorage." This was an unexpected turn: instead of an ongoing change from a "traditional" static system toward a more open "modern" configuration, a return to "tradition" emerged that, instead, allowed for new forms of mobility. Some of the young "autochthons" created roadblocks to extort money from "strangers," which they used to buy airline tickets to France.

Belonging and mobility can be articulated in paradoxical ways in present-day Africa. To understand such confusing developments, it is important to highlight that the main forms of group membership—"belonging"—in African history always allowed for considerable mobility. This is especially the case for what was (and still is) a very important criterion for group membership: kinship/descent. For Western readers kinship may be equated with fixedness and an "ascribed" place in the social constellation. By contrast, the enormous flexibility and openness of most African kinship terms, mentioned earlier, allows for the circulation of persons between groups that make any claim to belong relative and contingent. The same applies to another criterion for group membership: allegiance to a chief. Such allegiance was (and is) open to reconsideration—when land is an open resource, it is in the interest of a chief to attract as many people as possible around his court. Even in settings where more centralized formations emerged it was the "floating populations"—

traders, warrior bands, traveling scholars—that played a crucial role in the reproduction of such states. No wonder that these *populations flottantes* haunt the colonial archives (Roitman 2005). To the French and to others colonizers, they were a major challenge to colonial policies aimed at tying all the shifting groups to a definite place.

This reference to colonial archives shows, however, that the present-day tendency toward closure has a long history. In some respects the end of the last century—the post–Cold War moment—may have intensified this tendency but it fed on long-term developments during the colonial and postcolonial periods. After the colonial conquest, all colonial authorities, whatever their nationality, gave priority to "pacification," which in practice meant coercing the new subjects to remain in a specific place so as to facilitate collection of taxes and (forced) labor. The new administrative machinery had to be built on such stabilized settlements. Economic changes, notably the promotion of more permanent cash crops (cacao, coffee, cotton), reinforced this tendency toward permanent settlement and closure of the groups. A man's children became less and less prepared to accept cousins or even more distant "relatives" into the family since the latter could claim their share in these new and more permanent forms of wealth.

Paradoxically colonial policies throughout the continent were specifically shaped to take advantage of the mobility of colonial subjects. Despite their formal insistence on fixing these fluid populations, the colonials favored, in practice, migrants for all their larger projects. A fixed maxim for the French and the Belgians, as for the British and the Portuguese, was that migrants had more entrepreneurial spirit than the locals. A consequence is that behind all present-day conflicts over belonging and exclusion of "strangers" there is a colonial story of more or less forced migration. This applies as much to the great irrigation projects of the French (Office du Niger) or the British (Gezira in the Sudan) as to the Belgian *Mission d'Immigration des Banyarwanda* in East Congo; think also of the British support to migrant cacao farmers in Ghana and the French promotion of labor migration from "Upper Volta" to stimulate the plantation economy in southern Côte d'Ivoire—all regions that are now hotbeds of conflicts over "autochthony." Thus, colonials' formal emphasis on fixing the population was overtaken by new forms of mobility. Similarly, urbanization was formally discouraged but in practice promoted by various colonial policies. Toward the end of the colonial period, new possibilities to go overseas created a global diaspora of African-born elites.

Yet, even these new forms of mobility were intertwined with new forms of belonging. A striking aspect of urbanization in many parts of Africa is that, at least for quite some time, it did not lead to a definitive choice between city and countryside, but rather created what anthropologists have called "a rural-urban continuum." Urbanites, even those who are born in the city, are keen to maintain a base in the village, building a house and planning to retire there. Their insistence that they ultimately belong to the village has ideological overtones and is balanced by a certain averseness against village life in practice. And yet, the need to be buried there weighs heavily. It remains a point of great uncertainty, even for successful transcontinental migrants. The latter equally profess their belonging to the village, often organizing themselves to set up projects for its development. But, here again, new forms of transcontinental migration raise new problems in balancing belonging and mobility. In Anglophone Cameroon people now contrast the *America wandas* (wanderers), who left for America to study with scholarships and visas, to present-day *bush-fallers*, adventurers who try to cross the Sahara with just sheer luck (Alpes 2016). Wordplay is also at work here: *bush* stands now for Europe or any other rich part of the world (rather than for a backward place), while falling evokes the image of the hunter, who leaves on adventure and returns with a big prey. However, this metaphor has its flip side: there are many mythical stories about hunters who found a fertile spot in the bush and stayed there. So the relatives who stay behind double their efforts to make sure the *bush-faller* will not forget where he really belongs. New forms of mobility seem to engender new strategies of belonging.

Similar paradoxes between mobility and localization mark the emergence of new forms of religious belonging. In the early phases of conversion to Christianity—just prior to colonial conquest and during the first decades of colonial rule—this often meant moving to a new, separate settlement. In some areas missionaries tried to make the new converts live around the mission post—a theocratic version of the "wealth in people" principle—to such an extent that it led to conflicts with civil servants who complained that it became impossible for their chiefs to recruit laborers for the government's projects. In Islamized areas the *dar* (house) of scholars from the various brotherhoods could play a similar role: attracting especially young men (who, as among the Senegalese Murids, were not only taught to pray but also to work in the new cash-crop plantations of the *marabout*), the *dar* institution promoted new forms of settlement and colonization. With conversion becoming ever more common, local churches and mosques became centers that affirmed the coherence of existing villages. The recent success of new movements with fundamentalist claims—both Pentecostals and orthodox Muslims—again promote new visions of locality and mobility. Both appeal to a global vision of belonging to a worldwide community of believers. And, indeed, the support that global Pentecostal networks can offer to transcontinental migrants—just like the recent successful transformation of, for instance, the Murid brotherhood into a global credit association—gives this vision of religious belonging very concrete meaning. The deep distrust of many (but apparently not all) Pentecostal currents of the village and the family, as the obvious locus where the devil—often disguised as a witch—is hiding, could undermine the believers' commitment to local belonging. The implications of this religious distrust toward the village—in a certain sense, a return to earlier Christian convictions—are still far from clear, all the more so since they collide with other recent developments that reinforce the image of the village as the critical locus of belonging.

Indeed, the changing global context since the end of the 1980s—the end of the Cold War and concomitant changes in development policies favoring "bypassing the state" and decentralization—brought to many parts of the African continent an unexpected return of the village as a critical stake in national politics and therefore as a crucial focus for belonging. The example of Gbagbo's "National Operation of Identification" in Côte d'Ivoire, quoted earlier, had general relevance. The ability to identify with a village of birth became a precondition for proving one's "autochthony" and therefore one's citizenship.

A quick look at the genealogy of the notion of autochthony would be worthwhile for understanding how it could become a hallmark of belonging. The notion was likely introduced to the continent at the beginning of the last century by the French colonizers who gave it a central place in their plans for a new administration. For Maurice Delafosse, one of their main empire builders, the starting point of French policies should be that not all indigenes are autochthons. The colonial administration therefore had to build on the distinction between the autochtons, who really belonged where they lived, and other more mobile groups. The first task was to form homogeneous *cantons* of *autochtons* as a firm basis for the colonial administrative machine. But after independence (mostly around 1960), such distinctions between people who really belonged and latecomers—central also in colonial policies elsewhere—became anathema, at least formally. Then all emphasis was on nation building, national citizenship, and unity. In the 1990s terms like *autochtons* (versus *allogènes*) or "sons of the soil" (versus "strangers") returned with a vengeance, assuming a crucial role in many countries: in Côte d'Ivoire, Cameroon, and Congo as much as, for instance—albeit under different labels—in Nigeria, Kenya, and South Africa.

The example of Gbagbo's national operation of identification already suggested one important reason for this return of the village as a crucial stake in national politics: democratization. The restoration of multiparty democracy—in many countries around 1990—made it of great interest for politicians to mobilize the idea of a continuing solidarity between urbanites and their village in order to marshal votes. Of course, it was not accidental that this change coincided with the end of the Cold War, since this gave Western leaders more leeway to take a principled stand against the one-party states and military dictators they had supported until then. A crucial question became how the renewed stress on local belonging was to relate to other notions of belonging—to the idea of the nation, but also to ethnicity as a parallel expression of group membership, and to the restoration of notions of indigeneity that more recently came to affect Africa as well.

Alternatives: National, Ethnic, or Indigenous?

The strong emphasis on the village of origin as the lynchpin of belonging in the debates in Côte d'Ivoire may come as a surprise in view of this country's arduous efforts during the preceding decades, like those of many other postcolonial African states, toward nation building and the construction of national citizenship. In a city like Abidjan (of more than three million inhabitants) many people, migrants of the second generation, had been born in the city itself, not in the villages. Of course, locality and soil are shibboleths in most versions of nationalism. Compare, for instance, the evocative summing up of French nationalism by *maréchal* Pétain (the hero of the battle of Verdun who saved France in the First World War but in the Second World War collaborated with the Germans as president of the Vichy government): *La terre, elle ne ment pas* (the land does not lie). However, the national operation of identification of the 1990s brought a return to the soil that was different from the usual nationalist celebration of it. In the Ivorian version, the village and recognition by its elders were the hallmark of national citizenship.

For Gbagbo autochthony should coincide with the national: the nation had to be purified from "strangers." But there are also other articulations. In Cameroon autochthony is rather in competition with the national, creating a difference between citizens who live where they belong and others who are still recognized as Cameroonian citizens but have fewer rights in that particular locality. Nigeria can combine these two classes of citizen through its federal structure: in each federal state people of a certain group are "natives" (a colonial term, now often replaced by "indigenes"), and their "nativity certificate" makes them eligible for posts in the local administration. By contrast Nigerian citizens who are "natives" from other states can only serve there. Despite such variations, the different African trajectories all highlight alternative ways of relating local and national belonging to the "classic" trajectories of those followed by European and North American nation-states.

Even more complex and volatile is the relation of such classifications of people in terms of firstcomers and latecomers to ethnic ("tribal") distinctions that play such a large role in outsiders' interpretations of developments on the continent. As for notions of autochthony and similar expressions of belonging, it is important to emphasize the colonial background of ethnic classifications. Present-day ethnicity was to a large extent shaped by the bureaucratic need of the colonial state for classifying what seemed to be a chaotic anarchy of fluid, shifting groups with which the new power holders were confronted. Anthropologists—whether in service of the colonial government or not—often played a key role in creating such "order." Yet, as for notions of autochthony, it is important to emphasize that such colonial classifications built on older elements. In this sense they were not so much "invented" but were rather the product of a bureaucratic fixation of preexistent and much more "floating" distinctions. Even more important might be the fact that—again, as for autochthony—people were very quick to appropriate and remodel such colonial distinctions. Since access to the state was determined by these identifications, the "subjects" tried most actively to use them to serve their own needs.

One difference might be that, at least in some respects, autochthony and parallel discourses on claims as firstcomers are emptier and thus more easily adaptable to the rapidly changing situations of the post–Cold War moment. An ethnic group, too, may be a contingent historical construction, yet it can only serve as beacon for identification if it has at least some clear markers: a name, a specific history, often a language. By contrast, for a claim to be autochthonous, just a story about being a firstcomer suffices. Moreover, it can be easily generalized but also again restricted, depending on the groups that are to be included or excluded. It is striking how easily such groups switch from one "other" to the next "other." Just as the "autochthons" of the New Right in Flanders constantly hesitate between Muslim immigrants or Francophone co-citizens as their main "Other," Gbagbo's autochthonous Bete from southwest Côte d'Ivoire are never sure whose exclusion is more urgent: their "others" are not only the northerners but also the Baoule, who for a long time controlled the state. One can cite many more examples where the flexibility of such boundaries of belonging makes them all the more resilient in present-day circumstances. However, as always for Africa, there are many variations. For instance, in the Sahel, discourses on autochthony relate to older distinctions between people "of the land" and aristocrats who have come later. This gives more substance to the concept of autochthony. People debate over the different grounds on which claims to be autochthonous can be based and they therefore distinguish between different kinds of autochthony.

Another discourse on local belonging, that became current in the African continent only recently, is the one on "indigeneity." Of course, the term "indigenous"—like the parallel term "native"—has been around as long as the establishment of colonial rule. However, especially after independence, people increasingly attributed a pejorative slant to these terms. In Francophone areas the term *indigène* was particularly resented since it was equated with the special juridical status of African subjects, the *indigénat*, which allowed for harsh forms of exploitation (notably forced labor). After the abolition of this *indigénat* (at the conference of Brazzaville in 1944, to reward the role French colonies in Africa had played in the Second World War as a basis for de Gaulle's Free France against Vichy) both the French authorities and their African subjects were reluctant to use the term any longer. Under British rule the term "indigene" was already gradually replaced by the term "native." However, since the end of the 1970s, "indigenous" gained renewed popularity, owing to the successes of the United Nations Working Group of Indigenous Peoples. Africa was a relative latecomer to this forum. Initially many spokesmen from the continent—both politicians and intellectuals—stressed that in Africa all groups are indigenous, and that it would be dangerous to make distinctions between groups on such a basis. Toward the end of the 1980s, however, representatives of a few groups from the continent succeeded in getting recognized by the UN forum as "indigenous"—notably pastoralists, hunters-and-gatherers (Baka "pygmies" and San), and also some particularly endangered groups (like those from the Niger Delta suffering from the ecological damage caused by oil companies).

A complicating factor was that in 2007 the UN working group officially accepted the term *autochton* as the French translation of "indigenous" following the example from Québec where the First Nations had been labeled *autochtons* for quite some time already. However, for Africa, this translation created problems, since here the notion of *autochton* has a very different history and therefore quite specific connotations. Thus, in Cameroon people now tend to distinguish two kinds of *autochtons*: special groups of *autochtons vulnérables*—like the "pygmies" or some pastoralists whose way of life is under threat—and the *autochtons*, who are mostly in a relatively advantaged position, having special access to the state and enjoying protection of their land rights. As noted earlier, in Nigeria the term "indigenous" is now used to replace the colonial word "native," a term that in the post-independence period was used to distinguish in each of the federal states between those who belonged to a particular state and Nigerians from other states. The consequence is that here again very different notions of indigeneity have to be negotiated. For all Nigerian citizens it is vital to have the certificate of indigeneity of "their" state. But this is very different from the indigeneity claimed by certain groups—like the people in the Niger Delta—who are recognized as "indigenous" by the UN working group. The complications in Africa around concepts like "indigenous" and "autochthonous" highlight how important it is to follow the special trajectories of these notions in particular historical contexts. Just as claims to autochthony are always contested and relativized, so the notion of indigenous is never self-evident but always marked by power relations.

One thing all these versions of belonging have in common is their outspoken patriarchal tenor—in Africa as in many other parts of the world. Just as in *Blut and Boden* it is the man's blood and soil that is decisive—the *Mutter* role of the woman being emphatically seen as in service of the man—and it is the father's line that determines autochthony, ethnicity, or indigeneity. If in some African societies the mother's line at least formally takes precedence, it is still men—in this context, the mother's brother—who play a dominant role in a person's life. Yet here women are central in the genealogical constructions that confirm claims of belonging to a certain area.

The Funeral as a Festival of Belonging

The examples above—notably Gbagbo's national operation of identification—can give the impression that political manipulation from above plays a key role in the recent intensification of issues of belonging. It is certainly true that ambitious politicians play on these notions—just as they did and do with ethnicity—in order to marshal support for the ferocious competition at the national level. Moreover, democratization has certainly intensified this competition and therefore the political use of local notions of belonging. At the same time it is important to recognize that this political use of belonging falls on fertile soil. Indeed, one can say that this "politics of belonging" evokes such strong popular reactions that politicians often risk being swept off their feet by the popular emotions they engender.

In many African contexts, the funeral is a key moment to understanding the depth of emotion involved. There is a general proliferation of funeral rituals—of traditional appearance but in practice rather "neo-traditional"—that is directly linked to the increasing need to prove one's belonging. Thus, funerals turn into true festivals of belonging. Often the funeral has to take place "at home"—meaning in the village of origin. Even urbanites who have lived for several generations in the city insist that ultimately they must be buried in the village. Yet, it remains to be seen whether this can be realized in the future as well. Some groups from west Cameroon now send a stone rather than the corpse to be buried in the village. Elsewhere—for instance, in the larger Congolese cities—it has become acceptable to bury urbanites in their city of residence. But in many parts of the continent it remains a sign of social disgrace if someone has to be buried there (remember what Wayoro, the Ivorian director of identification, said about those who had forgotten where they came from).

The funeral in the village remains an important but also uneasy moment in the life of urbanites and transcontinental migrants. It is then that the precarious balance between belonging and distance is performed. For the villagers this is the moment to get even with the "sons of the village living elsewhere," who are often suspected of having forgotten about their "brothers" at home. In my research in east Cameroon I was always impressed how quickly urbanites, initially quite stiff and diffident, were swept away by the power of funeral rituals. Constant drumming, dancing, and drinking make it a hectic but very intense event, delirious mourning often alternating with ritual mockery and aggression, especially by in-laws. Thus, the funeral "at home" reaffirms most forcefully that even those who have left ultimately belong there.

Conclusion

The funeral, but also other examples above, highlight that the explosive mix of mobility and local belonging can be articulated according to different scenarios and trends. It is too simplistic to suppose that with the increasing scale of social relations a development will follow from local to national belonging, and then to growing cosmopolitanism. In Africa there has been a dramatic increase of scale in urbanization and migration, now also transcontinentally. But this insertion in broader frameworks was (and is) articulated in unexpected ways with a continued and perhaps even increasing emphasis on localist belonging. The ways in which such growing preoccupations with the local are expressed in many parts of the continent by notions like "autochthony" remind us of Arjun Appadurai's warning that open identities—like the emphasis on "wealth in people"—can easily become "predatory," cannibalizing other identities. We must better understand when such a switch, often quite sudden, will take place.

Suggested Readings

Alpes, Maybritt Jill. 2016. *Brokering High-Risk Migration in West Africa: Abroad at All Cost*. Aldershot, UK: Ashgate.

Appadurai, Arjun. 2006. *Fear of Small Numbers: An Essay on the Geography of Anger*. Durham, NC: Duke University Press.

Berman, Bruce, and John Lonsdale.1992. *The Unhappy Valley: Conflict in Kenya and Africa*. London: Currey/Heinemann.

Berry, Sarah. 2001. *Chiefs Know Their Boundaries: Essays on Property, Power and the Past in Asante, 1896–1996*. London: Currey/Heinemann.

Chauveau, Jean-Pierre, and Koffi Samuel Bobo. 2003. "La situation de guerre dans l'arène villageoise: Un exemple dans le Centre-Ouest ivoirien." *Politique africaine* 89: 12–32.

Geschiere, Peter L. 2009. *The Perils of Belonging: Autochthony, Citizenship and Exclusion*. Chicago: University of Chicago Press.

Goody, Jack. 1976. *Production and Reproduction: A Study of the Domestic Domain*. Cambridge: Cambridge University Press.

Marshall, Ruth. 2006. "The War of 'Who Is Who': Autochthony, Nationalism and Citizenship in the Ivoirian Crisis." *African Studies Review* 49 (2): 9–43.

Piot, Charles. 2010. *Nostalgia for the Future—West Africa after the Cold War*. Chicago: University of Chicago Press.

Roitman, Janet. 2005. *Fiscal Disobedience: An Anthropology of Economic Regulation in Central Africa*. Princeton, NJ: Princeton University Press.

Tsing, Anna Lowenhaupt. 2007. "Indigenous Voice." In *Indigenous Experience Today*, edited by M. de la Cadena and O. Stern, 35–68. Oxford: Berg.

3 BONDAGE

Gwyn Campbell

Issues of African bondage are conventionally subsumed under the term "slavery," while slavery studies, including analyses of enslavement, the slave trade, slavery, and the slave diaspora, has conventionally focused on Africa as the source of slaves, and Africans as slave trade victims. Throughout, definitions of slave and slavery are based on those applied by Moses Finley in his comparison of the classical Greek and Roman with New World slave systems. Thus Paul Lovejoy, in his standard reference on African slavery, defines slaves as chattel, the property of their masters who exercised full control over them, including the right to buy, sell, separate, and enjoy sexual access to them, and the fruit of their labor. Slaves were outsiders, whose skin color, language, and religion marked them apart. Even children of slaves, who inherited slave status, were regarded as outsiders. Violence characterized slavery, from enslavement to coerced work. A major difference was that in classical Greece and Rome, slavery was an open system, which meant, for example, that marriages between free widows and slaves were common in contrast to the closed system in America where intermarriage across the slave-non-slave divide was taboo (Watson 1980). Unlike their white masters, African slaves enjoyed no civil rights. It was literally a black and white divide that has left an indelible, troubled heritage on American, notably United States, soil. Even after abolition, members of the former slave-owning society stigmatized former slaves, who increasingly identified with a victimized African diaspora.

All societies have had slaves, but, according to Finley, slave societies are distinct in that slaves formed a high percentage—a minimum of around 30 percent—of the total population, they contributed significantly to surplus production, and slavery pervaded every aspect of the life of that society. Lovejoy prefers to focus on societies dominated by slave modes of production—the economies of which are dependent upon slave labor. Finley limited to five the number of genuine slave societies—ancient Greece and Rome, and colonial Caribbean, Brazil, and the American South—while, for Lovejoy, the Atlantic slave mode of production also embraced parts of West Africa.

Problems Posed by Conventional Definitions

Despite these preliminary qualifications for what constitutes bondage, major problems with conventional approaches to slavery studies prevail. The first is the common identification of "slave" with sub-Saharan Africans. This is understandable, given the predominance of American academe and focus in the United States on African American history, and the scale of the trans-Atlantic slave trade: some 12.8 million Africans were shipped across the Atlantic as slaves between the late fifteenth and late nineteenth centuries. Lovejoy concedes that Muslim countries north of the Sahara and in the Indian Ocean world (IOW) did import some non-African slaves, but emphasizes that Africans always constituted a significant proportion of the slave population (2012, 15). UNESCO considers only African slaves in its slave routes project, as did the 2007 bicentenary celebrations of the abolition of the slave trade. Thus conventional slavery studies focus almost exclusively on the particular type of servitude which dominated the Atlantic World from the sixteenth to nineteenth centuries. In this, the victims comprised predominantly West Africans, mostly young males, destined for New World plantations and mines, where their labor dominated the economy.

However, it is now clear that Africans were far from being the only servile human beings subject to trafficking or bondage. They constituted a majority of the servile labor force for the New World plantations and mines, but not elsewhere. In the IOW, for example, people of all skin colors and many different cultures were subjected to bondage and trafficked—far more in total than in the Americas. For instance, in 1841 Sir Bartle Frere estimated that in areas directly under British rule in India alone there were eight to nine million Indian slaves—representing from 62.5 to 70.3 percent of the total number of slaves shipped across the Atlantic, and double the number of slaves in the United States in 1860 (Caplan 1980, 181). The IOW traffic in servile humans included non-Africans shipped to Africa. For example, a trade in servile, probably female, Indians to

Egypt was almost certainly responsible for the arrival there of leprosy by 400 BCE, possibly earlier (Mark 2002). Again, some sixteen thousand Indian slaves (25 percent of the total) were imported into the Cape from 1657 to 1808 (Harris 2010, 150). Indeed, Africans constituted a minority of trafficked servile labor in the IOW, except along the western Indian Ocean rim. Even there, they formed a clear majority of victims only in the nineteenth century, when Black Sea sources for the Middle East dried up, and demand for servile labor expanded on the Mascarenes, Zanzibar, and Madagascar.

Additionally, conventional definitions, in which slavery is contrasted with freedom, and slave with free person, are ill-adapted to extra-European bondage systems. For Finley, slave labor was "work performed under compulsions other than those of kinship or communal obligations," while free labor comprised "free men working on their own (or leased) land or in their shops or homes as craftsmen and shopkeepers." He added that for Greeks "the condition of the free man is that he does not live under the restraint of another." For Lovejoy, a slave was a subservient dependent of the master who had total control over him/her, and had "absolute lack of choice." The slave was denied the rights and privileges granted to free people who as citizens of a particular society enjoyed the right to make decisions for themselves.

Such definitions are immensely problematical, as they conjure up concepts of modern democratic societies in which individual citizens are accorded legal guarantees protecting their right to freedom of travel, and choice of occupation and marriage partner. However, prior to the twentieth century, the concept of citizenship and individual freedom was largely unknown in non-European societies, and still is in many regions of the world. Lovejoy states that "the act of emancipation, when it existed, conveyed recognition that slave and free were not the same. Emancipation dramatically demonstrated that power was in the hands of the free, not the slaves" (2012, 2). However, in precolonial Egypt and Madagascar, the lot of the ordinary peasant farmer subject to forced labor for the state was often worse than that of most slaves, some of whom, in consequence, preferred slavery to freedom. Moreover, abolition of slavery failed to alter the condition of the overwhelming majority of people subject to bondage systems that Europeans did not recognize as slavery.

In most European languages the term "slave" derives from the same root and denotes chattel. Almost all Africanists and slavery studies experts apply, without question, the terms "slavery" and "slave" to myriad types of African bondage and the people subjected to them. However, this does not reflect historical or contemporary reality in Africa or in the wider IOW. Chattel slavery occupied but one extreme on a spectrum of types of human servitude. Even in non-Western societies that possessed a clear term for slave, as with the Arabic *abd* in Muslim countries, it did not carry the same meaning as the European term for slave. Under Islamic law children of a slave concubine and her master were accorded non-slave status, as was the slave mother should her master die before her. Moreover, manumission was considered a righteous act and was widely practiced. In pre-Islamic and non-Muslim African societies there existed multiple terms for different types of bondage, none of which derive from the European root for slave, and few of which carried the connotation of chattel (Eno 2005).

A further problem is the assumption that Africa's economic history centered on the slave export trade. Lovejoy, for example, states that from the earliest times Africa constituted a reservoir of cheap and plentiful slaves. He further considers that the Muslim Middle East was almost the sole external influence on the economy of Africa prior to 1450, after which Europeans became the dominant force. Consequently, first a Muslim slave mode of production developed in Africa, followed by a more dominant and deeply intrusive capitalist Western slave mode of production associated with New World slavery. A third slave mode of production emerged in Africa in the nineteenth century following the collapse of the trans-Atlantic slave trade.

However, it is increasingly evident that significant parts of Indian Ocean Africa (IOA: comprising approximately half of the continental land mass that lies along and east of a Cape-to-Cairo divide) formed an integral part of the wider IOW global economy, which emerged from about 300 BCE—over a millennium before the foundation of the European-dominated Atlantic world. From roughly 300 BCE, IOA participated in a vibrant trans-IOW (and wider) exchange network, with Africans as active rather than passive partners. Moreover, contrary to the conventional view, Africa's major contribution to the IOW global economy was almost always in commodities other than slaves, notably ivory, rhinoceros horn, and tortoise shell, and at times gold, iron ore, ambergris, mangrove wood, and cowries. Further, with rare exceptions, such as in the Nile Delta, population densities in IOA were low, and labor a scarce and valued factor of production. IOA slave exports were generally limited except at times of domestic crisis, as in Ethiopia from the seventh to ninth centuries, and again from the thirteenth century, and in equatorial East Africa in the long nineteenth century, when worsening environmental conditions, poor harvests, and disease provoked social and political disorder, and migration, impoverishing large swaths of the population and rendering them vulnerable to enslavement.

New Paradigms and Terminology

In all, it is clear that new terminology and paradigms are required in order to adequately analyze the wide variety of African bondage. It is proposed that, in the generic sense, the terms "slavery" and "slave" need to be replaced by "bondage" and "bondsperson."

The term "slave" is generally appropriate for victims of European systems of slavery—usually but not exclusively, enslaved Africans in the New World and European enclaves in Africa and the wider IOW. However, the trans-Atlantic slave trade, while highly significant, was not the chief component of African bondage. For most of history, Africans, as indeed all human beings, lived in societies in which individuals were bound in a social hierarchy in which each person had an allotted status that carried with it a multiplicity of rights and obligations. These hierarchies were subject to change and, according to local circumstances, statuses of groups and individuals could rise or fall. However, a person was always the dependent of another. In societies with no separation of the secular and religious, such dependency incorporated the spiritual world. Even elites were tied in bonds of dependency on otherworldly gods, spirits, or ancestors. Each category of bondsperson requires analyzing in terms of the language used to describe their status within a particular society at any given time, their position within the local hierarchy of dependence, and the nature and dynamics of their relationships with people of other statuses.

Second, the question of bondage needs to be critically reassessed. Issues of labor and control over labor need to be placed in context. In Africa, where land was generally plentiful, and labor and capital scarce, labor, both unskilled and skilled was at a premium. Women were generally the most valued, owing to their productive and reproductive capacities, and sexual services. With few exceptions this led to the elaboration of methods, chiefly by male elders, to control local females and obtain and incorporate females and children from other groups. These included marital alliances, kidnapping, and warfare. Through control of females, elders also commanded the allegiance and labor of younger males for manual labor and military service.

Wherever states emerged, more elaborate bondage systems developed. States such as Egypt and Aksum (in Ethiopia) emerged on the basis of innovations associated with the Neolithic Revolution. They developed centralized hierarchies, the top echelon of which comprised a numerically small elite that imposed coercive control over its subject population. The elite geographically restricted the movement of subject peoples, and directed their labor, chiefly into constructing and maintaining water control systems, cultivating crops, and building infrastructural projects. Enhanced agricultural productivity and grain storage capacity encouraged demographic expansion, greater specialization of labor, and trade. This further benefited the elite, who not only taxed peasants in produce and labor, but also imposed forced labor on skilled artisans, and often monopolized trade in the most valuable commodities.

Control over scarce and valuable long-distance trade could also encourage state formation in which similar patterns of control over and exploitation of servile labor developed. During the epoch of the trans-Atlantic slave trade, capture and sale of slaves formed a bedrock of some West African economic regimes, but in IOA, slave exports probably never formed the economic basis for states or ruling elites. For example, in the Great Zimbabwe complex from the eleventh to fifteenth centuries, gold and ivory were the most important exports. The East African slave export trade reached its zenith in the nineteenth century, but by then the burgeoning international economy had established demand for a variety of African plantation, forest, marine, and animal products—of which ivory was almost certainly the most valuable.

A priority for all states was to capture the resources of neighboring regions. Where unopposed, their armies generally left sedentary agricultural communities in place under the control of nominees who taxed and exploited the labor of the conquered peasants. When resisted, conquering armies generally killed male opponents, and captured women and children whom they brought back to the imperial capital. Often, they also imposed tribute in the form of valuable commodities, and servile, notably female, labor. The chief reason adult male opponents were killed is that they were more likely to resist and revolt, and required heavy surveillance and physical restraint (Goody 1980). They were also less likely than women and children to adopt the mores of the victor society. As labor for agricultural production and public works was generally satisfied by the existing subject population, most female and child captives and tribute entered domestic servitude in households of the ruling elite where they often served as objects of conspicuous consumption. Elites also established demand for highly priced exotic foreign and skilled servile labor, such as acrobats, magicians, unusually gifted craftsmen, singing girls, and beautiful girls and boys.

Debt and Bondage

Debt played a major role in *embondagement*. In small decentralized societies, where gift exchange was central to forging relationships, the inability of the less fortunate to reciprocate with gifts of the same value or status enabled the elite to cement allegiance, clientage, and the obligation to furnish labor when demanded. With the emergence of states, the link between debt and bondage grew in complexity. War captives literally owed their lives to the victors. Representing indebted bodies, they were obligated, and entered a life of perpetual servitude, to their conquerors. Thus in the late 1700s, Andrianampoinimerina, who emerged victorious in civil wars that embroiled Imerina, a landlocked kingdom in the highlands of Madagascar, tied newly subjected peoples—who owed their lives to the new sovereign (described as "god")—to the land and organized them into unremunerated forced labor (*fanompoana*) units (Campbell 2004).

Indebtedness was also probably responsible for most Africans embondaged through non-violent means. A universal phenomenon, indebtedness imposed obligations upon the debtor and his relatives to the creditor that, when formally witnessed and agreed to, were sanctioned by customary if not statutory law (Clarence-Smith 2013). In precolonial Madagascar, for instance, creditors could, through the application of law, embondage a debtor, his wife, and children (Campbell 2005a, 295–96). Exorbitant interest rates were common, and often caused debtors to default. Indeed, many seeking credit knew that it might well lead them to become embondaged—to the degree that for some it was tantamount to voluntary embondagement. In addition, certain crimes were punished by fines, which often led to indebtedness and subsequent embondagement. Should the debt be repaid, an embondaged debtor could regain his or her former status. Although males overwhelmingly contracted debt, the majority of those who were consequently embondaged, were—by choice of the male debtor—women and children—the most vulnerable members of a household, extended family or community and the most in demand as servile labor.

As embondaged debtors were removed from the taxable population, deliberate use of extortionate interest rates and other debt-inducing mechanisms could pose an economic challenge to the authorities. In this context, it is significant that societies governed by the Sharia—from the seventh century Islam spread from its Middle Eastern heartland across Northern Africa, into Sudan, West Africa, and down the East African littoral—forbade the embondagement of debtor Muslim, Jewish, and Christian subjects. Nevertheless, because of legal lacunae, or in regions where elements of pre-Islamic customary law were upheld, people often continued to become ensnared in forms of debt bondage.

There are also striking incidences of nineteenth-century indigenous states levying such heavy impositions on their subject non-slave population that it drove many into destitution, indebtedness, and forms of bondage. Egypt under Muhammed Ali and Imperial Madagascar under Radama I and Ranavalona I are major examples. Such a process was promoted by high legal interest rates—of up to 100 percent in nineteenth-century Madagascar. Consequently, defaulting on debts was common. European colonial regimes, through imposing monetary taxes, promoting commercialization, and enforcing credit contracts, facilitated a growth in indebtedness. At the same time, colonial authorities distinguished debt bondspeople from true slaves, whose condition they attributed solely to violent capture. As a result, debt bondage expanded considerably.

Ransom and indebtedness were also closely related. The ransoming of kidnap victims or war captives was customary in many traditional African societies. In the nineteenth century, with increasing Western abolitionist pressure and rising demand for servile labor, ransoming, often in the guise of redemption, assumed new proportions, and was extended to children. Ironically, the rationale for ransoming by Europeans stemmed from the widespread belief in Enlightenment Europe that members of "primitive" pagan societies required "domestication," and that slavery was the protected status best suited to that end. Ransomers, like slave owners, needed to discipline their undeveloped wards into accepting the physical and moral training necessary for the attainment of civilized virtues—which alone could justify "freedom." Thus some missionary groups in Africa redeemed slaves into mission villages to work off their redemption in situations of virtual bondage. Similarly, from 1839, the French in Senegal redeemed slaves, then made them work on fourteen-year contracts—a system extended from 1854 to other French West African enclaves and the French Caribbean (Northrup 1995, 48).

Abolitionist groups criticized such practices, as they did British exploitation of Prize Negroes—African human cargoes captured aboard slaving ships—and other liberated Africans. For example, between 1834 and 1867 about thirty-seven thousand Africans liberated from slavery were sent to the British West Indies (Northrup 1995, 48). Others were used in Africa: over two thousand were landed at Cape Town from 1806 to 1816. Prize Negroes were treated as confiscated property, transferred to British government agents who placed some in the military, but allotted most to serve prominent local whites (Worden, van Heyningen, and Bickford-Smith 2004, 109). Prize Negroes granted to Mauritian planters were leased back to the government for four days a year to perform public works (Anderson 2005).

Debt was also central to pawnship, a widespread form of African bondage, defined by Lovejoy as a system "in which labor was perceived as interest on a debt and the pawn as collateral for the debt." The debtor, generally an adult male, pledged a pawn, generally a girl, whose labor was commanded by the creditor until such time as the debt was repaid by her kin. Should the debt remain unpaid, she might become permanently embondaged to the creditor. Pawnship was particularly widespread among ordinary males as a means of raising credit. In Muslim societies, where debt bondage was forbidden, pawnship was nominally uncommon, but in reality, both pawnship and debt bondage were widespread. Muslim and, increasingly from the eighteenth century, European traders acquired pawns to subsequently sell as slaves. European colonial regimes did not normally recognize pawnship as slavery and it consequently remained in vigor until the mid-twentieth century.

The Rise of the International Economy

For a long time, antislavery movements focused their attention on the trans-Atlantic and Muslim slave trades in Blacks, and hence on Africa. European political and public opinion called for a civilizing mission to end the slave trade, emancipate slaves, and establish a free labor market. However, abolitionist pressure had an initially muted influence except in the Cape where the 1826 removal of protection for wine diverted investment into the far less labor-intensive wool-producing sector—a measure that effectively undermined slavery there. Abolition was enforced in 1833 and 1848 in British and French colonies, respectively. Elsewhere, however, despite abolition forming a central justification for the imperial thrust, the labor-intensive nature of the economy and lack of free wage labor led European regimes to rely on forms of forced labor.

This needs to be put in context. Preindustrial economies were heavily labor-intensive. The nineteenth century witnessed the emergence of capital-intensive production in the northern United States and Germany. However, in other industrializing regions, and in all nonindustrial zones, production continued to be largely labor-intensive. In Africa as elsewhere, the enhanced commercial opportunities offered by the burgeoning international economy greatly increased demand for labor required to cultivate tropical cash crops, collect forest and animal products, and extract minerals, as well as labor needed for porterage, storage, and manning ships. Simultaneously, indigenous and European powers engaged in state- or empire-building projects that involved large numbers of soldiers and workers, not least in indigenous industrial experiments, as in nineteenth-century Egypt and Madagascar.

However, growth in demand failed to result in a growth in the supply of labor, owing to uneven demographic growth and the prevalence of systems of bonded labor. Between 1750 and 1900, Africa's share of the global population fell from 13 to 8 per cent (Campbell 2008). Indeed, its demographic growth rates expanded significantly only from the 1920s (Cordell and Gregory 1987). Factors promoting low demographic growth included the slave export trade, adverse climatic factors, famine, and disease (Manning 1990a and 1990b).

Moreover, many indigenous authorities claimed the labor of all subjects. Indeed, some African states, such as Imerina in 1877, purposefully applied selective measures of abolition in order to "liberate" privately held slaves for state use. Given the lack of a free-wage labor force, Europeans in Africa initially depended largely on slaves to meet their labor demands. For instance, Robert Farquhar, governor of Mauritius, delayed anti-slave import measures in acknowledgement of the cheap labor requirements of local sugar planters (Anderson 2005). Also, in territories that were declared protectorates, officials could avoid enforcing some abolitionist measures compulsory in colonies.

Moreover, because European authorities needed to retain the goodwill of local indigenous elites who possessed servile labor, they adopted a gradualist approach to curbing bondage and human trafficking. In Somalia, the colonial regime initially permitted European settler farmers access to bonded labor and even returned bonded fugitives to their owners, and in the Sudan, effective measures to curtail bondage started only in the late 1920s (Eno 2005, 83–89; Miers 2005). European officials avoided confrontation with Islamic authorities on the issue of concubinage, and held debt bondage to be a benign form of private welfare. Pawnship, for example, weakened only during the post–Second World War boom. Again, because of a desire to meet the cheap labor demands of the oil industry, the export of African bonded labor to the Middle East, drawn into the British informal empire after the First World War, continued until the post-1945 era.

Even when emancipated, former slaves proved remarkably reluctant to work on European-run concerns. Thus European officials and colonists turned to traditional systems of bondage, and introduced new ones. Convicts had long been used as a source of servile labor. Prior to the nineteenth century, indigenous convicts were sent from Goa to Mozambique by the Portuguese and by the Dutch from Batavia to the Cape (Worden 2005). Use of penal labor increased in the transition years of abolition as slave labor progressively dwindled. For example, between 1815 and 1836 the English East India Company dispatched 1,500 Bengali convicts to Mauritius—where the migrant convict labor system lasted until 1851—ostensibly for public works but sometimes assigned, in return for payment, to private planters who often treated them as slaves (Anderson 2005). Penal labor was also widely used by indigenous authorities for the harshest types of work. For instance, the Merina regime in Madagascar used convicts in road construction, mining, and foundries.

Indentured labor was also a major form of bonded labor. Indentured labor was an old institution in Africa where it often overlapped with European concepts of indentureship and servant. For instance, indentureship was a significant feature of eighteenth-century Cape Society where it was either formalized by contracts, or imposed ad hoc, as with Khoi and San boys captured in the interior by Dutch farmers who forced them to work until the age of twenty-five, by which time they were often married, with sons who were subject to similar obligations. Many parents refused to abandon their children, and so remained tied to the farm for life. Following abolition of the slave trade in 1807, the Caledon Code of 1809 formalized indenture in the Cape through a pass system which bound victims to farms in a system of "virtual slavery." Thus, Nigel Worden argues, the first effective formal abolition in the Cape was not official abolition in 1834 but the 1828 repeal of the Caledon Code (2005). Again, upon abolition in the Cape and Mauritius, ex-slaves, who received no financial assistance, were declared to be apprentices and obliged to continue working for a fixed period for their old masters—in the Cape until 1838, and on Mauritius until 1839.

The failure to transform ex-slaves into pliant wage laborers resulted in the rise of a modified indenture system. A feature of British colonies from 1833 to 1920, it generally involved Indians and Chinese on five-year contracts. Of indentured Indians, some 453,000 were shipped to Mauritius, 152,000 to Natal, 32,000 to East Africa, 26,500 to Réunion, and 6,300 to the Seychelles. Contemporary observers and subsequent historians have underlined that the recruitment, transport, and living and working conditions of indentured laborers were often similar to those of slaves.

Indebtedness was a central feature of indentureship as indenture brokers advanced money to household or local agents through whom workers were recruited. Recruits were then obliged to remit sums to their home regions in order that such advances be repaid. Debtors also signed up in order to earn the money to repay their creditors. Recruits were additionally often obliged to repay the capital and interest on the cost of transport to their place of employment.

Further, colonial regimes introduced varieties of forced labor. These remained generally in place until 1945, but did not always have the intended impact. For instance, French *corvée* policies to promote cotton in Côte d'Ivoire failed because of a more successful indigenous cotton-producing and marketing system (Bassett 2001). In Madagascar, indigenous growers proved more efficient than Mascarene coffee planters, and when in 1946 the local French administration ordered them to perform *corvée* labor on European plantations, they rose in revolt (Campbell 2006).

Globalization, Child Labor, and the Sex Slave Trade

A major link between historical and modern bondage is the continued trafficking and exploitation of children—generally defined as those below the age of eighteen. Recent research indicates that complex elements are at work, including rural-urban and male-female employment, and matriarchal versus patriarchal family units. In Côte d'Ivoire, children as young as twelve may migrate to cocoa farms. However, most do so voluntarily and engage in light work. Exploitation is thus missing. By contrast, in rural Benin, traffickers, taking advantage of local traditions of children migrating to work as servants in wealthy urban households in return for education and training, trick parents into handing over their children who end up in forms of urban bondage (Manzo 2005, 397). Even less ambiguous is the case of child soldiers—a widespread phenomenon in Africa owing to the large number of civil conflicts. Most children are forcibly recruited and their labor ruthlessly exploited, often as frontline soldiers, and, in the case of girls, to sexually service males. The sex slave trade, a central feature of modern human trafficking, arose largely as a result of modern capitalist forces. Whereas the pre-1800 trade in people for sexual purposes was largely limited to a small traffic in beautiful, often highly trained girls for elite males, in the 1800s recognizably modern forms of sexual bondage developed. This was due to rising gender imbalance in key locations as a result of the commercial boom associated with the international economy, and military action associated with European imperialism. The most notorious case in Africa is possibly the Belgian Congo where sexual abuse and bondage were commonly inflicted on local women by European officials and soldiers. In late nineteenth-century Natal, some white planters controlled Indian male workers' access to women—wives and prostitutes—as a means of reward and punishment.

Again, civil wars and a breakdown of law and order have through the last decades of the twentieth and first decade of the twenty-first century greatly increased sexual violence, sex trafficking and sexual bondage in Africa. In South Africa, one of Africa's most dynamic yet troubled economies, mafia-type gangs commonly recruit both domestic African and foreign women and children for sexual trafficking. Victims are at high risk of contracting HIV and consequently of incurring sharply reduced living standards and life expectancy. Again, in West Africa, Ghana is a center for the distribution of Ghanaian and Nigerian women and girls to Europe, the Gulf States, and South Africa for sexual exploitation (Adepoju 2005, 77–78).

Conclusion

It is increasingly clear that conventionally understood models of Atlantic slavery are inadequate in explaining the full history of African bondage. Outside areas dominated by the Atlantic slave trade, myriad forms of human servitude existed, varying according to region and time. Colonial authorities tolerated many of these, notably forms of female servitude. Others, such as types of *corvée* labor, they adapted for their own purposes. In a few areas, they also tolerated chattel slavery. The collapse of colonial empires, and the post-1945 rise of Cold War tensions and more effective international organizations, spelled the end of most forms of chattel slavery. However, the rise of the international economy, and notably of globalization from the 1980s—in the context of feeble, corrupt, or uncaring governments—has encouraged a plethora of forms of human servitude and trafficking that continue to the present day, and continue to affect, in the main, the most vulnerable, notably women and children.

Suggested Readings

Campbell, Gwyn. 1988. "Slavery and Fanompoana: The Structure of Forced Labour in Imerina (Madagascar), 1790–1861." *Journal of African History* 29 (3): 463–86.

———, ed. 2005. *Abolition and Its Aftermath in Indian Ocean Africa and Asia*. London: Routledge.

Campbell, Gwyn, and Alessandro Stanziani, eds. 2013. *Bonded Labour and Debt in the Indian Ocean World*. London: Pickering & Chatto.

Clarence-Smith, William Gervase. 1989. *The Economics of the Indian Ocean Slave Trade in the Nineteenth Century*. London: Frank Cass.

———. 2011. "The Redemption of Child Slaves by Christian Missionaries in Central Africa, 1876–1914." In *Child Slaves in the Modern World*, edited by Gwyn Campbell, Suzanne Miers, and Joseph C. Miller, 173–90. Athens: Ohio University Press.

Honwana, Alcinda M. 2006. *Child Soldiers in Africa*. Philadelphia: University of Pennsylvania Press.

Kopytoff, Igor, and Suzanne Miers, eds. 1977. *Slavery in Africa: Historical and Anthropological Perspectives*. Madison: University of Wisconsin Press.

Lovejoy, Paul, and Toyin Falola. 2003. *Pawnship, Slavery, and Colonialism in Africa*. Trenton, NJ: Africa World Press.

Manning, Patrick. 1900a. *Slavery and African Life: Occidental, Oriental and African Slave Trades*. Cambridge: Cambridge University Press.

Miers, Suzanne, and Martin Klein, eds. 1999. *Slavery and Colonial Rule in Africa*. Portland, OR: Frank Cass.

Robertson, Claire C., and Martin A. Klein. 1983. *Women and Slavery in Africa*. Madison: University of Wisconsin Press.

Turshen, Meredeth, and Clotilde Twagiramariya. 1998. *What Women Do in Wartime: Gender and Conflict in Africa*. London: Zed.

Watson, James L., ed. 1980. *Asian and African Systems of Slavery*. Berkeley: University of California Press.

References

Adepoju, Aderanti. 2005. Review of "Research and Data on Human Trafficking in Sub-Saharan Africa." *International Migration* 43 (1/2): 75–98.

Anderson, Clare. 2005. "The Bel Ombre Rebellion: Indian Convicts in Mauritius, 1815–1853." In *Abolition and Its Aftermath in Indian Ocean Africa and Asia*, edited by Gwyn Campbell, 50–65. London: Routledge.

Bassett, Thomas J. 2001. *The Peasant Cotton Revolution in West Africa: Côte d'Ivoire, 1880–1995*. New York: Cambridge University Press.

Campbell, Gwyn. 2004. Introduction. *The Structure of Slavery in Indian Ocean Africa and Asia*, edited by G. Campbell, vii–xxxi. London: Frank Cass.

———. 2005a. *An Economic History of Imperial Madagascar, 1750–1895: The Rise and Fall of an Island Empire*. Cambridge: Cambridge University Press.

———. 2005b. "Unfree Labour and the Significance of Abolition in Madagascar, c. 1825–97." In *Abolition and Its Aftermath in Indian Ocean Africa and Asia*, edited by Gwyn Campbell, 65–82. London: Routledge.

———. 2006. "Coffee Production in Madagascar." In *Coffee under Colonialism and Post-Colonialism: The Global Coffee Economy in Africa, Asia, and Latin America, 1500–1989*, edited by William Gervase Clarence Smith and Steven Topik, 67–99. Cambridge: Cambridge University Press.

———. 2008. "Servitude and the Changing Face of Demand for Labour in the Indian Ocean World, c. 1800–1900." *Slavery and the Slave Trades in the Indian Ocean and Arab Worlds: Global Connections and Disconnections*. Proceedings of the 10th Annual Gilder Lehrman Center International Conference at Yale University.

Caplan, Lionel. 1980. "Power and Status in South Asian Slavery." In *Asian and African Systems of Slavery*, edited by James L. Watson, 1–15. Berkeley: University of California Press.

Clarence-Smith, William Gervase. 2013. "Debt and the Coercion of Labour in the Islamic Legal Tradition." In *Bonded Labour and Debt in the Indian Ocean World*, edited by Gwyn Campbell and Alessandro Stanziani, 21–30. London: Pickering.

Cordell, Denis D., and Joel W. Gregory, eds. 1987. *African Population and Capitalism: Historical Perspectives*. Boulder, CO: Westview.

Eno, Omar A. 2005. "The Abolition of Slavery and the Aftermath Stigma: The Case of the Bantu/Jareer People on the Benadir Coast of Southern Somalia." In *Abolition and Its Aftermath in Indian Ocean Africa and Asia*, edited by Gwyn Campbell, 83–93. London: Routledge.

Finley, Moses I. 1980. *Ancient Slavery and Modern Ideology*. London: Chatto and Windus.

Finley, Moses. I. 1959. "Was Greek Civilization Based on Slave Labour?" *Historia: Zeitschrift für Alte Geschichte* 8 (2): 145–64.

Goody, Jack. 1980. "Slavery in Time and Space." In *Asian and African Systems of Slavery*, edited by James L. Watson, 16–42. Berkeley: University of California Press.

Harris, Karen L. 2010. "Sugar and Gold: Indentured Indian and Chinese Labour in South Africa." *Journal of Social Science* 25 (1–3): 147–58.

Klein, Martin. 1994. "Simulating the African Slave Trade." *Canadian Journal of African Studies* 28 (2): 296–99.

Lovejoy, Paul E. 2012. *Transformations in Slavery: A History of Slavery in Africa*. New York: Cambridge University Press.

Manning, Patrick. 1990b. "The Slave Trade: The Formal Demography of a Global System." *Social Science History* 14 (2): 255–79.

Manzo, Kate. 2005. "Exploiting West Africa's Children: Trafficking, Slavery and Uneven Development." *Area* 37 (4): 393–401.

Mark, Samuel. 2002. "Alexander the Great, Seafaring, and the Spread of Leprosy." *Journal of the History of Medicine and Allied Sciences* 57 (3): 285–311.

Miers, Suzanne. 2005. "Slavery and the Slave Trade in Saudi Arabia and the Arab States on the Persian Gulf, 1921–1963." In *Abolition and Its Aftermath in Indian Ocean Africa and Asia*, edited by Gwyn Campbell, 120–36. London: Routledge.

Northrup, David. 1995. *Indentured Labor in the Age of Imperialism, 1834–1922*. Cambridge: Cambridge University Press.

Watson, James L. 1980. "Slavery as an Institution, Open and Closed Systems." In *Asian and African Systems of Slavery*, edited by James L. Watson, 1–15. Berkeley: University of California Press.

Worden, Nigel. 2005. "Indian Ocean Slavery and Its Demise in the Cape Colony." In *Abolition and Its Aftermath in Indian Ocean Africa and Asia*, edited by Gwyn Campbell, 29–49. London: Routledge.

Worden, Nigel, Elizabeth van Heyningen, and Vivian Bickford-Smith. 2004. *Cape Town: The Making of a City*. Cape Town: David Philip.

4 CITIZENSHIP

Francis B. Nyamnjoh

Citizenship can be a very nebulous concept. The idea of a citizen as an autonomous, rights-bearing individual who enjoys total freedom of choice in a legal and political sense, and who is answerable to none other than the constitution as supreme law of the land protected by a minimalist enabler state, sits uncomfortably with an Africa caught between corrupted cultural traditions and a blighted modernity. To insist that there are no intermediate solidarities and loyalties between the individual and the state, or to ignore such loyalties, which are actually more often determined by blood than by choice, is to force Africans to live a lie in the name of "freedom."

When it is scholars who insist as such, they demonstrably privilege a prescriptive scholarship of sterility and teleology that holds little bearing on the lived experiences of the citizens studied; as such, the impression given is that the shelf life of concepts is more important than their analytical relevance and empirical grounding. Yet, often isolated from the rights and privileges of those who "belong," "outsiders" tend to mediate barriers, borders, and boundaries in fluid and dynamic ways, producing identities that run across cultures, languages, and spaces in cities and within broader, national, contexts. The processes through which they engineer "composite" or "frontier" identities often escape a scholarship that uncritically reproduces taken-for-granted dichotomies and bounded notions of being and belonging. To fail to recognize such extensions to the conceptualization of citizenship, made possible by ordinary Africans immersed in popular traditions of meaning making, would be contrary to the very affirmation of autonomy of thought and representation accorded citizens (regardless of class or status). However schooled in Western modernity the state elite may be, to label and dismiss as a contradiction to citizenship all that is counter to their Western-inspired templates is to belie the very claim that their project is predicated on the principle of freedom of choice. It makes little sense to employ free-floating, untested assumptions about citizenship in the study of Africa where people, in their lived realities, have little room for neat dichotomies, even when their pronouncements or discourses might sometimes suggest otherwise. Just as we must taste our theoretical puddings to prove their worth, so is that true of citizenship studies as it is of every other facet of being and living in Africa.

A nuanced understanding of citizenship would be one that embraces instead of shies away from the complexity of being African. Identities on the continent, like identities elsewhere, are a permanent work in progress. Stereotypical evolutionism aside, human beings everywhere are complex and intricate, and identities are always the result of processes of becoming, best understood as flexible, fluid, and full of ellipses—an unfinished and unfinishable story in sociality and civility. Being and becoming citizens as works in progress require open-mindedness and open-endedness in encounters and the relationships they engender, reproduce, or contest. Particular contexts challenge us in particular ways to heighten or lower the bar and threshold of acceptability and tolerability in claims and denials of citizenship. It is through a simultaneous recognition of Africa's capacity to act on others as well as to bear the actions of others in time and space that an appropriate citizenship actualizes. Such a citizenship is far from possible in contexts where the myth of self-cultivation, self-activation, and self-management is uncritically internalized and reproduced with effortless abundance like an easily counterfeited, devalued currency. Citizens are not citizens in abstraction, but citizens through binding relationships and social action.

Reconceptualizing Citizenship

The future of citizenship in Africa and globally is in recognizing and providing for the truism that rights articulated in abstraction and without obligations do not amount to much. Throughout the world civic citizenship is facing hard times, as multitudes (ranging from women's movements to diasporas through youth movements and cultural communities big and small) clamor for inclusion by challenging the myopia implicit in the conservative juridico-political rhetoric and practices of nation-states. In Africa, social media–driven youth movements (such as the Arab Spring of North Africa) are involved in renegotiation of the exclusionary bases of citizenship that have fueled conflicts over belonging and representation. Women's movements are equally active throughout the continent, challenging the indicators of citizenship narrowly informed by the privileged biases of Western and African masculinities.

There is a clear need to reconceptualize citizenship in ways that create political, cultural, social, and economic space for excluded nationals and non-nationals alike, as individuals and collectivities. Such inclusion is best guaranteed by what anthropologist Aihwa Ong has called "flexible citizenship" unbounded by race, ethnicity, class, gender, or geography, and that is both conscious and critical of hierarchies that make a mockery of the juridico-political regime of citizenship provided by the coercive illusion of the nation-state. In this fluid and open-ended idea of citizenship, space should be created for its articulation at different levels, from the most global to the most local or autochthonous, from the ethnic to the civic, and from the individual to the collective. Just as cultural, economic, and social citizenship are as valid as juridico-political citizenship, so are collective, group, or community citizenship as valid as individual citizenship, to be claimed at every level, from the most small-scale local to the most mega-scale global levels. The idea of corporate, digital, electronic, cyber, global, itinerant, and related claims to citizenship are easily understandable and accommodated under the framework of flexible citizenship. The emphasis should be on the freedom of individuals and communities to negotiate inclusion, opt out, and opt in with total flexibility and reversibility of belonging in consonance with their realities as repertoires, melting pots, or straddlers of various identity margins.

Society is never monolithic, whatever the ambitions of some in this regard, and citizenship, as recognition and representation for pluralism and diversity, requires a delicate balancing of tensions between competing and often conflicting interests, aspirations, and truths. The more intricate the constellations of interests are, the greater the divergences in claims of citizenship, and the more imperative a case for a negotiated, accommodating consensus. Depending on the society in question and the disposition for mutual accommodation of its members, the interests are shaped by real or imagined identity, or boundary, markers. Articulated either as cast in stone or lines drawn in the sand, such markers may include the race or ethnicity, place or geography, class or status, gender or sexuality, generation or age of the individuals or groups competing for civil spaces and opportunities to activate and cultivate themselves to maximize, inter alia, their political, social, and economic dreams. Such factors comprise the basis on which privileges are claimed and contested, sought and maintained. Within a given social context, the fulfillment of citizenship is dependent on the relative advantage or disadvantage of each social category in relation to others in the interplay of hierarchies engineered by all or some of these factors and more. The interplays in turn result in hierarchies of interests legitimated by the relationships and dynamics of power between the social actors compartmentalized by these same factors. Histories and processes of encounters among social categories and between societies are critical for understanding changing configurations of citizenship.

Such an understanding of citizen and citizenship is a particularly relevant framework for Africa, in view of the phenomenal challenges facing current postcolonial attempts at crafting a common political and legal citizenship. It is in recognition of these challenges and tensions that Mahmood Mamdani invites us to recognize the bifurcated nature of citizenship in Africa by distinguishing between "ethnic" and "civic" citizenship. Overt tensions and conflicts within and between states speak of the unfinished and sometimes unstarted business of nation building around a shared or consensual set of core values. In many a situation, the state remains an extravagant irrelevance, with hardly any significant legitimacy beyond the handful of elite in power. Popular forms of citizenship and legitimacy with longer histories of practice, relevance, and suffrage are more likely to be expressed along lines of indigenous and endogenous forms of social organization and government than on the lines of political party and civil society organizations of voluntary membership that came with European colonialism or that mimic present-day Western associations. Given the very recent colonial past of the continent, and in view of the overwhelming grip of Western modernity on postcolonial state making, the challenges facing citizenship projects in Africa are particularly daunting.

Ethnic and Cultural Forms of Citizenship

In postcolonial Africa, where social action unfolds within a framework of interconnecting global and local hierarchies, communities large and small have both accepted and contested arbitrary colonial and postcolonial administrative boundaries and the dynamics of dispossession. Social movements and associations (voluntary and otherwise) concerned with the struggles for freedom and social justice of marginalized social categories and identities have proliferated across Africa, sometimes with the assistance of alternative and social media. Failing to achieve the idealized "nation-state" form and possessing relatively weak forces vis-à-vis global ones, African states have often sought to capitalize on the contradictory and complementary dimensions of civic, ethnic, and cultural citizenships. In this context, being a citizen in ethnic or cultural terms is much more than merely claiming to be, or being regarded as, an autochthon or an authentic son or daughter of a native soil. Under colonial and apartheid regimes, when technologies of dominance were perfected with policies and practices of divide and rule, to be called "indigenous," "autochthonous," or "native" was first to create and impose a proliferation of native, autochthonous, or indigenous identities circumscribed by arbitrary physical and cultural geographies. Second, the labels were to make possible not only distinctions between colonized "native" and colonizing Europeans but also between "native citizens" and "native settlers" among ethnic communities within the same colony. And, third, the objective of the label was to define the primitive, and therefore offer a perfect justification for the colonial *mission civilizatrice* (civilizing mission), for the dispossession of the indigenous and their confinement to officially designated tribal territories, homelands, or Bantustans; this was often done in callous disregard to the histories of relationships and interconnections forged with excluded others, or the differences and tensions even among the included.

In all, being an ethnic citizen was for the majority colonized "native" population to be shunted to the margins. These dynamics of classification and rule conceived of the "natives" through frozen ideas of culture and imagined traditions, or what Mamdani has termed "decentralized despotisms" in rural areas, while the town and city were reserved for the minority colonial settler population and their purportedly "modernizing," "cultured," and "detribalized" African servants and support staff. Today, towns and cities are still instinctively perceived as the places and spaces well suited for citizens, while rural areas and villages are the reserve and preserve of ethnic citizens and strangers confined or subjected to the diktats of culture and tradition under chiefly authority. Few, even among critically minded scholars, are ready to entertain the prospect that Africans are active agents, busying themselves domesticating imported ideas of citizenship by bringing them into conversation with endogenous ideas of citizenship, some of which predate the continent's subjection to the whims and caprices of European ambitions of dominance.

If the negative colonial and apartheid history of ethnic or cultural citizenship continues to shape the highly critical stance of African intellectuals and nationalists toward all claims of autochthony, it has also, quite paradoxically, tended to render invisible the everyday reality of postcolonial Africans (including those same intellectuals and nationalists) who straddle civic, ethnic, and cultural citizenships on the one hand, and multiple global and local cosmopolitan identities on the other hand. The baby of ethnic and cultural citizenship does not have to be thrown out with the bathwater of colonialism and apartheid.

With growing uncertainties and the questioning of the inadequacies of civic citizenship and its illusions of autonomy, rigid and highly exclusionary affirmations of being indigenous have become prevalent among majority and minority communities alike within various states in Africa. An outcome is covert or overt confrontation and conflict over territoriality and access to power and resources. The logic of ever-diminishing circles of inclusion dictates that the next foreigner or stranger is always one layer below the obvious one.

South Africa, where xenophobic eruptions against migrants from elsewhere in Africa are commonplace, offers excellent illustrations of this obsession both in a song by popular Zulu musician Mbongeni Ngema, released in May 2002, and in a diversity advertisement released by Nando's, a restaurant chain, in June 2012. Titled AmaNdiya, Ngema's controversial song claims to "begin a constructive discussion that would lead to a true reconciliation between Indians and Africans," and accuses South African Indians of opportunism and of enriching themselves to the detriment of blacks. In the song Ngema goes on to say that if Indians are to be taken seriously as belonging to South Africa, they must display greater patriotism and stop straddling continents. Implied in his song is that Indians risk losing their South African citizenship should they refuse to change their ways. And if and when Indians are gone in this bizarre nativity game of exclusionary violence and South Africa's problems are still unsolved, the next target is just a layer below.

This regressive logic and the scapegoating of perceived outsiders are also well captured by the Nando's diversity advertisement. The ad articulates an idea of identity and belonging in South Africa that is both conscious and cognizant of the histories of mobilities of peoples that have made South Africa possible. The ad starts with black Africans illegally crossing a barbed-wire border fence into South Africa. There is a voice-over and each time the voice calls out a name, the group of people who represent that particular identity are transformed into a cloud of smoke, as follows:

> You know what is wrong with South Africa: all you foreigners. You must all go back to where you came from—you Cameroonians, Congolese, Pakistanis, Somalis, Ghanaians and Kenyans. And, of course, you Nigerians and you Europeans. Let's not forget you Indians and Chinese. Even you Afrikaners. Back to Swaziland you Swazis, Lesotho you Sothos, Vendas, Zulus, everybody.

In the end, only one person is left standing, a San man who, armed with a bow and arrow and ready to explore the wilderness, confronts the voice-over with these words: "I'm not going anywhere. You found us here." The ad concludes with the voice-over saying: "Real South Africans love diversity. That's why we have introduced two more items: New peri-crusted wings and delicious Trinchado and chips."

To my mind, far from promoting xenophobia, this ad challenges narrow and parochial identities, or ideas of being and belonging as a zero-sum game. It plays with exclusionary obsessions by demonstrating the absurdity of ever-regressive logics and ever-diminishing circles of being South African in a world characterized by the flexible mobility of people. It invites us to contemplate what it is to be South African, if every color of its current rainbow configuration must go back to their Nazareth and be counted. If belonging is articulated in rigid exclusionary terms, where everyone, however mobile, is considered to belong to a particular homeland somewhere else, a place they cannot outgrow and which they must belong to regardless of where they were born or where they live and work, then South Africa can only belong to one group of people, those who were there before everyone else: the San—they, who know only too well that they are the bona fide sons and daughters of the South African soil and its resources, the only authentic South Africans. These examples demonstrate that citizenship is negotiated from an unfolding history of encounters between different people and ideas, and among a diversity of interests and aspirations.

Conviviality

States and policy makers, inclined to police rather than facilitate mobility and a flexible disposition to citizenship, stand to learn from the forging of everyday conviviality in urban Africa. Urban life in Africa depends on the extent to which Africans circulate or are circulated. The city, urban transport most especially, offers us a privileged site to fathom how Africans in their flexible mobility negotiate their citizenship through relationships.

Citizenship and belonging are negotiated in spaces of public transit, such as trains, taxis, and buses, and are dependent upon a fine line of conviviality. As a multitude of travelers pass in, out, and through each day, zones of mobility and public transport become places of intense negotiation and interaction. Conviviality emerges in the frequent interplay between dynamics of group autonomy on the one hand and interdependent communalism of groups on the other hand. Tensions are often put aside out of mutual necessity to make one's way throughout the city. Conviviality emerges out of the necessity to earn one's living, to surmount the tensions and divisions of inequality with attempts at flexibility propelled by the need to get by. Conviviality, in many ways, results from compliances with cultural implications of power. Its intricacies in the lived everyday are, in fact, steeped in tensions.

Understanding the sense of belonging that citizens feel, display, mobilize, invest in, and invariably ambiguate is essential to the challenge of exploring and theorizing what Edgar Pieterse terms "African cityness." An analytical focus on conviviality in the everyday narrative of "insiders" and "outsiders" and their relationships as "intimate strangers" demonstrates the thorny paradoxes of intimacy and mutuality, representative of contestations of belonging taking place in urban African crucibles of becoming. Conviviality rests on the nuances inscribed and imbibed in everyday relations—the micro-trends of socialization. Conviviality makes possible interdependence among humans whose tendency is to seek autonomy even at the risk of losing dependency. Urban conviviality has little room for neat dichotomies emphasizing distinct places and spaces for different social categories and hierarchies, as urbanites, like porcupines compelled to huddle together to keep warm in winter, can ill afford to insist rising above the messiness of everyday realities. The entangled, interconnected, or even mangled lives of urbanites suggest an approach at understanding them that seeks to marry the emotional and the rational which they embody as social and relational beings.

How simple or complex, bounded or flexible—indeed, how convivial or not—we are in our articulation of what constitutes citizenship in Africa is informed by whom we are ready to include in our shopping basket as "an African." In this regard, critical interrogations such as the following demonstrate the intricacies involved in establishing the attributes of being and belonging as a citizen in Africa:

What does it mean to be African? Who qualifies to claim Africa? Is being African or claiming Africa an attribute of race and skin color (black, white, yellow), birth (umbilical cord, birth certificates, identity cards, passports), geography (physical spaces, home village), history (encounters), culture (prescriptive specificities), economics (availability and affordability, wealth and deprivation), sociology (social configurations and action, inclusion and exclusion), psychology (mindsets), philosophy (world views), politics (power relations), or collective memory (shared experiences and aspirations)—to name just a few of the many possibilities that present themselves? These are questions which have deep roots in debates on citizenship and identity—and, therefore, in the definition of rights, entitlements, duties, and responsibilities. The questions, of course, are not uniquely African—indeed, similar issues have been posed and debated with considerable passion in other parts of the world both historically and contemporaneously, and contestations around them have also often been played out in violent communal confrontations, civil wars, and interstate conflicts. And while they may seem straightforward to answer, the questions have been rendered much more complex by the dynamic interplay of race, ethnicity, gender, and religion in the structuring and exercise of power and opportunity. Precisely for this reason, they are not questions that can be addressed in the abstract.

In Africa, like everywhere else, aspirations for and claims of purity, authenticity, and primary and often parochial identities coexist with notions of the nation-state and its logic of large-scale, exclusive communities. This would suggest that citizenship is necessarily bringing the parochial and the cosmopolitan into conversation aimed at providing for and encouraging a citizenry that negotiates and navigates conviviality from the intersection of myriad identity margins. Yet, everywhere in the world, we are all familiar with the question: "Where do you come from, originally?," which seems ready for no answer short of the land of your birth, or the birth of your father. Here is an exchange which reportedly took place between an English woman and a black British girl:

ENGLISH WOMAN: Where were you born?
BLACK GIRL: Manchester.
ENGLISH WOMAN: I mean before that.

Similarly, when people I meet for the first time seem to think they know where I come from with questions like, "Are you from X?"—X standing for the village, town, city or country of their guesswork—I usually leave them perplexed when I answer, "Not yet."

Within the framework of hierarchies among nationals as insiders and between nationals and non-nationals in Africa, even where citizenship is granted to mobile outsiders, the emphasis in official documentation on "original country of birth" means that naturalized citizens are always haunted by the potential inferiority of "legal citizenship" to "citizenship by birth," as claims of authentic belonging as "sons and daughters" of the "native" soil—autochthons—can always be invoked to exclude those who belong only by force of the law. We have seen manifestations of this almost everywhere in Africa—ranging from "Ghana Must Go" in Nigeria and "Cam No Go" in Cameroon, to "Makwerekwere" in Botswana and South Africa, through "Nyak" in Senegal and "L'Ivoirité" in Côte d'Ivoire. In this sense, the law facilitates violence against those seen not to be lawful or official rights bearers. To make a case about who belongs, states do not hesitate to explore and embrace the distinction between "handheld and heartfelt" citizenship and indicators of belonging. It is not enough to carry official documentations of belonging and wave the national flag of a given country; you have to be seen to belong by hard core or bona fide blood and umbilical cord insiders who arrogate to themselves the prerogative of ultimate legitimizers of belonging.

Such bureaucratic and legalistic indicators and the opportunism they excite notwithstanding, it is however safe to say that to most ordinary people in Africa, citizenship is more than just a birth certificate, an identity card, or a passport. For them, to be African and belong to a country or a community is not simply to be labeled or merely defined as such bureaucratically and for purposes of administrative control. It is to be a social actor enmeshed in a particular context that has been and continues to be shaped by unique histories marked by unequal encounters and misrepresentations often informed by the arrogance and ignorance of the economically and politically powerful, who take the liberty also to attribute a cultural superiority to themselves. For many an ordinary African, being and belonging anywhere in Africa is above all a lived reality, one that is constantly shaped and reshaped by their toil and sweat as subjected and devalued humanity, even as they struggle to live in dignity and to transform their societies progressively. For these people, the fact of their belonging and citizenship is neither in question nor a question.

A citizen, therefore, is a person who has attained considerable social visibility within the community to which they belong. Such visibility may come from the responsibilities that person assumes in their community. Fulfilling responsibilities entitles the person in turn to seek rights from and protection by the institutions that govern everyday life, practices, and processes in the community. There is nothing, however, to suggest that such relationships of obligation and reciprocity can or may only be fulfilled under and by a state or a particular form of state. This point is worth insisting upon as states are the product of history, whose form and transformation are dictated by contextual specificities and the encounters and relationships that shape and are shaped by them. Every community, state and stateless, large-scale and small-scale, seeks to reproduce itself through shared values and aspirations by insisting on rights and obligations from those it recognizes and purports to represent or those who aspire to be recognized and represented by it. The status of citizen can be claimed under group identities that are not necessarily static or large-scale or common in origin. Belonging and being a citizen are more flexible identities than we have the habit of admitting when we define and confine them in abstraction.

Conclusion

Being a citizen is a permanent work in progress. It is part of a lifelong quest to be human in the world. Although being incomplete is the normal order of things and calls for interdependence and conviviality, it is a common tendency for some to mobilize coercive violence in an illusory and elusive quest for independence to accumulate with reckless abandon while policing others' aspirations. Citizenship is an attribute of being and becoming human through constant awareness and provision for the normalcy of incompleteness in how one claims rights in full cognizance of one's obligations to oneself, to others, and to the imperatives of society. Citizenship is a capacity, technique, or technology of self-cultivation and self-activation through relationships of sociality and civility. But given the ambitions of dominance of those in power who may or may not act on behalf of the communities or societies they purport to lead, citizenship is also a technology, technique, or capacity of ownership and control of mechanisms of belonging. It is in this sense that apparently emancipatory technological innovations in the fields of information and communication are often paradoxically employed by states and corporations to police the circulation of people, ideas, and things. Citizenship in this sense becomes the power to mobilize and immobilize, recognize and ignore with impunity. It is the dictatorship of being privileged and in charge. Thus, not surprisingly, for example, African states are just as keen as states elsewhere in using the emerging computerized identification and biometric technologies to define, confine, and monitor for disciplinary purposes the flow of people, things, and ideas within and across borders. As a system of social recognition and social control, citizenship pertains to the whole complex of power, privilege, obligations, and responsibilities of being a citizen in time and space. However, to confine or reduce citizenship to the beck and call of zero-sum games of power and dominance is to impoverish the creative innovation of being human through rights and responsibilities.

Citizenship thrives on a balance of tensions between centripetal and centrifugal forces in the lives of individuals and societies. It is simultaneously open-ended and close-ended, inclusive and exclusive, real and aspirational. It is as much a mark of birth, an observatory for navel gazing as it is about creative innovation, achievement, and choice. Even as a birthmark, citizenship can be formed, transformed, and reformed, configured and reconfigured with changing encounters and the myriad possibilities they inspire. Citizenship is a thirst for which there is no final quencher, a quest whose successes are measured not in definitive answers, but rather in the ever-new ways of questioning it engenders. The story of citizenship the world over is the story of how actively and successfully those claiming it are open to balancing the possibilities and tensions between nature and nurture, ascription and achievement, blood and choice, autonomy and sociality, independence and dependence, us and them, here and there, the familiar and the profane. It is the story of the making of conviviality by turning adversaries into intimate strangers.

It is evident that such flexible citizenship is incompatible with the prevalent illusion that the nation-state is the only political unit permitted to confer citizenship in the modern world. Nor is it compatible with a regime of rights and entitlements that is narrowly focused on the illusion of "the autonomous individual." The price of perpetuating these illusions has been the proliferation of ultranationalism, chauvinism, racism, and xenophobia that have consciously denied the fragmented, multinational, and heterogeneous cultural realities of most so-called nation-states. The tendency has been for the citizenship thus inspired to assume the stature of a giant compressor of, especially, cultural differences. Almost everywhere, this narrow model has cherished hierarchies based on race, ethnicity, class, gender, and geography, which have tended to impose on perceived inferior others the decisions made by those who see themselves as more authentic or more deserving of citizenship. The citizenship that hails from such a celebration of insensitivities is clearly not a model for a future of larger mobility and increased claims for rights, recognition, and representation by its individual and collective victims. Flexible citizenship informed by flexible mobility, on the other hand—a reading of citizenship whose relationship with the nation-state is open-ended and convivial—renders citizenship and belonging as truly cosmopolitan and in tune with the age-old reality of composite identities and societies in Africa.

Suggested Readings

Chachage, Seithi L. C., and Karuti Kanyinga, eds. 2003. Special issue: "Globalization and Citizenship in Africa." *Africa Development* 28 (1 and 2).

Comaroff, John L., and Jean Comaroff, eds. 1999. *Civil Society and the Political Imagination in Africa: Critical Perspectives*. Chicago: University of Chicago.

Dawson, Marcelle. 2010. "The Cost of Belonging: Exploring Class and Citizenship in Soweto's Water War." *Citizenship Studies* 14 (4): 381–94.

Englund, Harri. 2006. *Prisoners of Freedom: Human Rights and the African Poor*. Berkeley: University of California Press.

Englund, Harri, and Francis B. Nyamnjoh, eds. 2004. *Rights and the Politics of Recognition in Africa*. London: Zed.

Geschiere, Peter, and Francis B. Nyamnjoh. 2000. "Capitalism and Autochthony: The Seesaw of Mobility and Belonging." *Public Culture* 12 (2): 423–52.

Halisi, C. R. D., Paul J. Kaiser, and Stephen N. Ndegwa, eds. 1998. "Rethinking Citizenship in Africa." *Africa Today* 45: 3–4.

Kopytoff, Igor. 1987. *The African Frontier: The Reproduction of Traditional African Societies*. Bloomington: Indiana University Press.

MacGaffey, Wyatt. 1995. "Kongo Identity, 1483–1993." *South Atlantic Quarterly* 94 (4): 1025–37.

Mamdani, Mahmood. 1996. *Citizen and Subject: Contemporary Africa and the Legacy of Late Colonialism*. Cape Town: David Philip.

Manby, Bronwen. 2009. *Struggles for Citizenship in Africa*. London: Zed.

Nyamnjoh, Francis B. 2006. *Insiders and Outsiders: Citizenship and Xenophobia in Contemporary Southern Africa*. London: CODESRIA/Zed.

———. 2007. "From Bounded to Flexible Citizenship: Lessons from Africa." *Citizenship Studies* 11 (1): 73–82.

Ong, Aihwa. 1999. *Flexible Citizenship: The Cultural Logics of Transnationality*. Durham, NC: Duke University Press.

Werbner, Richard, and Deborah Gaitskell, eds. 2002. Special Issue: "Minorities and Citizenship in Botswana." *Journal of Southern African Studies* 28 (4).

Yuval-Davis, Nira, and Pnina Werbner, eds. 1999. *Women, Citizenship and Difference*. London: Zed.

5 COLONIALISM

John L. Comaroff and Jean Comaroff

Did "Europe's colonization of the world," as Herbert Lüthy (1964, 36) once claimed, really mark "the painful birth" of the modern? The jury is still out on this question. For one thing, colonialisms of various kinds long preexisted modernity. For another, it depends on what, precisely, is meant by the modern. And what by colonialism. To be sure, the relationship between them remains the subject of contention. This is in spite of the fact that much has been written about the former, colonialism, over the past forty or so years, a good deal of it in revisionist mode. It has become commonplace, for example, to observe that the term covers a range of historical phenomena far broader, and older, than is often allowed; also that, since the fin de siècle, there has been a sea change in approaches to its analysis, partly at the insistence of those once colonized. Alongside older forms of modernization theory and their Marxist antitheses—whose traces remain strong in Western thought—there has arisen a growing concern with colonialism's contingent, constructed, cultural dimensions (e.g., Dirks 1992); with its conceptualization and its historiography (Cooper 2005); with the making of colonial subjects through dispersed disciplinary regimes (e.g., Mitchell 1991) and the circulation of commodities (e.g., Mintz 1985); with its retrospective narration by those subjects (Scott 2004); with the forms of violence implicated in it (e.g., Taussig 1987); with the sorts of subjection and citizenship to which it conduced (Mamdami 1996); with the reciprocal impact of the agency of the colonized on European lifeways (e.g., Trotter 1990, 5f); with the fact that it may not ever have ended (Azikiwe 2014); and with the impossibility of Euro-capitalist modernity, ab initio, without the racial others in relation to which it constituted itself and its enchantments (Dube 2009).

Colonialisms

None of these perspectives offers a unified theory of colonialism. Each refers to different moments in, different perspectives on, different aspects of, its workings over the long run. Taken together, they point to a clutch of foundational, only partially resolved, questions: What exactly *is* colonialism? One thing or many? How is it to be conceptualized? What is distinctive about it? How does it differ from imperialism? Does it refer to a unique species of governance (or, as some would prefer, governmentality), inscribed in unique institutions, practices, forms of power, or is it no different from any other mode of domination?

Once upon a time, the answers seemed self-evident. True, the term itself has always been difficult to pin down, having had a history of "shifty, changing meaning" (Etherington 1984, 2–3). Still, least until recently, both scholarly and popular imaginings clustered around one basic axiom: that colonialism, over the past two centuries, has had to do, above all, with the extension of "modern" political and economic control by European powers over non-European others—although the status of Europe as the originary site of modernity has been deeply questioned of late (Chakrabarty 2000). As one standard dictionary definition puts it, the term denoted the "acquisition and exploitation of [underdeveloped, distant lands] for the benefit of the mother-country" (*Penguin Concise English Dictionary* 1991, 147)—to which scholars have added the exploitation, also, of racialized "native" peoples (e.g., Magdoff 1978, 118f.) and the imposition of sovereign authority over them (e.g., Nederveen Pieterse 1989, 15ff.). This, of course, could apply as well to imperialism which, as many have pointed out, has also had a history of "shifty, changing meaning," its connotation depending on its political deployment (Kemp 1967, 1) and the historical epoch to which it refers.

Notwithstanding dictionary definitions, the nature and extent of the exploitation inherent in colonialism has been debated since the very beginning. So, too, has the question of who benefited from it, how, and in what measure (cf. Phillips 1989, 1ff.). That debate continues today. But, in general, colonization has long been associated, on all sides, with spatial distance and racial difference, represented typically in the argot of center-and-periphery, enlightenment-and-barbarism; with overrule by an imperial state, usually through the offices of a local colonial bureaucracy; with the active presence of colonists, among them, missionaries and, in many places, expatriate settlers; and with the imperatives of political economy. Its moral dimensions might have been a matter of argument across the ideological spectrum, but even those who disagreed on this tended to concur on its mechanics.

As we have already intimated, none of these certainties seem quite so assured nowadays. For a start, it has long been demonstrated that colonization was everywhere more than merely a process in political economy—or one vested primarily in the colonial state (e.g., Thomas 1994). We ourselves have argued that it was as much about, among other things, bodily regimes, aesthetics, ethics, and the management of time as about the brute extraction of labor power or raw materials; as much about cartography and the remaking of landscape as about the practical logic of capitalism; as much as anything else about "inscribing in the social world a new conception of space, new forms of personhood, and a new means of manufacturing the real" (Mitchell 1991, ix).

But this is not all.

Few would insist any longer that colonization necessarily involves physical distance between centers and peripheries, rulers and ruled; to invoke an aphorism from Homi Bhabha (1994, 6), colonized populations might have occupied ex-centric spaces in the imperial imagination—the pun is at once pointed and poignant—but that does not mean they were always geographically elsewhere. Some time ago, Hechter (1975) used the term "internal colonialism" to underscore the similarities between the Celtic fringe of the United Kingdom and Britain's overseas territories. Even closer to home, the inner cities of nineteenth-century England, like those of twentieth-century Europe and America, were regarded not so differently from colonies abroad. These inner-city "jungles" (Hebdige 1988, 20) were also sites from which value, primarily in the form of labor, was extracted—and into which the cultural outreach of the civilizing mission stretched in an effort to remake their allegedly uncivil inhabitants (Comaroff and Comaroff 1997, 314ff.). Today those inner cities are the ground on which the spatial and temporal coordinates of the past converge, on which the metropole and the margins of empire fold into each other. It is here that former colonial subjects-turned-immigrants live, typically along the edges of a political economy that increasingly offers them little prospect of formal employment, or recognition or rights. And that situates them beyond the sight lines of polite society.

The conflation of inner city with imperial fringe suggests, in turn, that the association of colonialism with race (Stoler 1995) was inflected, in complicated ways, by the facts of social class. What made the uncivil denizens of a nineteenth-century Manchester slum into a colony of savages, and demanded that they be "taken in hand," had its roots, patently, in their destitution. Their lack of material and cultural capital, which was attributed to their lack of self-possession and self-discipline, made them radically different—indeed, unthinkable, said E. M. Forster's fictional imperialist, Henry Wilcox (1992, 58). Often, this difference was seen to have physical effects, especially among those who were ethnicized as Other. The Irish are a celebrated case in point (e.g., Muldoon 1975), just as, as in colonial South Africa, were the Boers, a hybrid population of Europeans, largely small farmers, who, at times, were likened unfavorably to Africans by the English (e.g., Livingstone 1974, 75). The elision of race, class, physicality, and political subordination was implicit in the *real* sociology of colonialism everywhere.

The point? That, while political domination and economic exploitation, spatial distance and racial difference might have been features of most colonial situations, they cannot be taken, a priori, to separate colonialism from other forms of dominion and overrule. To be sure, there are those who have argued that they cannot be taken as defining features at all, being merely the crude motifs of an imperial narrative, cast as a story of heroic humanitarianism, that Europe told itself. This, at least, is a corollary of some postcolonial efforts to rewrite that narrative—sometimes as revisionist history, sometimes as literary criticism, sometimes as fiction, sometimes as anthropology, sometimes as all of them at once (e.g., Boahen 1987; Ndlovu-Gatsheni 2013; Scott 2004)—in order to assert the agency of colonial subjects (see, e.g., Kolapo and Akurang-Parry 2007). Of course, agency is itself an elusive abstraction; always an attribution after the fact, it cannot be measured or easily established. Note, in this respect, how viscerally ambivalent were the likes of Frantz Fanon and Albert Memmi, Ken Saro-Wiwa, and Steve Biko, articulate "native" voices all of them, in speaking about the contradictory experience of being colonized. Those voices were much darker, more concerned with what it meant to be acted upon than were many of the more romantic advocates of African agency—especially those associated with the nationalist histories (see Limb 2011, 20–23)—that were to gain purchase in the academy during the late twentieth century.

What is important about revisionist accounts of colonialism is *not* whether they are factual or fanciful. It is that, taken together and placed alongside older ones, they chart the diverse perspectives on the same historical moments. For some of those who were its subjects and objects, colonialism *was* about domination and violence, invasion and exploitation; for others, an ongoing struggle in which they sometimes gained and sometimes lost; for yet others, an ambiguous process of making themselves and their worlds anew—and, in varying degree, on their own terms. For some, it appeared to be primarily about the material conditions of existence, about the alienation of their land and their labor; for others, it was equally an encounter with European modernity, with its truths, its technologies, and its modes of representation. For some it was all of these things, for others it was few of them. But for everyone it involved a distinctive experience: the experience, offered by Sartre (1955, 215), of coming to feel, and to *re-cognize* one's self as, a "native."

Colonialism, in other words, has always been everywhere the same yet everywhere different (cf. Memmi 1965, xff). This is why it is so difficult to pin down conceptually; why, also, it resists easy capture in a general theoretical statement. From the first, it was a constantly unfolding, mutating, unruly process *and* an infinitely intricate order of evanescent, often enigmatic, *relations*; indeed, the practical effort to define and control its terms was often part of that process, those relations. Nevertheless, while a unitary theory of colonialism, sui generis, may be an impossible pursuit, we may characterize some of its common features in the propositional voice.

Seven Propositions on Colonialism

Let us offer seven propositions, then, as we have done before (1997, 14–29). We are not the first to note them, of course—although, in truth, they have all loomed larger in programmatic discourse than in analytic practice. While they do not address the question of historical origins, and are confined to the past two hundred years, these propositions do, we believe, point the way to a grasp of colonialism as an epochal, world-making process. We begin with the most familiar, the most straightforward, if not the least contentious.

> The First: Colonialism was simultaneously and inseparably a process in political economy and culture, a process embedded at once in materialities, moralities, and mentalities. This is not to say that it had political-economic and cultural dimensions that played themselves out in parallel, and/or in some proportion to each other. To the contrary: they were ontologically conjoined, mutually constitutive, phenomenally interdependent.

This point is critical. In treating colonialism as a "cultural formation" (Dirks 1992, 3), a discursive field (Seed 1991), or a "regime of power/knowledge" (Stoler 1995, 5f)—or in focusing on consciousness, representation, subjectivity, textuality—it is easy to lose sight of political economy: or, at best, to relegate it to the background rumble of realist history. Which is *not*, by and large, how colonization was experienced. Conversely, to explain it purely in terms of the historical logic of European capitalist expansion is also to miss the point, even if the conception of capitalism is broadened to include its cultural fascia. Empire was always also a corollary of the post-Enlightenment worldview entailed in liberal modernity (e.g., Nederveen Pieterse 1989, 20). For example, the campaign of colonial evangelists in South Africa to transform indigenous agriculture was, *indistinguishably*, about moral imperatives *and* modes of production: about the inscription on the landscape of imaginative, tactile geometries, about upright bodies engaged in disciplined labor, *and* about crops, fertilizer, irrigation, and machines. Reciprocally, for their part, many "natives" refused to allow a wedge to be forced between the material and symbolic planes of their own world, between *its* spiritual and temporal dimensions.

In sum, it may be that efforts to account for colonialism in terms of the laws of capitalist development, or the material imperatives of modernization, have been discredited; that Marxist world systems and dependency theories have been shown to be flawed; that their Weberian alternatives, grounded in liberal political economy, have proven no more persuasive. But this is *not* to say that colonization had nothing to do with the growth of industrial capitalism, that it was not about the exploitation of cheap labor and the extraction of raw materials, that underdevelopment did not occur, or that political and economic forces had no effect on colonized peoples. Any such claim would be absurd. But so is the counterclaim that a cultural or discursive or dialogical approach explains all. Colonialism, Christianity, capitalism, and modernity constituted and played off each other as *both* political economy and culture, albeit in different ways at different times and in different places.

The next proposition, a negative one, refers to the colonial state.

> The Second: To the extent that colonization effected a change in the state-of-being of "native" populations, it typically depended as much, if not more, on non-commissioned agents of empire—among them, missionaries, men of business, settlers, soldiers of fortune—than it did on the colonial state; this contra the very general scholarly tendency to place the latter at the driving center of the imperial project. Even when these states were at their

> most elaborate, their instrumental capacity to control the everyday lives of their subjects, either by administrative or by violent means, was always incomplete, sometimes quite limited; which is why they relied heavily on techniques of representation, often highly ritualized, to assert their presence.

The colonial state varied a great deal in its institutional elaboration, the reach of its sovereignty, its technologies of governance, its economic infrastructure, and the sorts of coercion, even terror, it perpetrated (J. L. Comaroff 1998). To be sure, it is difficult to think of it as a singular object at all: *vide* the contrast, for example, between the protectorates of Bechuanaland or Basutoland in the early twentieth century and India at the height of the Raj. What is more, some colonial polities were, at times, remarkably disordered, inchoate, internally conflicted; indeed, barely governed at all. It hardly needs saying that each major theoretical tradition has had its own take on the colonial state, from Marxism, according to which it was primarily the political armature of capital, to modernization theory, for which it was a vehicle of enlightened development and the rule of law. But one thing can be said. It picks up on a well-worn double entendre: that state refers at once to a species of political authority and to a condition of mind-and-being.

In many contexts, government was a fairly latecomer on the scene: a state of colonialism—effected by nongovernmental agents of empire—often preceded the colonial state by decades. This, by turn, conduced further to the secondary role of the latter in colonization, a point that resonates oddly with Gallagher and Robinson's (1953) once controversial notion of the informal empire. In British Bechuanaland, for example, overrule occurred ninety years after the arrival of Europeans. After the discovery of diamonds in South Africa in the 1870s, moreover, waves of "natives" moved, at their own volition, to the diggings in search of employment; this *before* Britain annexed the territory, *before* a British administration began to organize the flow of labor. Nonconformist evangelists, who themselves had ambivalent relations with officialdom, had set in motion processes that, over the long run, reoriented indigenous perceptions of money and goods, work, and wants (J. Comaroff 1985). It did not take the state to create the conditions for an industrial labor supply. It took a state of mind, itself the product of forces—set in train by the arrival of the missions and settlers, expanding trade networks, regional warfare, and the like—much more far-reaching than those entailed in the practice of colonial government.

A footnote here.

The refusal to presume the primacy of the state is integral to a view of colonialism that stresses the everyday rather than the epic—and everything in the space between them. This, we hold, accords with the way in which the encounter was apprehended by most colonial subjects: the European embrace typically presented itself less in the form of methodical stately, governmental action—that would, it is true, gain momentum with time, but was always uneven across the landscape—than in the quotidian: in interactions and transactions between Europeans and Africans, in the entry of the latter into the labor market, in their dealings with the institutions that arose at the edges of empire. This is not to deny that global economics and politics, or indeed the state, had a major impact on the colonized. They clearly did. But it was from the bottom up, through a myriad of mundane exchanges, that the forms of European modernity first found their way onto African and Asian landscapes, there to become the object of the protracted process—that curious mix of consent and contestation, desire and disgust, appropriation and accommodation, refusal and refiguration—subsumed in the term "the colonial encounter."

That encounter was ineluctably dialectical: it remade all parties involved in it. Which leads us to our next proposition.

> The Third: Colonialism was as much involved in making metropolitan modernity, and modernist citizens, as it was in (re)making colonial subjects. Colonies were typically locales in which modernist ways and means—themselves often insecure, precarious, contested—were subjected to experimentation, refined, and reimported for domestic use. In short, Europe itself became modern—to the degree that it realized its own ideological aspirations in that respect—in the process of the colonial encounter, not prior to it.

Much has been made of this. As Delavignette (1964, 8–9) noted a half-century ago, "Colonization has had a transforming effect on metropoles at all levels . . . the countries colonized have had just as much influence on the colonizing powers as these prided themselves on spreading overseas." It was the act of colonization, he added, that actually created the metropolis, not vice versa. Similarly Sartre (1965, xxv–xxvi, after Memmi 1965) offers: "The colonial situation manufactures colonizers as it manufactures colonies."

So far so good. But still too general. There are three quite separate senses in which colonialism constructed colonizers, beyond the fact, as

George Orwell (1962, 108f.) long ago observed of Britons, that they regularly reconfigured themselves and their social standing while abroad. Most obviously, first, expatriates abroad tended, often despite themselves, to be profoundly affected by their interactions with indigenous peoples. The worlds that they forged at colonial frontiers bore the strong imprint of "native" cultural forms—reaching into everything from the aesthetics of architecture and attire, through such domesticities as diet and daily ablutions, to relations of production—many of which they themselves condemned as primitive. Second, "at home" in Europe, modernity, as an ideologically scaffolded order of signifying practices, was achieved in major part with reference to the colonies: through the imaginative resources they provided for self-discovery and the production of potentially powerful knowledge; through the kinds of cultural and physical trial-and-error that they permitted away from metropolitan oversight; through the forms of governmentality, legality, and material production that were developed in them and then repatriated. And, third, those colonies became models of and for the improvement of underclasses back in Europe—imaginative vehicles, that is, for representing their condition, for remaking them, and for rendering them tractable—especially in the fast-growing industrial cities. For the rising bourgeoisies of Europe, the greatest threat to civilization, and to their own ascendancy, was a population living in unruly poverty. Hence they felt the need to instill in the poor a proper sense of morality, patriotism, and decency, a respect for property and prosperity, a measure of self-control and modest ambition. Without these things there was little assurance of social order, let alone of a well-regulated labor force. In Britain, for example, the new Christian elites of Africa were held up as a template for the reconstruction of the lowly at home: the elevation of the former, so recently "savages," served both as an example and an admonition to the latter—and as the justification for a civilizing mission into the terra incognita of the inner city.

Thus far we have spoken of colonizer and colonized in the singular, as if each were a historical type. It is now time for refinement.

> The Fourth: Despite their cogency as discursive tropes, and their political deployment, neither the colonizer nor the colonized represented an undifferentiated, discrete sociological reality. Nor did the opposition between them. Despite being invoked in the cause of imperial overrule and in struggles against it, both the categories and the contrast between them were repeatedly ruptured, their boundaries blurred and their content reinvented.

"The colonizer" typically consisted of cadres divided by social, economic, and political situation, by ideological disposition, and by various sorts of interest. Nor did they always share a language or a culture. Moreover, over time, they often came into conflict with one another. Likewise the colonized, who, apart from their own prior cultural diversities, were also differentiated by status—and, as the European presence made itself felt, by processes of ethnicization and class formation.

With time, too, an intricate web of ties came to transect the imaginative—and, later, political and legal—cleavages between colonizers and the colonized, both now in the plural. This did more than merely create creolized identities. It also yielded counter-stereotypic affinities and alliances. In South Africa, some British missionaries confessed themselves much closer to black Christian elites, whom they likened to respectable whites, than to Boer settlers, whom they portrayed in pejorative terms. For their part, the Africans sometimes spoke patronizingly of their uncivilized compatriots (e.g., Molema 1966, 307ff.), and entered easily into the society of liberal English expatriates, especially under the aegis of the church. This sociology of sameness and difference had analogues everywhere. It underlay the pluralities and polyphonies of all colonial societies—and was crucial in establishing what kinds of difference differences in kind really made as worlds apart were conjoined.

And yet, for all the entanglements of colonial worlds, their own internal dynamics yielded to imaginative simplification, to the objectification of stark, irreducible contrasts.

> The Fifth: Despite the internal complexity of colonial societies, they tended to be perceived and represented, from within, in dualist, oppositional terms—terms that solidified the singularity of, and distance between, ruler and ruled, white and black, modernity and tradition, civilization and savagery. The reification of this order of differences was intrinsic to colonization itself. To the extent that European hegemonies took root, they underlay a grammar of distinctions that insinuated itself into the world of the colonized, into their own self-construction, and into the ways in which they forged and inhabited their identities (cf. Fanon 1963 and 1967; Memmi 1965).

It is, of course, against just these distinctions and dualities—these ideological fictions on which the political economy of empire depended—that much postcolonial writing has been directed. And against which much anti-colonial resistance pitted itself.

But, as we have said, in practice, colonies rarely consisted, for any length of time, of two discrete worlds, each whole unto itself. Nor were they founded on dual economies, one precapitalist and the other capitalist. Those economies were increasingly integrated totalities, their parts bound together ever more indivisibly. In industrial revolution Britain, the country and the city were figuratively set apart in rough proportion to the degree that they became structurally fused (Williams 1973). So it was with the worlds of colonizer and colonized. And, as "at home," each came to stand, iconically, for a clutch of signs and practices. Interestingly, in light of the comparison with Britain, the country-city distinction was also exported abroad: "native" life was designated "traditional," while English expatriate society cast itself as urban—even though, in the nineteenth century, some African "villages" were larger and more elaborate than were most colonial towns.

It is easy to offer a functionalist explanation for all this. Something like: the more that "natives" became an indispensable part of colonial society, the more that black elites rose and syncretic identities were fashioned; the more that social barriers were ruptured, the more it became necessary for Europeans to legitimize and enforce their dominance—which they could only do by disclaiming the capacity of colonized peoples to assume responsible control over their own worlds or to determine their own destiny. Nor is such an explanation entirely wrong; after all, colonial authority *did* ground inequality in this kind of logic, forcing black-and-white contrasts in the face of sociologies that confounded them. But it is incomplete. The construction of a binary, racialized universe had a cultural archaeology: it was traceable back to the way in which post-Enlightenment Europeans had come to represent difference (cf. Achebe 1978), congealing fluid local identities into stereotypic, named forms of otherness. Reciprocally, given the existential challenge from those Europeans to their lifeways, it is not surprising that colonized peoples should have erected their own Manichean alterities, their own tropes of otherness—a.k.a. vernacular traditions, customs, cultures, economic practices—that stood in binary opposition to those of the colonizers. These afforded a means of asserting some control, imaginative as well as material, over their ruptured worlds. In short, the symbolic politics of dualism and difference were a refraction, in the colonies, of the general tendency of overrule to force ever deeper conceptual wedges into ever more articulated, indivisible orders of relations.

The next proposition ought to be self-evident. The need to state it at all arises from the fact that non-Western societies are still portrayed, both within and beyond the academy, in reductive, monochromatic, ahistorical terms. Even in colonial historiography, these societies are often said to be patriarchal and gerontocratic, kinship-based, communal, pervaded by ritual and magicality, and so on. And so:

> The Sixth: Contrary to long-standing archetypes, non-Western societies were never closed, traditional, or unchanging. Nor were they founded simply on kinship, communalism, ascriptive status, patriarchy, chiefly despotism or any other such principles. They tended, rather, to be complex, fluid social worlds, each situated in a more-or-less extensive universe of, among other things, trade networks, political alliances, and cultural exchanges, each caught up in their own intricate dynamics, the workings of which had a direct effect on the terms of the colonial encounter.

In Southern Africa, for example, indigenous polities evinced a great deal of fluidity in their manifest social arrangements from long before the arrival of Europeans (J. L. Comaroff 1982); this was partly a product of political and economic tensions deeply embedded in their internal organization, partly a function of their external relations. And they expressed themselves in a wide range of social and cultural arrangements on the ground. As a result, some of them congealed, for long periods, into large centralized chiefdoms, others diffused into scattered peasant communities, and yet others fell somewhere in between. And all of them changed over time. This, in turn, affected the terms on which they entered into the colonial political economy, the intensity with which they were subjected to land expropriation and violence, and the ways in which their social arrangements were transformed. It also influenced the ways in which colonized peoples dealt with the presence of whites, from whom many actively adopted and recast new ways and means, toward whom others reacted with resigned or resentful compliance, and against whom some sought to seize economic, political, military, religious, and cultural initiative. All of which may be read as a corollary of our final proposition.

> The Seventh: Modern colonialism was founded on a series of contradictions. Having arisen in tandem with industrial capitalism, it promised to bring modernity but perpetuated the mythos of the premodern; promised an enlightened legal system but enforced customary law; promised that its civilizing mission would convert "natives" into sovereign citizens of empire, but made them into ethnic subjects in a racially divided world; promised prosperity but

> left a legacy of poverty; promised to save colonized people from the prison-house of tradition but, in fact, actually built and buttressed that prison-house; promised to remove difference but reinscribed it ever more deeply across the social and physical landscape.

These contradictions—which have been spelled out alike by Marxist *dependistas*, postcolonial *literati*, social historians, cultural critics, and political activists—lay bare the material, moral, and social physics that underpinned technologies of imperial overrule. But, even more importantly, it was in the fissures and interstices of the European outreach, in the seams made visible by its inconsistencies, that the counteractions of colonized peoples first took root; here that their readings of the encounter yielded legible signs on which to muse. And to act.

Conclusion

The seven propositions come together in our central contention here: that, far from being reducible to a historical physics of domination and resistance—though both occurred in more or less explicit, more or less intentional forms—colonial encounters everywhere consisted in a complex, open-ended dialectic: a dialectic, mediated by social differences and cultural distinctions, that transformed everyone and everything caught up in it, if not in the same way; a dialectic that yielded new identities, new hybridities, new frontiers, new signifying practices—and reproduced some older ones as well; a dialectic animated not only by brute acts of conquest, even if violence was always immanent in it, than by attempts to alter existing modes of production and reproduction, to reshape the taken-for-granted surfaces of everyday life, to remake consciousness; a dialectic, therefore, founded on an intricate mix of visible and invisible agency, of word and gesture, of subtle persuasion and brute force on the part of all concerned. This, again, is why colonialism escapes easy definition. Or reduction to bland generalities or monolithic motives. Nineteenth-century colonizers, it is true, typically tried to gain control over the lifeways through which their would-be subjects constructed themselves and their worlds. But the very act of so doing set in motion processes much too complicated and ambiguous of outcome to be rendered as a grand Eurocentric narrative of modernity-in-the-making, although modernization was its most frequent, euphemized rationale on the part of colonizers and their elite subalterns. Nor, inversely, is it plausibly portrayed as an unvarnished romance of refusal, resistance, even *ressentiment* on the part of colonized peoples. Like all historical processes of this order of complexity, its effects are still with us. They will be for a long time to come.

Author's Note:

This essay draws on—but is an abbreviated, heavily amended, and updated version of—a section in the introduction to Comaroff and Comaroff (1997).

Suggested Readings

Asad, Talal, ed. 1973. *Anthropology and the Colonial Encounter*. London: Ithaca Press.

Césaire, Aimé. 1972. *Discourse on Colonialism*. Translated by Joan Pinkham. New York: Monthly Review Press.

Cohn, Bernard. 1996. *Colonialism and Its Forms of Knowledge: The British in India*. Princeton, NJ: Princeton University Press.

Comaroff, John L. 1998. "Reflections on the Colonial State, in South Africa and Elsewhere: Factions, Fragments, Facts and Fictions." *Social Identities* 4 (3): 321–61.

Cooper, Frederick, and Laura Ann Stoler, eds. 1997. *Tensions of Empire: Colonial Cultures in a Bourgeois World*. Berkeley: California University Press.

Cooper, Frederick. 2005. *Colonialism in Question*. Stanford, CA: Stanford University Press.

Dirks, Nicholas B., ed. 1996. *Colonialism and Culture*. Ann Arbor: University of Michigan Press.

Fanon, Frantz. 1967. *Black Skin, White Masks*. Translated by C. L. Markmann. New York: Grove.

McClintock, Anne. 1995. *Imperial Leather: Race, Gender, and Sexuality in the Colonial Context*. New York: Routledge.

Memmi, Albert. 1965. *The Colonizer and the Colonized*. Translated by H. Greenfeld. New York: Orion.

Mitchell, Timothy. 1991. *Colonising Egypt*. Berkeley: University of California Press.

Stoler, Ann Laura. 1992. "Rethinking Colonial Categories: European Communities and the Boundaries of Rule." *Comparative Studies in Society and History* 31 (1): 134–61.

Taussig, Michael. 1987. *Shamanism, Colonialism, and the Wild Man: A Study in Terror and Healing*. Chicago: University of Chicago Press.

Thomas, Nicholas J. 1994. *Colonialism's Culture: Anthropology, Travel and Government*. Cambridge: Polity, in association with Blackwell.

Vaughan, Megan. 1991. *Curing Their Ills: Colonial Power and African Illness*. Stanford, CA: Stanford University Press.

References

Achebe, Chinua. 1978. "An Image of Africa." *Research in African Literatures* 9: 1–15.

Azikiwe, Abayomi. 2014. "Neo-Colonialism and the Changing Nature of Imperialism in Africa." *Global Research*, June 5. http://www.globalresearch.ca/neo-colonialism-and-the-changing-nature-imperialism-in-africa/5385713.

Bhabha, Homi. 1994. *The Location of Culture*. London: Routledge.

Boahen, A. Adu. 1987. *African Perspectives on Colonialism*. Baltimore: Johns Hopkins University Press.

Chakrabarty, Dipesh. 2000. *Provincializing Europe: Postcolonial Thought and Historical Difference*. Princeton, NJ: Princeton University Press.

Comaroff, Jean. 1985. *Body of Power, Spirit of Resistance: The Culture and History of a South African People*. Chicago: University of Chicago Press.

Comaroff, John L. 1982. "Dialectical Systems, History and Anthropology: Units of Study and Questions of Theory." *Journal of Southern African Studies* 8 (2): 143–72.

———. 1998. "Reflections on the Colonial State, in South Africa and Elsewhere: Factions, Fragments, Facts and Fictions." *Social Identities* 4 (3): 321–61.

Comaroff, John L., and Jean Comaroff. 1997. *Of Revelation and Revolution*. Volume 2, *The Dialectics of Modernity on a South African Frontier*. Chicago: University of Chicago Press.

Cooper, Frederick. 2005. *Colonialism in Question: Theory, Knowledge, History*. Berkeley: University of California Press.

Delavignette, Robert. 1964. *Christianity and Colonialism*. Translated by J. R. Foster. London: Burns & Oates.

Dirks, Nicholas B. 1992. "Introduction: Colonialism and Culture." In *Colonialism and Culture*, edited by N. Dirks. Ann Arbor: University of Michigan Press.

Dube, Saurabh. 2009. "Modernity and Its Enchantments: An Introduction." In *The Enchantments of Modernity: Empire, Nation, Globalization*, edited by Saurabh Dube. New York: Routledge.

Etherington, Norman. 1984. *Theories of Imperialism: War, Conquest and Capital*. London: Croom Helm.

Fanon, Frantz. 1963. *The Wretched of the Earth*. Translated by C. Farrington. New York: Grove.

———. 1967. *Black Skin, White Masks*. Translated by C. L. Markmann. New York: Grove.

Forster, E. M. 1992. *Howards End*. Edited by O. Stallybrass. London: Penguin. First edition, 1910.

Gallagher, John, and Ronald Edward Robinson. 1953. "The Imperialism of Free Trade." *Economic History Review* (2nd ser.) 6: 1–15.

Hebdige, Dick. *Hiding in the Light: On Images and Things*. New York: Routledge, 1988.

Hechter, Michael. 1975. *Internal Colonialism: The Celtic Fringe in British National Development, 1536–1966*. Berkeley: University of California Press.

Kemp, Tom. 1967. *Theories of Imperialism*. London: Dennis Dobson.

Kolapo, Femi J., and Kwabena O. Akurang-Parry, eds. 2007. *African Agency and European Colonialism: Latitudes of Negotiations and Containment*. Washington, DC: University Press of America.

Limb, Peter. 2011. "Terence Ranger, African Studies and South African Historiography." *Historia* 56 (1): 1–25.

Livingstone, David. 1974. *David Livingstone: South African Papers, 1849–1853*. Edited by I. Schapera. Cape Town: Van Riebeeck Society.

Lüthy, Herbert. 1964. "Colonization and the Making of Mankind." In *Imperialism and Colonialism*, edited by G. H. Nadel and P. Curtis. New York: Macmillan. First published in 1961 in *The Journal of Economic History*, Supplement [The Tasks of Economic History] 21 (4): 483–95.

Magdoff, Harry. 1978. *Imperialism: From the Colonial Age to the Present*. New York: Monthly Review Press.

Mamdani. Mahmood. 1996. *Citizen and Subject: Contemporary Africa and the Legacy of Late Colonialism*. Princeton, NJ: Princeton University Press.

Memmi, Albert. 1965. *The Colonizer and the Colonized*. Translated by H. Greenfeld. New York: Orion.

Mintz, Sidney Wilfred. 1985. *Sweetness and Power: The Place of Sugar in Modern History*. New York: Viking.

Mitchell, Timothy. 1991. *Colonising Egypt*. Berkeley: University of California Press.

Molema, Silas Modiri. 1966. *Montshiwa, 1815–1896: Barolong Chief and Patriot*. Cape Town: Struik.

Muldoon, James. 1975. "The Indian as Irishman." *Essex Institute Historical Collections* 3: 267–89.

Ndlovu-Gatsheni, Sabelo J. 2013. *Empire, Global Coloniality and African Subjectivity*. Oxford: Berghahn.

Nederveen Pieterse, Jan P. 1989. *Empire and Emancipation: Power and Liberation on a World Scale*. London: Pluto.

Orwell, George. 1962. *The Road to Wigan Pier*. Harmondsworth, UK: Penguin.

Phillips, Anne. 1989. *The Enigma of Colonialism: British Policy in West Africa*. London: James Currey.

Sartre, Jean-Paul. 1955. *Literary and Philosophical Essays*. Translated by A. Michelson. New York: Criterion.

———. 1965. Introduction. In *The Colonizer and the Colonized*, by A. Memmi. New York: Orion.

Scott, David. 2004. *Conscripts of Modernity: The Tragedy of Colonial Enlightenment.* Durham, NC: Duke University Press.

Seed, Patricia. 1991. "Colonial and Postcolonial Discourse." *Latin American Research Review* 6: 181–200.

Stoler, Ann Laura. 1995. *Race and the Education of Desire: Foucault's* History of Sexuality *and the Colonial Order of Things*. Durham, NC: Duke University Press.

Stoler, Ann Laura, and Frederick Cooper. 1997. "Between Colony and Metropole: Rethinking a Research Agenda." In *Tensions of Empire: Colonial Cultures in a Bourgeois World*. Berkeley: California University Press.

Taussig, Michael. 1987. *Shamanism, Colonialism, and the Wild Man: A Study in Terror and Healing*. Chicago: University of Chicago Press.

Thomas, Nicholas J. 1994. *Colonialism's Culture: Anthropology, Travel and Government.* Cambridge: Polity, in association with Blackwell.

Trotter, David. 1990. "Colonial Subjects." *Critical Quarterly* 32 (3): 3–20.

Williams, Raymond. 1973. *The Country and the City*. London: Chatto and Windus.

6 DESIGN

Suzanne Preston Blier

In the mid-1920s, Texas-based Presbyterian missionary Conway Wharton traveled by motorbike for a special meeting with the Kuba king. After the royal audience concluded, in the savanna of Congo's Kasai region where this polity was located, Wharton remounted his bike, leaving a dust cloud in his wake as he headed home. We know from Conway's later account that the Kuba court was little impressed with Wharton's display of this new technology. They saw little in the utilitarian potential of the motorbike's design for carrying people or goods sizable distances at greater efficiency and speed. They saw little of the commercial potential that could transform regional trade for their benefit. It was another aspect of the vehicle's form that impressed them far more—namely, the design pattern left by the motorbike tires in the ground where Conway had ridden it. Soon a copy of this pattern was made by the Kuba royal sculptors; they named it *nyimi*, after the individual who first saw this pattern and recognized its unique appearance (Mack 2012).

Similarly today, when one enters many African markets, negotiating the narrow pathways between seller stalls, merchandise, and clientele, we can see the important role played by design. The market seller (usually a woman) arranges her goods (cloths of different hues and patterns, piles of tomatoes, bowls—whatever) to attract the attention of each passerby. Market women are not only skilled negotiators but also design critics, cognizant of how design impacts different groups of shoppers. The design of each presentation is based on capturing the interest of potential buyers to one's own merchandise rather than others'—even though similar goods are available at a comparable price from a compatriot nearby. Recognition of the importance of design has a long history in Africa, a history that

European manufacturers of goods (beads and textiles among other things) readily noted, forwarding new products on a regular basis consistent with changing African markets and tastes.

This chapter addresses the ways in which the core design features of African forms, be they clothing, jewelry, furniture, housing, or religious paraphernalia are imbued with larger sociopolitical features, such that they merge a range of values—among these, aesthetic choices, need (functionality), and both individual and social identity. Addressing design within the larger African milieu allows us to see the larger discourse on African art, architecture, and aesthetics in different view, bringing to the foreground new ways of looking at and thinking about form here more generally. Design theory speaks of such works as comprising a language of vision, a visual communication system that is similar to but different from verbal languages (although the two may intersect) (Lupton 2009). As early as 1919, the artist Vasily Kandinsky would speak about the laws of visual forms as forming a graphic language, a theory developed further in his writings on the 1919–1933 Bauhaus design movement in Germany. In this sense, design functions as a site of ongoing individual and societal engagement, a liminal site of empowerment and play that addresses an array of political, moral, and other considerations. Sometimes design elements serve as a vehicle of contestation, at other times they can convey accord. Whatever these forms of design reveal they are a critical part of both rural and urban life.

It is hard to imagine any walk of African life in which design is not a core feature. One of the first to recognize its aesthetic importance was Margaret Trowell whose 1960 volume, *African Design: An Illustrated Survey of Traditional Craftwork*, is still a classic. Divided largely by medium and genre—metal, ceramics, calabash, wood, textile, bead, ivory, mats, and wall decoration—she also focuses our attention on the powerful yet relatively simple ways in which slight variations or irregularities in the details or handling of form carry textural effect, adding a sense of visual pleasure that "is meant to be enjoyed for its own sake alone." She also observes the ways that certain oral traditions—among these allegories, proverbs, and adages—may inform a design's symbolic grounding.

In the aftermath of Trowell's text, an array of exhibitions and richly illustrated catalogues have appeared that focus our attention on African design in various ways. Among the most important of them was the groundbreaking 1974 exhibit and catalogue, called *African Textiles and Decorative Arts*, that Roy Sieber mounted for the Museum of Modern Art in New

York. A long series of exhibitions, books, and articles by other scholars followed on everything from stools and jewelry to hats, clothing, and contemporary fashion arts. Among the most recent is a 2015 Dapper Museum exhibition in Paris titled *Design en Afrique: S'asseoir, se coucher, et rêver* ("Design in Africa: To sit, to sleep, and to dream")—the last word, *rêver*, given visual emphasis to highlight the creative and imaginative qualities that design evokes. In much the same way, Tapiwa Matsinde's 2015 *Contemporary Design Africa*, has emphasized the originality of African artists creating notably functional objects, as they reimagine and reshape diverse traditional forms. As Matsinde insists, African art and design are deeply creative works of individual artists (despite the legacy of Western-defined anonymity), which in part have left these artists at the margins of the international art market.

These and other biases still remain and must be addressed in a subject of this importance. One example suffices. In a 2013 essay, titled "What Can African Design Teach Us," business consultant and design science researcher Soren Petersen points to Africa as "a blank white spot on the international designers' map." Taking both a dated and a stridently Eurocentric stance he insists that "due to resource, infrastructure, and financial constraints, the hallmarks of African design are simplicity, practicality and ruggedness." Design, now as in the past owes very little to economic variables—whether in Africa or elsewhere. His next statement is even more problematic: "African design is founded on Primitivism and is concerned with raw form, childlike lines, and references to wildlife, earthly hues, and the color orange." Peterson insists, incorrectly for the most part, that "most, if not all of African designs, have their roots in spiritualism. The customs and traditions driving the designs are closely tied to the living and breathing souls [of] their chiefs or tribal heads." Yet his tempered praise of African design at the conclusion of his piece holds broad interest—and not just here: "If one can marry all the aforementioned values, create a good looking product, produce it economically and, if the end result is exceptionally tough, easy to use and something that people actually love to use,—then that is quintessential African Design!"

A Motorbike Tire Track: Kuba Design Primacy

In addressing this remarkable motorbike tire design story highlighted at the outset of this chapter, a number of issues could be brought into play. One might delve more deeply into the narrative of Belgian colonial power and its support by American missionaries and the US government. A somewhat different lens might be focused on the violence that was a central part of Euro-American rubber production intended largely to support new Western commercial products such as motorbike, pedal bike, and car tires, and sporting events on a global scale. But this is equally, and in some ways more importantly, a story about design and the ways that design intersects closely with local African ideas of value—political, utilitarian, and aesthetic.

A 1971 study of Kuba textile traditions authored by David Crowe adds further insight to this striking episode from the vantage of Kuba art and history more generally. Crowe, a mathematician, determined that an extraordinary 66 percent of all known design possibilities are employed by Kuba artists within their raffia cut cloth patterns. Considering this fact, it is not surprising that on the day Reverend Wharton arrived here, it was *not* the motorbike's transport potential but rather the unique track that its tires left that served as the primary indices of this event. Kuba design patterns are strikingly complex and can be found in a broad array of local art works, from textiles to woven building walls, from carved drinking vessels and boxes for precious goods to various forms of masks. So striking are these patterns of interlocking lozenges, crosses, diamond shapes, and meandering lines that they also feature prominently in studies of the importance of African fractals as models of computing (Eglash 1999). As Matisse would say of the Kuba textiles in his own collection: "I never *tire* of looking at them for long." Clearly the complexity of these patterns carries resonance not only in elite Kuba contexts but also in other arenas.

There is more to the significance of design among the Kuba and other African cultures than this striking event reveals. Among other things this example offers insight into the importance of artistic innovation and creativity in African society more generally, be it sculpture, dress forms, music, religious beliefs, or practices of healing. Despite the historical bias that in most of Africa "tradition" and "custom" are the norm, the remarkable diversity of objects and styles in African art and architecture tells a very different story, both in the more recent period and historically. These works reveal that innovation has been a centerpiece of how African individuals and societies have engaged their own worlds and those of others.

Kuba textiles and related patterns here too offer important insight. The names of these patterns are as diverse as their designs. Some reference individuals such as a ruler or the artist who invented a specific design—making clear that individual recognition and accomplishment are important. This too contrasts with the long history of Western claims that African social and community values are so dominant that the individual has little place (or impetus) in which to act independently. Still other Kuba patterns reflect forms seen in nature (smoke, fish, or eyebrows) or in myths such as the oft-referenced Kuba founder, Woot. Both observed phenomenon and more abstract concepts are clearly important. In the very diversity of these patterns and themes, they offer us core insight into why design creation have figured so centrally in Kuba life and why Conway Wharton's motorbike tire left such a striking imprint on the minds of the individuals who saw it.

To understand this more deeply we also need to turn to Kuba social history in the late nineteenth and early twentieth centuries. While the coastal Kongo regions suffered extensively from the violence of forced labor as part of the plantation rubber economy, in the Kasai region of the Kuba to the east, early travelers reveal a rich court life defined in part by heated competition between titled individuals that involved prestigious displays. Among these were elaborately woven and embroidered raffia fabrics and carved palm-wine drinking cups, many of which carried striking design motifs. In this era, perhaps half the Kuba royal men held titles and as such competition for added status and influence was considerable (Vansina 2010). Palm-wine drinking vessels became objects not only of striking beauty but also individual status. Demonstrating one's position through largesse, specifically through one's ability to distribute large quantities of palm wine to one's supporters and family added to the "weight" of self-fashioning status needs in tangible ways. New, creative, complex designs on associated apparel framed this dynamic of public competition for influence in important ways as well.

Since many of these same titled men acquired their own high-status positions through plantation agriculture contexts that included forced labor (palm production especially), there also was a certain complementarity at play between the local and colonial worlds despite notable scale and other differences. For members of the Kuba court who were present for the arrival and departure of Conway Wharton's motorcycle, the new design pattern was not only an important means of recalling this event, but also positioned Wharton and his motorbike within the vocabulary of local status competition.

African Design Terms

A variety of terms for "design" exist within local African languages. Like the Latin word for design, *designo*, signifying at once "to mark, represent, point out, denote, designate, describe, and brand," African terms also often carry references to the individual, the designer of a form, and the distinguishing mark or signature that is part of the form itself. In short, this term frequently carries significance not only for the design itself (as a noun), but also qualities conveyed through good form (an adjective), and the very processes of its creation (the act of designing—a verb). In some cultures we find multiple terms at play, suggesting how important design is within related communities.

In the Yoruba language, for example, the term *ọnà* not only means "design," "pattern," "shape," and "art," but is also used to reference artistic embellishment, ornamentation, and beauty (Adepegba 1991). The same term, *ọnà*, is also found in the term for "artist," *ọlọ́nà*, as well as for specific groups of the later—leather workers and embroiderers among these. The Yoruba have a further array of other terms that convey notions of design. One such term to mean design is *ìrò*, "imagination" (the root *rò* itself signifying "to plague" or "to bother"). Another design-linked term is *ìmò*, "knowing"—specifically, that which one experiences firsthand, with one's own eyes. A related word, *ìtumò* (*ìtú ìmò*), evokes the unwrapping of (encoded) knowledge.

To these Yoruba terms we can also add *àpẹrẹ* (imitation) and *awòran* (representation). The reference for artist, *ẹnití nyà àwòrán*, has its root in the related, *àwòrán*, "beholder." Without belaboring the point that among the Yoruba there exist multiple related terms, what is important to emphasize here is that design, and related ideas of embellishment, imagination, encoded knowledge, and representation reveal a sophisticated engagement with a wide variety of values that individually and together help us understand the primacy of design in this society. Among the Yoruba, too, it is not only "design" itself that is imperative, but also the idea of form as a segmented or serrated "discontinuous aggregate" of units, as exemplified in everything from the composition of ceremonies, to door patterns and overall textile motifs, to the wearing of a specific cloth pattern by groups of individuals (as, for example, in memorial ceremonies) (Drewal and Drewal 1987).

Other African cultures also have an array of terms offering insight into the local importance of design. In Zulu the word is *linganisa*, which also means "to equalize, match, or balance," suggesting larger shared aesthetic and societal values at play. Another Zulu term, *kutengeneza*, means "to make, create, or construct," having its complement in the verb *kutunga*, "to compose." In Swahili the general term for design is *kubuni*, a word that also references invention and improvisation, evoking the importance of imagination within the larger design conception here.

Often, as with the Kuba, designs incorporated into textiles or other forms constitute a visual language, one that is known to key members of the society. A range of ideas and philosophical values are conveyed through these patterns. In Ga (Akan) textile patterns, from Ghana, various proverbs come into play. This is particularly the case with *adinkra*, stamped mourning cloth designs. Among the notably abstract patterns that are used in these textiles it is the diversity of referents that stands out. Among these is an X-motif "the fence" (signifying strength and authority), a palm tree (symbolizing wealth), a set of imbedded concentric circles (standing for the king), a watery plant (for chastity, fortune), two crossed swords (for bravery), a spider web (for wisdom), a drum (for praise), a double drum (for unity), and a house (for security), to name just a few. Woven *kente* cloth patterns from this area are equally diverse. Some *kente* designs honor specific individuals, especially rulers, queen mothers, artists, and their families. Other patterns refer to plants, animals, everyday objects, and themes such as wealth, poverty, peace, and well-being. Still others have their basis in the event or occasion on which the cloth was first worn. Design complexity is another important name reference in these designs, as in one cloth called "skill is exhausted."

Nsibidi patterns (designs) in Eastern Nigerian Igbo communities are found in contexts ranging from body paintings to wall paintings and stone menhirs, some of the latter dating to circa 300 CE. In the early- to the mid-twentieth-century examples, Nsibidi designs display an array of forms and ideas, ranging from animals (the leopard, crocodile, and lizard) to drums, gongs, staffs, and manila currency, each referencing some aspect of wealth and authority. Still others convey philosophical values such as peace, harmony, welcomeness, and friendship, or specific familial and social situations that may cause problems such as a man and his sweetheart, a man and woman in bed who are tired of each other, a man sleeping with another's wife, iron money for the market, a torch and whip (punishment), fetters (an unfaithful lover), and a dead person on a mat. (See Dayrell 1911; "Inscribing Meaning" 2007.)

The Politics of Design and New Commercial Markets

In some cases today these same design terms have been taken up to identify new design consortia and collectives created to bring questions of design to the forefront in transforming the community or world more generally. For example, in Nigeria, the Igbo word for design or manufacture, *imewe*, is redeployed in an endeavor known as *imewe ụwa*, "design world." In another example from the Igbo, one known as Ulism, a group of artists centered in Nsukka draws on the elegant body patterns called *uli*, worn by Igbo women. These forms, also used to decorate temple walls here, share a visual vocabulary that has deep socio-philosophical grounding. As Christopher Adejumo points out, here and elsewhere in Nigeria, similar design concepts have been employed to evoke the "shared vision or philosophy" that brings groups of artists together on projects for the common social good, projects that advance social responsibility through various aspects of design (Adejumo 2002, 185). Adejumo also discusses another project known as Onaism, centered with artists working in Ile-Ife, that takes its name after the Yoruba term *ọnà*, for design, decoration, or pattern.

Yet another recent movement, *Africa Is Now 2015* (a project of Design Indaba), addresses both people and process in promoting creativity in different African regions (Egypt, Kenya, Senegal, and Angola) and in diverse media (film, architecture, design, and others)—collaborations intended to fuel societal change. In one of these groups from Dakar, Senegal, known as Les Petites Pierres (the small stones), a network of performance and other visual artists who see the city itself as their canvas are instituting a new wave of artistic innovation, in the course of which they make their art available to Dakar citizens more generally. Their name references the means by which, little by little, they can improve the world by encouraging the population to contribute to this common building (design) platform. In some ways this draws on the historic Dakar community-based mural painting traditions discussed by Elizabeth Harney.

Leaving a social imprint is a core part of these new design movements. In Luanda, Angola, the architectural firm Beyond Entropy Africa uses research from key neighborhoods to address the everyday realities of urban living, promoting the use of informal settlements (*musseques*) in part as a response. Some of Africa's new architects, among these the Aga Khan award winner Diebedo Francis Kere of Burkina Faso, forge a path between tradition and the contemporary by supplanting concrete technologies of the colonial era with earthen brick structures that empower the community by emphasizing not only local materials and labor but also structures that offer better air circulation as part of a similarly active design agenda. Zimbabwe architect Mick Pearce draws instead on the model of termites, to create a system of ventilation that moves air through buildings by way of tubes in an equally cost-effective way. Another architect, Mokena Makeka of Cape Town, South Africa, has begun to use design to redress history, specifically that of apartheid segregation. His redesign of the Cape Town railway station, which historically had two separate entrances (one for black and one for white passengers), is a key example of this.

While some of these design movements owe something to the legacy of Western art practices, such as the Bauhaus movement, it is also true that historically in Africa similar kinds of movements were at play, bringing together artists and community members to work on key projects for the common good. Among these examples is the building of palaces for newly enthroned kings in centers ranging from Kuba (Congo) to Bamun (Cameroon). Another noteworthy example is the yearly replastering of the Djenne mosque (Mali) that brings together community men from all walks of life. Going back in time, an equally impressive context comprises the ancient Ife bronzes and terracottas that appear to have been commissioned by King Obalufon II in the aftermath of a circa 1300 civil war; these works served as furnishings for temples dedicated to the leaders of both sides of this conflagration.

More recently, one needs to look no further than the April 2015 decision by the University of Cape Town in South Africa to take down the statue of the British imperialist Cecil B. Rhodes after it had been vandalized by students who defaced it with red paint and human excrement, wrapping its head in paper. While the empty plinth stands as a marker of the sculpture's trace, so does the fact that the land on which the campus itself was built had been owned by this same vilified mine owner prior to his donating it for the creation of this university. With male members of a white Afrikaner solidarity group in pseudo military attire calling for protection of monuments linked to their heritage, it is clear that the context in which design engagement occurs also carries a heavy political imprint.

Elements of African Design

Theodor Adorno, in his work *Minima Moralia*, has provided a list of elements he identifies as important in addressing subjectivity. This reads as an elaborate shopping list of ideas that pinpoint core values: "fish in water," "antithesis," "separated-united (marriage)," "*Inter pares* (among equals), "Gaps," "Inner and Outer," "*plurale tantum* (only in the plural)," etc. In some ways we might see this as similar to the sign taxonomy of Charles Peirce in his theory of semiotics. A complementary model is taken up by Jacques Bertin in his "Semiology of Graphics," a system addressing design (here graphics) as a kind of "transcription" of ideas that moves beyond easy interpretation in standard visual terms. In much the same way, György Kepes's work on the *Language of Vision*, which draws in part on the visual "laws" promoted by the Bauhaus, applies a grammar of form to the designed object as a kind of diagram of ideas and expressions. Elsewhere I have highlighted the core set of design elements in the Batammaliba architecture of northern Togo, forms that also address key aspects of social engagement (Blier 1995b). Here they include six core features: nesting (transposing a series of elements or ideas into a nest of parts); silhouetting (defining an object through its distinctive profile); skeuomorph (use of material other than the original); synecdoche (elements standing for the whole); reversal (overturning what is considered normal); and condensed forms. Each of these carries different metaphoric properties: for example, reversal is often linked to death. Some of these also hold meaning in other African art and ritual contexts, and there are others, specific to design, that also come into play. Key among these are the following:

Contrast and Variability, Balance and Asymmetry: The historic color palette of Africa (red, black, and white) is seen in African wall paintings, beaded jewelry, and other forms. In addition to holding metaphoric values (for example, life/danger, night/poser, and purity/ancestry), these hues when positioned together also highlight the importance of contrast and variation. Similar kinds of contrasts can be seen in African sculpture, works that, while also emphasizing balance, frequently incorporate subtle elements of asymmetry (Adams 1978). These ideas are also seen in contemporary works from the stunning photographs of Mali photographer Seydou Keitu (with their bold textile contrasts) to the fashionable attire of Kongo *flâneurs* (dandies) in urban Kinshasa. In their own way, the redolent contemporary global designs of Ghanaian architect David Adjaye incorporate similar kinds of visual complexities through their contrasting textures, hues, and features.

Shine, Coolness, and Attraction versus Roughness, Heat, and Repulsion: Shine—referencing newness, presence, status—figures prominently in many African arts, focusing the eyes and thoughts: through, for example, the incorporation of mirrorlike mica chips into early Ife (Nigeria) terracotta figures, or the regularly polished brass of Yoruba *edan* Ogboni figures, or the polished silver of royal Fon Nesuxwe elephant and lion figures; or through the insertion of bright porcelain plates into walls, the oil baths accorded Bamana sculptures or Kongo and other power figures, or even of the repainting of Yoruba Gelede masks with shimmery Western pigments. Shine is a key feature of the highly glamorous interior decorations of many modern African elites, as showcased in modern Congolese canvases by Cheri Samba. A Cape Town–based textile company called Shine Shine (created in 2007 by Tracy Rushmere) has introduced the kind of richly playful graphic designs, derived from local forms that speak to a new glam-seeking clientele (Matsinde 2015). Not surprisingly, in some of these same cultural contexts, idioms of roughness and repulsion also are important, as seen, for example, in the tangle of binding cords and nails in Kongo Nkisi figures or Fon *bocio* sculptures. These works, and others, such as Bamana *boli* figures and Komo masks (in Mali) speak to power (and necessary protection) in an equally visceral way. Jean-François Bayart speaks to much the same cultural dynamic in addressing the "politics of the belly" (Bayart 1993). In these contexts, the anti-aesthetic within design often carries important aspects of protest. Contrasting Yoruba idioms of cool and heat, beauty and anti-aesthetics, are part of this same dynamic (Thompson 1973; Doris 2011).

Presence and Absence: Most of us who have traveled in rural Africa readily recognize the regular predawn sweeping of women and children of the household, bent over with short straw brooms to clean the face of the earth, leaving in their wake elegant fans of semicircle markings on the earth they sweep. Over the course of the day these get covered over by daily activity. This pattern of delicately curving lines represents an absence that is also a presence—evoking cleansing, culture, and honor to the earth and the array of ancestors and spirits therein. Similarly striking design elements of this type can be seen in the hanging of cloth frames to delimit the spaces where royals sit during outdoor ceremonies (a room that is not a room), or in the "cleaning" of walls and communities of urban Dakar to renew the city through the addition of white paint and richly painted scenes. Adeline Masquelier addresses some of these same elements of dirt, undress, and difference as vital social referents.

Assemblage and Recycling: Pablo Picasso is widely recognized today for inventing a new form of art known as assemblage. In truth he discovered the technique in African art works from the Dahomey kingdom, among these a metal bird owned by his friend Guillaume Apollinaire that was built from various pieces of brass and iron, and the famous iron figure of Gur, the god of metal, war, and creativity from this same kingdom. The latter work was made in part from recycled materials—European iron bolts and screws, along with a locally made gong, machete, and an array of miniature tools. From this use, too, Picasso drew key insight. Contemporary artists living in what is today Benin Republic (once Dahomey) employ similar forms of assemblage/recyclage in their works. Whether evoking the importance of social assemblage to state formation here, or the passage of time, or even the detritus left from the colonial encounter, these forms continue to have primacy. Similar elements can be seen in Dahomey *bocio* figures, Kongo power figures, and the *boli* and Komo masks of Bamana artists. While the contexts differ, complementary ideas about power and protection, and knowledge and ignorance, as well as matters of individual and sociological import, come into play.

Tradition and Innovation: The standard view of African art and design long perpetuated in the West speaks to the primacy of heritage and tradition at the expense of creativity and innovation. In key respects this framing belies the frequent use in Africa of what Henry Maine once characterized as "Legal Fictions," those forms or truisms that are widely acknowledged and even accepted but which often cover very different kinds of actions and realities. In African terms, much like in traditions of Malikite law in Islam, this often means a return to the well of tradition (ideas of the past) to fashion a new way forward. In African sculptural form we see frequent references to the past even in works that evince striking innovation. Igbo Mbari sculptures and mask forms are key examples of this (Cole 2012). Traditional Ndebele wall paintings in apartheid South Africa similarly conveyed the impression of tradition and harmonious family life, even as local men worked long months in the mines. Illustrations of playing cards (chance) and airplanes (flight) were often included in "traditional" Ndebele wall designs by local women, suggesting the difficulties their lives held and their desires for a different future.

Stasis and Movement: Frequently shown in a standing posture, feet together, with hands at the sides, many historic African figural arts evoke ideas of stability and permanence. Yet these elements often are countered in the same figures by equally strong emphases on the bending of legs, suggesting the primacy of both dance and movement. Similar concerns with movement against a broader shared emphasis on stability are frequently seen in African palace architecture—from the Kuba of Central Africa to the

Yoruba, Benin, and Dahomey kingdoms in West Africa. While the interiors are often defined by complex mazelike plans, difficult for even the most familiar to navigate (in part to protect the king from human and spiritual harm), palace facades often are distinguished by their high, thick, windowless walls and well-guarded portals, forms evoking permanence and power. In other African architectural contexts where relatively ephemeral materials of earth and vegetable fiber find frequent use, similar qualities of stasis and movement are evoked through the rebuilding of houses in long-settled locales. Architects have recently begun using mobility and stasis in new ways. Nigerian architect Kunlé Adeyemi's floating A-frame school, built on pontoons made from empty barrels near the long-standing Lagos Makoko slum area, is one such example.

Basic Form and Complexity: Elements of design often are defined around core elements—a point, line, circle, triangle, diamond, swirl, or zigzag. Such patterns often are repeated, for example, on a stool seat or the incised markings of the body. Similarly elemental motifs are found in many of Africa's traditional inscribed language symbols—Nsibidi among these. Design complexity also is highly appreciated, as exemplified not only in the rich patterns of Asante *kente* cloth (Ghana), the rich raffia textiles of the Kongo and Kuba (Congo), or the complex male and female hair coiffures worn by the Fulani (Niger, Mali), Igbo (Nigeria), Luba, and Chokwe (Congo), among others. One particular pattern, the "unending knot" (found in Hausa, Akan, and Kongo contexts) suggests the kind of complexity that can never be undone (a motif referencing ideas of both deep thought and long life). This same form is found in Coptic textiles in Egypt, suggesting its deep history and broad diffusion.

Society and Individual: The person and the community are also addressed through design. Forms of housing in acephalous (nonhierarchical) societies, such as the Batammaliba of northern Togo, share the same basic ground plan (suggesting every community member occupies the same social position), while both the size of this plan and facade details (shrine and healing elaborations) speak to the existence and valuation of individual differences. In Bamana mud-cloth traditions (Bogolanfini) similarly, although the patterns of a given cloth suggest an overall design and pattern unity, key elements of asymmetry (mistakes) are introduced as marks of an individual maker. In some of the most striking examples of colonial architecture, in the Yoruba and Igbo areas of Nigeria among others (Afro-Brazilian and other traditions), new design models and technologies are taken up to create works that are strikingly individualistic.

Conclusion

As we have seen, design plays a central role in African life. Often it plays an active social role. Rather than a formal conclusion, I wish to highlight a February–March 2016 event in Ouagadougou (Burkina Faso) called "Design for Peace." The event was intended to draw attention to traditional artist techniques (textiles and leather among these) in order to bring together local artists and the growing group of refugees (from Mali and elsewhere). The stated objective of the organizing group, Afrika Tiss, was to share knowledge and reinforce related artisan skills in order to advance a socioeconomic agenda, such that the various participants would gain financially as new local and international markets for their works were sought; here, the combination of aesthetic primacy and sociopolitical need had the potential to bring broad benefit.

Suggested Readings

Adams, Monni. 1978. "Kuba Embroidered Cloth." *African Arts* 12 (1) (November): 24–39 and 106–7.

Adejumo, Christopher. 2002. "African Art: New Genres and Transformational Philosophies." In *Africanizing Knowledge: African Studies Across the Disciplines*, edited by Toyin Falola and Christian Jennings. New Brunswick, NJ: Transaction.

Adepegba, Cornelius Oyeleke. 1991. *Yoruba Metal Sculpture*. Ibadan: Ibadan University Press.

Blier, Suzanne Preston. 2015. *Art and Risk in Ancient Yoruba: Ife History, Power, and Identity c. 1300*. New York: Cambridge University Press.

Cole, Herbert M. 2012. *Invention and Tradition: The Art of Southeastern Nigeria*. New York: Prestel.

Harney, Elizabeth. 2004. *Art, Politics, and the Avant-Garde in Senegal, 1960–1995*. Durham, NC: Duke University Press.

Masquelier, Adeline, ed. 2005. *Dirt, Undress and Difference: Critical Perspectives on the Body's Surface*. Bloomington: Indiana University Press.

Matsinde, Tapiwa. 2015. *Contemporary Design Africa*. London: Thames and Hudson.

Peterson, Soren. 2013. "What Can African Design Teach Us." *Huffington Post*, June 27. http://www.huffingtonpost.com/soren-petersen/what-can-african-design-t_b_3820623.html. Accessed November 1, 2015.

References

Adams, Monni. 1978. "Kuba Embroidered Cloth." *African Arts* 12 (1) (November): 24–39 and 106–7.

Adejumo, Christopher. 2002. "African Art: New Genres and Transformational Philosophies." In *Africanizing Knowledge: African Studies Across the Disciplines*, edited by Toyin Falola and Christian Jennings, 185. New Brunswick, NJ: Transaction.

Adepegba, Cornelius Oyeleke. 1991. *Yoruba Metal Sculpture*. Ibadan, Nigeria: Ibadan University Press.

Adorno, Theodor. 1951. *Minima Moralia*. https://www.marxists.org/reference/archive/adorno/1951/mm/ch01.htm. Accessed November 1, 2015.

"Afrika Tiss: Le fils solidaire." http://www.afrikatiss.org/. Accessed November 1, 2015.

"Aninkra: Cultural Symbols of the Asante People." http://www.stlawu.edu/gallery/education/f/09textiles/adinkra_symbols.pdf. Accessed November 1, 2015.

Bayart, Jean-François. 1993. *The State in Africa: The Politics of the Belly*. London: Longman.

Bertin, Jacques. 2010. *Semiology of Graphics: Diagrams, Networks, Maps*. Redlands, CA: Esri Press.

Blier, Suzanne Preston. 1995a. *African Vodun: Art, Psychology, and Power*. Chicago: University of Chicago Press.

———. 1995b. *The Anatomy of Architecture: Ontology and Metaphor in Batammaliba Architectural Expression*. Chicago: University of Chicago Press.

———. 2003. "Assemblage: Dahomey Art and the Politics of Dynasty." *Res: Anthropology and Art* 45: 186ff.

———. 2015. *Art and Risk in Ancient Yoruba: Ife History, Power, and Identity c. 1300*. New York: Cambridge University Press.

Brent, Joseph. 1998. *Charles Sanders Peirce: A Life*. 2nd ed. Bloomington: Indiana University Press.

Cole, Herbert M. 2012. *Invention and Tradition: The Art of Southeastern Nigeria*. New York: Prestel.

"Creative Collectives in Africa." http://www.designindaba.com/articles/creative-work/creative-collectives-africa. Accessed November 1, 2015.

Crowe, Donald. 1971. "The Geometry of African Art: Bakuba Art." *Journal of Geometry* 1 (12): 169–83.

Dayrell, Elphinstone. 1911. "Further Notes on 'Nsibidi Signs with Their Meanings from the Ikom District, Southern Nigeria." *Journal of the Royal Anthropological Institute* 41 (July–December): 521–40.

Design en Afrique: S'asseoir, se coucher, et rêver. 2015. Musée Dapper.

Doris, David T. 2011. *Vigilant Things: On Thieves, Yoruba Anti-Aesthetics, and The Strange Fates of Ordinary Objects in Nigeria*. Seattle: University of Washington Press.

Drewal, Margaret Thompson, and Henry John Drewal. 1987. "Composing Time and Space in Yoruba Art." *Word and Image: A Journal of Verbal/Visual Enquiry* 3 (3): 225–51.

Eglash, Ron. 1999. *African Fractals: Modern Computing and Indigenous Design*. New Brunswick, NJ: Rutgers University Press.

Harney, Elizabeth. 2004. *Art, Politics, and the Avant-Garde in Senegal, 1960–1995*. Durham, NC: Duke University Press.

"Inscribing Meaning." 2007. Smithsonian National Museum of African Art. http://africa.si.edu/exhibits/inscribing/nsibidi.html. Accessed September 3, 2014.

Lupton, Ellen. 2009. *Modern Design Theory*. http://elupton.com/2009/10/modern-design-theory/. Accessed November 1, 2015.

Kandinsky, Vasily. 1919. "Little Articles on Big Questions." In *Vasily Kandinsky, "Little Articles on Big Questions: On Line."* Reprinted and translated in *Kandinsky: Complete Writings on Art*, edited by Kenneth C. Lindsay and Peter Vergo. Boston: G. K. Hall, 1982.

Kepes, György. 2012. *Language of Vision*. Whitefish, MT: Literary Licensing.

Mack, John. 2012. "Making and Seeing: Matisse and the Understanding of Kuba Pattern." *Art Historigraphy* 12, n.p. https://arthistoriography.files.wordpress.com/2012/12/mack.pdf. Accessed November 1, 2015.

Maine, Henry. 1861. *Ancient Law: Its Connection with the Early History of Society*. London: John Murray.

Masquelier, Adeline, ed. 2005. *Dirt, Undress and Difference: Critical Perspectives on the Body's Surface*. Bloomington: Indiana University Press.

Matsinde, Tapiwa. 2015. *Contemporary Design Africa*. London: Thames and Hudson.

Peterson, Soren. 2013. "What Can African Design Teach Us." *Huffington Post*, June 27. http://www.huffingtonpost.com/soren-petersen/what-can-african-design-t_b_3820623.html. Accessed November 1, 2015.

Sieber, Roy. 1972. *African Textiles and Decorative Arts*. New York: Museum of Modern Art.

Thompson, Robert Farris. 1973. "An Aesthetic of the Cool." *African Arts* 7 (1) (Autumn): 40–43, 64–67, and 89–91.

Trowell, Margaret. 1960. *African Design: An Illustrated Survey of Traditional Craftwork*. London: Farber & Farber Ltd.

Vansina. Jan. 2010. *Being Colonized: The Kuba Experience in Rural Congo, 1880–1960*. Madison: University of Wisconsin Press.

Wharton, Conway. 1927. *The Leopard Hunts Alone*. New York: Revell. Cited in John Mack, "Making and Seeing: Matisse and the Understanding of Kuba Pattern," *Art Historiography* 12 (2012). https://arthistoriography.files.wordpress.com/2012/12/mack.pdf. Accessed November 1, 2015.

7 ENVIRONMENT

Maano Ramutsindela

In everyday language, the term "environment" generally refers to the surrounding of a living organism and its interaction with it. Due to this entanglement, the environment is not a thing but is instead a concept embedded in complex social relations. It is a product of the relations people have with their dynamic biophysical surroundings. Thus, there can never be a singular meaning of the term "environment" because humans, as organisms living in the environment, are involved in multiple ways of coproducing quite different environmental conditions, even as that environment impacts their way of living. This process is not limited to the urban or rural settings but can, through human agency, unfold across the rural-urban divide. The scholarly literature is, however, replete with analyses that treat urban and rural environments as distinct spheres. Such a distinction is rooted in scholarly traditions and professional specializations that tend to locate socioecological dynamics in particular settings even though ecosystems, the food chain, and environmental problems transcend the boundaries between the urban and the rural. Both the urban and the rural are integral to, as well as a product of, multiple cultural, economic, and political forces operating at various scales. In most African countries people's lives circulate between the urban and rural. Given this caveat, how do we uncover the multiple meanings of the environment within the wider economic and political systems in which they evolve?

I suggest that the meanings of the environment are best discovered by linking environmental ideas and practices to specific contexts in time and space, and by paying greater attention to intervening processes such as infrastructure development that fundamentally reconfigure human-environment interactions, determine the fortunes of national economies, impact on the provision of services, and affect environmental health. Such processes also lead to the emergence of new environments and social identities. Our understanding of the environment as a site of human interaction could be enhanced by appreciating the relational meanings of the term encapsulated in terminologies such as environmental security, environmental citizenship, and so on. These terminologies have gained currency in scholarly discussions, policy formulations, and environmental activism.

Landscape, Wilderness, and Wildness

Despite its lack of a universal meaning, the term "environment" is one of the big ideas of the twentieth century that has significantly challenged and shaped human behaviors. It has become a way of thinking about social relations and the relations between society and nature, and also an avenue through which governmentality is imposed or enacted. It serves as an indicator of inequality in society and between regions of the world. The environment is a prism through which the futures of society and that of the planet are imagined, reorganized, and protected, but also manipulated by powerful groups and nations in pursuit of their social, political, and economic interests. It also offers a platform on which control, access, and distribution of natural resources are contested but also resisted through collective social action. These make the environment an important political terrain.

Social scientists across disciplines have shown that humans, like other organisms, have created and shaped their own environment throughout history, and that the environment, too, has influenced humans in different ways. Though humans, animals, and their biophysical environment are mutually constitutive, this entanglement has been undermined by ideas and discourses of landscapes and wilderness that thrive on social hierarchies often underpinned by a set of moral assumptions. These hierarchies manifest in the built environment in the form of access to land and social services like the provision of water, sanitation, public transport, and housing. In cities, the built environment is a bifurcated space in which different forms of urbanism are discernible. It is a space often inhabited by two kinds of citizenship: one that consumes the fruits of colonial urbanism and capitalist accumulation, and the other that is wounded by these processes. While this duality can be traced to settler colonies and to the inability of the post-independence state of the Global South to transform it, most cities around the world have also been divided along a variety of axes by site-specific and global processes.

The social hierarchies of landscape are a product of power relations through which a hegemonic meaning of landscapes is imposed onto other societies and cultures. Like landscapes, the notion of wilderness expresses dominant ideas of the environment but is also a lens through which the other is given a particular place in the world. It relies heavily on two constructs, namely, the sublime—where wilderness is seen as an act of creation—and the frontier representing the border between civilization and primitivism. A common denominator between landscape and wilderness is that they are both produced by and favor powerful actors and nations who use various instruments and platforms to present their ideas as universal. African societies have long been depicted as having no interest in landscapes even though they produce particular landscapes with aesthetic consciousness and artistic images as has occurred with other cultures. It could be argued that the social stratification inherent in the idea of wilderness has remained intact despite the shifts in the meanings of the term over time. For example, the initial conception of wilderness was associated with hostile environments inhabited by the so-called noble savage and wild beasts considered to be in need of Western civilization and conquest. Subsequently wilderness became less repulsive and was romanticized as spaces of quietness and tranquility for the elite.

The meanings and the creation of wilderness formed the basis of epistemic violence on indigenous peoples. Out of wilderness emerged a Eurocentric representation of indigenous peoples as a mirror of the failures of Western industrial society and as a symbol of backwardness. The earlier conception of wilderness in which indigenous people were considered part of the wild meant that the natives were categorized as wild beasts of the human kind, who could be hunted for sport by colonial hunters just like wild animals. Another way of treating indigenous people as part of the wild played out in colonial administration structures in which the natives were managed together with the zoos. It was at this moment in the history of wilderness that Africans were overtly equated with wildlife and also described in zoological terms. It has also been common to describe the behavior and attributes of Africans through plants and insects. The shift in the meaning of wilderness from hostile environments to the imagined paradise unleashed another form of epistemic violence in the form of forced removals. The removals are symbolic of the pacification of ecotourism spaces as well as the closing of the door of that paradise for the natives, who would only be allowed to reenter as cheap conservation labor.

Notions of landscape and wilderness underpin the big idea of nature conservation. That is to say, conservationists have drawn on narratives of landscapes and wilderness to promote the vision of pristine nature or a slice of the biblical Eden that needs protection from people, especially the poor and the natives. The ideal of the picturesque of the natural landscape is realized by putting aside land, forests, plants, and fisheries in the form of national parks, marine parks, nature reserves, botanical gardens, conservancies, and so on. These conservation areas are found in both urban and rural areas though in different sizes and quantities. Most national parks and nature reserves are found in the rural geographical peripheries of the state as the remnants of nature that needed to be saved from the juggernaut of industrialization. This pattern has since changed with the growing attention to the wilding of cities in the form of urban green spaces and corridors considered the lungs of the city.

In the face of heightened anxieties caused by climate change, the ideology of green urbanism has taken root in the city with the aim of reducing environmental damage and the environmental impact of cities. The concerns with the impact of climate change on cities gave rise to the need to make cities green, which in turn calls for massive capital investment in infrastructure and energy as part of the wider green economy. This ecological impulse accounts for a tree-planting ethic, which is in turn anchored on romantic views of nature that are no different from those of nature in rural landscapes. Literature shows that the rationales for greening cities are many and varied. For example, tree planting in cities could be motivated by the need to govern urban populations, to manage crime, to give the city an orderly form, to give city streets a material character, and so on. While green urbanism deepens capital penetration, the emergent network of infrastructure is appropriated by various actors, including marginalized groups and immigrants, who use it to create a virtual system that transforms the city and its landscape.

Environmental Racism

Inspired by Western thought that underpins the current hegemonic society-nature dualism, and armed with environmental science, conservationists reconstituted existing socioecological relations in pursuit of predetermined environmental goals. In the main, Western nations have used environmental problems as an avenue to influence domestic policies of African states. Solutions to environmental problems are also used to justify dispossession even as they disempower and create or revive social stratification. Take the problem of dwindling wildlife in Africa that was mainly caused by commercial and sport hunting by settlers but laid on the shoulders of Africans who often hunted for the pot, and who assisted Europeans with hunting skills. Despite all these, hunting by Africans was outlawed in order to prevent them from participating in the lucrative wildlife trade. Generally, wildlife laws were spurred more by the need to regulate hunting and wildlife trade than by the need to conserve animal species for their own sake. As in the past, sport hunting remains an exclusive activity dominated by whites and the elite. These exclusionary practices are part of a wider environmental racism.

Whereas environmental racism in the North American context manifests mainly in the form of differential exposure to harm, especially toxic wastes, it has a much wider meaning in African contexts, where environmental deterministic assumptions about the relationship between culture and nature, and between nature and the environment, are prominent. It is worth noting that environmental determinism subscribes to the culture-nature dualism, and holds that cultures are shaped by the biophysical environment in which they exist. In doing so, environmental determinism promotes cultural relativism—that is, the assumption that people experience the world through culturally given categories. The racial undertone of this relativism emerges as the environment becomes a prism through which socioecological relations are directly linked to racial superiority and class. Indigenous people and the poor in developing countries are routinely blamed for environmental degradation, even though the human-induced destruction of the environment is linked to the global capitalist system. Their methods of, say, fishing and cultivation are generally categorized as environmentally inefficient and destructive.

The racist logic here is that since human achievement and development are determined by environmental conditions, African societies have limited scope of advancement given deteriorating environmental conditions on the continent. The most recent manifestation of this version of racism is found in analyses of climate change that describe African societies as the most vulnerable group due to their supposedly inherent weak institutions, weak environmental ethic, lack of skills, and so on. These assumptions undermine the ways in which African societies have dealt with harsh environmental conditions in their history. The point here is not to deny the threats posed by global environmental change to Africa in the twenty-first century. Rather, it is to foreground enduring stereotypes of African societies as the weakest link in the human race. Racial inclusivity in environmentally related actions has been rare in the African continent. This practice can be traced back to the colonial enterprise that determined that the knowledge and management skills required for effective environmental protection were lacking in or even absent from African societies.

Environmental racism in African contexts further manifests in the denial of the contribution that Africans have made toward biodiversity conservation. African culture is seen through the Western gaze as inherently lacking environmental ethics despite Africans having preserved forests through, say, sacred groves, some of which are currently designated as UNESCO World Heritage Sites, and as important areas for biodiversity conservation. In its crude form, environmental racism has led to racialized ownership of and access to natural resources in much of the developing world. While tenure arrangements over natural resources depend on both the resource in question and existing institutional governance, a general trend is that resource ownership is structured in ways that disadvantage certain population groups or nations.

Resource Sovereignty

Natural resources are a source of struggles and violence in most parts of the world, even as they are one of the pillars of state sovereignty. The question of sovereignty over natural resources took center stage when Chile introduced the concept of permanent sovereignty over natural resources into the debates on the Human Rights Covenants of the United Nations in 1952. The debates culminated in the United Nations Declaration on Permanent Sovereignty over Natural Resources adopted by the General Assembly of the United Nations on December 14, 1962. Accordingly, the declaration confirmed the rights of people and nations to permanent sovereignty over their natural wealth and resources, and the exercise of those rights by states in the interest of national development and the general well-being of their citizens. Sovereignty as a legal and political concept however derives its meaning from the ability of the state to exercise power and control over territory, and over its people and natural resources. There is no such thing as exclusive and absolute sovereignty precisely because sovereignty involves the exercise of power by the sovereign entity such as government in the domestic sphere while the legitimacy of a sovereign power or authority depends on whether it is recognized by other sovereign states in the international system. Thus resource sovereignty may be territorial and inward as when only the state and internal actors own the resources in the form of, say, nationalization (a form of domanial ownership). Nationalization and indigenization of resources should be understood as a reassertion of national sovereignty over resources found in the state's territorial space. The system of domanial ownership leads to state monopoly over natural resources that could either be used for the advancement of national economies or for self-enrichment by those in leadership. Resource sovereignty may also be relational as when power over and control of resources are influenced by extraterritorial forces. This regalian system of ownership stems from the idea that a resource belongs to whoever discovered it rather than to the authority who controls the area in which it is located. Regalian ownership enables private/external actors to subvert national sovereignty over the resources.

A pertinent question for Africa relates to the nature of sovereignty over territory and how it translates into resource sovereignty. It could be argued that while liberation struggles in the continent delivered territorial sovereignty most African governments have been and still are struggling to achieve resource sovereignty envisaged in United Nations Declaration. A number of reasons can be advanced to explain this condition. Daron Acemoglu and James Robinson have argued that post-independence governments are caught in a vicious cycle in which colonial-era extractive institutions are maintained to the disadvantage of the working class and national economies. Such a process is more pronounced in Africa owing to competition over natural resources key to the workings of the global capitalist economy, and to the geopolitical positioning of powerful nations and groups within and outside of the continent. For instance, the majority of coltan that the lucrative mobile phone industry relies on comes from the Democratic Republic of the Congo.

External investment into Africa's extractive industries ensures that resource sovereignty in the continent is not territorially circumscribed but that it is shared with global networks. A case in point is Africa's natural resources such as oil and minerals that not only lead to resource extraction but also enable the territorialization of resources—that is, the allocation and beneficiation of mineral wealth to certain individuals, companies or countries to the detriment of national economies. These processes are embedded in the exploitative capitalist economy, and are challenged by ordinary citizens in two main ways. First, growing unemployment, entrepreneurship, and reforms in mineral policies have motivated ordinary people to get involved in artisanal and small-scale mining in Africa. This sector has grown despite efforts to control it through force and regulation (such as institutionalizing mineral titles), or by providing alternative sources of livelihoods to artisanal mining through strategies such as re-agrarianization. Second, mine workers have intensified their struggle for a living wage and better conditions of employment in extractive industries. These struggles challenge the foreignization of mineral wealth, and seek to disrupt the exploitative relationships between mining houses, national governments, and the elite in labor unions.

Notions of the global environmental crisis as a war for human survival have been used to frame citizenship and security, and to suggest wider responsibilities toward the environment. People have used the environment to rediscover or claim their identities and to think about their roles and responsibilities toward the planet and its inhabitants. From the national to the global, the environment is seen as being imbued with the curative properties of nature that can be mobilized toward a peaceful coexistence of nations or people in conflict-ridden countries. Thus, environmentally inscribed citizenship operates at the national, regional, and global levels, but also across these levels. This is made possible by the fact that environmental problems are hardly confined to a particular level. Moreover, environmental change and ecological conditions are products of broader political processes that are inseparable from the workings of the global capitalist economy. For analytical purposes, we can scrutinize environmentally inspired citizenship at various levels to make sense of a set of responsibilities at hand. At the global level, the notion of environmental crisis is mobilized to promote the idea of a global citizen, whose responsibility is to look after the health of the planet. Critical scholarship has questioned whether giving environmental problems a global profile is not in fact to succumb to the political and economic interests of powerful nations, who use international platforms to parade national concerns as global issues.

Peace Parks and Environmental Security

Environmental issues are increasingly being incorporated into regional integration plans, with the hope that environmental concerns could facilitate transfrontier regionalism: a regional integration process underpinned by environmental concerns and that has as its geographical location the borderlands. The result of this process has not only been to develop regional environmental agendas and responses, but also to forge some kind of regional identity. Since the 1990s, a regional and continental citizenship has developed in Africa in the name of the environment. It was spurred by the emergence of peace parks in Southern Africa that sought to amalgamate contiguous protected areas across two or more countries. These transnational parks were touted by nongovernmental conservation organizations, governments, and the private sector as appropriate mechanisms for protecting and managing ecosystems, for developing shared environmental responsibilities, for fostering peaceful coexistence among African nations, for facilitating regional integration, and for promoting socioeconomic development, especially in economically depressed rural areas. In reality the only "citizens" free to enjoy the regional space are the wildlife, as well as tourists who visit these transnational parks, rather than ordinary people living in these countries. Such freedom of movement of wildlife is facilitated by the physical and symbolic removal of fences marking international boundaries at the edge of protected areas, and also by the removal of people living in areas designated for peace parks. This way, regional environmental actions and responsibilities sponsored by the private sector and nongovernmental organizations become the basis on which the rights of animals to move freely across international borders are placed above human ones.

The idea of peace parks evolved from being the project of nongovernmental organizations and interested individuals to a continental plan. This was made possible when local and international conservation lobby groups and their funders pushed the agenda of peace parks into broader regional and continental projects. The first stage in this process was to insert the notion of transfrontier conservation area into the Protocol on Wildlife Conservation and Law Enforcement signed by member states of the Southern African Development Community in 1999. The protocol was meant to forge a common regional position for the Convention on International Trade in Endangered Species of Wild Fauna and Flora (CITES). Thereafter conservationists touted the idea of peace parks as a regional initiative and Southern African governments used it to show the world that they cared about nature conservation. The institutionalization of peace parks as a regional project resulted in Southern African states signing memoranda of understanding and treaties on peace parks in the name of regional integration, environmental stewardship, and development. This way, the parks became symbolic of Africa's aspirations as articulated in the Action Plan for the Environment Initiative that was launched in Algiers in December 2003. The Action Plan was part of the New Partnerships for Africa's Development (NEPAD) project championed by former presidents Thabo Mbeki (South Africa), Olusegun Obasanjo (Nigeria), and Abdoulaye Wade (Senegal).

The launch of this plan was historic in that African leaders met in the context of NEPAD to discuss environmental strategies at a continental level. These strategies were meant to promote sustainable use of Africa's natural resources; to strengthen public and political support for subregional and regional environmental initiatives; to support the implementation by African countries of their commitments under the global and regional environmental conventions and other legal instruments to which they are party; to promote the integration of environmental issues into poverty reduction strategies; to foster regional and subregional cooperation in addressing environmental challenges; and to improve the institutional framework for regional environmental governance. These strategies were incorporated into peace parks and were sealed as an environmental agenda for Africa through a number of instruments: the Sirte Declaration on the Environment and Development (June 2004); the Dakar recommendations of the Conference of Ministers on resource mobilization (October 2004); and the Dakar Declaration for the Enhanced Partnerships in the Implementation of the Action Plan for the Environment Initiative of NEPAD. As part of a continental agenda, peace parks were expected to translate the dream of an African Renaissance into reality.

In addition to the role it could play in regionalism, the environment was firmly placed at the center of security discourses after the end of the Cold War. In the post–Cold War era, the threat posed by nuclear warfare was replaced with that of the environment in crisis. The crisis in turn became an avenue for the securitization of the environment—a process by which environmental issues form part of wider national and global security concerns and strategies. This process became more prominent after the 9/11 attacks in the United States. The infusion of the multifaceted concept of security into the environmental domain has broadened meanings of security that have huge implications for African states. Effectively, a combination of the end of the Cold War and growing concerns with global environmental protection created conditions under which national security was redefined to encompass environmentally induced threats such as dwindling resources for livelihoods, environmental refugees (the mass migration of people on account of deteriorating environmental conditions), environmentally induced conflict, and so on. It is understood that climate change disrupts and also undermines the sustainability of life and therefore poses one of the greatest security risks of the twenty-first century. The argument goes that those disruptions and conflicts have the potential to create conditions for social disorder at the national and international levels. Nationally, states stand to lose their legitimacy due to escalating environmentally related socioeconomic problems and as a result of lack of capacity and infrastructure, and weak military capabilities to manage those problems. According to this narrative, the net effects of such environmental crisis would be felt beyond the borders of individual states.

Proponents of environmental security have used Africa as a microcosm of the coming environmentally induced chaos. According to such a scenario, the scarcity of resources caused by global environmental change and unprecedented population growth in Africa would result in massive human displacement and migration. It has been argued that such mass migration would disrupt key social institutions and provoke ethnic clashes that could destroy weak governments in Africa while threatening social order in countries of the Global North. This scenario harks back to the colonial discourse of uncivilized Africa. It is based on a construction of the world ignorant of centuries of exploitative and unequal relations between Africa and the Global North.

Though the environment blurs the boundaries between national and global security, the link between security and the environment is tenuous. Environmental threats are framed such that they enable nations to engage in violent actions such as military intervention even as these put the biophysical environment at risk. Africa has been one of the laboratories for the militarization of protected areas, which includes testing new technologies and tactics of green wars. Expressed differently, the threat posed by commercial poaching in national parks and in private game reserves opened up possibilities for militarizing conservation areas in Africa. Conservation goals have become integral to global security through the narrative of poacher-as-terrorist. In the Cold War environment poaching and the so-called communist threat were conflated, especially in Southern Africa where a well-established anti-communist environmental movement was determined to hunt down liberation armies by framing them as poachers. African wildlife became embroiled in Cold War politics as state security establishments used proceeds from wildlife products to financially support anti-government insurrectionary forces. Current concerns with poaching of rhinos and elephants in different regions of Africa have reignited the controversial link between poaching and terrorism. The antiterrorism campaign spurred by the growth of terrorist networks and their brutal actions around the world considers wildlife trafficking—defined by the White House as the poaching of protected species and the illegal trade in wildlife and their derivative parts and products—as one of the key sources of financing terrorism. Thus, illicit wildlife trade is considered a global security risk. Africa occupies a special place in that campaign, not least because of the abundance of wildlife on the continent. Wildlife trafficking is also seen as fueling political instability in countries such as the Central African Republic, Chad, the Democratic Republic of the Congo, South Sudan, and Sudan, even as the political fortunes of these countries are determined by a multitude of factors.

Conclusion

Much of the debate on environmental problems and their possible solutions revolves around the links between society and nature in time and space. A critique of this dualism remains incomplete if social research does not uncover its varied impact on society, especially on marginalized groups around the world. A full understanding of the environment as a political terrain could be gained by scrutinizing environmental ideas and related policies and practices. Understanding how these ideas are rooted in urban and rural areas of Africa and their impact on African societies is crucial for the study of Africa. The notion of environment has been deployed by powerful groups and nations to fundamentally reconfigure the ownership of natural resources, to restructure urban landscapes, and to undermine existing socioecological relations in Africa and elsewhere. These practices are rooted in broader ideologies that coalesce around notions of difference. In green urbanism such difference is magnified by the existence of slums and suburbs side by side, by unequal infrastructures, and by skewed investments trends. There is nothing inherently wrong with difference but such difference becomes a problem when it is used to construct a superiority complex and stereotypes that feed into existing social and racial categorizations. Much of these categorizations inform the historical and contemporary production of negative images of Africans and their environments.

From a global perspective, environmental ideas not only shape socioecological relations but also contribute significantly to the idea of Africa as a wild continent. They keep Africa open to external influences and actors, who use green agendas as a political paddle on which attempts are made to determine the direction and speed of African development. Historical configurations of social relations by environmental ideas and practices demand a recontextualization of environmental justice in Africa that goes beyond the right for everyone in society to live in a healthy environment and to benefit from it, irrespective of gender, class, or race. It should instead be expanded to include resource sovereignty, restitution, resource rights and access, and the restructuring of resource governance. Thus, a progressive notion of environmental justice can only become meaningful in the continent when it addresses the legacy of the exploitation of people and their resources, and the consequent poverty and loss of dignity.

Suggested Readings

Cronon, William. 1995. "The Trouble with Wilderness: Or, Getting Back to the Wrong Nature." *Environmental History* 1 (1): 7–28.

Dalby, Simon. 2009. *Security and Environmental Change*. Cambridge: Polity.

Hall, Peter. 2014. *Cities of Tomorrow: An Intellectual History of Urban Planning and Design since 1880*. Chichester, UK: John Wiley & Sons.

Neumann, Roderick, P. 2004. "Moral and Discursive Geographies in the War for Biodiversity in Africa." *Political Geography* 23 (7): 813–37.

Okoye, Ikem S. 2016. "Good Bush, Bad Bush: Representing Our Natures in Historical Southern Nigerian Landscapes." In *Cultural Landscape Heritage in Sub-Saharan Africa*, edited by John Beardsley, 263–92. Washington, DC: Dumbarkton Oaks.

Ramutsindela, Maano. 2007. *Transfrontier Conservation in Africa: At the Confluence of Capital, Politics and Nature*. Wallingford, UK: Cabi.

Simone, AbdouMaliq. 2006. "Pirate Towns: Reworking Social and Symbolic Infrastructures in Johannesburg and Douala." *Urban Studies* 43 (2): 357–70.

———. 2016. "It's Just the City after All!" *International Journal of Urban and Regional Research* 40 (1): 210–18.

Swilling, Mark. 2013. "Reconceptualising Urbanism, Ecology and Networked Infrastructures." In *Rogue Urbanism: Emergent African Cities*, edited by Edgar Pieterse and AbdouMaliq Simone, 65–81. Auckland Park: Jacana.

8 EVIDENCE

Luise White

Is there such a thing as African evidence? Can there be facts specific to a continent that necessitate continentally specific methods to study them? No one anywhere would disagree with the fact that Ghana became independent on March 6, 1957, with Kwame Nkrumah as its first prime minister, but how can we assess the nature of evidence that is more than dates and names? We need to ask, Does a fact found in Africa mean the same thing in Africa as it does in Europe and North America? The date of Ghana's independence certainly means the same thing everywhere, but how do we understand things that are literally concrete, like a shard of Chinese celadon pottery or a nine-hundred-year-old wall? There is no disputing they were found in Africa, but what are they evidence of and does their meaning change over time and space? A pottery shard may be proof of twelfth-century international trade or it may be a souvenir removed from ground that has remained undisturbed for years. A nine-hundred-year-old wall may be evidence of an ancient royal enclosure or it may be an impediment to ploughing. How can we know which it is? Naming the pottery shard an artifact requires knowing the history of the pot it originally was part of and knowing something about the other material objects found beside it. A shard of Chinese pottery found near glass beads might mean one thing while a shard of Chinese pottery found next to modern metal cooking pots would mean something very different. Assessing the meaning of an artifact tells us what it is evidence of, and sometimes how different groups assess that evidence. A pottery shard found beside a nine-hundred-year-old wall in Africa might be evidence of a rich and exploitative dynasty for those who toiled building the structure, but it can mean wealth and international trade when studied as an artifact. What a pottery shard proves—

what it is evidence of—depends on the questions we ask about it. Those questions are based on where it was found, what was found near it from the same time period, and how much can be ascertained about its use. In short, facts become evidence by their context and, in this case, that context is African.

But is a social fact the same kind of evidence an artifact is? Do stories told about witches or extractive authorities or shape shifting animals constitute evidence? If they are, is that evidence the same in 1920s Nigeria and 1950s Mozambique, for example, or even in 2015 Florida? The answer is, probably not. Evidence does not stand alone: social facts are indeed social, situated in relationships, in local situations and local struggles. Sometimes those struggles involve chiefs who are overzealous in their collection of tax monies, and sometimes they involve the drought-stricken farmers who claimed that the goat they sold to an unscrupulous merchant turned into a snake. Some facts involve a world visible to Africans but not easily seen by Western academics, as when dead ancestors provide freedom fighters with gifts of tobacco or when they sicken runaway slaves until they purchase their freedom. Are these facts evidence? I argue that they are, and that what they are evidence of is layered; the fact has a meaning on the ground far deeper than anything we would ascribe to it.

Early Methods and Participant Observation

Let me start with E. E. Evans-Pritchard's eighty-year-old observation of how Zande people understand an event. On a hot afternoon a granary collapses, injuring the men who were sitting beneath it to escape the heat of the day. Every Zande knows (as we do) that termites often eat through the wooden poles supporting a granary; even the best maintained granary may collapse after years of service. This fact might have been enough for you and I but for Zande people it is the entry point for a new, more detailed set of questions: what caused the termites to eat through the poles of that particular granary at the exact moment when those particular men rested beneath it? Evans-Pritchard argues that the point is not that Zande people believe in magic or have a great fear of supernatural powers, but that their idea of evidence contains causation; a fact must have agency behind it. In more modern contexts these ideas did not disappear but were honed. Years later in South Africa the young, educated research assistant of an anthropologist stated as much, suggesting that the facts of science did not adequately explain why one person falls ill and another does not. He knew that typhus was caused by lice, but "who sent the lice?" Stories about the spread of infectious disease—that influenza was shot from guns fired at the end of World War I, or that HIV/AIDS was spread by white doctors—were not facts nor were they evidence of contagion. Instead they were evidence of deep and abiding anxieties about how and why European power has been deployed in Africa.

The development and deployment of evidence in African studies has never been as rich as it was on the ground in Africa. The academic study of Africa sought to make African ideas and experiences comprehensible to Western eyes. Africa was to be presented to the wider world as a continent of culture and reason, proving that fictions of African savagery and ideas about African superstition were wrong. As the academic study of Africa expanded over the years it became as complicated and contested as any explanation for why a granary collapsed, but it has had its own history and its own specific concerns about the nature of evidence and, perhaps unique in the academic world, the way evidence has been obtained. The academic study of Africa began with the ethnography of Africa. Insights like those of Evans-Pritchard were based on participant observation, on the fact of his being there: authority came from what the author saw, what he or she learned from speaking to people. It was understood that the analysis was not invented by the author alone, but was the result of observation, experience, and consultation with local people. It was this consultation that made the evidence of ethnography reliable and arguably more important, different from the eyewitness accounts of slave traders, explorers, and colonial officials, whose writings were read far more critically than those of anthropologists were. Being there transcended notions of insider and outsider knowledge; it applied to Jomo Kenyatta's 1938 ethnography, *Facing Mount Kenya*, even if he had not been in Kenya for many years and to Marcel Griaule, who did live in Dogon country before publishing an ethnography in 1948. Indeed, when ethnographers were criticized it was most often for their heavy-handed ways of finding things out or for what they had failed to acknowledge. The first generation of anthropologists was later criticized for being too close to African kings and ruling lineages and a later generation often criticized themselves for unwittingly being too close to the regimes they studied, but whatever those anthropologists did not reveal at the time, they made up for it by what they saw and wrote about.

Evidence from Africa, like all forms of evidence, even the evidence based on never-to-be-repeated personal observations, is unstable. African history began in earnest as an academic discipline in the 1960s; its first task was to separate itself from the history of European empires. African history was to be about African agency, not the agency of causation as Zande people understood it, but the agency of Africans actors, doing things in Africa: it was not the history of Europeans in Africa. Its second task was to separate itself from anthropology, the discipline that had been studying Africans in Africa for more than forty years. African history was to be the study of the African past in all its dynamism and glory: Africa had states and trade and factional struggles long before the slave trade or colonial conquest. The African past was not static. A generation of African historians turned to the huge body of literature written by slave traders and explorers—men who had been there—and to the innovative research method pioneered by Jan Vansina, oral tradition. Although a generation of African historians was trained to insist that oral traditions were as reliable as documents, the actual practice of interpreting oral traditions was to doubt what was in them: scholars had to identify what was a cliché and what was not, they had to be critically aware of when discrete events or the accomplishments of several kings were telescoped into one miraculous reign, and they had to know when to disregard stories of burning lakes and talking buffalo and queens whose pregnancies lasted for years so as to get to the political events hidden within them. Historical evidence could be found in oral tradition if a scholar was willing to peel the onion, to disregard the layers of untruth to get to the truth it held. Oral traditions were charters of legitimacy for states and kingdoms: dissertators were advised to establish lists of kings and to keep a list of solar eclipses handy to help with establishing firm dates. They had to be especially attentive to language: not just the one Africans spoke presently, but the origins of words. Learning where words came from and what concepts were embedded in them allowed scholars to see the movement of peoples and the movement of their ideas. Oral traditions required work: young researchers had to find the keeper of the tradition (usually male), they had to record it, and then he or she had to ask the questions that justified its claims. They were expected to know the archaeology of the region and to understand local cosmologies so as to turn oral traditions into historical evidence.

Years later scholars complained that these methods made African culture appear static, but these methods and the publications they produced gave us a history of Africa before 1900 that is perhaps one of the great successes of African studies. In 1960, for example, little was known about the politics and livelihoods of Africa before 1900, but by 1980 histories of what is still called the precolonial past filled the shelves of university libraries. The work based on oral tradition and local archives demonstrated a history of economic growth, political thought, and political change. Contemporary criticisms chided these scholars for their narrowness; they had not consulted metropolitan archives and tended to write about Africans and what they did in Africa, missing an opportunity to write about African's relations with broader regions in Africa and with Europe. Such criticisms missed the point, that this was a new African history, the goal of which was to reconstruct the history of Africans in Africa. Its motivations were political; it was to give a deep history to the independence of African states. It was, in the words of one of its earliest Nigerian proponents, "history for self-government." In such a history there was no reason to study what Africans did with or for European traders and North African herdsmen: Africa had a history that was important in and of itself. Even as scholars recuperated the history of African kingdoms and empires from sources in Africa, historians of the Atlantic (and later the Saharan and Indian Ocean) slave trade used evidence and wrote histories that would link the history of Africa to that of the wider world. It was a history that was based on sources found on two and often three continents; the main body of evidence did not come from Africa, nor was it based on research done there.

"African" Evidence and Inclusionary Methods

A range of concerns, both about the present and the past, transformed the historical study of Africa in the 1970s. There was a growing awareness that the histories of Africa's past grandeur did not empower Africans to address challenges of contemporary Africa and there was scholars' engagement with the emerging field of social history in the broader discipline as a way to widen the scope and subject matter of historical analysis. If African historians had been cautioned away from the study of colonialism—it was, in the words of a pioneering Nigerian historian, "the blink of an eye" in Africa's long history—they now began to embrace it. Not only did it appear that colonialism held the key to the problems and inequalities that befell Africa in the 1970s, but studying the colonial era fit well with the new concerns of social history. This was history from below, the study of poor and marginal people who had been ignored by previous generations. Scholars charged themselves with rescuing the unskilled and the unschooled from the "condescension of the present" to bring them into an historical narrative that had been forged without them. For historians of Africa, the opportunity to link political economy to social history encouraged a new vision of how the African past might best be interrogated. Scholars turned to the newly accessioned archives for the colonial period and read them critically, to see the experiences of slaves, women, workers, and peasants. African beliefs and motives could be found in the most regressive of colonial texts: indeed it was reading for African ideas within Europeans' suppression thereof that the historiography of resistance was born.

The discovery of African resistance in colonial texts was part and parcel of a broader transformation in how scholars of Africa used evidence. Put simply it became dogma that the people who were excluded from the historical record should be included, and that inclusion required attention to new kinds of evidence and more often than not new methodologies with which to collect and use that evidence. Historians of African women, like historians of women elsewhere in the world, sought ways to bring women's experience to the fore. In Africa, however, perhaps more than anywhere else, this required oral history. This oral history was positioned in opposition to the state-centered study of oral tradition: this was the history of ordinary folk, of slaves and ex-slaves, all of whom were historical agents in African history. For two very basic reasons it became essential to interview, to collect oral histories. First, historians researching in Africa in the 1970s and 1980s had a huge reservoir of informants to choose from, since most of the people scholars wanted to interview had lived in colonial times. Second, it was taken for granted that most Africans could neither read nor write, which meant there was no other means to record their lives. This, too, was in opposition to the study of oral tradition; events within living memory could be checked by documents; there was no need to look for clichés or the formulaic elements in someone's life story; dates and chronologies could be easily ascertained if not by the informant then by well-known events. Perhaps for this reason there was a notion that oral histories could be equated with the kinds of facts social science recognized. Scholars wrote of their data as if was a statistical sample that had been derived from interviews conducted with men and women who were "representative" of a specific time and place. In a very short time, however, the idea that there could be a singular kind of colonial experience that would bring women, and former slaves, and mine workers into the historical record could not withstand the complicated lives and imaginings of the women and men who were interviewed. What began as a straightforward task of inclusion became one of changing what we knew about the past: the words of women and former slaves told new and different stories about twentieth-century Africa. The belief in the transformative power of oral interviews meant that nothing a woman or a peasant said required the careful interrogation reserved for oral tradition. Indeed, scholars began to insist that women's or peasants' words were the most reliable chronicle of colonial experiences, that those words should be privileged over the writings of district officers and mission doctors. African women's history did more than restore agency to African women, however: it successfully located the history of African women into the broader, worldwide histories of women and gender.

Oral Histories

This emphasis on speech, on women's words, was usually bundled into the idea of voices, as in African voices or women's voices. Many scholars saw the idea of "voices" as a logical step in the inclusive practices that had long shaped African history, but the notion of someone's voice providing an irrefutable window into the past marked a sea change in ideas about evidence. The interview, which had never been a significant part of African history methodology, became central to the production of historical evidence. Interviewing women and men was declared a much more reliable endeavor than collecting folktales or gossip about an informant, which had been standard ethnographic practice. More important, perhaps, was the recognition that the interview was an act in itself, requiring ethics and empathy. This was an era of positionality, the idea that who a researcher was—white, female, married, privileged—shaped the evidence in ways earlier generations had not understood. Interviews contained all the power relations of the postcolonial world, and for that reason there was no doubting an informant; if they could speak for themselves it was assumed they would recount their experiences accurately. Such an interview required being there, of course, but it also required being unobtrusive: the researcher's task was not to ask questions like an inquisitor or a policeman, but to create a space in which ordinary Africans could speak without constraint or criticism. Almost by accident, that space created some self-reflective moments in which a former slave remembered when he bought his first pair of shoes but not when he was freed, for example, or when women in Nairobi recalled the years in which the fire department captured Africans and took their blood. Such evidence opened up, and legitimated, new areas of enquiry. If informants spoke of the clothes available to them after the abolition of slavery, or said that it was the yellow fever department in Uganda that took Africans' blood, those were questions worth studying. There were two issues of evidence at play here. First, in an interview in which Africans "spoke for themselves," everything was evidence. Second, evidence took the back seat to the fact of speaking, to the African voice. The voice hardwired agency into our historical writings. When Africans spoke for themselves, their agency was recuperated. And if that voice told us about shoes and bloodsucking firemen, so be it: the voice had to be respected.

The opposite of the voice, of Africans speaking for themselves, was silence, a singular notion that could not contain all the things that were unspoken and unseen. Unmediated voices, albeit in translation, were given a special status. The life history, a well-established but neglected anthropological method, was revived in the 1990s with the widespread production of African women's life histories. In these texts women spoke for themselves: summarizing women's words was problematic, in large part because it denied them their voice; but letting Africans speak in long, indented quotes that were then contextualized and interpreted by an author gave voice to the people imagined to be voiceless. Informants ceased to be informants and became life historians. Nevertheless, the genre contained a grave contradiction in that its foundational texts were based on written life histories, and composite life histories paid greater attention to women who left a paper trail than those who did not.

African voices can still be heard but they seem to have receded in significance as a form of evidence. There is not any single reason for this, but starting in the early 1990s there were critiques of the whole idea of experience. Such critiques were never fully embraced by African historians but the overall sensibility that words alone could not always convey what was important in peoples' lives undermined the authority of individual testimony. At the same time, many scholars looking at medicine or law in colonial Africa began to reread colonial texts with critical care. They did not identify an African voice, but rather Africans subjects whose experiences were known through colonial categories. This research offered a new understanding of how African experiences were shaped and constrained as well as new insights into how colonial categories were shaped and constrained by the experience of ruling Africans. In 1994, South Africa became an African-ruled country and was open for research as it had never been before. Once there it was impossible to ignore African's long engagement with writing the way scholars had ignored literate Africans in West Africa, for example. South African scholars were quick to point out that the scholarly fixation with oral history amounted to an obsession with the authority and authenticity of specific kinds of evidence, as if the media in which information was presented determined how true and how useful it was. The idea of unmediated speech made no sense in worlds in which people who could neither read nor write routinely engaged with published texts. Across the continent scholars became aware that informants spoke back to fictional or cinematic portrayals of events in which they had participated.

The impact of these ideas was not immediate but within a few years there was a shift in how scholars approached evidence in Africa: a narrow focus on an oral history that was synonymous with interviews was no longer possible. By the start of the twenty-first century it became obvious that Africans wrote and Africans read what they wrote. Scholars began to examine the small but steady flow of literary productions coming out of Africa since the nineteenth century. By the twentieth century some parts of Africa experienced a flood of literary production in the form of accounts of local histories and customs and self-help literature. In the 1990s the donor-driven pressure for multiparty democracies in Africa encouraged activists and dissidents—some recently released from prison—to write their memoirs. These, like newspapers in African languages and self-help books and texts recording local customs, were published locally and read locally: the idea that Africa was a continent whose history could only be recuperated by attending to the spoken word was no longer credible.

This shift may have been accelerated by events in Africa that seemed to require new modes of interrogation, new ways of looking for and at evidence. Nowhere is this clearer than Stephen Ellis's imploring his readers to see the torture of Liberian dictator Samuel Doe as Liberians would, to understand that Doe had to be mutilated to prevent him from turning into a bird and flying away. Being there became once again critical to how a scholar obtained evidence; it was how scholars learned that the unspoken and the unseen were not silences, but active forces that determined the politics of the day. If an earlier generation of historians had turned away from the glories of the precolonial past because they believed that in colonial history they could see the origins of the poverty and inequality they saw around them, another generation began to tackle the problems of postcolonial history. However obvious it seemed that Africa's recent past was best studied though oral history, scholars turned, or returned, to written evidence to understand the complexities of events in Africa after 1960. This was an unexpected development made even more bewildering by the absence of organized postcolonial archives on the continent. Historians had to traipse around the world to find documentation about events in the 1960s and 1970s, visiting not only metropolitan archives but private and local ones as well. This seems to have brought about a new interest in and respect for archives: new approaches to written documents argued that they were not simply records, but narratives constructed to manipulate a specific audience at a specific time, which made metropolitan or corporate or local archives all the more interesting.

This reevaluation of what could be found in a written text, be it colonial or postcolonial, coincided with scholars beginning to doubt the evidentiary authority of interviews. Starting in the late 1990s there was a gradual disinclination to claim that African voices provided special or specific truths. One reason was the situation in Africa: scholars had to confront the fact that the people they asked to speak for themselves did not always believe they could speak freely, and those who did often spoke in clichéd and formulaic accounts of charged events. And why not? What was the right answer to a question posed in the early twenty-first century about one's participation in anti-colonial revolts or the slaughter of one's neighbors who were of a different tribe? By contrast, the postcolonial era generated texts that foregrounded many of the complexities that oral history had flattened. There were trials and commissions of inquiry into the murders of politicians, all of which presented a density of evidence that showed how fractured and fragmented truths were and that no single true version of any event could be found, nor could any single voice speak such a truth. Courtroom trials and commissions of inquiry were spaces in which the dead and the living spoke in one venue, but the dead constrained what the living could say, and the living refashioned the dead as they spoke. Commissions of inquiry were sites in which what could be said and what was unspeakable came together, as South Africa's Truth and Reconciliation Commission revealed the extent to which what could be known, and what could be said, was more than a matter of speech.

New Technologies and the Future of Evidence in Africa

Even as truth commissions met, new technologies changed how evidence could be used and interpreted. The Atlantic slave trade had long been the subject of acrimonious disputes, over how many slaves left Africa and how many arrived in the Americas. As the logs of slave ships were digitized it became possible to see not only how many slaves survived the Middle Passage, but the age at which they were enslaved. This material allowed scholars to establish the ratio of male to female captives, and to assess slaves' health when they disembarked in the Americas. New ways of interrogating evidence changed what that evidence could reveal. They also undermined the notion that scholars could distinguish between evidence produced in Africa and that found in metropolitan archives: facts and physical conditions traveled, sometimes in chains, but always provided evidence for the embodied histories of African peoples.

This is not to say that new technologies make research in Africa and the evidence so obtained obsolete. On the contrary, new technologies improve our ability to address and contextualize evidence. Just as the technologies available in modern laboratories can tell us the age of a pottery shard from the Kenya coast, digitized newspapers can be searched to find individuals whose obscurity would have made them invisible to historians only a few decades ago. But the issue is not one of which technologies a scholar uses, but of how those technologies are used and the kinds of local knowledge that are brought to bear on the findings derived from an oral interview or a digitized census. Facts in Africa are not simply there to be plucked; just like pottery shards they become evidence by their context, where they were produced and to whom they mattered; that evidence becomes knowledge by the broader context of how many facts were produced and what they meant to communities and social groups. With the possible exception of the date of a country's independence, no fact stands alone. No pottery shard or witch belief or recollection of late colonial labor practices exists in isolation.

Scholars who have studied Africa may well have anguished over the right way to do so, but that anguish emerged (and continues to emerge) from the persistent question of what is the right way to understand Africa, a question that has always come from events on the continent: questions of understanding African societies gave way to questions about what kinds of knowledge best served African societies when they became independent nations precisely because Africa changed. Concerns about the quality of that independence gave rise to a range of social and cultural histories that were grounded in the everyday lives of ordinary Africans. That there were debates about how those lives could be recuperated and which method could be relied upon to encourage Africans to speak openly is not evidence of indecision or an inability to settle on the one correct way to study Africans: these debates were situational and that they continue is proof of an engagement with events in Africa. The complicated lives of African men and women who live in difficult and rapidly changing times are best recovered through a variety of methods.

Suggested Readings

Barber, Karin, ed. 2006. *Africa's Hidden Histories: Everyday Literacy and Making the Self*. Bloomington: Indiana University Press.

Cohen, David William, and E. S. Atieno Odhiambo. 1992. *Burying SM: The Politics of Knowledge and the Sociology of Power in Africa*. Portsmouth, NH: Heinemann.

Ellis, Stephen. 1999. *The Mask of Anarchy: The Destruction of Liberia and the Religious Dimension of an African Civil War*. New York: New York University Press.

Evans-Pritchard, E. E. 1937. *Witchcraft, Oracles and Magic among the Azande*. Oxford: Clarendon.

Geiger, Susan. 1997. *TANU Women: Gender and Culture in the Making of Tanganyikan Nationalism, 1955–1965*. Portsmouth, NH: Heinemann.

Miller, Joseph C. 1980. *The African Past Speaks: Essays on Oral Tradition and History*. Hamden, CT: Archon.

Vansina, Jan. 1985. *Oral Tradition as History*. Madison: University of Wisconsin Press.

Vaughan, Megan. 1991. *Curing Their Ills: Colonial Power and African Illness*. Cambridge: Polity.

White, Luise. 2000. *Speaking with Vampires: Rumor and History in Colonial Africa*. Berkeley: University of California Press.

White, Luise, Stephan F. Miescher, and David William Cohen. 2001. *African Words, African Voices: Critical Practices in Oral History*. Bloomington: Indiana University Press.

Wright, Marcia. 1984. *Women in Peril: Life Stories of Four Captives*. Lusaka, Zambia: NECZAM.

9 GENDER AND SEXUALITY

Marc Epprecht

Research, arts, and activism around gender and sexuality in Africa are increasingly engaged with global, transnational, and transdisciplinary debates. The days of writing about tribal puberty rituals, marriage customs, and fertility in splendid ethnographic isolation are thus long and deservedly gone. Such writing nonetheless has a stubborn and sometimes insidious afterlife that needs to be considered carefully in contemporary interventions that aim to improve sexual health, to "empower" women and to foster human rights on the continent. Moreover, there are compelling reasons to be alert to the issues aside from the intrinsic merits of better health and social justice. As Ghanaian population expert Fred Sai coolly explains, current trends in population growth—the highest in the world concentrated in the poorest countries with the worst gender development indices—in the context of climate change and the broad environmental harms that Africa is facing, pose an enormous risk to Africans' development aspirations, with likely knock-on harms globally. For that reason even conservative donors and banks now claim to "mainstream" things like gender equality, girls' education, and sexual minority rights. The World Bank has taken an especially strong lead with cost-benefit analyses of sexual and reproductive rights (Beyrer et al. 2011), which indeed the African Commission on Human and Peoples' Rights itself now explicitly affirm. Yet, as I will argue in this chapter, there are also dangers to mainstreaming gender and sexuality.

Definitions

Gender refers to the ways that societies attribute differential norms and ideals for appearance, behavior, language, division of labor, and other social roles according to physical sex. The naturally predominant dimorphism of human beings led most cultures in the world to conceive of gender roles in a binary way. On the one hand, hegemonic femininity sets out the parameters of what a "real" or proper woman should do and look like in order to align social expectations with her physical body. Hegemonic masculinity similarly defines how people with anatomically male bodies should behave in order to conform to gendered norms. Age and aging, health and able-ness, and many other factors qualify those norms over a person's life cycle. Alternative or counter-hegemonic femininities and masculinities also generally allow for some diversity within that broad binary, while some cultures further recognize a "third gender" in which the hegemonic gender identity of one sex maps onto the physical body of the opposite (transgender in modern terms—that is, a masculine-identifying person with a female body or a feminine-identifying person with a male body). People born with ambiguous genitalia (intersexed, formerly known as hermaphrodites) are commonly "assigned" a gender, sometimes by a physical operation to remove uncertainty.

Gender is often thought of as belonging to the sphere of culture, the colorful enrichment of our mundane lives. In fact gender is at root an apparatus for organizing and displaying power through to the most intimate relationships: who gets to make decisions about the distribution of resources, the identities and mobilization of people, the relationships between humans and the biophysical world, and so forth. That helps to explain why people often defend "African culture" so strongly when talking about gender issues but don't particularly care about music, masks, divination, or any number of other aspects of culture. To question gender relationships, roles, and identities is indeed a highly political act that is potentially threatening to people who currently hold power, and who often fight hard to protect inherited privileges. Since gender roles are overdetermined by many factors, they can be policed through multiple strategies—law, violence, culture, religion, policy, diet, and pay, notably. One can win a battle for gender equality in one area (constitutional protections) only to have gains compromised by losses in another (internalized sexist or homophobic cultural stereotypes). South Africa today provides a stark illustration. As Mark Hunter and Allison Goebel among others detail, despite South Africa's highly progressive constitution and massive, female-centered welfare system, it still has some of the highest levels of gender-based violence and sexual ill health in the world.

In a historical and transcultural sense, the overwhelming tendency in gender relations has been for marked disparities in power that are skewed toward senior men—that is, patriarchy. Under patriarchy, power flows to those who master (or appear to master) approved aspects of masculinity such as decisiveness, assertiveness, gravitas, self-control, and willingness/ability to use violence. The early scholarship on gender in Africa tended to assume that those qualities inhered more or less naturally in male-bodied people, but a growing field of critical masculinity studies exposes the fragile and fraught relationship between physical manhood and cultural manliness. From infancy, lessons, attire, shaming, myths, rituals, sports, work, peer pressure, role models, and ultimately violence guide boys along the path to approved expressions of manliness, and not all follow that path with equal comfort or success. Scholars like Robert Morrell, Lahoucine Ouzgane, Lisa Lindsay, and Stephan Miescher have also shown how boys and men are significantly crafted as gendered beings through the coaching and critical eye of girls and women.

Some women also possess the approved qualities of hegemonic masculinity and many examples of "female kings" can be discerned in African history. However, patriarchy fundamentally disempowers most women and the many men who do not show the approved qualities of masculinity. This raises an apparent contradiction. Why are the victims of patriarchy often among its most avid defenders (it is overwhelmingly older women who perform female genital cutting [FGC] on girls, for example, and, as Marina Mancuso reveals, who today control some of the most invidious forms of sex trafficking of young African women into Europe). The answer to that is that patriarchy reserves some confined spheres of power and moral claims for autonomy and dignity for women who perform their subaltern roles in the approved ways. To challenge their inferior status by claiming human rights may expose them to even greater harms. For example, the right to divorce on paper does not necessarily benefit women who cannot read or afford a lawyer while exposing them to high economic risks; the right to legal title in land may undermine usufructory rights or moral claims to use the land; sexual rights and freedoms for young women may threaten older women; abolition of FGC may undercut women's claims of moral authority, and so forth.

The point is that gender is complex in and of itself but is also intertwined with other social markers of difference like class, race, age, and ethnicity. This can make change extremely difficult and fraught with unanticipated consequences. Researching gender also poses far greater methodological and ethical challenges than (as early anthropologists once imagined) just finding the women. That said, and as I hope to have demonstrated in my own earlier work, simply finding out about the experiences and perspectives of women, sexual minorities, and subaltern men that are largely obscured in conventional sources is a critical first step.

Sexuality poses even greater research challenges since, whereas gender is mostly a public, social performance, sexuality is mostly private, indeed, often so secretive that it is in effect hidden even from the individuals who possess it. By sexuality we mean the ways people feel, understand, express, control, and experience the diverse naturally occurring forms of sexual desire. In the past most societies regarded sexuality as a largely natural or god-given phenomenon dictated by one's physical sex. In this view, male or female sex organs impel attraction to the opposite sex, while the anatomical structure of the respective genitalia "fit" together in such a way as to demand heterosexual desire. Observed exceptions were sometimes explained as arising from spirit possession (for example, the spirit of a deceased male occupying the body of a living female and controlling her sexuality to suit his presumed natural needs). In the modern West, exceptions tended to be seen as willful choices; hence the word "unnatural" was commonly used to describe deviations from the ideal. We now know, however, that sexuality is significantly affected not only by spirits (if you prefer), genes, and hormones, but also quite strongly by environmental factors including birth order and in utero hormonal influences. These make the idea of choice deeply misleading (Bailey et al. 2016).

Gender is one such environmental factor, and unquestionably among the strongest to shape the nonheritable aspects of sexuality. Gender teaches us powerful lessons about which sex we should desire, what physical or other attributes are attractive in another person, and when, where, and how we may express such desire or perform our identities in order to attract sexual partners (or not). This means that sexuality, like gender, is subject to change over time. That history of change often relates to other changes affecting culture, society, and political economy. Poverty and hunger, notably, have huge impacts upon the ways people feel sexually and make decisions about sex. How poverty and hunger are unevenly distributed and experienced in a society, as well as the options people have to address them through marriage or sex work, is meanwhile powerfully gendered. Desire may need to be adjusted in the circumstances. Indeed, as Melissa Hackman examines in her provocatively titled ethnography of the so-called ex-gay movement in South Africa, when gender ideology, physiology, sexual orientation, and political economy do not match up in individuals as heteronormative expectations demand, desire may require quite hard work to conjure and sustain.

Africa, it sadly still needs to be emphasized, is not different from the rest of the world in the above respects. The scientific racism that predominated intellectual life in the late nineteenth and early twentieth centuries maintained otherwise, of course, and that black people were inherently different and inferior to white people. One marker of that supposed inferiority was sexuality. Blacks, typically seen as a single entity (The Native or The Negro), were in this view more primitive and closer to animal nature than people from Europe or Asia. Their sexuality was largely governed by their hyperdeveloped genitals and thus not open to homosexual practices, non-procreative sex play, or even "higher" emotions like romantic love. Such thinking was thoroughly demolished in intellectual terms by the mid-twentieth century, but it continues to have some pernicious echoes even today. One politically influential school of African cultural nationalism in particular maintains as a point of pride that Africans (usually undefined but again assumed as a single entity) are essentially different from other people in the world. This is captured by the commonplace claim that "homosexuality is un-African" or in the sometimes spluttering or chuckling responses of African leaders to questions about oral sex, masturbation, or celibacy.

Many stereotypes of "African sexuality" are not only deeply misleading but also imply serious harms for public health, social justice and economic development. Most obviously they disproportionately expose young girls to sexual exploitation, gender-based violence, and sexually transmitted infections including HIV. For men, impossible expectations of virility can be profoundly alienating to the many who long for—but cannot admit—something more to intimate relationships with women than multiple ejaculations. Legal discrimination and social stigma arising from the "homosexuality is un-African" stereotype meanwhile drive people to hide or to profess "cures" for their non-normative desires, with many tragic consequences. Much of the scholarship on gender and sexuality in Africa since the 1970s self-consciously aimed to challenge such damaging stereotypes and to support gathering initiatives to minimize their influences upon public discourse and policy formation.

History

Gender and sexuality are endlessly fascinating to most people anywhere, especially when they evoke titillation, scandal, or the exotic Other. Descriptions and speculation about specific local gender relations and sexual mores are thus as old as any writing about Africa, and even older if we consider cave paintings or tomb art from ancient Egypt. Over the centuries, many hundreds of written accounts attested both to the great variety of gender and sexual norms in African cultures and to some strong underlying commonalities. This is not to restate the "Africa is a country" notion, but simply to recognize the fact that societies across a vast area had to adapt to shared environmental conditions with similar levels of technology. The central political question over the millennia in which Africa was settled was thus how to organize people to ensure survival in very challenging biophysical environments. Across the continent, political systems, religious traditions, and cultures developed to enable groups to survive and sometimes prosper through the vicissitudes of drought, epizootics, pests, wild animal migrations, and other potential dangers.

Kinship stretching back in time through lineage and revered ancestors, and forward through abundant offspring emerged in this environment as a core strategy for assuring loyalty and mutual, moral obligations to a group. Kinship had to be nurtured and protected against many threats, but the risks posed by uncontrolled sexuality were especially compelling. Control over sexuality was thus a strong imperative, but it required a fine balance. For example, women's fertility was essential to meet kinship and labor needs, but too many pregnancies threatened women's and their children's health. So too, senior men's decision-making power was important to kinship structures but disgruntled wives and children threatened social harmony. Sex itself was good for physical, emotional, and mental health, but sexual jealously and disputes over paternity could quickly spiral into violence. Different societies developed myriad ways to achieve the aspired balance between such potentially disruptive forces: polygyny, long postpartum abstinence, child betrothals, sexual "outercourse" (thigh sex), genital cutting, herbal abortificents, incest and other taboos (plus ritual transgressions thereof), gendered divisions of labor/ crops/ spaces/ rituals, fictive marriage, matrilyny, viri- or uxorilocality, ad infinitum.

One common practice across a very wide swath of the continent distinguished most African kinship systems from European and Asian cultures. Bridewealth linked the control of human sexuality to the biophysical world through the exchange of cattle and other forms of wealth for marriage. Bridewealth is the opposite of dowry. It compensates the family of the bride for the loss of her labor and fertility to the groom's family. Bridewealth, or bride service in some cases (where the prospective groom provides an equivalent in labor to the family of the bride, a kind of probationary period before formal marriage), marries families rather than individuals and honors ritual ties over time to strengthen social solidarity. Healthy herds of cattle thus meant healthy kinship ties. Healthy herds of cattle required attentiveness to the land that sustained them.

One final general point to make about traditional African cultures was their high degree of empiricism (responsiveness to observed evidence). This allowed for what Ifi Amadiume (1987) called a "flexible" or fluid sex-gender system. For example, the theory may have said that senior men should be in charge, but if a person with a female body had the qualities of a good chief then she could be one, although more commonly just call the shots from behind a male figurehead. The theory said a man should be virile, but if he was not he could still appear to be by allowing his wife or wives to be impregnated by a trusted relative. The cattle (or other forms of wealth) exchanged in marriage protected the impotent (or "gay"?) husband from any doubts about paternity. The theory said women had to be married but if a widow or otherwise independent woman owned the cattle to do it, she could herself marry, taking a wife or wives to be impregnated by a trusted male. The cattle insured the offspring belonged to her. The theory said such and such a medicine or sacrifice would cure a husband of infidelity or neglect, or a daughter of tomboyish tendencies, but if it didn't then something else might. And so on, in a living customary law that allowed for constant adaptation, experimentation, and acknowledgement of the diversity and mystery of human nature, within the kinship paradigm.

Islam as it spread across the Maghreb, across the Sahara and along the eastern coast over many centuries, basically accommodated to the preexisting sex/gender systems. Less is known about ancient forms of Christianity practiced in Nubia and Ethiopia, but we may infer from the harsh judgments of Portuguese missionaries in the latter, and from the female autonomies that Wendy Belcher and Michael Kleiner recount, that indigenous forms of Christianity were also more accommodating of preexisting practices than European Catholic dogma allowed. This began to change not so much from the imposition of religious doctrine from outside, but from Africa's growing entanglement in the emerging world capitalist system. The slave and ivory trades were particularly disruptive to African gender relations and sexual mores, not least of all by stimulating the rise of centralized kingdoms and professional armies. New forms of the state were led by Big Men with sometimes hundreds of wives of varying status. They asserted control over young people's sexuality away from natal families, including by withholding young men's right to marry until they had performed service for the state in war or slave/ivory hunting expeditions.

For centuries, Europeans trading along the coast were mostly unaware of developments in the interior of Africa, although the gathering violence served their interests by ensuring a steadily growing flow of slaves into their hands. By the early nineteenth century, however, changes in the global political economy led by Britain's industrial revolution created a political space for a humanitarian movement against the slave trade and eventually slavery itself. This became a key motivating force in the establishment of colonial rule. Ironically (in retrospect), Europeans commonly justified the use of violence against Africans in this era on the grounds that it was needed to protect African women and children from the violence of African and Arab men.

Colonial rule in most cases lasted well under a century, seemingly a blip in the long trajectory of African history. But combined with changes brought by an expanding cash economy, new technologies, and the proselytization of ideas and practices like Christianity, consumerism, nationalism, romantic love, and science, colonial rule had a very profound impact on Africa. This era has attracted much of the most interesting and revealing scholarship about gender and sexuality, which closely examines, for example:

- Tensions and changes wrought by the colonial state's suppression (or not) of perceived barbaric customs like slavery/pawnship, twin murder, child betrothals, witchcraft, and FGC
- The male migrant labor system and legal prohibitions against women in cities
- The codification and enforcement of so-called customary law by bureaucratized male chiefs
- New freedoms, opportunities, and risks both for "loose women" and male youth in growing urban spaces
- The encouragement of male commercial agricultural production and legal property ownership over women's subsistence farming and usufructory rights
- Differential education including education for domesticity for girls

- The rise of a class of Westernized *assimilés* or *évolués* and contestations among Africans over the gendered meanings and performances of modernity or respectability
- The emergence of commercial sex work and public health initiatives that targeted (indeed, often pathologized, even demonized) "African sexuality"
- New fashions, diets, and body ideals
- Selective demographic interventions by the state, for example, through racially differentiated policies on abortion or access to birth control, and the differential criminalization of certain sexual practices or relationships
- Differential impacts on women and men of new crops, animals, and technologies
- Female-led forms of resistance or rebellion, and the list goes on.

It is impossible to generalize about this era. In some ways under some regimes, colonialism, cash, and accompanying ideologies were manifestly emancipating to women, in others, disastrously disempowering. One thing we can say for certain, however, is that the transition to political independence preserved many of the economic and ideological contours laid out by the colonialists. Indeed, one very powerful and widespread legacy of colonialism was the small class of *évolués* who took control of the state after independence. These men may have been politically radical in some cases but they were often very socially conservative. As such they resisted women's efforts to achieve liberation from oppressive neo-traditions or forms of capitalist enterprise that were immiserating to the majority of women but were lucrative to the new elite and their foreign friends. In some cases rights and ideals of gender equality were made rhetorically but then betrayed by bureaucratic practice and masculinist assertions of national or ethnic identity. A common feature of the era, for example, was "women's leagues" that demagogic, corrupt regimes exploited to shore up popular support. Populism could also take the form of homophobic scapegoating. According to S. N. Nyeck's revealing study of postcolonial Cameroon, for example, neocolonialism and elite moral corruption were partially obscured by new, explicit anti-homosexual laws. This is not to deny that progress toward primary health care, female literacy, and other basic needs was sometimes impressive in the early postcolonial era. Such gains, however, often came at great cost—debt, dictatorships, economic malaise, and civil strife often targeting minorities. The messes created in the so-called development decades of the 1960s–1970s thus opened the door to a new form of de facto colonialism from the early 1980s: structural adjustment.

Structural adjustment programs were ostensibly gender-blind. They sought to instill fiscal discipline, provide better incentives for market production and exports, and encourage more democratic forms of governance. In many cases donors recognized the harmful impacts upon economic efficiency of inherited traditional, colonial, and neocolonial values or practices around gender and sexuality, and they included some elements of women's rights in the program backed by feminist-inspired research. The International Monetary Fund, for example, for a time specified that affected African governments needed to set targets to eliminate FGC as part of their financial aid packages. Yet it fairly quickly became apparent that austerity, "user-pay" and other economic reforms tended more commonly to undercut girls' education, health, and employment opportunities. For many women and a growing number of street-connected children, sex work became a necessity for survival. At the same time, rising unemployment for men in the formal sector, and declining hope to achieve traditional markers of masculine dignity like marriage and fatherhood, metaphorically emasculated a generation. This created a perfect storm of conditions to enable a hitherto unknown and marginal disease to explode to devastating levels in Central, Eastern, and Southern Africa. Survival sex work, multiple concurrent sex partners, scapegoating of ethnic and sexual minorities, substance abuse, gender-based violence, high levels of migration and incarceration, and a profound distrust if not cynicism toward development—and particularly public health and human rights discourse—fueled the rapid transition of HIV/AIDS from localized hotspots to regional pandemic.

The decades of structural adjustment have by now seen some positive results in economic growth terms, and witnessed significant reforms to offset the earlier free market fundamentalism. The Millenium Development Goals also achieved important successes in addressing some of the most harmful burdens of inequality for women and children, while anti-retroviral therapy has mostly contained, if not solved, the HIV/AIDS crisis. Yet loss of faith in the promise of progress under neoliberal economic strategies has been profound. That loss of faith attracts growing numbers of people to alternative development visions expressed in evangelical Christianity and Islamist movements. These typically propose, and sometimes enforce with considerable brutality, neo-patriarchal gender and sexual norms which fundamentally contradict both human rights aspirations and sexual health needs. Rudolf Gaudio's remarkable ethnography of "sexual outlaws" in northern Nigeria, for example, suggests a looming intolerance of gender and sexual diversity that threatens to derail HIV programs. New technologies like social media and pharmaceuticals, explicit sexuality instruction and web-accessed pornography, and "technologies of self" like confessionals add to the volatile mix. In this often fraught context, gender and sexuality are likely to remain a central arena of struggle in the decades to come.

Debates

Writing about gender and sexuality in Africa has changed in tone and intent throughout its history. Early missionary anthropologists typically described gender and sexuality in Africa in morally normative language. This implied—and sometimes explicitly demanded—colonial intervention to emancipate African women from oppression and drudgery, and to civilize African men out of their lazy, lascivious and/or barbaric ways. Subsequent professional researchers were more attuned to the need to appear scientifically and politically objective, and could be quite sympathetic to African dignity and anti-colonial aspirations. They sought to explain gender and sexuality with reference to their imputed functions within the identifiable structures that sustained a harmonious society, or their dysfunctions under conditions of racial capitalism and rapid urbanization. The advent of HIV brought intense focus on pathological aspects of gender and sexuality, with sometimes furious debates about implicit moralism or even racism in the process of knowledge production.

By now, an array of studies has found and analyzed sources and limitations of women's power/agency, and discerned nuances in local cultures of gender and sexuality that were previously hidden in masculinist, heteropatriarchal idioms. My sketch of history above draws upon a small fraction of that scholarship, which acknowledges many unresolved questions and disputes. I now want briefly to look at three of the latter that are especially pertinent to current initiatives to address the gender inequalities and sexual injustices that HIV so painfully reveals and amplifies.

First, in the mid-1980s a critique of Western feminist approaches and assumptions began to emerge, with a group of female Nigerian intellectuals based in the West at the forefront. They proposed that gender was not as significant a factor in African societies as Western feminists insisted, but rather, that age and merit were traditionally valued more to produce social hierarchies. Postmenopausal women became elders or honorary men with real power, while wives had their own parallel institutions and rituals that nullified the argument that African women were historically oppressed and exploited. It was the colonialists and missionaries, with their sexist and racist obsessions, who undermined women's traditional autonomies and constructed the modern forms of gender oppression. Oyèrónkẹ́ Oyéwùmí pushed this further by arguing that the concept of gender is itself a form of epistemic colonialism foisted upon Africa by Western feminist scholars. Since gender, indeed even the categories of woman and man, did not exist in Africa prior to colonialism, the intellectual energy poured into asserting that they did frustrated the reemergence of a decolonized, genderless, or even matriarchal pan-African culture.

This argument has been strenuously challenged in empirical and logical terms. Oyéwùmí bases much of her case, for example, on the fact that many African languages do not possess gendered pronouns. By that logic, the English (who do not have gendered nouns) must be less sexist than the French (who have two genders) who in turn are even less so than the Germans (three). The error is compounded by reliance on an ideologically sanitized ethnography that, ironically, suppresses the sophisticated gender awareness of one of Africa's first professional anthropologists (Nathaniel Fadipe, whom Tola Olu Pearce rescues). The underlying critique nonetheless remains attractive to many scholars of gender and sexuality. At the very least it makes a political point about the continuing unequal relationship between the producers of knowledge about Africa, still based mostly in the Global North, and the providers of raw data in Africa. It is a point abundantly worth underscoring as it suggests a continuing colonial-type relationship that needs to be addressed. The fact that I am the sole author of this essay could be taken as a corroboration of that critique (although to be fair, I began the work with an African partner who fell away for reasons that cannot easily be explained by inherited structures).

Evan Mwangi makes a similar point in his critique of a strong Eurocentric tendency in postcolonial analyses of African literature. He finds a powerful underlying assumption in that scholarship which sees African writers to be primarily concerned to "write back to empire"—that is, to create fictional depictions of gender and sexuality in Africa that are intended to counter pernicious and insidious stereotypes about Africans constructed by Europeans in the colonial or apartheid eras. Even scholarship that is ostensibly anti-imperialist or queer in its politics, may unwittingly place Europeans at the heart of its analysis. In part by directly accessing literary works in African languages, Mwangi unseats that eurocentrism. African authors' main concern is not to trouble Western audiences and inherited stereotypes about African simplicity or pathology, but to push other Africans to think about African agency in gender-based violence or homophobia, and thence inspire indigenous initiatives to build better societies.

Joseph Massad extends the debate over the salience of gender into the realm of activism over sexual minority rights. Unlike politicians and religious leaders who have baldly claimed that homosexuality is un-African, Massad concedes that forms of same-sex intimacy existed in Egypt and the wider Islamic world that of course includes much of Africa. These relationships were mostly unnamed, invisible, and hence non-threatening to—and tacitly accepted by—heteronormative culture. His concern arises from Western activists who now insist upon publicly naming and personal coming out as the *only* ways to modernize, to achieve human dignity, and to exercise appropriate personal responsibility for health care. But by inciting Egyptians to come out as gay and lesbian in terms that are clearly identifiable by modern Western standards, Western activists are exposing those individuals to severe reaction by the Egyptian state and intensifying social stigma. It is a new form of cultural imperialism that costs the activists nothing and may even benefit Western donors' self-branding as progressive, but which potentially ruins the lives of the people to be saved. By extension, scholarship that reveals sexual secrets in Africa to non-African audiences, or that assumes the universality and indivisibility of human rights, is colonizing.

Like Oyéwùmí, Massad probably overstates his argument (are Egyptians in 2018 forever to remain in patriarchal closets or secrets that may have worked well in 1518, or perhaps even 1988?). But he underscores a similar concern about the imbalance of power between scholars/activists/donors in the West and people on the ground in Africa who have to bear the direct consequences of ill-considered initiatives to apply neat, liberatory theory to messy, lived reality. When, how, where, and why to make one's sexual orientation and gender identity visible as a political gesture remains a burning question for sexual rights advocates throughout the continent. Allies in the West thus need to be sensitive to the local context and perhaps more humble, an argument that Robert Lorway and Ashley Currier persuasively explore in their analysis of nascent LGBT activism in Namibia and South Africa.

The third debate I want to highlight hinges on the potential of mainstreaming gender and sexuality to produce real change—that is, of incorporating awareness of the issues into *all* analysis and policy responses in order to eradicate gender inequalities and related injustice. On the one hand, some point to evidence that mainstreaming works. Twenty years ago the formal reins of power in Africa were almost exclusively in men's hands. Today African women are presidents, ministers of finance, police generals, top judges, bankers, and other high-profile leaders, a stunning transformation guided in part by women's own activism in collaboration with donors and international solidarity groups. The "homosexuality is un-African" ideal has also been significantly eroded. Where once sexual minorities in Africa could only be heard in isolated and easily marginalized venues, now their claims are embraced by many of the most powerful state actors and multilateral institutions in the world including, after much resistance, the African Union (at least on paper, recognizing sexual orientation as a human right). With the abolition of FGC, the enactment of legal and constitutional rights, the promotion of maternal and child health, and on many other fronts, the struggle for gender equality has seen remarkable progress in the majority of African countries in the years since gender mainstreaming became a clarion call.

On the other hand, a case can be made that these signs of progress belie a deeper stability to gender injustice. Gender mainstreaming in practice is often interpreted as the mitigation of absolute poverty for women through, for example, microcredit loans or direct welfare benefits to them *as mothers*. These relieve suffering but also stabilize an economic system that entrenches and exploits existing gender roles and class disparities. Similarly, much of the current sexual rights agenda is hidden within euphemistic language including an alphabet soup of depoliticized acronyms and jargon ("MARPs," "MSM," "MCPs"), and public health or economistic arguments and statistics (condoms in prison cost so much, lives of men saved from HIV are worth so much, therefore . . .). Does this actually challenge the power disparities which are at the heart of gender and which ramify via gender inequality through to so many other aspects of global inequality and unsustainable models of economic growth? One can look to evidence of "rape culture" and widening income disparities along racialized lines within even the richest, most developed, and ostensibly postfeminist countries in the West for evidence that such limited interventions do not in fact challenge much, though they may save lives. The right to same-sex marriage in South Africa has also very evidently not mitigated crimes like so-called corrective rape against lesbians, let alone pervasive rape that affects all women and many young men and boys in the continent's most developed country. In Uganda, government-commissioned scientific research on the causes of homosexuality appeared to move the debate there into the realm of reasoned, evidence-based discourse. Yet it was immediately used by the government to justify enacting a harsh new anti-homosexuality law and to denounce hectoring, hypocritical donors. Clearly, mainstreaming research in and of itself is no guarantee of an enlightened outcome.

Conclusion

Bad or misguided research on gender and sexuality in Africa has a long and ignoble tradition that has underpinned some very poor policy choices, formerly under the name of a civilizing mission and now as development, globalization, or science. Uganda's scientific statement on homosexuality is only one of the most recent examples. Yet such research can also spark healthy debate leading in turn to better questions, more sensitive research tools and methods, and a growing ability to assess local or regional struggles around gender and sexuality in relation to the transnational or even global context. Where this will lead in linking the issues to climate change, emerging technologies, and transnational movements remains to be seen. An intriguing example, however, still undecided at the time of writing, is a lawsuit brought by Ugandan activists against an American preacher in the United States for his role in promoting homophobic hate speech in Uganda. That case is powerfully supported by light shed upon the Christian Right in the US by Zambian researcher Kapya Kaoma. A victory in this case would drive a nail into an odious expression of gender ideology that has purchase in the halls of power in the most powerful country in the world, and in that sense Americans will also benefit from Africans' research and activism. It is a different form of globalization than critics generally allow, and we should be cautious about its potential. We can say, however, that mainstreaming gender and sexuality will probably have more political traction in the future in Africa when the stream is finally seen to flow both ways.

Suggested Readings

Aderinto, Saheed. 2015. *When Sex Threatened the State: Illicit Sexuality, Nationalism, and Politics in Colonial Nigeria, 1900–1958*. Urbana: University of Illinois Press.

Aidoo, Ama Ata, ed. 2007. *African Love Stories*. Banbury, UK: Ayebia Clarke.

Amadiume, Ifi. 1987. *Male Daughters, Female Husbands: Gender and Sex in an African Society*. London: Zed.

Boddy, Janice. 2007. *Civilizing Women: British Crusades in Colonial Sudan*. Princeton, NJ: Princeton University Press,

Cole, Jennifer, and Lynn Thomas, eds. 2009. *Love in Africa*. Chicago: University of Chicago Press.

Currier, Ashley. 2012. *Out in Africa: LGBT Organizing in Namibia and South Africa*. Minneapolis: University of Minnesota Press.

Epprecht, Marc. 2013 [2004]. *Hungochani: The History of a Dissident Sexuality in Southern Africa*. 2nd ed. Montreal: McGill-Queen's University Press.

Hackman, Melissa. 2018. *Desire Work: Ex-Gay and Pentecostal Masculinity in Democratic South Africa*. Durham, NC: Duke University Press.

Hunter, Mark. 2010. *Love in the Time of AIDS: Inequality, Gender and Rights in South Africa*. Scottsville, South Africa: UKZN Press.

Jean-Baptiste, Rachel. 2014. *Conjugal Rights: Marriage, Sexuality, and Urban Life in Colonial Libreville, Gabon*. Athens: Ohio University Press.

Kalipeni, Ezekiel, Susan Craddock, Joseph R. Oppong, and Jayati Ghosh, eds. 2004. *HIV/AIDS in Africa: Beyond Epidemiology*. Oxford: Blackwell.

Kaoma, Kapya. 2012. *Colonizing African Values: How the U.S. Christian Right Is Transforming Sexual Politics in Africa*. Somerville, MA: Political Research Associates.

Klaussen, Susanne M. 2015. *Abortion under Apartheid: Nationalism, Sexuality, and Women's Reproductive Rights in South Africa*. Oxford: Oxford University Press.

Lindsay, Lisa A., and Stephan F. Miescher. eds. 2003. *Men and Masculinities in Modern Africa*. Portsmouth, NH: Heinemann.

Lorway, Robert. 2015. *Namibia's Rainbow Project: Gay Rights in an African Nation*. Bloomington: Indiana University Press.

Miescher, Stephan F. 2005. *Making Men in Ghana*. Bloomington: Indiana University Press.

Mwangi, Evan Maina. 2010. *Africa Writes Back to Self: Metafiction, Gender, Sexuality*. Albany: State University of New York Press.

Nyeck, S. N., and Marc Epprecht, eds. 2013. *Sexual Diversity in Africa: Politics, Theory and Citizenship*. Montreal: McGill-Queen's University Press.

Ouzgane, Lahoucine, and Robert Morrell, eds. 2005. *African Masculinities: Men in Africa from the Late Nineteenth Century to the Present*. London: Palgrave.

Oyéwùmí, Oyèrónké. 1997. *The Invention of Women: Making an African Sense of Western Gender Discourses*. Minneapolis: University of Minnesota Press.

Spronk, Rachel. 2012. *Ambiguous Pleasures: Sexuality and Middle Class Self-Perceptions in Nairobi*. New York: Berghahn.

Tamale, Sylvia, ed. 2011. *African Sexualities: A Reader*. Cape Town: Pambazuka Press.

Uganda Ministry of Health. 2014. *Scientific Statement on Homosexuality*. http://www.boxturtlebulletin.com/btb/wp-content/uploads/2014/02/UgandaScientificReportOnHomosexuality.pdf. Accessed January 20, 2015.

References

Amadiume, Ifi. 1987. *Male Daughters, Female Husbands: Gender and Sex in an African Society*. London: Zed.

Bailey, J. Michael, Paul L. Vasey, Lisa M. Diamond, S. Marc Breedlove, Eric Vilain, and Marc Epprecht. 2016. "Sexual Orientation, Controversy, and Science." *Psychological Science in the Public Interest* 17 (2): 45–101.

Belcher, Wendy, with Michael Kleiner. 2015. *The Life and Struggles of Our Mother Walatta Petros: A Translation of the Earliest African Biography of an African Woman*. Princeton, NJ: Princeton University Press.

Beyrer, Chris, Andrea Wirtz, Damian Walker, Benjamin Johns, Frangiscos Sifakis, and Stephan D. Baral. 2011. *The Global HIV Epidemics among Men Who Have Sex with Men*. Washington: World Bank. http://siteresources.worldbank.org/INTHIVAIDS/Resources/375798-1103037153392/MSMReport.pdf. Accessed September 8, 2015.

Currier, Ashley. 2012. *Out in Africa: LGBT Organizing in Namibia and South Africa*. Minneapolis: University of Minnesota Press.

Goebel, Allison. 2002. "'Men These Days, They Are a Problem': Husband-Taming Herbs and Gender Wars in Rural Zimbabwe." *Canadian Journal of African Studies* 36 (3): 460–89.

———. 2015. *On Their Own: Women and the Right to the City in South Africa*. Montreal: McGill-Queen's University Press.

Hackman, Melissa. 2018. *Desire Work: Ex-Gay and Pentecostal Masculinity in Democratic South Africa*. Durham, NC: Duke University Press.

Hunter, Mark. 2010. *Love in the Time of AIDS: Inequality, Gender and Rights in South Africa*. Scottsville, South Africa: UKZN Press.

Kaoma, Kapya. 2012. *Colonizing African Values: How the U.S. Christian Right Is Transforming Sexual Politics in Africa*. Somerville, MA: Political Research Associates.

Lindsay, Lisa A., and Stephan F. Miescher, eds. 2003. *Men and Masculinities in Modern Africa*. Portsmouth, NH: Heinemann.

Lorway, Robert. 2015. *Namibia's Rainbow Project: Gay Rights in an African Nation*. Bloomington: Indiana University Press.

Mancuso, Marina, 2014. "Not All Madams Have a Central Role: Analysis of a Nigerian Sex Trafficking Network." *Trends in Organized Crime* 17 (1–2): 66–88.

Massad, Joseph A. 2007. *Desiring Arabs*. Chicago: University of Chicago Press.

Miescher, Stephan F. 2005. *Making Men in Ghana*. Bloomington: Indiana University Press.

Morrell, Robert. 1998. "Of Boys and Men: Masculinity and Gender in Southern African Studies." *Journal of Southern African Studies* 24 (4): 605–30.

———, ed. 2001. *Changing Men in Southern Africa*. Pietermaritzburg, South Africa: University of Natal Press; London: Zed.

Mwangi, Evan Maina. 2010. *Africa Writes Back to Self: Metafiction, Gender, Sexuality*. Albany: State University of New York Press.

Nyeck, S. N., and Marc Epprecht, eds. 2013. *Sexual Diversity in Africa: Politics, Theory and Citizenship*. Montreal: McGill-Queen's University Press.

Ouzgane, Lahoucine, and Robert Morrell, eds. 2005. *African Masculinities: Men in Africa from the Late Nineteenth Century to the Present*. London: Palgrave.

Oyéwùmí, Oyèrónké. 1997. *The Invention of Women: Making an African Sense of Western Gender Discourses*. Minneapolis: University of Minnesota Press.

Pearce, Tola Olu. 2014. "Dispelling the Myth of Pre-Colonial Gender Equality in Yoruba Culture." *Canadian Journal of African Studies* 48 (2): 315–32.

10 GOVERNANCE

Brenda Chalfin and Omolade Adunbi

Governance within contemporary Africa has been an intellectual focus across academic disciplines (Doornbos 1990; Mudimbe et al. 1993). The meaning of governance in much of the Africanist literature has shifted significantly from consideration of the colonial mode of governance epitomized by Britain's indirect rule system and questions of native administration, to analyzing the character of the postcolonial state based on what Mahmood Mamdani (1996) called "decentralized despotism." Mamdani suggests that the South African apartheid system is more norm than outlier and argues that African leaders who inherited the authoritarian political structures of colonialism were despots. Despite being elected into office based on procedural democracy, their ascent laid the foundations for political instability and discontent to come.

Good governance and its corollaries—rule of law, accountability, transparency, anti-corruption, elections, democratization, human rights, political participation, and multiparty rule—took hold of scholarly, policy, and donor discussions of African politics in the mid-1980s. As the touchstone for interventions into the African political scene, both the reach and fallout of good governance initiatives expanded over the ensuing decades and continue to shape Africa's political landscape in the twenty-first century.

The construct of good governance turned African polities into a field for external monitoring and rehabilitation. This was as much a reflection of new analytic outlooks as of new facts on the ground. Brought into being via an explosion of academic workshops, policy platforms, survey instruments, international advisory commissions, and multilateral aid programs, the birth of good governance is attributable to processes occurring within Africa and without. They include the changing landscape of geopolitics and multilateral aid as the Cold War waned, a concomitant spike in domestic political crises across the African continent, and the expanding influence of Africanist political science. Sometimes mutually reinforcing, the triple inheritance of good governance moved this platform of evaluation and intervention in diverse directions. Good governance, like other grand schemes "to improve the human condition" in less industrialized and empowered regions of the world (Scott 1998), spawned political dilemmas and configurations little anticipated within the confines of its original formulation.

Good governance is uneasily and imperfectly aligned with broader processes of democratization. Although it is largely represented and delivered in technopolitical terms by external agencies, it has become an integral component of political struggles across the continent. This is due to the legitimacy and material resources that come with it as well as the tensions induced by its simultaneous buildup of executive authority and disaggregation of governing functions within and beyond the state. In the wake of good governance initiatives, in many African states the result is a rise of ancillary and competing arenas and arms of governance. Whether NGO governance, insurgent governance, corporate governance, or the expansion of agencies devoted to governmental oversight (i.e., the governance of governance), the diffusion of governmental bodies and responsibilities fostered by the good governance agenda makes increasingly remote the possibility of strong states capable of internalizing the concerns of their populations and delivering services to them.

Good Governance and Threats against It

Between 1960 and 1982, 90 percent of forty-five independent African states experienced a military coup or coup attempt, which facilitated, in turn, the rise of military regimes and the suppression of democratic participation and popular rule (Jenkins and Kposowa 1992; McGowan 2003). General Eyadema took power in Togo in 1963, barely two years after independence; Ghana's Nkrumah was overthrown in a military coup in 1966, followed by a coup in Nigeria that same year. From 1975 to 1985 more coups than any decade since independence dashed all expectation of stabilization over time. The majority of African states were characterized by one-party systems, with the rare if short-lived exceptions of Upper Volta (now Burkina Faso), Ghana, Senegal, and Uganda.

Perpetuating the ills of colonial inheritance, prevailing regimes tended toward authoritarian, personalized rule where corruption was high and accountability low, such as the despotic rein of Idi Amin in Uganda, Hastings Banda in Malawi, Siad Barre in Somalia, Mobutu Sese Seko in Zaire (now the Democratic Republic of Congo), Daniel Arap Moi in Kenya and Sekou Toure in Guinea. Many regimes fed into the superpower politics of the period where aid was tied to alliances built on Cold War divisions. Africa became a major theater for the prosecution of the war, and regime sustenance depended on playing its politics (Clapham 1997). For many African states, regimes bolstered their power with entitlements to aid from former colonial powers and interested superpowers engaged in cold war competition in efforts to attract diplomatic and strategic supporters. They did not gain political authority primarily from internal legitimacy, bureaucratic efficiency, nurturing of local revenue sources, or attractiveness to foreign investors. Governance became entrenched in human rights violations, the absence of democratic practices, civil conflicts, and the rise of insurgent regimes across the continent.

African citizen-subjects and Africanist academics, reflecting on the status of African states after two decades of political independence, considered the situation dire. Responding to a sense of continent-wide crisis, political scientist Richard Sklar presciently noted in his 1983 presidential address to the US-based African Studies Association: "The democratic project or the process of redemocratizing African politics is becoming the hegemonic issue in African studies" (Fatton 1990, 455). Among political scientists disciplinary consensus centered on building the right institutions of representative rule within and through state bodies.

At the same time, but not always for the same reasons, Africa claimed a renewed presence within international aid organizations. As early as 1981, Africa gained new ground in the multilateral agenda. The much-discussed World Bank "Berg Report," published at the end of the reign of long-serving president Robert McNamara, made African development central to the World Bank mission. This report was titled *Accelerated Development in Sub-Saharan Africa: An Agenda for Action* (World Bank 1981), and although it was largely economic in focus (Loxley 1983), issues of good governance lurked in the background. Avoiding consideration of external economic constraints and the lingering impacts of the debt and oil crises of the 1970s, the report focused on retooling domestic policy and reining in overextended states in order to reach national development goals. Under this rubric, international aid was plentiful but came with strict rules and recipes for application as well as repayment (van de Walle 2001). Requirements put forth by donors centered on fiscal policy, management of state assets and enterprises, and opening national economies to competition and international trade. The report thus ushered in the era of "structural adjustment" in which capitalist "market-oriented" reforms were central.

As an example of Africa's situation at the forefront of global trends, a chronology of good governance indicates its initial formulation in the context of sub-Saharan Africa prior to being broadcast elsewhere in the world (Santiso 2001, 3). Over the course of the decade, the perspectives of academics on Africa's political and economic problems and prospects impacted multilateral agency outlooks. Reflecting a temporary convergence of concerns across academe and policy, influential interlocutors included African scholars and intellectuals Claude Ake, Nakhtar Diouf, and Ali Mazrui as well as other leading analysts of African politics, such as Goran Hyden. Attuned to their insights, a forthright program of political reform became a pillar of multilateral and bilateral involvement in Africa.

The oft-quoted World Bank report *Sub-Saharan Africa: From Crisis to Sustainable Growth*, published in 1989, bluntly attributes the obstacles to Africa's economic growth to political ills: "Underlying the litany of Africa's development problems is a crisis of governance" (1989, 60). In the report's preface, World Bank president Barber Conable states:

> A root cause of weak economic performance has been the failure of public institutions. Private sector initiatives and market mechanisms are important but they must go hand in hand with *good governance*—a public service that is efficient, a judicial system that is reliable, and an administration that is accountable to the public" (World Bank 1989, xii; italics ours).

Indicative of the growing emphasis on political explanations, sections of the report are devoted to "Deteriorating Governance" and "Political Renewal." Most remarkable is the transmutation of political reform into a requirement of aid. Foreshadowing the growing grip of political—not just economic—conditionality, the last page reads: "Increased flows of foreign resources cannot be expected without profound political reforms that establish governance for development . . . external agencies providing aid have the right to insist on such matters" (World Bank 1989).

By the early 1990s the dissolution of Cold War coalitions and enmities endowed the state and donor-centric outlooks of the emerging good governance paradigm with legitimacy and necessity anew, enabling its firm advance. Superpower support of repressive regimes was no longer tenable, whether it was Mobutu's Zaire, Banda's Malawi, apartheid South Africa, or Somalia—all in the US camp—or the USSR-aligned Ethiopia, Angola, Mozambique, Benin, and Guinea-Bissau. With multilaterals, not Cold War allies, now the prime arbiters of governmental assistance, political reforms across the continent centered on the implementation of "structural adjustment programs" (SAP). Dominating intellectual discourse, SAP's proponents argued it would make governance much more efficient through the shrinking of the state and the empowerment of the private sector (Bienen and Herbst 1996). To the opponents, SAP would further entrench a prebendal state detrimental to the general population.

Cutting across the two camps, SAP spawned mass protests in dozens of countries. With many countries implementing economic reforms but resisting political liberalization, collective outcries against economic hardship galvanized opposition to dictatorial regimes. Cameroon's Social Democratic Front, established in 1990, organized marches calling attention to the devastating effects of SAP and triggered the formation of National Coordination Committee of Opposition Parties addressing a wide arc of political grievances against the state (Konings 2011). Reflecting new modes of political mobilization emerging on the heels of SAP, human rights organizations in Nigeria allied with labor and civil society groups to form the Campaign for Democracy. In Benin, civil society successfully agitated for a national conference, paving the way for democratic rule. In contesting the monopoly of the state over governance, such popular mobilizations became a defining feature of the post–Cold War turn. Although their impacts were often frustrated, pace the staying power of Paul Biya in Cameroon and the rise of Laurent Kabila in the Democratic Republic of the Congo, governance transformed from an exclusive preserve of the state to the modus operandi of many organizations and groups.

Also contributing to the reformatting of domestic political order in the Cold War's wake was a new sort of Africanist political science in the offing. Distilling a different essence of the still nascent notion of good governance, this incarnation of African political science was keen to apply and identify universal rules and principles trumping claims of Africa's uniqueness. This development was exemplified by the rise of working groups linking academe and policy. In the US, the Carter Center's African Governance Program, established in 1989 in collaboration with Emory University, was a formative manifestation. The very title of the 1989 inaugural seminar, "Perestroika without Glasnost in Africa," situated Africa as part of a global wave of post–Cold War and post-socialist political transitions. Reflecting broader shifts in the world and the academy, democracy took its turn at the fore of the discipline among Africanists and well beyond. Good governance in this iteration was virtually equated with democratization. Said Adejumobi (2000, 3) remarks:

> From the 1980s when a new tide of global democratic change resonated in most parts of the world, the emphasis of academic discourse on the linkage between democracy and development shifted to the object and purposes of democracy. Democracy has become the independent variable, and economic development, dependent. The political import is that democracy can now be accepted, tolerated and promoted for all societies.

These claims were broadcast and refined through new institutes and outlets. The National Endowment for Democracy initiated publication of the *Journal of Democracy* in 1990. Putting Africa's democratic prospects on par with other world regions, all four issues of the journal's inaugural run addressed Africa. Following suit came the journal *Democratization*, making special reference to "democratization in the developing world and post-communist societies." On the ground, within the span of just a few years, elections in African countries grew exponentially, numbering ten in 1990, fifteen in 1991, and over thirty in 1992 (Bratton 1998). The reach of political transformation extended to the usually conservative Southern Africa, with Namibia gaining full independence in 1990 and by 1991 the South African government dismantling the legal legacy of apartheid and minority rule.

Yet at the moment of its coalescence across academic, donor, and African institutions, the good governance platform was already in the throes of fracture. Some analysts attributed this to the shallowness of democratic reform. Richard Joseph (1997, 368) remarks, "By the end of 1992 most leaders learned how to control the process of competitive elections so they can win a grudging seal of approval from Western donors but still hang on to power." It is perhaps more accurate to ascribe this turn of events to the narrowing of the conceptual and practical levers of good governance at the very instant they were more widely and systematically broadcast.

Development and Good Governance Interventions

The crux of this structural realignment is contained in the World Bank's signature statement on good governance, *Governance and Development*, released in 1992, in which good governance is explicitly defined. Not restricted to Africa, it bundles governance concerns in the continent with Asia, the Middle East, Europe, and Central Asia. Most significant, the report puts forth a surprisingly restricted reading of good governance, stating, "Good governance is synonymous with sound development management" (World Bank 1992, 1). Touting the Bretton Woods founding mandate that agency activities must be driven by economic ends alone, governance is described as a "framework for the conduct of private and public business and the promotion of economic and financial performance" (1–2). Excepting questions of rights, representation, and political mobilization, good governance is reduced to six factors: public sector management, accountability and fiscal management, rule of law, transparency, corruption prevention, and administrative decentralization. Along with formalizing what Baylies (1995) calls a "new aid regime," the conditionality of aid is reiterated and intensified through the institution of negative sanctions and promise of assistance only to those governments who conform, cooperate, *and* show results.

With this turn, good governance interventions intensified the administrative logics of the state and devolved the provision of government—whether public goods, social protections, or channels of participation—to donor-driven projects. Fostering a different form of governmental "disaggregation" than the protest movements that also marked the era, donor projects transformed the nature of the state in such a way that actors outside of the state become "rent-seekers" while the donors are "rent-givers."

In this move the fundamental paradoxes of the multilateral good governance program are laid bare. Despite the claim that political institutions matter critically to development prospects, the political agenda is narrowly construed and good governance transposed to a "technopolitical" template. To borrow the language of Timothy Mitchell (2002), it is rendered bureaucratic, tied to experts and expert knowledge, and essentially depoliticized. As Brenda Chalfin (2010) demonstrates in her analysis of anti-corruption initiatives within Ghana's Customs Service, good governance is turned into an administrative problem hinging on procedure and the replication of international models and best practices, not deliberative process. This is not too different from the sort of "anti-politics" James Ferguson (1994) describes in the case of earlier World Bank development interventions in Lesotho where the power struggles shaping the state apparatus are steadfastly avoided by development planners. But unlike the program discussed by Ferguson, the multilateral good governance agenda was all about deliberately remaking the state in order to serve economic ends, all the while sidestepping politics.

In this iteration, good governance at once propels and masks what Claude Ake (1991, 37) recognizes as the abiding "donor fallacy of equating destatization with democratization." Namely, good governance mediates—or more accurately, obscures—the contradiction between the fading political project of the developmental state and the rise of the neoliberal polity. Addressing this slippage, Thandika Mkandawire (2007, 681) maintains, from the perspective of the multilaterals, that "it was important that the democratic institutions that might come with good governance were not used to undermine economic policy." Noting the cross-purposes of this agenda, he goes on to remark, "This was ensured by introducing institutional reforms that effectively compromised the authority of elected bodies through the insulation of policy technocrats and the creation of 'autonomous' authorities." For these and other African intellectuals who once endorsed it, good governance so construed was anything but.

Here we see yet another form of political "disaggregation" emerging in the wake of good governance initiatives. Selective investment in state building via the promotion of electoral processes narrowed the grounds of political give and take, ultimately reducing executive accountability and public goods delivery. Evidence on the ground was not hard to find. Deborah Bräutigam and Stephen Knack (2004), revealing a paradox of melding the means and ends of multilateral-led economic development and good governance—and drawing on longitudinal evidence from across the continent, including Senegal, Mali, Tanzania, and Mozambique among others—show that the massive influx of aid and long-term aid dependence, even with the obligations of implementation, actually stymy state capacity and political accountability. T. Hagmann and Filip Reyntjens (2016) likewise provide evidence of collusion between one-party regimes and dictatorships, speaking of the aid-authoritarian nexus.

Further complicating the relationship between professed intentions and actual outcomes of multilateral good governance agendas are the realities of political conditionality. In a fine-grained study of civil service reform in Malawi, Gerhard Anders (2010, 35) explains that multilateral donors foster domestic buy-in by commuting conditionality into "country ownership" of reform. Though governed by public international law, in practice these arrangements are legally ambiguous. Hard-and-fast rules of compliance give way to a battery of indeterminate assessments and audits. Generating a veritable industry devoted to what might be called the "government of good governance" (to play on Michel Foucault's [2010] notion of "reflexive government"), these include qualitative and quantitative performance criteria and ongoing program reviews. Suggesting that this is by no means an even playing field despite the ostensible transparency of reports and evaluations made accessible to all, Anders shows they are used and interpreted largely at the discretion of donors.

In Malawi and elsewhere in Africa, rather than streamlining government as the good governance paradigm purports, "Monitoring and Evaluation" for each and every domain of donor assistance has become an added layer of governmental function. Ramah McKay (2012, 545) vividly illustrates this point in her examination of health care in Mozambique, where the proliferation of monitoring and evaluation tools and data sets leads to a "multiplication of medical governance." The outcome is a variety of overlapping but largely uncoordinated governing authorities in which the collection of data overrides the provision of services and becomes a proxy for results. A side effect not fully acknowledged by policy makers, this arrangement at once augments the state apparatus and fosters the formation of hybrid governmental bodies melding state and international functions and functionaries.

In these examples the criteria of both development and governmental capacity are altered, in turn putting a premium on reflexive knowledge. Privileging data production over social improvement renders "projectization" an "art of (good) governance," to again paraphrase Foucault (2010). Whether regarding electoral practices or project delivery, good governance comes to hinge on the ability of practitioners to derive figures and craft measurable outcomes. In this double-sided move, the on-the-ground institution of good governance involves the "governmentalization" of the state and the "projectization" of state service delivery, often by non-state actors.

Harnessing civil society activism came with post–Cold War transitions to this new institutional field (Hearn 2007), and an explosion of nongovernmental organizations across the continent was a definitive side effect of broadcasting the good governance platform. In a recursive replication of governing functions outside the state apparatus, both local and international NGOs took up the task of carrying out and evaluating projects and monitoring service delivery and evaluation.

Along with the technocratic functions of project execution and evaluation, growing international awareness and activism around human rights made rights-based organizations and discourses increasingly central to the execution of good governance initiatives by NGOs (Reif 2000). In Ghana, for instance, the Committee on Human and Peoples Rights emerged alongside the state-allied bodies like the Commission for Human Rights and Administrative Justice and the work of transnational groups such as the International Commission of Jurists and Human Rights Watch. The insertion of human rights into the good governance paradigm built on earlier preoccupations with accountability and also renewed the moral orientation of a platform increasingly associated with austerity and technical proficiency. NGOs—especially those marshaling the language of rights, good governance, and neoliberal economic and political policies—were imbued with the capacity to not only rule but also shape the rules of engagement within the state.

The marriage of NGOs and human rights is succinctly described in Gregory Mann's (2015) account of the rise and dissolution of state capacity in Mali. Here, human rights organizations and rhetoric, including their enunciation in culturally distinctive idioms, lured international interest and capital. But they also pulled human rights advocacy and democratic activism out of the sphere of the sovereign state, ultimately contributing to a process Mann calls "nongovernmentality." In Mali and elsewhere, such collaborations between international intergovernmental and nongovernmental organizations altered the nature of states and of governance.

Elections and Democratizing

Elections continued to hold pride of place in the good governance agenda, and they set off a parallel stream of political transformation, although the pursuit of democratic rule and representation was pushed outside of official IFI (international financial institution) interventions in strict adherence to Bretton Woods agreements. The closing years of the 1990s and well into the 2000s were electoral boom times across Africa. Elections were promoted by African leaders, citizenries, and interest groups and were a principal preoccupation of scholars in and of Africa (Lindberg 2006).

Bankrolled by bilateral initiatives and aligned with US foreign policy interests, elections emerged as a centerpiece of the US Agency for International Development (USAID) Africa portfolio. Seeding and supporting ancillary organizations like the International Foundation for Electoral Systems (IFES) and National Democratic Institute for International Affairs (NDI), USAID pursued a project- and procedure-based approach well in line with multilateral models. USAID investment in democracy and governance programs in Africa tripled between 2001 and 2008, going from $89.2

to $274.4 million (Cooke and Morrison 2009, 102). Examples include programs for electoral officials across Southern Africa, establishing standards and competencies for electoral commissions in Ghana and Ethiopia, training domestic observers in Kenya and Zimbabwe, and providing hardware and capacity for results tabulation in Zambia and Nigeria, among many other initiatives (Azpuru et al. 2008)

Various European partners joined in this effort. The UK, Germany, Sweden, Denmark, Netherlands, and European Union devoted a large share of total overseas assistance to sub-Saharan Africa. All developed programs around democratization and governance in which elections were central. Extending to material and logistical support and external observer missions, these initiatives continued to grow well into the millennium with new commitments to funding and harmonization, and with total aid from 2000–2009 reaching 560 million Euro (Motsamai 2010).

From the start, Africa's electoral "third wave" attracted critics. Mkandawire (1999) pegged them "choiceless democracies" where "accounting to external agencies takes the place of accounting to legislatures and electorate." Crawford Young (1999) likewise considered them "tributary to [the] international system." Scott Taylor (1999), analyzing the situation in Mugabe's Zimbabwe, described electoralism as a new tack for autocratic rulers to consolidate power within the state. Revealing the enduring trade-offs between the priorities of neoliberal economic reform and commitments to good governance, Stephen Brown's (2001) close reading of Kenya's 1992 and 1996 elections shows that despite the presence of internationally trained election commissions and monitors, ultimately beholden to donors' economic priorities, gross electoral abuses went unsanctioned. All the while, new NGO and civil society organizations focused on democratization took root, buoyed by the resources and rhetoric of good governance and the failures of real political reform. Indeed, as Moi's human rights record in Kenya faltered, the Kenya Human Rights Commission gained ground.

Marked by more elections, more election programs, promotions, and NGOs, and a growing academic interest in elections, the putsch of electoralism sealed its place in the good governance paradigm. Blurring the line between the academic and policy arena, by the mid-1990s academics were invited to serve as Democracy Fellows at USAID with European institutions soon following suit (Barkan 1997, 385). Moving past the conventional wisdom that "elections matter" to the mantra "elections matter most, for good or ill," electoral studies became a growth industry. Attention to elections overwhelmed Africanist political science, with the claim that democratization could not only be gauged, but moreover, determined by elections increasingly accepted.

Again allying scholarship, international and in-country programming, the electoralist wave was buoyed by new fields of measurement and statistical analysis. Drawing on academic expertise and contributing to it, new and larger indicators and indexes of electoral practice and democratic progress were devised and popularized, among them: Freedom House, Economic Intelligence Democracy Index, Democracy Ranking Association, Afro-Barometer, and others. Pegging electoral success to the scope of reportage as much as electoral participation, statistical production on the national and local level was made a mark of internal accountability (Bogaards 2000).

Champions of electoral accountability, such as the International Institute for Democracy and Electoral Assistance (IDEA), emerged on the scene. They too "projectized" notions of electoral success and governance in Africa. The institute's 2005 handbook details the process of choosing an electoral system, the impact that system has on a country's political and institutional frameworks, and an electoral system's broader impact on numerous issues of governance (Reilly et al. 2005). Figures representing successful conduct of elections (rates of registration, voting, lack of electoral violence, tabulation of results) became a marker of good governance more generally. Migrating from academe to policy and back again, these figures now populate databases utilized by academic researchers, such as the Comparative Study of Electoral Systems out of the University of Michigan (Comparative Study of Electoral Systems n.d.), the Elections Database Macro Data Guide compiled by the European Statistical Service (MacroDataGuide n.d.), or the Yale University–based National Elections across Democracy and Autocracy (Hyde and Marinov 2012).

Though formally separated from IFI activities, the technopolitics of electoralism thus share the procedural orientation of multilateral good governance initiatives. They too are conjoined with social science methodologies in which ongoing large-scale surveys are valorized. Propelled by scholarly investments, the generation of survey data is treated as a political act in its own right (Bratton and Mattes 2001), effectively conflating governmental means and ends.

These disciplinary alliances and conceptual elisions would have direct impact on the discipline of political science. On the one hand, they promoted abstraction, as the compilation of large data sets became a research methodology in its own right, reducing for many scholars the importance of fieldwork or historical analysis. On the other, the growing intellectual intimacy across academic and policy worlds made it difficult to critically evaluate the merits of the research questions and techniques in play. Experts are slowly becoming aware of the risks of such conceptual involution. Once a leading democracy advocate, the Carnegie Foundation's Thomas Carothers (2015, 65), in a frank reanalysis of the democratization industry, remarks: "Aid providers do carry out program evaluations. But they are deeply wary of outside critical scrutiny and too rarely fund the sort of in-depth independent studies that examine the underlying assumptions, methods and outcomes."

In the wake of these developments, the precedence of the electoral piece of the good governance paradigm is facing a crisis of reproduction, threatened from within and without. After two decades of democracy promotion there is a mounting backlash coming from civil society discontent with policies that continue to promote executive might and state consolidation in the absence of public provisioning and representation (van de Walle 2016). Whether in large, highly populated countries like Nigeria, territorially large countries with small populations such as Mali, or small nations with low populations such as Liberia, elections have all the trappings of procedural success but say little about the capacity to rule or govern, as recent crises in all three countries make clear. Revealing the gap between the governmental and the democratic, there is entrenched resistance of state and party leaders to move beyond the shallow markers of electoral reform. Despite claims of "state consolidation" via new administrative practices and efficiencies, state capacities wane as governance functions are increasingly devolved to nongovernmental organizations. Consequently, the advancement of state-based electoralism becomes less and less significant in terms of revenue, representation, or access to public goods.

A Continent in Transformation

Threats to state-based democratic rule in Africa are further compounded by the failure of democratic transformations, exemplified by the violence and insecurities generated by the Arab Spring. The niceties of electoral proceduralism cannot combat the overwhelming rise of political forces and insurgencies that are both nondemocratic and nongovernmental, whether the Movement for the Emancipation of Niger Delta, Front for the Liberation of the Enclave of Cabinda, Islamic State or Boko Haram. As Jean-François Bayart and Stephen Ellis (2000, 226) remind us, "the fairy-story called Democracy is a new case of what might be termed 'transformism,' so characteristic of both the colonial and postcolonial state" that it serves merely as an instrument of internal legitimacy and a form of *conformism* with international norms. The failure of widespread but largely superficial democratic transformation to address social inequality, limited economic opportunity, arbitrary resource extraction policies, and their environmental fallout all undermine state monopoly over legitimate governance.

A notable outcome of the uneven buildup and breakdown of state capacity wrought by good governance initiatives and their penchant for procedural reform and outsourcing of state accountabilities is the rise of new political alliances and configurations outside or at the edge of the state. Loosely instituted and largely non-hierarchical, identified by Omolade Adunbi as "complex actors," they align NGOs, corporations, insurgents, and communities in networks that extend beyond locality, nation, and continent to articulate claims and counterclaims within and beyond the state.

The emergence of such political agents is particularly evident in the resource-rich territories of Sierra Leone, Liberia, and Nigeria. In Nigeria, residents of the oil-rich Niger Delta share in a form of "insurgent governance" where militants turned human rights activists such as the Movement for the Emancipation of Niger Delta People seize control of oil infrastructures and redistribute the proceeds derived from the sale of oil (Adunbi 2015). The rise of "rebel rulers" in Congo and South Sudan share some of the same characteristics (Mampilly 2011). At the same time, transnational corporations collaborate with NGOs to turn communities into their business partners, effectively rekindling Frederick Lugard's (1922) indirect rule system in a bid for domination and pacification. These modes of corporate-cum-communal governance operate through regional development councils, a tactic at once invoking the state and challenging state monopoly over governance.

By no means restricted to hot zones of intensive extraction, three interrelated factors shape these new articulations of good governance, suggesting that they are or will become more common. They include the spread of transnationally networked human and environmental rights campaigns across the continent. Second and closely connected is the rise of civil society and nongovernmental organizations as appendages of transnational networks. The third is the rise of insurgencies outside of existing patronage systems in the face of the sheer attenuation of state capacity and near collapse of state governance structures.

Conclusion

Over its thirty-year life span in the annals of African studies, good governance emerges as an enduring yet unstable political formulation. In tandem with geopolitical shifts and more localized struggles over power and resources, the quest for good governance has dramatically reshaped the function and organization of state bodies across Africa. Equally significant are the impacts of good governance interventions on nonstate bodies and the distribution of governance outside of the state. Indeed, good governance as a widespread paradigm and policy platform is twice rendered, both within and without the state.

In the first instance, in a host of African countries good governance initiatives have reorganized the executive apparatus of rule around elections and democratic procedure. This process is fundamentally enabled and naturalized—that is, made to appear necessary and self-evident—by the democracy industry in close alliance with the political science discipline. The state, in turn, is strengthened, but unevenly so. Namely, the process of state building is paired with the intensively orchestrated process of state dismantling and disaggregation, redistributing state functions to other entities and actors.

Whether short-lived donor projects, well-institutionalized NGOs, flashy investments in corporate social responsibility, or underground insurgencies, they hark back to the "decentralized" and often "despotic" (i.e., unchecked) political configurations described by Mamdani (1996) during the colonial period. But rather than enabling the "hegemony on a shoe string" (Berry 1993) of an earlier era of indirect rule, they are characterized by the proliferation of governing bodies and strategies of governing, of governing governance, of non-governing, and of governing non-governance. Much more than wordplay, Africa's political map is being remade in part resulting from the pressure of heavy-handed interventions of good governance. This is not about redrawing boundaries of sovereign territory but about reconfiguration of the terms of *legitimate* and *illegitimate authority* and the resources, rights, and recognition that come with it.

Suggested Readings

Ake, Claude. 1996. *Democracy and Development in Africa*. Washington, DC: Brookings Institution.

Bayart, Jean-François. 1993. *The State in Africa: The Politics of the Belly*. London: Longman.

Boone, Catherine. 2014. *Property and Political Order in Africa: Land Rights and the Structure of Politics*. Cambridge: Cambridge University Press.

Chabal, Patrick. 1986. *Political Domination in Africa*. Cambridge: Cambridge University Press.

Cheeseman, Nic. 2015. *Democracy in Africa: Successes, Failures and the Struggle for Political Reform*. Cambridge: Cambridge University Press.

Clapham, Christopher. 2000. *Africa and the International System: The Politics of State Survival*. Cambridge: Cambridge University Press.

Comaroff, Jean, and John L. Comaroff. 2012. *Theory from the South: Or, How Euro-America Is Evolving toward Africa*. Boulder, CO: Paradigm.

Englund, Harri. 2006. *Prisoners of Freedom: Human Rights and the African Poor*. Berkeley: University of California Press.

Ferguson, James. 2006. *Global Shadows: Africa in the Neoliberal World Order*. Durham, NC: Duke University Press.

Herbst, Jeffrey. 2000. *States and Power in Africa: Comparative Lessons in Authority and Control*. Princeton, NJ: Princeton University Press.

Reno, William. 1999. *Warlord Politics and African States*. Boulder, CO: Lynne Rienner.

von Schnitzler, Antina. 2016. *Democracy's Infrastructure: Techno-Politics and Protest after Apartheid*. Princeton, NJ: Princeton University Press.

References

Adejumobi, Said. 2000. "Between Democracy and Development in Africa: What Are the Missing Links?" Paper Presented to the World Bank Conference on "Development Thinking in the Next Millennium." Paris, June 26–28.

Adunbi, Omolade. 2015. *Oil Wealth and Insurgency in Nigeria*. Bloomington: Indiana University Press.

Ake, Claude. 1991. "Rethinking African Democracy." *Journal of Democracy* 2 (1): 32–44.

Anders, Gerhard. 2010. *In the Shadow of Good Governance: An Ethnography of Civil Service Reform in Africa*. Leiden: Brill.

Azpuru, Dinorah, Steven E. Finkel, Aníbal Pérez-Liñán, and Mitchell A. Seligson. 2008. "Trends in Democracy Assistance: What Has the United States Been Doing?" *Journal of Democracy* 19 (2): 150–59.

Barkan, Joel D. 1997. "Can Established Democracies Nurture Democracy Abroad? Lessons from Africa." *Democracy's Victory and Crisis* 93: 371–403.

Bayart, Jean-François, and Stephen Ellis. 2000. "Africa in the World: A History of Extraversion." *African Affairs* 99: 217–67.

Baylies, Carolyn. 1995. "'Political Conditionality' and Democratisation." *Review of African Political Economy* 22 (65): 321–37.

Berry, Sara. 1993. *No Condition Is Permanent: The Social Dynamics of Agrarian Change in Sub-Saharan Africa*. Madison: University of Wisconsin Press.

Bienen, Henry, and Jeffrey Herbst. 1996. "The Relationship between Political and Economic Reform in Africa." *Comparative Politics* 29 (1): 23–42.

Bogaards, Matthijs. 2000. "Crafting Competitive Party Systems: Electoral Laws and the Opposition in Africa." *Democratization* 7 (4): 163–90.

Bratton, Michael. 1998. "Second Elections in Africa." *Journal of Democracy* 9 (3): 51–66.

Bratton, Michael, and Robert Mattes. 2001. "Support for Democracy in Africa: Intrinsic or Instrumental?" *British Journal of Political Science* 31 (3): 447–74.

Bräutigam, Deborah, and Stephen Knack. 2004. "Foreign Aid, Institutions, and Governance in Sub-Saharan Africa." *Economic Development and Cultural Change* 52 (2): 255–85.

Brown, Stephen. 2001. "Authoritarian Leaders and Multiparty Elections in Africa: How Foreign Donors Help to Keep Kenya's Daniel Arap Moi in Power." *Third World Quarterly* 22 (5): 725–39.

Carothers, Thomas. 2015. "Democracy Aid at 25: Time to Choose." *Journal of Democracy* 26 (1): 59–73.

Chalfin, Brenda. 2010. *Neoliberal Frontiers: An Ethnography of Sovereignty in West Africa*. Chicago: University of Chicago Press.

Clapham, Christopher. 1997. "International Relations in Africa after the Cold War." In *After the Cold War: Security and Democracy in Africa and Asia*, edited by William Hale and Eberhard Kienle, 99–113. London: Tauris Academic Studies.

"Comparative Study of Electoral Systems." University of Michigan. Accessed November 17, 2016. http://www.cses.org/.

Cooke, Jennifer G., and J. Stephen Morrison. 2009. *US Africa Policy beyond the Bush Years: Critical Challenges for the Obama Administration*, vol. 31. Center for Strategic and International Studies.

Doornbos, Martin.1990. "The African State in Academic Debate: Retrospect and Prospect." *Journal of Modern African Studies* 28 (2): 179–98.

Fatton, Robert. 1990. "Liberal Democracy in Africa." *Political Science Quarterly* 105 (3): 455–73.

Ferguson, James. 1994. *The Anti-Politics Machine: "Development," Depoliticization, and Bureaucratic Power in Lesotho*. Minneapolis: University of Minnesota Press.

Foucault, Michel. 2010. *The Birth of Biopolitics: Lectures at the Collège de France, 1978–1979*. New York: Palgrave Macmillan.

Hagmann, Tobias, and Filip Reyntjens. 2016. "Introduction: Aid and Authoritarianism in

Sub-Saharan Africa." In *Aid and Authoritarianism in Africa*, edited by Tobias Hagmann and Filip Reyntjens, 1–19. London: Zed.

Hearn, Julie. 2007. "African NGOs: The New Compradors?" *Development and Change* 38 (6): 1095–110.

Hyde, Susan D., and Nikolay Marinov. 2012. "Codebook for National Elections across Democracy and Autocracy." http://www.nelda.co. Accessed November 17, 2016.

Jenkins, J. Craig, and Augustine J. Kposowa. 1992. "The Political Origins of African Military Coups: Ethnic Competition, Military Centrality, and the Struggle over the Postcolonial State." *International Studies Quarterly* 36 (1): 271–91.

Joseph, Richard.1997. "Democratization in Africa after 1989: Comparative and Theoretical Perspectives." *Comparative Politics* 29 (3): 363–82.

Konings, Piet. 2011. *The Politics of Neoliberal Reforms in Africa: State and Civil Society in Cameroon*. African Books Collective. Leiden: Leiden African Studies Center.

Lindberg, Staffan. 2006. *Democracy and Elections in Africa*. Baltimore, MD: Johns Hopkins University Press.

Loxley, John. 1983. "The Berg Report and the Model of Accumulation in Sub-Saharan Africa." *Review of African Political Economy* 27/28: 197–204.

Lugard, Frederick. 1922. *The Dual Mandate in British Tropical Africa*. London: Blackwood.

MacroDataGuide. Norwegian Centre for Research Data. Accessed November 17, 2016, http://www.nsd.uib.no/macrodataguide/index.html.

Mamdani, Mahmood. 1996. *Citizen and Subject: Contemporary Africa and the Legacy of Late Colonialism*. Princeton, NJ: Princeton University Press.

Mampilly, Zachariah Cherian. 2011. *Rebel Rulers: Insurgent Governance and Civilian Life during War*. Ithaca, NY: Cornell University Press.

Mann, Gregory. 2015. *From Empires to NGOs in the West African Sahel: The Road to Governmentality*. Cambridge: Cambridge University Press.

McGowan, Patrick J. 2003. "African Military Coups d'état, 1956–2001: Frequency, Trends and Distribution." *Journal of Modern African Studies* 41 (3): 339–70.

McKay, Ramah. 2012. "Documentary Disorders: Managing Medical Multiplicity in Maputo, Mozambique." *American Ethnologist* 39 (3): 545–61.

Mitchell, Timothy. 2002. *Rule of Experts: Egypt, Techno-politics, Modernity*. Berkeley: University of California Press.

Mkandawire, Thandika. 2007. "'Good Governance': The Itinerary of an Idea." *Development in Practice* 17 (4–5): 679–81.

———. 1999. "Crisis Management and the Making of 'Choiceless Democracies.'" In *State, Conflict, and Democracy in Africa*, edited by Richard Joseph, 359–76. Boulder, CO: Lynne Rienner.

Motsamai, Dimpho. 2010. *The European Union's Electoral Assistance: Perceptions of African Democracy Building*. Stockholm: International IDEA.

Mudimbe, V. Y., Robert Bates, and Jean O'Barr. 1993. *Africa and the Disciplines: The Contributions of Research in Africa to the Social Sciences and Humanities*. Chicago: University of Chicago.

Reif, Linda C. 2000. "Building Democratic Institutions: The Role of National Human Rights Institutions in Good Governance and Human Rights Protection." *Harvard Human Rights Journal* 13 (1): 1–70.

Reilly, Ben, Andrew Ellis, and Andrew Reynolds. 2005. *Electoral System Design: The New International IDEA Handbook*. International Institute for Democracy and Electoral Assistance.

Santiso, Carlos. 2001. "World Bank and Good Governance: Good Governance and Aid Effectiveness: The World Bank and Conditionality." *Georgetown Public Policy Review* 7 (1): 1–137.

Scott, James C. 1998. *Seeing Like a State: How Certain Schemes to Improve the Human Condition Have Failed*. New Haven, CT: Yale University Press.

Taylor, Scott. 1999. "Race, Class, and Neopatrimonialism in Zimbabwe." In *State, Conflict, and Democracy in Africa*, edited by Richard Joseph, 239–66. Boulder, CO: Lynne Rienner.

van de Walle, Nicolas. 2001. *African Economies and the Politics of Permanent Crisis, 1979–1999*. Cambridge University Press.

———. 2016. "Democracy Fatigue and the Ghost of Modernization Theory." In *Aid and Authoritarianism in Africa*, edited by Tobias Hagmann and Filip Reyntjens, 161–77. London: Zed.

World Bank. 1981. *Accelerated Development in Sub-Saharan Africa: An Agenda for Action*. Washington, DC: World Bank.

———. 1989. *Sub-Saharan Africa: From Crisis to Sustainable Growth*. Washington, DC: World Bank.

———. 1992. *Governance and Development*. Washington, DC: World Bank.

Young, Crawford. 1999. "Democratization in Africa." In *State, Conflict, and Democracy in Africa*, edited by Richard Joseph, 15–38. Boulder, CO: Lynne Rienner.

11 HEALTH

Susan Reynolds Whyte

In the Preamble to its Constitution, signed in 1946, the World Health Organization famously defined health as a state of complete physical, mental, and social well-being, and not merely the absence of disease or infirmity. It thus recognized the contrast between a narrow biological conception of health and a broad view of welfare that embraces all of life. As complete well-being, health is a dream, a utopia, a nearly unachievable ideal anywhere in the world. But ideals are not to be dismissed merely because they are beyond reach. They animate imagination and striving.

Not the absence, but the presence, of disease in Africa has fired minds and motivations since the first medical missionaries began their work there in the nineteenth century. The negative picture of African suffering has been the justification for interventions by religious organizations, policy makers, humanitarians, and researchers aimed at alleviating, even eradicating, disease. The image of Africa as "disease-ridden" and blighted by debility has dominated Western perception for nearly two centuries. The dangers posed to Europeans by the deadly fevers of the "white man's grave" were already feared in the nineteenth century. Since then, attention has focused on syphilis, leprosy, sleeping sickness, malaria and tuberculosis, malnutrition, and the mutilations of war. Epidemics of AIDS and Ebola demand emergency responses, while endemic conditions ebb and flow. The NTDs (Neglected Tropical Diseases like guinea worm, bilharzia, and river blindness) seem to be diminishing while NCDs (non-communicable diseases such as hypertension, diabetes, and cancer) are on the rise everywhere on the continent. Some scholars claim that the concentration on disease and suffering supports the use of Africa as a living laboratory, where researchers carry out experiments in medicine and public health. As the field of global health expands in high-income countries, collaboration with African research and health institutions offers access to sick populations eager for health care. Because disease brings misery, and health is an unassailable value, such interventions are rarely questioned.

The focus on sickness and the need for disease-specific interventions appeal to health professionals, politicians, and external humanitarian agencies. Yet the struggle for well-being in the broader sense—the never fully reachable goal of social and spiritual, as well as physical, well-being—is in many ways the more important concern for ordinary people. In several East African languages, the word for health has these broader connotations. In Luganda, *obulamu* also means life; in Kiswahili, *uzima* has the sense of being in good health, whole, entire, alive. Well-being is the hope. Melioration is what may actually be possible. In imagining improvement, in trying to overcome problems, or at least finding a way to live with them, people and societies reveal their particular genius. It is these attempts to manage and improve life in the face of adversity that have preoccupied nonmedical scholars of health in Africa, from the early classic works on divination to the most recent studies of living with HIV. Social scientists are concerned with what African families, health workers, and communities *are doing* to achieve better lives, as well as with what *is being done to* African populations in the name of intervention and experimentation.

It is widely recognized that health and disease are biosocial phenomena. That is, the biological conditions we know as sickness and infirmity are heavily determined by social, economic, and political factors. Likewise, it is generally acknowledged that meaning and morality intertwine with scientific understandings of bodily and mental conditions and affect the response to them. In African societies this sociality and morality of suffering and alleviation are explicit in characteristic ways that have been explored by generations of scholars. Sociality and morality are relevant to illness and debility in at least three ways: in considerations of cause; in the search for treatment; and in the provision of care. The critical terms for health as a social condition can be framed as accountability, connections, and concern.

Well-Being and Social Accountability

The attempt to account for misfortune is an enduring theme in the study of African societies. Accounting and accountability denote both explanation, as in giving an account of what happened, and allocating responsibility, as in holding someone to account. Notions of "social accountability" informed the landmark studies by E. E. Evans-Pritchard; his view of actors as moral agents continues to this day. Scholars document the ways that people account for the failure of well-being and allocate responsibility for affliction. In very many African settings, misfortune is found to result from problems in relationships with other people, living and dead, spirits, and anonymous forces underlying the moral order. This view sees misfortune, and by implication well-being, as relational. It fits with an understanding of personhood as a social condition of dependence and interdependence. Classic examples show how people attribute the death of their children to those with whom they have conflicts, or mental disorder to the vengeful spirits of people who died badly or the birth of malformed babies to parental transgression of moral injunctions. Because illness and infirmity are common forms of misfortune, it could be said that accounting for them was fundamental to cosmology, moral order, and social relations. But fortune and misfortune were never limited to biological disease; ideals of vitality and fertility corresponded to broad notions of social and mental well-being including livelihood and security.

The classic studies of accountability explored divination, rituals of healing, and attempts to restore social and spiritual relationships. The beings and forces held accountable were identifiable powers that could be named and addressed, openly or secretly. More recently, other questions about accountability are being raised—partly through the influence of biomedically inspired campaigns. To what extent are individuals responsible for their own (failures of) well-being? Is it your own fault if you are infected with HIV through careless sex? Do you make yourself vulnerable to hypertension and diabetes through overeating and underexercising? In contrast to assertions of individual accountability, others point to general conditions of contemporary life as "sickening." War, poverty, lack of jobs, corruption, and increasing inequality combined with indifference are forces for insecurity. They are social and moral issues, but because they are anonymous and impersonal, they require another kind of accounting than the personalistic assertions about sorcery and spirits.

Social accountability is not simply an intellectual exercise in explaining the occurrence of health and misfortune. Questions of accountability arise in response to problems and exigencies that call for action. Holding some identifiable person, being, or force to account is a possibility for doing something. But that action may not resolve the problem and people pragmatically try other possibilities until they find improvement or accept that they cannot change the situation. This pragmatic trying out of accounts and accountability is based on a disposition of uncertainty, hope, tentativeness, and doubt captured by the grammatical concept of subjunctivity—the mood expressing what is imagined or wished or possible. Recognizing the subjunctive aspect of social accountability counteracts the danger of seeing people as fixed on culturally given ways of accounting. It brings into view readiness to try different ways of improving situations and the tentative, open attitude toward sociality.

Traditional Healing and Western Medicine

Moving to alleviate misfortune may entail addressing questions of accountability by identifying a possible agent and adjusting relationships through words, exchange, or ritual action. More and more, as biomedicine becomes African medicine, it means accessing drugs for an individual body, leaving aside the question of social accountability. But no matter what move is made, it will most likely involve connections with other people. The quest for therapy is almost always a social affair; giving advice, referring a patient to a known source of treatment, and relating to a health care provider are about personal connections between people.

John Janzen captured the sociality of treatment seeking in the concept of the "therapy managing group," by which he meant the people who took responsibility for the patient and suggested treatment alternatives. He recognized that social support in finding help is a universal phenomenon, but emphasized that the nature, size, and significance of such groups—or better, networks—varies. Janzen originally used the concept in conjunction with an exploration of medical pluralism in Kongo society, showing how therapy managers guided recalcitrant illnesses to different kinds of therapy and therapists: the healer, the kin collective, the spirit cult, and Western medicine. Different treatments have different relational consequences. There are economic, emotional, and social stakes in joining a Pentecostal church or kneeling to ask forgiveness from an annoyed mother's brother or traveling to a distant hospital. These play into guidance and decisions, together with the all-important assessment of which therapy works effectively in alleviating the problem.

Many of the classic early studies concentrated on "traditional healing," where the dimensions of social accountability were clearly evident in both explanations of misfortune and actions taken to address it. At first glance biomedicine seemed different—more individualistic in its application, less personalistic in its construal of the causes of suffering, more focused on disease and its treatment than on broader well-being. But closer examination reveals equally fundamental issues of sociality, together with new questions about belonging and global connections. In order to grasp the sociality of biomedicine, it is necessary to recognize the providers as well as the users, and to consider the relations between them.

The Western medicine introduced by missionaries in the nineteenth century and colonial authorities in the twentieth became African medicine in practice, if not in name, as Africans increasingly provided and consumed it. They worked with European doctors, first as low-status apprentices, then as medical assistants, nurses, and midwives trained in mission hospitals. They constituted what Nancy Rose Hunt (1999) called the "middle figures," those who mediated European agencies and biomedicine to local societies. After the First World War, opportunities expanded for "tribal dressers" and nurses in government service; and after the Second World War, government institutions were training African doctors. In the developmentalist era of the 1960s and 1970s, independent African states expanded biomedical services, together with education and economic development. Health was part of an ideal of national welfare, in principle for all citizens.

The image of health workers was playfully incorporated on ceremonial occasions as representing vitality, order, and discipline—characteristics of general well-being beyond the fight against disease. By the 1950s, the anthropologist J. Clyde Mitchell observed that *kalela* dancers on the Copperbelt included in their teams someone dressed as a doctor in a white coat to encourage the dancers and another in the uniform of a nursing sister carrying a mirror so dancers could check if they were neat and tidy and a handkerchief to wipe the sweat from their brows. By 2014, in southern Uganda, the introduction (*okwanjula*) of the groom and his family to the bride's home sometimes included a set of young women in nurses uniform, who welcomed the guests by "vaccination," pinning red ribbons to their festive clothes. From the *kalela* dance to the wedding introduction, it is good to have health workers on the team.

Trained health workers were professionals with specialist knowledge, held to standards and subject to institutional regulation. But they did not maintain a monopoly on biomedicine. Their knowledge, procedures, and most of all their *materia medica* were popularized. During the 1980s and 1990s, as the global economic downturn and structural adjustment policies were felt in the public health care system, the business of pharmaceuticals flourished in the private sector. As commodities, medicines were made common, sold by small drug shops in trading centers, hawkers on buses, and pharmacies in towns. Families were able to buy medicines directly and take them according to the advice of retailers and neighbors, often a much more convenient arrangement than seeking help at formal medical facilities.

This was the period when influential international organizations and powerful donors adopted the discourse of community participation and made efforts to provide "health for all" through training village health workers and traditional healers. It is striking that so few authorities recognized that retailers of medicines were the real community health workers in many areas. These folk providers of biomedicine were similar in some ways to other folk specialists; their success depended on inspiring confidence and pleasing their customers.

By the turn of the millennium, government health care was drastically underfunded in most African countries. In some, patients paid fees in public facilities; even in countries like Uganda where the government had abolished user fees, many services were only available for money. The inequities of a system where treatment depended on ability to pay were clear. Health workers too were dissatisfied with their conditions of work, and they were criticized for corruption and indifference.

Under these conditions, the relations of therapy managing groups to health workers are of keen interest. They take a variety of forms, from intimacy to distance, from brief to enduring. At one extreme is the situation, fortunate for the patient, where a health worker is a close friend or relative and is actually part of the therapy-managing group. For health workers, the expectations and demands of extended families and more or less close acquaintances becomes a burden—one that is seldom recognized by policy makers and researchers. For patients, being able to rely on a knowledgeable person with good contacts in the health care system is a boon.

However, most patients are not in that privileged situation. They and their supporters seek treatment here and there, according to the nature of the problem and how much money and time they have. A child's acute fever may require no more than purchasing some antimalarials at a shop in the trading center. The child's mother buys them as a customer, from a shopkeeper she may or may not know, but who will probably treat her with courtesy and sell her what she asks for. More chronic conditions lead to longer therapeutic journeys, where those close to the sick person try one treatment after another. They may buy "African medicine," do a spirit exorcism ceremony, and visit different biomedical facilities, where consultations are brief and follow-up is rare. They shop around until the condition improves or until they give up trying to alleviate it and just live with it.

Family Care and Public Welfare

Members of a therapy-managing network advise and guide the patient to sources of treatment. They are concerned about arranging medicines and rituals. But they may not necessarily be involved in the long-term everyday care of infirmity or in structural aspects of providing care. Concern and the related term care point to relatively lasting dispositions: being attentive, worried, and emotionally involved. They are about minding in the sense of being aware, thinking and feeling about something or someone. Matters of concern are not only about immediate treatment; they include health in the larger sense of life. They are about caring about and caring for.

Concern and care are evident in relation to chronic conditions of disease, disability, and infirmities of aging. Daily support in the form of nursing, feeding, and conversing is everywhere primarily a family matter. It is also a moral matter in that ideals of amity and solidarity enjoin sustaining those weakened by debility. Such ideals are not always realized, but they are part of how people imagine their societies used to be or should be. Studies of disability show that despite assertions of stigma and discrimination, persons with impairments are generally cared for by family members. They may not be given the extra care implied in the term "handicap," but they are included in the maintenance and support provided to all household members. As captured in the title of an article about Maasai care for disabled children, "a child is a child." In principle, all children should be treated equally. The ideal of care provision by family members is iconized in a statue at the entrance to the WHO headquarters in Geneva. It represents a blind old man being led by a child, presumably his grandson.

The reality of family care is more problematic. That little boy guiding his grandfather should be in school. The burden of daily care for debility falls disproportionately on women. Families are not static consolidated units and members distance themselves geographically and socially. Moreover, there are aspects of care that need structural interventions beyond what families alone can provide. Newer research asks questions that open the issue of concern and care beyond families and local communities. To what extent do African states care for their citizens? Who are the publics of public health? What are the concerns of international donors? Nongovernmental organizations? Patient groups?

The weakness of African states in providing welfare for their citizens has been a theme since the global economic downturn of the 1980s. Insufficiencies in public health care are matched by inadequacies in education, employment, and infrastructure. Dispensaries are empty facades, schools are overcrowded, jobs are in short supply. Reports of callous nurses, midwives demanding money, and health worker absenteeism are rife. Yet this Afro-pessimistic view is being tempered in two ways. One is by attending to those public health workers who struggle in place and show concern under adverse conditions, such as those Livingston (2012) portrays in her study of an oncology ward in Botswana, or those Malawian medical students with a "heart for the work" of serving their countrymen, whom Wendland (2010) describes. The other modification of Afro-pessimism follows from recognition of all the new possibilities for providing health care that are being explored.

African states have never been alone in attempting to improve the lives of their citizens. Missionaries had their vision of the good life, which included biomedicine with its assumptions and requirements. After independence, as new states sought development, bilateral and multilateral donors stepped in. From the 1980s, these were supplemented by national and international nongovernmental organizations, and in the health domain, by global health research institutions. Moreover, neoliberal policies welcomed private enterprise, in health care as elsewhere, from small businesses to large hospitals and pharmaceutical companies. Critics point to the weakening of the state, its dependence on external resources, and the fragmentation of initiative as the welfare landscape became increasingly "projectified"—dotted with endeavours undertaken by different agencies, each with its own agenda, and all with limited time horizons. What might have been state functions are spread among many different actors. We should note however, that this is not merely a question of weakening state concern. The functions themselves, as well as the expectations and hopes around health care, are far more diverse and complicated than they were in late colonial and early post-independence times.

African health care workers and African publics have appropriated, even created, new opportunities in the shifting landscape of care. Staff in government health facilities that host donor projects appreciate the extra benefits (though not the extra paperwork); projects may provide equipment and medicines, transport for outreaches, and allowances for attending training workshops. Beyond the extra money, health workers value the exposure and recognition they obtain through projects. Some health workers obtain employment with NGOs as an alternative or supplement to government service. Health workers are concerned about their own well-being and that of their families. But they also appropriate discourses of care promoted by donors and projects that emphasize the welfare of patients or "clients" as they are sometimes called. While projects are often focused on specific conditions or target groups, health workers find ways to carry over benefits and new knowledge to other areas.

The landscape of care and concern features patient groups in some places. They are not as common as in the Global North, but they figure significantly here and there. Partly they are a consequence of interventions that facilitate contact and common consciousness among people with similar conditions or treatment regimes. Sometimes they are encouraged by donors and projects; sometimes they are energized by health professionals. Eric Silla wrote the history of a leprosarium originally started by missionaries in Mali. It drew patients from the whole region, who remained in the neighborhood after the facility closed, developed a niche in trade, and eventually formed a patient advocacy group. In coming together, dispersed individuals not only received treatment but also forged a common identity, first as lepers and later as people with disabilities.

Identities are always multifaceted and situational. Nationality, ethnicity, clan, family, and religion may each be a basis for interaction and self-consciousness in a given situation. Identification and mobilization on the basis of a biomedical diagnosis or treatment are relatively new in the African scene. But support groups for people with chronic conditions have a precursor in the cults of affliction that existed in many African cultures. They brought together those in distress attributed to the same spirits, which were addressed in performances of possession. Today "biosociality"—relationships cultivated around a biomedical characteristic—assembles people with diabetes, sickle cell, cancer, and other conditions. Since 1981, the International Year of Disabled Persons, national organizations of people with disabilities have emerged. Some were based on specific disabilities such as visual or hearing impairments; others were umbrella organizations that included all kinds of debilities and proposed an identity—"the disabled"—that had never existed in African societies. These groups and identities are more common in urban areas, and appeal most to more educated people with some resources. Even so, they have wider consequences in raising awareness and sometimes in advocacy. They offer another sense of belonging beyond inclusion based on kinship, religious faith, or ethnic affiliation.

Epidemics and Accountability

Starting in the mid-1980s a strange affliction began to spread suffering and death in large regions of Africa. First recognized in Uganda as "Slim" disease because of the way it wasted its victims, it was soon identified as AIDS (Acquired Immune Deficiency Syndrome) caused by the Human Immunodeficiency Virus (HIV). It took millions of lives, devoured family resources, and imposed crushing burdens on health systems, particularly in Eastern and Southern Africa, where HIV prevalence was, and still is, highest.

For at least ten years, there was no medicine to control the virus. It became available in the late 1990s, but was inaccessible for practically everyone in Africa because it was too expensive. Around 2004–5, with immense funding from countries of the Global North, antiretroviral therapy (ART) was "rolled out"; it was provided for free through NGOs and public health facilities. A whole generation of HIV-infected people who had expected to die got a second chance to live. But their chances depended on their adherence to treatment—taking medicine every day for life—and on the quality and sustainability of the programs providing therapy. A growing social science literature documents the depredations of the disease and the political, social, and cultural dimensions of the response in various countries. Three decades on from the first reports of Slim disease, the shifting shape of AIDS as a social phenomenon makes a fascinating story, not least in Uganda which has been an AIDS pioneer in so many ways.

Accountability is a critical term in the history of AIDS in Uganda. Explanations of AIDS have changed over time, but they have persistently been infused with moral undertones. The mysterious new disease was first evident in southwestern Uganda at a time of political instability, not long after invading forces from Tanzania defeated Idi Amin's army. Illicit trade across the border with Tanzania was rife, some traders were getting rich on smuggling, and people were quick to attribute the wasting disease to sorcery machinations. As AIDS made its deadly way to other parts of the country, sorcery, or sometimes spirit affliction, figured in the accounts of affliction on an individual level. Assigning blame to a malicious person or insistent spirit allowed families to take pragmatic action against the presumed cause. When there was no remission, even after resources had been expended on rituals and "African medicine," families sometimes admitted that they were simply uncertain about how to account for the suffering and death.

The enormous effort to prevent the spread of HIV through informing the Ugandan public bore results. People learned that the virus was transmitted from mother to infant, through cuts and injections, and most of all through sexual relations. The injunction "to love carefully" was promulgated again and again: ABC—abstain, be faithful, or use a condom. Health education placed responsibility for protection on individuals, and, for some at least, AIDS was an indication of moral failure. But it soon became clear that HIV was an eminently social disease in several ways. You could not always guard against a partner's partners. Faithful married women also contracted the virus. And social patterns, such as gender inequality, transactional sex, and wealth disparities, were also to blame. Social conditions as well as individual behavior were held accountable for the spread of HIV. Given the value attached to health, these insalubrious social patterns were cast in moral terms, at least by some.

Those who fell sick over and again might first have attributed their afflictions to the malice of a sorcerer, or to some indisposing spirit. Before the advent of ART there was little motivation to test for HIV; a positive test was a certain death sentence while uncertainty left room for hope and trying out explanations that suggested ways forward. But once treatment was possible, those who tested positive and managed to improve on ART tended to look back regretfully on their earlier attempts to account for their illness. Many felt that they had wasted money on "witch doctors." Accepting the biomedical explanation for infection and adopting the discourse of testing, treating, and "living positively" became an indication of enlightenment and modernity.

The many different donor supported projects that rolled out ART saw themselves as institutions providing therapy to individuals. Those members of the first generation who benefited from the treatment spoke as if they achieved it through connections to other people, rather than accepting it from impersonal programs. Recounting their therapeutic journeys, people told of friends and relatives who had advised them to take an HIV test. Before testing was routine for in-patients and out-patients, it was voluntary, which meant making a decision and taking an initiative. In this, individuals were often encouraged by someone they knew well. Those who tested positive had to enroll in a treatment program. Later they remembered who had put them in touch with an ART clinic and who had referred them to organizations providing material benefits to those who tested positive for HIV. Neighbors with connections, family members who were already on a treatment program, someone who knew someone working in a relevant organization—members of the first generation drew on such links.

The concept of the therapy managing group expanded the notion of a health system to include those who helped the patient to navigate between options. Having a health worker on that team was always an advantage. But the advent of ART changed the game and the relation between patients and health workers. For it was not only a matter of locating treatment, but of staying on it. Patients had to join a treatment program and attend the same clinic regularly for monitoring and medicine refills. They had to *belong* to a program, which kept their files and was their exclusive source of treatment. Repeated visits meant that patients developed personal relations to their health care providers, upon whom they depended for the lifesaving medicine. Tellingly, staff in AIDS clinics spoke of their patients as "clients" and they were indeed clients in a double sense. They were consumers of professional services on a long-term basis, not just customers making a one-off purchase. And they were dependents of programs and professionals, who were their patrons in that they availed scarce and necessary resources in exchange for loyalty. "Therapeutic clientship" is a new kind of connection in Ugandan health care; the enduring relation to a treatment program supplements the continuing connections of family and friendship that sustain HIV positive people. "Therapeutic citizenship," the term used by Vinh-Kim Nguyen to denote the relationship to more distant sovereign polities providing resources, is a less personal, more abstract kind of dependency.

International concern about AIDS has far exceeded attention to other health problems in Africa. Scholars write of "AIDS exceptionalism": the emphasis on AIDS as a unique challenge requiring a massive and exclusive response. Critics find the reaction disproportionate; it unbalances health care systems and draws resources and awareness away from other conditions. However, in countries like Uganda, where the epidemic was so devastating, AIDS exceptionalism did not seem misplaced, at least not initially. When Yoweri Museveni and his National Resistance Movement came to power in 1986, after a protracted guerilla war, he immediately confronted the epidemic of Slim disease, making him exceptional among African heads of state. He welcomed the concern of international agencies; their interventions helped to give his new regime legitimacy. The intertwining of efforts, national and international, over thirty years has kept AIDS as a high priority in Ugandan health care, but concerns have shifted and widened as time has passed. The early focus on prevention problematized partnerships and sexual relations, while the advent of treatment added the dimension of clientship. For those who have achieved ART, immediate cares about sickness have been replaced with trying to get on with life, albeit a life with medication and a weakened body. They have moved from preoccupation with disease to concerns about health in a broad sense.

The AIDS epidemic coincided with the period when Uganda, like many African countries, saw a florescence of NGOs. TASO—The AIDS Support Organization—was one of the first to provide counseling and material support to people with AIDS, while also addressing stigma and advocating for better care. TASO was a home-grown organization, started by concerned Ugandans. In time, the influx of external resources for AIDS activities encouraged the multiplication and growth of such organizations. Uganda was one of the countries to benefit most heavily from PEPFAR (the US President's Emergency Program for AIDS Relief), as well as from many other donor programs. That has meant a proliferation of projects, groups, clubs, HIV testing campaigns, Safe Medical Circumcision, Prevention of Mother-to-Child-Transmission programs, orphan support, and all the clinic days and home visits for people on ART.

What began as an effort to deal with a disease became a source of livelihood—one in which the disease itself became a qualification. Health workers could not cope with the growing numbers of clients and the many new tasks of HIV education, counseling, home visits, monitoring, and paperwork. HIV positive "expert patients," mainly those with some education, were recruited to assist. They started as volunteers with the prospect of allowances for lunch, transport, and attending workshops. They hoped that they might later receive an actual salary, and some did—at least for a time. HIV prevention and care efforts are infused by a discourse of enlightened concern, empathy, and acceptance, whether carried out by health workers, expert patients, or NGO employees. These values might not always be realized in practice, but the ideals are frequently expressed. The stated principle of client-centered care, adopted by TASO early on and facilitated by external resources, is an important contribution of the AIDS response to healthcare in Uganda.

The concerted efforts of national and international actors to prevent and treat AIDS brought forth new forms of belonging, obligation, and responsibility. Therapeutic clientship and therapeutic citizenship are terms that mark these spheres of concern. But biosocial relations based on interventions supplemented rather than replaced those enduring links of kinship and friendship that form the fabric of everyday life. Much has been written about "the African family" in the era of AIDS, underlining both its assumption of the burden of care and its fragility.

Studies in Uganda contribute two perspectives to this discussion. The first is the intensification of preexisting patterns of care and concern. The fostering of AIDS orphans continues an old practice of sending children to stay with relatives for shorter or longer periods. The return of ill married women to their consanguineal homes is a long-standing mode of providing chronic health care that reveals the lasting obligations of blood relationships. As one man reminded his wife, when he brought his sick sister to stay in their home, "We must care well for her, for she may survive and care for us when we fall ill." The second perspective on "African families" arising from the years of experience with the epidemic, is that families are best seen as shifting networks of potential support. People needing care look to those strategically located relatives with resources who also show most concern. Once they have improved they are able to assume their own places in the networks of care and obligation that go under the name of family.

The response to the AIDS epidemic is thus more than a reaction to a disease. Through new and old forms of accountability, connections and concern, people are striving for health in the sense of physical, mental, and social well-being, utopian as that may be. This is, as I have argued, in keeping with the African emphasis on a state of complete physical, mental, and social well-being as opposed to a more narrow focus on medical treatment or cure.

Suggested Readings

Dilger, Hansjörg, and Ute Luig, eds. 2010. *Morality, Hope and Grief: Anthropologies of AIDS in Africa*. New York: Berghahn.

Feierman, Steven, and John M. Janzen, eds. 1992. *The Social Basis of Health and Healing in Africa*. Berkeley: University of California Press.

Geissler, P. Wenzel, ed. 2015. *Para-States and Medical Science: Making African Global Health*. Durham, NC: Duke University Press.

Hunt, Nancy Rose. 1999. *A Colonial Lexicon: Of Birth Ritual, Medicalization, and Mobility in the Congo*. Durham, NC: Duke University Press.

Janzen, John M. 1978. *The Quest for Therapy: Medical Pluralism in Lower Zaire*. Berkeley: University of California Press.

Livingston, Julie. 2012. *Improvising Medicine: An African Oncology Ward in an Emerging Cancer Epidemic*. Durham, NC: Duke University Press.

Nguyen, Vinh-Kim. 2010. *The Republic of Therapy: Triage and Sovereignty in West Africa's Time of AIDS*. Durham, NC: Duke University Press.

Prince, Ruth J., and Rebecca Marsland, eds. 2014. *Making and Unmaking Public Health in Africa*. Athens: Ohio University Press.

Silla, Eric. 1998. *People Are Not the Same: Leprosy and Identity in Twentieth-Century Mali*. Martlesham, UK: James Currey.

Wendland, Claire L. 2010. *A Heart for the Work: Journeys through an African Medical School*. Chicago: University of Chicago Press.

Whyte, Susan Reynolds, ed. 2014. *Second Chances: Surviving AIDS in Uganda*. Durham, NC: Duke University Press.

12 HUMANITARIANISM

Rogaia Mustafa Abusharaf

In recent years, civilians in African wars have expressed considerable concern toward humanitarian organizations working in their midst. In an interview I conducted with displaced people in Khartoum in 2004, a few months after the onset of political violence in Darfur, Sudan, many stressed that humanitarian aid was not dispensed on the grounds based on dire need as they were led to believe, but rather on the basis of the ethnic affiliation of the applicant. "If you are not Zaghawa, Masaleet, or Fur, you don't receive help," one interviewee averred. Ethnic affiliation with these "three indigenous African tribes" as preconceived by humanitarian organizations is, therefore, the main perquisite for one's eligibility for aid. These humanitarian organizations, working in Darfur, have grown to be part of the greater "knowledge network" about classifying needy populations as victims or villains by virtue of ethnicity and regardless of their position in the conflict. As this crisis continues to be viewed as a war between Africans and Arabs, these partial knowledge circuits ignore that categories are highly charged and overgeneralized political positions that exclude on the basis of a perceived homogenous identity. In this context, humanitarian Manicheanism is exactly what ails it as politics and practice. Similar encounters are abundant throughout African societies in the throes of war.

The Global and African Evolution of Humanitarianism

According to Michael Barnett (2011), humanitarianism is approximately two centuries old. It was roughly at the turn of the nineteenth century that humanitarianism became part of people's ordinary vocabulary.

Barnett starts his delineation of the trajectory of humanitarianism with the story of Geneva businessman Henry Dunant, whose 1862 memoir about the aftermath of the battle of Solferino during the Second Italian War of Independence motivated the creation of the International Committee of the Red Cross (ICRC) and the Geneva Convention. Dunant had traveled to Italy, hoping to gain the support of government officials for his planned commercial ventures in Algeria. While there, he witnessed the carnage and the miseries of injured French and Austro Hungarian soldiers, who had been abandoned to die on the battlefield near the village of Solferino after fighting for their countries' control of Italian states. Appalled, he organized local townspeople to treat the wounded regardless of their nationality. The spirit of volunteerism animating Dunant, Barnett avers, was a watershed moment in the history of modern humanism.

More generally, the concept and practice of humanitarianism can be situated within a broader international politics. A voluminous literature traces the origin of humanitarianism and its cardinal precepts to activities carried out in the aftermath of slave revolts, earthquakes, and wars across the globe. The abolitionist movement in the United States in the eighteenth and nineteenth centuries has also been recorded as a watershed event that helped translate humanitarianism into concrete actions thought to assuage human suffering.

Barnett identifies three stages of humanitarianism: (a) imperial humanitarianism, beginning with the onset of colonization and the missionary work that accompanied it until World War II; (b) neo-humanitarianism, beginning roughly at the end of World War II and continuing through the end of the Cold War; and (c) post–Cold War liberal humanitarianism, which he describes as "alchemical," when aid became linked to involvement in the underlying causes of conflicts that generate the need for it in the first place.

In the African context, comparisons between the discourses and practices of contemporary humanitarianism with those of its colonial counterpart thus cannot be helped. Nineteenth- and twentieth-century missionaries practiced a brand of humanitarianism designed to civilize and Christianize the presumably godless, atavistic populations scattered over an uncongenial African terrain. They and their colonizing allies were very clear about who was or was not civilized, and who had the potential of becoming civilized. In colonial Sudan, for example, the British encouraged Christian missionaries to introduce health care and education to local populations, initiatives that became an important factor in the formation of a Southern Christian educated elite who were allied with the British colonial government and, after independence, took part in the government, even when it waged war against the South. The colonially supported missionary work was part of a larger policy adopted ostensibly to protect poor, benighted, black Africans from exploitation by Arab merchants and the influence of Islam and to render them capable of dealing with the modern world on terms the British thought proper. Both the "colonizability" and "civilizability" of Africans were justified as protection and rescue, an attitude that continued in the dispensation of aid in the post–Cold War area.

In *Humanitarianism Contested*, Barnett and Thomas Weiss elucidate the core doctrines of modern humanitarianism as being rooted in the ethics of "humanity, impartiality, neutrality, independence, voluntary service, unity, and universality" (2011, 9). Only lately have scholars been drawn to the exercise of unmasking humanitarianism's marked ideological character and the political nature that has prevailed in the post–Cold War period, with negative effects on the countries whose suffering humanitarians are attempting to allay.

The existential conditions warranting humanitarian response in postcolonial Africa are incontestably real. However, the ordeal of African suffering as seen by the humanitarian sensibility inspires the irresistible urge to recycle narratives of othering that animated encounters with Africans throughout the colonial period and have persisted with tenacity into the postcolonial present. In a critical analysis of humanitarianism that draws from African situations, Roberto Belloni argues that it demonstrates propensities to broadcast sweeping generalizations, misapprehend reality, fan the flames of political violence by prompting people to escalate violence, and prolong war and distress. In addition, it supports organizational dysfunctionality, highlights associations with perpetrators of violence if need be, and reproduces the pervasive inequalities it professes to thwart when unconditionally giving undivided attention to all victims. Using the examples of Sudan and Rwanda, he suggests that humanitarianism has more to do with power and containment than it does with altruism, and that, rather than addressing the problem of human suffering, humanitarianism is as best useless and at worst harmful. Humanitarianism's core ethos of neutrality vis-à-vis the needs of others is thus forfeited.

Within the humanitarian structures being set up in Africa, limitations abound. Humanitarian agencies often handle perpetrators of civil violence in order to effect aid delivery. They are often selective in reporting crises if the perpetrators happen to fall within their notions of the appropriate victim. And they may work with entities (as happened in Somalia) to secure their own continuing presence in the country. For example, John Prendergast, the president of the nonprofit organization Enough and a founding member of the Save Darfur Coalition, has, in numerous reports and testimonies, stressed the need for intervention in Darfur, the region in western Sudan where observers have described the presence of genocide and ethnic cleansing since 2003, when armed groups attacked government facilities there. Two days after Barack Obama was elected to the US presidency in 2008, Prendergast and his colleagues wrote him a letter urging decisive action toward Darfur and encouraging military intervention. By not intervening in the conflict, they insisted, the US became complicit in the perpetration of violence. Similar calls were made before the United States Senate Foreign Relations Committee as well as the House Appropriation Subcommittee that same year. Enough's calls for rescue of the "indigenous black tribes of Fur, Zaghawa, and Massalit" of Darfur from Arab militants highlight a persistent pattern of humanitarianism's embeddedness in a broader international order tolerant of the reductive labeling of victims and villains.

The Position and Problems of Humanitiarianism in Africa

Unquestionably, the descent of a growing number of postcolonial countries in Africa into internal conflicts, territorial partition, and social inequality has intensified the need for humanitarian aid aimed at mitigating the suffering of postcolonial subjects. However, in the large body of literature written since the 1990s, the concept of "failed" or "fragile states" has gained momentum and served as a pretext for intervention. African spaces now depicted as collapsing, fragile, or failing are deemed to be "ungovernable," a danger to themselves and others beyond their frontiers. The "Fragile States Index," published in *Foreign Policy Magazine* in 2014, identified fifty-nine states as "failed." Strong evidence indicates that the knowledge stable governments and triumphant states produce about the failure of other states omits the formers' support of repressive regimes and their imposition of sanctions that have prevented ordinary citizens access to the bare necessities of life. Despite the boon of independence, the colonial oppression the continent endured has been reincarnated in postcolonial elites' perpetuation of poverty, socioeconomic disparities, hierarchy, and the reproduction of the colonial episteme. Despite the historic roots and ongoing existence of these problems, humanitarianism in Africa has focused on crises warranting intervention as if they were irrational and unpredictable events, a perspective only exacerbated by media images of Africa's postcolonial victimhood. The conflation of myth with reality remains.

Humanitarians' continued use of forceful language, replete with verbs like "should" and "need," and escalating to "must," coupled with their increased calls for military intervention throughout the continent, further expose the highly ideological nature of a concept that is supposed to be based on ideas of inalienable, universal humanity and illustrate the inextricable link between humanitarianism and politics. That this sort of rhetoric and appeal to militarism resemble the *Pax Britannica* imposed during the colonial era was not lost on the Paris surrealists as early as 1932, when they authored "Murderous Humanitarianism," a statement expressing concern about the perils of colonialism and humanitarianism in Africa. A *Pax-Humanitariana*, if we can call it that, seems at this political juncture a successor to the colonial effort to pacify and subdue ungovernable and rebellious bodies. In his *Disaster Gypsies*, John Norris demonstrates how humanitarian aid flow to Sierra Leonean refugees in Liberia masked international support of despotic rule in Liberia, which itself was a cause of the crisis in West Africa. Recent calls to intervene on behalf of the dominant Hema in their conflict with the Lendu in the Democratic Republic of Congo and on behalf of the Tutsi in their conflict with the Hutu in Rwanda further exemplify the way contemporary humanitarianism both creates and supports polarizing categorization among African peoples. Regardless of this tendency, activists consider themselves to be the arbiters of truth and the ultimate authorities on the nature and causes of conflicts they purport to ameliorate.

Humanitarian myths are further rendered hollow when producers of these categories assume they are authorized to speak on behalf of victims, appropriating their suffering for their own purposes and denying them the right to tell their own stories. Since humanitarians are acting as arbiters of truth, the representations of the continent that they perpetuate are critical. V. Y. Mudimbe asks probing questions in other contexts that are germane to Africa: "Who is speaking about it? Who has the right and the credentials to produce it, describe it, comment on upon it, or at least represent it"? (1988, x). When a Sudanese translator accompanied a Dutch team to Darfur to collect stories about rape perpetrated by Arabs as a weapon of war, an interviewee mentioned that she was sexually violated by another refugee. Once this information was translated to the team of humanitarians, the translator was rebuked for her perceived failure to ask the victim to confess that her rapist was "Arab" and "Janjaweed" (personal communication Durham, UK, in July 2007), rather than a fellow refugee from a non-Arab ethnic group. The assumption that the interpreter had failed to get her to name the "real" criminal exemplifies how humanitarians reject stories that do not conform to their worldviews.

We can also consider here the position of humanitarians vis-à-vis Ethiopia. The brutal Italian invasion of 1935 did not inspire humanitarian organizations such as the International Committee of the Red Cross to provide aid, as sympathy lay largely with the Italians who were seen as saving the Ethiopians from the threat of Bolshevism. In the early 1980s, facing the prospect of famine, aid agencies managed to create what they called an early warning system, which gave them advance warning of a likely famine. However, when the system predicted famine, Cold War alignments caused the administration of US President Ronald Reagan to shun proposals for aid. The Ethiopian government also resented calls for intervention in domestic programs of resettlement and decided to undertake massive evictions of the ICRC's personnel. Observers noted that the effectiveness of humanitarian responses to the famine, including that of the ICRC, was minimal.

The negligible response of the ICRC in Ethiopia, however, was not necessarily characteristic of its responses in another African situation. During the war Igbo speakers waged to gain independence from Nigeria and establish the Republic of Biafra, the organization challenged the Nigerian government's blockade of aid to starving Biafrans, an act that incited the killing of humanitarian workers. On June 5, 1969, Nigeria shot down an ICRC aircraft, and the ICRC continued to provide aid in spite of these challenges. This response itself raises several questions that get at the heart of the humanitarian dilemma today. Do we consider the ICRC's challenge to the Nigerian blockade of aid a positive or negative thing? Do we view the ICRC's decision to continue flights without the consent of the government admirable or not? The ICRC's evasion of the blockade was the beginning of calls for military intervention by European and American forces. Is such intervention a humanitarian act? The extent of the involvement of ICRC and the extent to which they challenged the Nigerian government demonstrate how this situation was more than a humanitarian issue.

During the civil war in Rwanda, calls for humanitarian response and military intervention by NGOs far outweighed the actual response by the international community. Later, the devastation that occurred in Rwanda haunted the West. Barnett has argued that it is what happened in Rwanda that has motivated Rwandans to see themselves as invested with the "responsibility to protect." Survivors were atoning for their sins while keeping alive the memory of the dead. However, these sentiments have done little to mitigate massive violence elsewhere on the continent.

Discussion of humanitarianism in Africa requires a closer look at the way representations of Africa and Africans affect specific forms of humanitarians' power and knowledge. Humanitarians' presumed expertise, asserted because they have witnessed conditions in Africa firsthand, makes them arbiters of truth. But the limitations on their ability to grasp events in their totality only highlight the politicized nature of the knowledge to which they lay claim. Examples of the effect of such claims on victimization and suffering cut across a large swath of the continent. In the Sudan, Ethiopia, and Somalia, humanitarians' involvement in foreign policy, ranging from calling for military invention to giving eye-witness testimony in support of one faction against another, led to their systematic eviction and denial of their own ability to provide aid. Humanitarian projects, in deciding whom to focus on, espouse dichotomies and classifications of African populations hailing from different ethnicities, a tendency that again belies humanitarianism's core precepts of neutrality and impartiality. Prescriptively oversimplified perspectives on the racialized victim not only rest on binary representations of victim and villain, good and evil, but also further the continued polarizing of Africa's polities and identities.

What, then, can we glean from the facts on the ground, and the realities of humanitarian discourse and practice? In *Forces of Compassion*, anthropologists Erica Bronstein and Peter Redfield draw upon examples from the work of Médecins Sans Frontières (MSF) in Africa and elsewhere to demonstrate the difficulties arising from claims to impartiality that nonetheless gloss over competing interpretations, histories, contexts, and practices. When Somalia unraveled as a state, for example, MSF relied upon clans for aid delivery when it was politically expedient to do so, despite the clans' controversial role in the perpetuation of violence. Impartiality, understood as a fundamental belief in a universal humanity, is thus relational rather than absolute: the conditions that render it possible or impossible cannot be extracted from the specificities of the political contexts in which it is enacted. In these and other cases, humanitarians' partisan actions under the guise of their "responsibility to protect" exceed their insistence on allaying suffering. Riina Yrjölä (2009) identifies how this language serves as an instrument of power. She argues that by presenting humanitarianism as a moral duty, these discourses not only provide a justification for continued Western intervention in Africa but also reproduce a certain vision of the world in which the Global South remains subordinate to the Global North.

There is yet another problematic which remains organic to the humanitarian discourse. It is a question of how victimhood gets defined. Conversely, the needy victim's worthiness is largely determined by reductive reasoning that defines recipients and bestows aid on the basis of imagined tribal differences among various African communities rather than that on the immediacy of need. Humanitarian discourse that seems on the surface to be justifiable often only serves to perpetuate oversimplifications. Dichotomous thinking was clear in the humanitarian invention of ethnic categories in Darfur, identifying Darfurians as either African or Arab. Within this classification, the Darfur Arabs were represented only as colonizing settlers within the region and presumed guilty of war crimes regardless of their position in the violence. All were thought to be either Janjaweed, those "devils on horsebacks," or Janjaweed sympathizers, epithets that denoted ethnic identities devoid of context, which the international community has taken little trouble to learn.

As their relationship to the conflicts in Africa changed from the delivery of emergency aid to activism for intervention, humanitarians also increasingly relied on images of victimization and suffering to garner necessary support. In particular, they involved celebrities interested in embracing the power of humanitarianism to burnish their images. After actor George Clooney became involved in the Save Darfur movement and his subsequent visit to the region, Maeve Sharlaw pointedly asked in *The Guardian* whether his heavily mediatized intervention had actually changed anything in the lives of people in Darfur. With a few exceptions, responses from the public expressed considerable skepticism. If posed to cultural critic Lilie Chouliaraki, her reply would have been squarely positioned in a neocolonial context to read as follows:

> The neocolonial argument situates celebrity humanitarianism within an orientalist discourse of the "white man's burden": images of beautiful people in stark contrast to the African poor perpetuate historical relationships of power. . . . In so doing, the celebrity seeks to conceal a scandalous contradiction: by appearing to care for the "wretched of the earth" whilst enjoying

> the privilege of rare wealth, he or she glosses over the ongoing complicity of the West in a global system of injustice that reproduces the dependence of the developing world through acts of charity (2012, 4).

As the involvement of a number of celebrities suggests, in recent decades humanitarian organizations have increasingly adopted corporate modes of operation, including competition for funding, the replacement of volunteers with highly paid professionals, and the drive to establish spheres of influence within Africa similar to those established by earlier missionaries. Even as humanitarians continue to present themselves as experts of local conditions and therefore able to maintain an apolitical stance, corporatization and commodification of compassion and the creation of a humanitarian establishment in Africa increases. What happens when "morals and money" become inextricably linked? Agencies largely understand that by publicizing the suffering of some to generate the financial support needed to relieve the suffering of many, they run the risk of exploiting those they seek help. Yet they see the commodification of suffering as a necessary evil.

The corporatization of humanitarianism as played out in Africa thus reflects a burgeoning enterprise in which compassion and charity become subject to the ebb and flow of market relations. Funding represents what Ian Smillie and Larry Minear call a "political calculation," including whether or not to cooperate with military governments. Humanitarian action is influenced by the interests of givers, which are so diverse as to preclude any attempt to catalogue them. This constellation of contradictory relations helps explain the commodification of the needy African and unravel some of the inequalities among competing victims. In Darfur, for example, unfolding hierarchies spawned a selectively inscribed humanitarian definition of the worthy recipient of aid as indigenous black Africans, including Zaghawa, Fur, and Masaleet. Conversely the non-worthy victim was defined as any community or individual outside these three groups, including Arabs.

Conclusion

An anthropological perspective on gift giving and receiving is relevant here, where gift giving is anchored in the unequal relationship between the affluent giver and the beseeching recipient. The superiority of the giver, although implicit, is critical in this transaction. Examined from this vantage point, the political construction of emotions embedded in humanitarianism is unmasked. As the Somali novelist Nuruddin Farah argues in his *Gifts*, the knotted web of the self-interests of the giver and the hopelessness of the receiver cannot be treated in the absence of power politics. And in this, the internal logic [or structure] of contemporary humanitarianism is not all that different from the colonialism of the previous era.

The moral sentiments of compassion and pity are impossible to apprehend in isolation from humanitarians' claims to authority and involvement with governmental regimes in Africa. The existential realities of Africa prevent Africans and humanitarians from coming together as equals. The exchange between the two is one of asymmetrical power. The emotions of pity and compassion peddled by the humanitarian industry carry what linguist Anna Wierzbicka calls "the whiff of superiority." Of necessity, the kind of humanitarianism practiced in Africa depends for its very existence on victims and on the longevity of their victimhood within an enterprise that has become more professionalized and corporatized and long given up any semblance of "neutrality." The underlying emotions of compassion that animate humanitarian response are rooted in specific rescue regimes that bear a striking resemblance to the paternalism of colonialism vis-à-vis formerly colonized subjects.

While acknowledging the conditions that have called forth humanitarian aid, at its root humanitarianism, especially in the context of African conflicts, is a postcolonial encounter. Contradictory to their core principles of neutrality and impartiality, humanitarians' application of dichotomous typologies and classifications, divides up societies as either victim or villain, good or evil. Salvationist sentiments notwithstanding, these descriptions are in a similar vein to those of colonists in the continent. Mahmood Mamdani (2009) is correct to refer to such production as an example of "writing race into history." Humanitarians' asserted expertise on African conditions highlights the politicized nature of the very knowledge to which they lay claim and prompts questions as to whether it is a rendition of colonialism for the postcolonial era.

Suggested Readings

Abusharat, Rogaia Mustafa. 2013. "Seeds of Secession." *Transition: An International Review* 110: 73–89

Barnett, Michael. 2011. *Empire of Humanity: A History of Humanitarianism*. Ithaca, NY: Cornell University Press.

Barnett, Michael, and Thomas G. Weiss. 2011. *Humanitarianism Contested: Where Angels Fear to Tread*. New York: Routledge

Belloni, Roberto. 2007. "The Trouble with Humanitarianism." *Review of International Studies* 33 (3): 451–74.

Bornstein, Erica, and Peter Redfield. 2011. *Forces of Compassion: Humanitarianism between Ethics and Politics*. Santa Fe, NM: School for Advanced Research Press.

Césaire, Aimé. 2001. *Discourse on Colonialism*. Translated by Joan Pinkham. New York: Monthly Review Press.

Chandler, David. 2004. "The Responsibility to Protect? Imposing the 'Liberal Peace.'" *International Peacekeeping* 11 (1): 59–81.

Chouliaraki, Lilie. 2012. "The Theatricality of Humanitarianism: A Critique of Celebrity Advocacy." *Communication and Critical/Cultural Studies* 9 (1): 1–21.

Kennedy, David. 2004. *The Dark Side of Virtue*. Princeton, NJ: Princeton University Press.

Mamdani, Mahmood. 2009. *Saviors and Survivors: Darfur, Politics, and the War on Terror*. New York: Pantheon.

Norris, John. 2007. *The Disaster Gypsies: Humanitarian Workers in the World's Deadliest Conflicts*. Westport, CT: Greenwood.

Patrick, Stewart. 2011. *Weak Links: Fragile States, Global Threats, and International Security*. New York: Oxford University Press.

Reiff, David. 2003. *A Bed for the Night: Humanitarianism in Crisis*. New York: Simon & Schuster.

Smillie, Ian, and Larry Minear. 2004. *The Charity of Nations: Humanitarian Action in a Calculating World*. Bloomfield, CT: Kumarian Press.

Styan, David. 2012. "EU Power and Armed Humanitarianism in Africa: Evaluating ESDP in Chad." *Cambridge Review of International Affairs* 25 (4): 651–68.

Weiss, Thomas G. 2004. "The Sunset of Humanitarian Response? The Responsibility to Protect in a Unipolar Era." *Security Dialogue* 35 (2): 135–53.

Wierzbicka, Anna. 1999. *Emotions across Languages and Cultures: Diversity and Universals*. Cambridge: Cambridge University Press.

Yrjölä, Riina. 2009. "The Invisible Violence of Celebrity Humanitarianism: Soft Images and Hard Words in the Making and Unmaking of Africa." *World Political Science Review* 5 (1). Published online 2009-11-17. ISSN (online) 2363-4782; ISSN (print) 2363-4774. https://doi.org/10.2202/1935-6226.1072. Accessed October 14, 2016.

13 LABOR

Jane I. Guyer

Our analytical concepts in the political and economic domains of African studies derive largely from European languages, where their use first developed specifically within European history, and were then applied to Africa through trade, colonial rule, and the demands of international reporting after independence. The terms we use became an enduring lingua franca for all formal domains of life, in countries where the populations speak a diversity of languages in daily life, and where exact precision in translation from African to European terms can be impossible. Such concepts, however, have also not been consistently stable in the European contexts in which they were developed over the centuries. Labor falls into that category. It has a history and variability of application, and there were debates and discussions over a very long period, particularly in England, during which its applications developed from the English language tradition where the terms *labor* and *work* were applied differently, in both the social and economic spheres. These two terms also changed over time, under shifting political regimes, especially in formal quantitative and legal contexts. Consequently, the exact use of both terms in public and intellectual life needs to be examined in each case, and particularly where the economic dynamics of value creation and measurement, and the politics of control, are at stake.

The Terms "Labor" and "Work"

As a critical concept, whose diverse and changing uses deserve very close attention, we start from the European crafting of the term *labor*, over time, then move to its application in African public life and intellectual analysis, and then to the specific concepts within Africa's own societies and languages. We bring up the question of whether African languages and cultures make similar, or completely different, conceptual distinctions, and therefore how the terms that were developed in Europe have been engaged in African political and economic life. The two main themes here, then, are both focused on how the conceptual terms differ in different milieux: (1) in places, times, and politico-theoretical contexts; and (2) for populations who derive their concepts from different languages and cultural histories.

Labor has a long history in European social theory and public life, from which it was applied to the colonial world. In English, the concepts of *labor* and *work* derive from different etymologies. *Labor* comes from the Latinate legal vocabulary of the dominant class (the Norman-French aristocracy of England, after the Conquest), applying simply to physical effort. For example, the Africans who were traded into slavery did slave *labor*. *Work*, by contrast, is from old German, deriving from the craft trades, and thereby implies skill. These two terms have not always been used either consistently or precisely, but both have been brought forward into the present. In more detail: from its origin, the term *labor* derives from the verb *labourer* which refers to tilling of the ground, and where it is used in distinction from *travail*, which is usually translated into English as "work." In modern French, so also in the francophone African world, *travail* is used in many of the sociopolitical senses where *labor* would be used in English, such as *Ministère du Travail* (Ministry of Labor); *travail forcé* (forced labor).

The concept of *work*, by contrast with *labor*, in English depicts what people actually do and make, in all its variety, including by gender and social class: housework, office work, craftwork, and so on. The most straightforward way to understand a literature that may use the concept of *labor* in varied ways—by place, topic, and theoretical orientation of the scholar—is by simply following the words and examining how they are used, both intellectually and in the world. Here Marx offers a valuable guide. As a native speaker of German, he noted the English propensity to "use a Teutonic word for the actual thing, and a Romance word for its reflexion" (that is, for abstraction) (footnote 1 in chap. 1 of Capital). His own signal example is "worth" (in Teutonic terms) and "value" (in Romance terms). Here we have "labor," in the Romance vocabulary, and "work" in the Germanic vocabulary. *Labor*, then, implies a measurable variable, to be controlled and counted, whereas *work* depicts the multifarious actual tasks that people do.

Over the transition from feudal to industrial production, and then to financial capitalism, labor came to designate measurable human effort, among the factors of production: land, labor, and capital. These are all acquired on the factor market, and combined and controlled to produce goods for the commodity market. *Labor*, as a term, thereby became most applicable to contexts where measurement and comparison were the technical purpose, and where control and management were the social and political purpose. This promoted the use of inclusive terms such as *labor force*, *wage labor*, and *labor laws*, created for analysis and administration. There developed ministries of labor (in government, for supervision of conditions), labor economics (a field within the economics profession), and concepts in regulatory law—for example, child labor—with respect to legal conditions.

Theory could then become generally applicable, such as the labor theory of value (Adam Smith, Karl Marx): that the value of commodities derives from the "socially necessary" labor time to produce them. Work remained in the vernacular register of meaning, in the practical world of place, skill, personhood, and cooperation (working men's clubs). In the public sphere, however, the term *labor movement* was taken up by advocates for better conditions and stronger representation. Labor parties were founded in democratic political life, so political dynamics were also implied by the word *labor*, from the nineteenth century onward.

As an increasingly inclusive concept, *labor* could then be divided into subcategories according to conditions of mobilization, control, and productivity. The idea of a whole productive process composed of different parts gave Emile Durkheim, considered a major founder of modern social science, a much broader image of society, as in his *The Division of Labor in Society* (1893) (*Travail*, in the original French). The social dynamics of organization and control implied in the concept of "division of labor" is later applied to the sexual (later, gender) division of labor, as gender studies developed.

Over these shifting political and analytical uses of the vocabulary, labor came to have a certain social class implication, whereas the poor and the craftsmen still referred to themselves as "the industrious classes" in the late eighteenth century or "the working class" (see E. P. Thompson 1963) in the nineteenth century. The difference between work and labor became an explicit philosophical theme in the mid-twentieth century. For example, in Hannah Arendt's analysis, in *The Human Condition* (1958), the difference between *labor* and *work* is defined such that the former is repetitive, concerned with reproduction and necessities, and the latter can be aspirational and creative, creating tangible products beyond necessity, including the products of intellectual work.

So *labor* is a concept to be understood broadly and historically, and also to be examined carefully in each particular use. For example, categories of work are generally depicted as labor when it is their status relative to the law, rather than what they actually do, that is at stake: slave labor, migrant labor, indentured labor, domestic labor, farm labor, child labor, seasonal labor, day labor, and others. When the tasks that they actually fulfill are at stake, the words *work* and *worker* are more often deployed. In summary, the overlap, and yet also distinction, between *labor* and *work* in English is important to pay attention to, since it carries political and analytical implications that are particularly relevant when examining closely their application outside Europe, across different languages, and under rapidly changing political-economic conditions, as in the colonial and postcolonial worlds. How did these conceptual shifts apply to African economic change?

The Literature on Labor and Work

The most voluminous literature that deploys the concept of labor in African studies is historical, since it is concerned with the colonial project of creating a labor force from a population of independent producers and traders. Critical social historical scholarship would refer to the West's gains as extractive processes that used outright violence or colonial domination to establish inferior status and thereby a nonmarket, or only partially market-governed, process of value creation. The foothold of capitalism in Africa has a specific history: the purchase and sale of people themselves as commodities, as slaves; the acquisition of land mainly by conquest or states' rights, without purchase, including for highly profitable mineral extraction; a long colonial history of forced recruitment for large public projects; the recruitment of African men into proletarian status in essential sectors such as plantations and ports (Cooper 1980; 1996); the intricate, racially discriminatory legal regimes for the supply of labor to large businesses, such as the mines, in Southern Africa (Murray 1981).

Into the present, much of the commodity supply economy is still defined as "informal," so outside of formally defined factor markets and considered recalcitrant to the frameworks of the law and status, such as taxation, standards, and reporting. This is rarely referred to as labor. There are, therefore, and even in European and American scholarship, some theoretical variations in how the term "labor" is used. One emphasis is largely sociopolitical with respect to labor as a political category, with its own subdivisions. The other one extends the analytical potential with respect to measurement and comparison of hours worked, productivity, earnings (returns to labor), and the cost of their constant reproduction.

Bill Freund made a comprehensive review of the history of this literature in 1984. He points to the first major compendium on the topic, published in 1928: Raymond Buell's *The Native Problem in Africa*. The problem was always the inconstancy of the labor supply. As long as Africans had access to land, their rhythms of work would be set by their own targets in life and livelihood. The "freedom" of labor that had been produced by the enclosures in Britain was in fact a constraint for the workers themselves. Constraints would be put in place to free up "labor" for deployment in colonial enterprises. W. Arthur Lewis, Caribbean winner of the Nobel Prize in economics in 1979, developed a theory that did justice to the worker's perspective when he developed the concept of "the backward-bending supply curve of labor," using colonial data, showing that free workers who have their own means of production are target-workers when it comes to labor for others. The higher the wage the sooner they may return to their own livelihoods. He aimed to depict "economic growth with unlimited supplies of labor" (1955). The political economic logic of profit and control by large enterprises and the state would then favor precisely the kinds of constraint and low wages that Freund and Frederick Cooper both document for African history.

Cooper's (1996) comprehensive history of the labor force, labor policy, and labor organizations during the independence period moves from the imperial legal framework to the nationalist framework for labor laws and negotiations. He addresses the new regimes of sovereignty and the challenge of creating the kind of "free labor" that classic European working-class history had been based on, on a continent where work for companies and governments had rarely been based on regimes of freedom and on labor markets for recruitment and wage-setting.

The Southern African history of labor pays particularly close attention to dispossession and the legal framing of forms of citizenship that required labor migration and personal documentation through pass laws for travel, segregated residence, and labor in a large formal economy, including in domestic service for the elite, usually white (Hansen 1989). One source on dispossession that offers details of the implementation of a project that purposely created systematic conditions of land shortage and livelihood uncertainty for the people, and labor constraints on the terms of their participation in the economy is a study entitled *The Surplus People Project* (1983), whose name evokes the "reserve army" concept. It documents, in five volumes of detail, the eviction of African landowners, and others, from what were called "black spots" in desirable farming areas for the white population, in South Africa under apartheid. James Ferguson's (1999) ethnography of unemployed miners in Zambia in the postcolonial period examines the fate of labor that had been recruited under colonial conditions, now in a post-wage era.

These postcolonial sources give complementary empirical accounts of the formal sector labor force, which is now actively present in political life. A major innovation in the use of the concept of labor for the present, particularly the post-industrial economies of the twenty-first century, is Ferguson's (2015) book on "the new politics of distribution" in South Africa. Ferguson treats labor, in the wage sense, as a historical creation, and then extends the concept to include the supervision and mediation of the new economy of cash distribution, which he terms "distributive labor." This is labor in the sense of organized, measurable effort within the whole economic system; its functioning is central to the money-mediated economy as is production; and indeed—in the new economy in particular, but also more generally—the capacity to produce at all is dependent on effective redistributive mechanisms of the many formal and informal kinds which keep resources and money circulating and nourishing productive endeavors (2015, 45). Here the term "labor" still implies system and organization, but it also combines with the use of work to describe what is actually done, in all its detail and qualitative variety. For example, one subheading is "Distributive Labor and the Hard Work of Dependence" (94).

In African studies, then, the status designation of labor can allude to slave labor, forced labor, migrant labor, female labor, child labor, seasonal labor, and others, depending on the scholar, the legal framework of the case, and the topic under study. The term designates status in general, and also occupations such as mine labor and farm labor. For self-employed occupations, "work" is more commonly used, such as market workers, transport workers, and so on, in informal and short-term employment. "Laborer," however, is more commonly used for those whose work falls under the authority of others and who—if not slaves—are directly paid, in cash or in kind.

These categories facilitate the grouping of different cases across time and space, in ways that make possible comparison and analysis, including eventually with other parts of the world and in relation to theory itself. In some economic studies, this also allows the quantitative value of the work done by people who fall into that category to be studied and compared. For example, in the 1970s, feminist economics turned the "housework" of wives into "domestic labor," and started to quantify the monetary value that women add by "stretching the wage." In African studies, however, most of these categories of labor have been set up for analytical purposes that have focused on the *conditions of control* under which people work and their *social status*, rather than on analyzing the monetary value of the work itself ("returns to labor"), which can be exceptionally complicated to do across currency zones, eras of history, and self-employment situations. Slave labor varies widely in the value it produces, depending on the products; forced labor for colonial governments was a kind of tax, for public infrastructure projects for which no other labor force was available; the value produced by migrant labor, and its remuneration, depends entirely on its political control and the kind of work that it does.

Measurement becomes a challenge for scholarship, as well as for the authorities, especially for self-employed populations, but the concern with gender differences encouraged further thought. Following the publication of Ester Boserup's highly influential *Conditions of Agricultural Growth* (1965), comparative interest intensified in the kind of farming system common in historical Africa: under conditions of low population density with women playing an important enough role for some of these to be depicted as "female farming systems." Ken Swindell's (1985) summary entitled *Farm Labour*, a short but highly informed book focused on domestic organization, is a very good source on both the descriptive work on African farming at that time, and also on the deployment of the terms "labor" and "work." Where "mobilization, control and organization of farm labour" (3) is the theme, "labor" is the term used. Where its distribution by task and season is graphed, "work" is discussed, according to "patterns" in the tasks. When Swindell turns back to numbers of hours, crop yields, and conditions of hire, he uses "labor" again, as, for example, in his graph on "labor bottlenecks" (164) taken from a paper by J. Karimu and Paul Richards (1980).

In the 1980s there was a burst of empirical studies published about women in African economies, which focused not only on what women did as workers, but on their own control of the produce and income from their labors. The move toward quantification in farming and the informal sector allowed terms such as "returns to labor" and the "division of labor" to open up comparison: between men and women, and between different occupations. A paper of my own (Guyer 1980) compared the complementarity of male and female work and income control in two cocoa-producing societies. Another (Guyer 1988) reviewed the ways in which female labor had been combined with male labor, over time, in relation to value and control. Several further contributions focused on income itself, but only implicitly referring to women's control of their own "labor." The expansion of the ethnography of trade and informal sector enterprise, such as Clark's (1994) study of Ghanaian market women, hardly used a concept with the analytical weight of "labor," and indeed we might see the gender issues as reopening the question of "work" for European scholars, which then complements an African scholarship that moves away from labor in order to bring to the fore Africans' own conceptions of work.

Moving closer to current studies on labor, as a subject of research and concept for analysis, we can point to the innovations being produced as now opening up much closer attention to Africa's own concepts, which so far have fallen mainly under the English term "work." As exemplified above, the concept of labor tends to imply that tasks are undertaken under authoritative control of some kind. Even where this is not the guiding definition, as in Swindell's book, "organization" still lies at the heart of the topic. By contrast, there is an interesting revival in certain key African studies scholarship of the use of "work" to open up the question of self-direction and innovation, in action, by those who have the expertise and the latitude to be inventive, for themselves and in their own ways. In this usage, the "actual," to which Marx drew attention, is the moment when all the faculties of a person's mind, skills, and toolsets meet with the tangible contexts in which action is called for. In some domains of life, the uncertainty of things—weather, markets, health, ecological shifts, and so on—makes people's capacity to invent and develop new trajectories, however mundane, in productive life, of central importance. I had this orientation in mind in my article entitled "Traditions of Invention" (Guyer 1996), although it was not focused primarily on production itself, or on work/labor defined as such. People were seen as doing all kinds of expressive works that had social implications: carving spoons and images, forging iron, applying medicinal cures, building houses and canoes, hunting, conversing with the spirits of the forest, dancing, fishing, and so on.

At this frontier of thinking, particularly by African scholars, we find the term "labor" used in reference mainly to a politics of resistance and "work" in the context of local innovation. Elias Mandala's history of *Work and Control in a Peasant Economy* (1990) blazes a trail in this regard, as one can see from his chapter titles: "Resistance to Capitalist Colonial Labor Regimes, 1875–1923" (chapter 3); "The Land, Work, and Workers in Cotton Agriculture" (chapter 4, section 1), which the peasants themselves integrated with their patterns of production for millet and other food crops, evading the strict rules of blueprints sent to them by the colonial government, and creating possibilities for themselves. Agricultural laborers were experienced in running multi-crop and intercropping systems, with their own practices of fallow; hence the idea of a mono-crop and a singular labor regime was not only a political imposition on them but an ignorant intervention into an ecological microcosm, where "soil types, rainfall patterns, crop diseases and ecological fluctuations . . . can affect the labor process in many significant ways . . . often ignored in the literature" (1990, 271).

Clapperton Mavhunga's (2014) book on people's ecological management of game and the environment in Zambia and Zimbabwe goes even further in examining the actual science of those continual adaptations in what he calls *Transient Workspaces*. *Work* here refers to tasks and innovations, undertaken by "the professoriate of the hunt"—that is, people with profound learned and experienced knowledge of the uncertain, complex, and changing environments that they share with other beings of all kinds: flora, fauna, and human neighbors. He offers very detailed descriptions of the kind of "work" that "innovation" is, and he offers us terms within the Shona language that translate with difficulty into European concepts, so they do indicate the divergence in our understandings of the complex of dynamics around understandings of work. The word *nzira* "means a way (of doing things)"; "mobility as creative work . . . a quest for opportunities, or simply an anticipative mode," "technology as a way of doing . . . [a]s expertise, *unyanzvi* is a combination of *shavé* (spirit), *chipo* (talent. pl. *zvipo*), *zvidobi* (skills) and *ruzivo* (knowledge)." All of these practices depend on the guidance of the ancestors, consultation with the spirits of the dead, and observation of codes of conduct (taboos). People also developed collaborative modes through what they called *hlengwe*, gathering (Mavhunga 2014, 17–18). He calls the whole complex one of "everyday innovation." This frontier of appreciation for work and knowledge within Africa is a growing area, and is very unlikely to be designated as "labor," since it configures many qualities, rather than searching for a single variable to measure.

Conclusion

To reiterate, the one place where daily innovation has been accepted as constitutive of economic life is in what was designated as "the informal sector," so altogether outside of direct central control. Markets and small-scale specialist expertise have generally been described in terms of work, and they may well have been less subjected to case study for explicitly comparative and theoretical purposes than those domains depicted as labor. Nevertheless, they have always been important in the creation of livelihoods, and may well be expanding in importance.

We can infer a guide to future studies from this direction of change. With the shifts in emphasis in African economies toward enterprise and self-employment, which tap into certain past modes of organization, there may well be a change in empirical and analytical attention toward a greater inclusion of work in the sphere that used to be depicted as labor studies, and to people's own concepts for the configuration of their own inputs: effort, skill, imagination, collaboration, and so on. States will still deal with labor policy, and with labor unions, since there will always be a comparative nexus in the international political and economic world. But the new expansion in small-scale business and self-employment within Africa may well offer the terrain on which new analytical innovations will have to be made vis-à-vis the old concept of labor, and these will be informed increasingly by Africa's own concepts and practices, in which innovation and improvisation already figured.

Suggested Readings

Allan, William. 1965. *The African Husbandman*. Westport, CT: Greenwood.

Bay, Edna G., ed. 1982. *Women and Work in Africa*. Boulder, CO: Westview.

Berry, Sara S. 1975. *Cocoa, Custom and Socio-Economic Change in Rural Western Nigeria*. Oxford: Clarendon.

Brautigam, Deborah. 2015. *Will Africa Feed China?* New York: Oxford University Press.

Bryceson, Deborah, ed. 2016. *How Africa Works: Occupational Change, Identity and Morality*. London: Practical Action Publishing.

Clarke, Gracia. 2010. *African Market Women: Seven Life Stories from Ghana*. Bloomington: Indiana University Press.

Guyer, Jane I. 1997. *An African Niche Economy: Farming to Feed Ibadan 1968–88*. Edinburgh: Edinburgh University Press; London: International African Institute.

Hansen, Karen Tranberg. 1997. *Keeping House in Lusaka*. New York: Columbia University Press.

Iyam, David Uru. 1995. *The Broken Hoe: Cultural Reconfiguration in Biase Southeast Nigeria*. Chicago: University of Chicago Press.

Lindell, Ilda, ed. 2010. *Africa's Informal Workers: Collective Agency, Alliances and Transnational Organizing in Urban Africa* (Africa Now). London: Zed.

Murray, Colin. 1981. *Families Divided: The Impact of Migrant Labour in Lesotho*. Cambridge: Cambridge University Press.

Reynolds, Pamela. 1991. *Dance Civet Cat: Child Labour in the Zambezi Valley*. Athens: Ohio University Press.

Robertson, Claire. 1997. *Trouble Showed the Way: Men, Women and Trade in the Nairobi Area 1890–1990*. Bloomington: Indiana University Press.

Ross, Alec. 2016. *Industries of the Future*. New York: Simon & Schuster

Saunders, Richard, and Tinashe Nyamunda. 2016. *Facets of Power: Politics, Profits and People in the Making of Zimbabwe's Blood Diamonds*. Harare, Zimbabwe: Weaver Press.

Spear, Tom. 1997. *Mountain Farmers: Moral Economies of Land and Agricultural Development in Arusha and Meru*. Berkeley: University of California Press.

Swindell, Ken. 1985. *Farm Labour*. Cambridge. Cambridge University Press.

References

Arendt, Hannah. 1958. *The Human Condition*. Garden City, NY: Doubleday.

Booth, Charles. 1892. *Life and Labour of the People in London*. London: Macmillan.

Clark, Gracia. 1994. *Onions Are My Husband: Survival and Accumulation by West African Market Women*. Chicago: University of Chicago Press.

Cooper, Frederick. 1980. *From Slaves to Squatters: Plantation Labor and Africulture in Zanzibar and Coast Kenya, 1890–1925*. New Haven, CT: Yale University Press.

———. 1996. *Decolonization and African Society: The Labor Question in French and British Africa*. Cambridge: Cambridge University Press.

Ferguson, James. 1999. *Expectations of Modernity: Myths and Meanings of Urban Life on the Zambian Copperbelt*. Berkeley: University of California Press.

———. 2015. *Give a Man a Fish: Reflections on the New Politics of Distribution*. Durham, NC: Duke University Press.

Freund, Bill. 1984. "Labor and Labor History in Africa: A Review of the Literature." *African Studies Review* 27 (2): 1–58.

Guyer, Jane I. 1980. "Food, Cocoa and the Division of Labor by Sex in Two West African Societies." *Comparative Studies in Society and History* 22 (3): 355–73.

———. 1988. "The Multiplication of Labor. Historical Methods in the Study of Gender and Agricultural Change in Modern Africa." *Current Anthropology* 29 (2): 247-72.

———. 1996. "Traditions of Invention in Equatorial Africa." *African Studies Review* 39 (3): 1–2.

Hansen, Karen Tranberg. 1989. *Distant Companions: Servants and Employers in Zambia, 1900–1985*. Ithaca, NY: Cornell University Press.

Karimu, J., and Paul Richards. 1980. "The Northern Area Integrated Agricultural Development Programme." Occasional Paper no. 3 (new series). SOAS, Department of Geography.

Lewis, W. Arthur. 1955. *The Theory of Economic Growth*. London: Allen & Unwin.

Mandala, Elias. 1990. *Work and Control in a Peasant Economy: A History of the Lower Tchiri Valley in Malawi, 1859–1960*. Madison: University of Wisconsin Press.

Marx, Karl. 1907. *Capital*. Vol. 1. Edited by Friedrich Engels. Translated by Samuel Moore, Edward Aveling, and Ernest Untermann. Chicago: H. C. Kerr & Co.

Mavhunga, Clapperton. 2014. *Transient Workspaces: Technologies of Everyday Innovation in Zimbabwe*. Cambridge, MA: MIT Press.

Murray, Colin. 1981. *Families Divided: The Impact of Migrant Labour in Lesotho*. Cambridge: Cambridge University Press.

Surplus People Project. 1983. *Forced Removals in South Africa*. Vols. 1–5. Cape Town: Surplus People Project.

Thompson, E. P. 1963. *The Making of the English Working Class*. New York: Pantheon.

14 LIBERATION

Elisabeth McMahon

In 1822, a ship carrying ex-slaves and freeborn African Americans landed at the Cape of Mesurado in Western Africa with the intention of settling a colony for the descendants of former American slaves in Africa. Several different colonies were developed along the "Pepper Coast," which eventually came together to declare themselves the country of Liberia in 1847. These freedmen and women chose to base the name of their new country on the ideal of liberty—what they sought in leaving the United States, a country whose founding documents enshrined white privilege. Liberia has come to represent many of the linguistic illusions and problems of using a Western framework of liberation to establish an egalitarian society in the African continent. The first citizens of Liberia, known as Americo-Liberians, ostensibly liberated themselves from racism by moving "back to Africa." However, the history of discrimination that developed among Americo-Liberians against the indigenous populations of the region reflects the problem of Western liberty—it was always achieved by privileged groups at the expense of less privileged groups. This legacy of eighteenth-century liberation continued through the twentieth century in Africa.

The terminology of liberation, emancipation, and freedom came to Africa through Western interaction with the continent; as European societies enacted their ideas about religion, civility, and power, Africans sought to find a remedy to these new impositions on their societies. While the ideas of freedom or liberty are seemingly universal, at the same time these concepts, as introduced into Africa by Westerners, carry much baggage in how they represent power globally. These ideas almost always imply constraint in some way—freedom from whom or what? Who is doing the liberating? What requirements do emancipators put on liberation? Western traditions offer that freedom, emancipation, and liberation are all positive ideas. Yet, these ideas, foundational to Western ideas of democracy and liberty, impose particular limitations on Africans. In the nineteenth and twentieth centuries Africans mobilized the language of liberation in their efforts to fight against the imposition of Western cultures and political control. Nonetheless, the framework that defines "liberation" as a freedom from the constraints of others in Western societies still lingers in reifying the power imbalance between the West and Africa. Just as the Americo-Liberians' treatment of other Liberians demonstrated the seemingly universal idea that some groups will seek power over others regardless of racial, class, religious, or gender commonalities, their example also reflects the systemic racialized structures that come with the conceptual structure of liberation.

Liberation and the Enlightenment

The ideas of liberty and liberation in Western societies developed in the eighteenth-century revolutions of the United States, France, and Haiti. These three revolutions had a founding impact on later understanding of liberation in Africa. The foundations of liberty used in the eighteenth-century revolutions tied together European cultures with racial politics in a way that has shadowed Africa over the past three centuries. All three revolutions sought to liberate a subset of the population of those countries from the political and economic control by elite, European men. In all three cases, the revolutions did liberate members of the local male elite and middle classes, yet enslavement and servitude continued in various forms within all three countries. Much like in Liberia, in Haiti a subset of African-descended men dominated the larger African-descended populations. While racial identity did not connote power (or lack of power) it did indicate global privilege in the post-Revolutionary world. Haiti and Liberia were both economically isolated regions within the white-dominated global economy of the nineteenth and twentieth centuries. "Liberation" and "freedom" were gendered and racialized economic terms and had little resemblance to the Enlightenment ideal of liberty of the individual.

The modern notion of freedom developed during the Enlightenment in Europe as "freedom from the constraints of the state" (Benjamin Constant quoted in Cranston 1997). Liberty meant having the freedom to be your own authority; free individuals were under their own control. Central to this notion of liberty is a singular individualism that disregarded the greater communal good. Understanding the structure of Enlightenment liberty is crucial to seeing how Thomas Jefferson could write that "all men were created equal" in the US Declaration of Independence and at the same time allow for a clause in the constitution that counted enslaved people as three-fifths of a person for the purposes of legislative representation. Individuals had a right to liberty only if they were white and male. When Europeans began bringing their ideas of liberty and liberation to Africa in the early nineteenth century, two key components of Western liberty remained: freedom for the individual was more important than freedom for the community and liberty was racialized and gendered. These two aspects of Western liberty clashed with African percepts of what freedom meant. *Ubuntu*, a term from Southern Africa often translated as "I am because we are," is a concept that offers an African understanding of freedom that focuses on communal power rather than individualism. The idea of *ubuntu* was first recorded in the nineteenth century but became popularized in the 1950s among African nationalist leaders. For African communities, the individualism of Western "liberty" directly contradicts their cultural interpretation of what "freedom" means. It is this inherent contradiction between the two cultural ideas of liberty that explains the inability of Western liberation to work in African contexts. Consequently, when Americo-Liberians set up a colony along Cape Mesurado, they brought a Westernized notion of liberty with them, making it almost impossible for "freedom" to exist for indigenous Africans in the territory.

Tunde Adeleke explored the contradictions of freed African Americans who immigrated to Liberia but dominated the indigenous populations in the country. He argued that "what pushed them [African American immigrants] in the direction of Africa was not the paramount importance of African identity but the rejection, subordination, and exploitation of blacks in the United States" (1998, 113). He goes on further to explain that the group of black nationalists (as he calls them) who sought liberation in their move to Liberia supported instead a Eurocentric society with "negative and racist values" that allowed Americo-Liberians to justify their domination of indigenous Africans. The example of Liberia demonstrates the disturbing reality of what imposing a Western-centric ideology of liberation, soaked in the privileging of Western societies, looks like on the ground in Africa. It begs the question—could other terms be more effective for describing African agency in the nineteenth century? Could "freedom" or "emancipation" be more effective terms than "liberation"?

Emancipation was the terminology used to describe abolitionist efforts in nineteenth and twentieth century Africa and the pre–World War II nationalist movements advocating for the end of slavery and independence from European powers respectively. The problem with "emancipation" as a term is that it gives sole credit to Westerners in "freeing" Africans and removes any agency on the part of Africans seeking their emancipation from enslavement. Just as Europeans justified colonialism in Africa through a framework of emancipating the continent from African slavery, African nationalists implied that colonialism was enslavement with their calls for emancipation. World War II interrupted nationalists' efforts to use the concept of emancipation to frame their calls for independence. The language used by nationalists changed after the war. "Liberation" as a term came into usage in the post–World War II period, after Europe was "liberated" by the Allies, Jews were "liberated" from concentration camps, and African Americans in the United States sought their liberation from Jim Crow and other discriminatory laws (Cooper 2014). Frederick Cooper suggests that the usage of liberation as a concept encompasses an element of pan-Africanism and can indicate the period when the aspirations of African and African American people came into concert in the 1950s and 1960s. All of these examples demonstrate that language carries histories that may or may not be intentionally referenced by the people promulgating the terms.

Liberation as Emancipation

A significant portion of the African population in 1800 was enslaved in some form or another. Whether it was the obligation to perform specific work for others, temporary enslavement through pawning, patriarchal control over women, or instead the limitations on mobility placed upon individuals, a sizable African population found itself with little to no control over their movement, labor, or bodies. For Africans whose lives had been made perilous by slave trades and enslavement, liberation was a complicated matter. What did liberation really look like? Was it the same as "freedom," and whose idea of freedom was being used? Numerous scholars of African slavery over the years have argued in some form that freedom from enslavement was not "freedom" in the Western sense of liberty, but rather "belonging," being a full member in a community or living in a state of *ubuntu*. As Cooper, Thomas Holt, and Rebecca Scott (2000) note in their work *Beyond Slavery*, even if belonging was the opposite of slavery (as posited by Igor Kopytoff and Suzanne Miers), belonging was still not liberation. Part of the problem with using the term "liberation" in an African context is that the meaning of liberation comes from a non-African cultural context.

The first example of the notion of "liberation" being applied widely to a group of Africans living in the continent was when the British ended their participation in the transoceanic slave trades from Africa to other continents in 1807. While the end of the slave trade did not end slavery itself in British colonies (or any other European or African controlled spaces), Africans were "liberated" by British naval vessels off of slave ships. These "liberated" Africans were either returned to Sierra Leone or dropped off on St. Helena Island in the middle of the Atlantic Ocean. Liberated Africans landed at St. Helena were eventually transported to the Caribbean colonies as "indentured" servants, but those Africans landed in Sierra Leone were handed over to European missionaries to be educated in the "civilized" ways of Europeans—this civilizing was viewed by Europeans as the real liberation of Africans. "Liberated Africans" were not given the opportunity to live freely on their own once they were released by the British Navy; instead they either worked as indentured laborers or lived on a Christian mission station under the auspices of European supervision. Both systems introduced "liberated Africans" to European culture and values and put them under the direct authority of Westerners.

A well-known "liberated African" from the slave ships in the nineteenth century was Samuel Ajayi Crowther. He was taken off a slave ship in 1822 as a teenager and deposited by the British navy in Freetown with the Church Missionary Society. Crowther quickly proved himself adept at learning English and within four years he was sent to England on one of several trips to study. He was the first student to register at Fourah Bay College in Sierra Leone in 1827 and he soon became a teacher. However, Crowther is better known for his work with the pioneering British Niger Expeditions of 1841, 1854, and 1857 and his founding of the Niger Mission in 1857. This mission was unique at the time among the Church Missionary Society because of its all-African staff, most of which were from the community of liberated Africans living in Sierra Leone. In 1864 Crowther was consecrated as the first African Anglican bishop for the territory of Western Africa outside of the "Queen's control."

Samuel Crowther wrote of his initial experience of freedom in an 1837 account. He recounted:

> "They [other liberated Africans] assured us of our liberty and freedom; and we very soon believed them. But a few days after our arrival at Bathurst, we had the mortification of being sent for at Freetown, to testify against our Portuguese owner . . . notwithstanding all the persuasion of Mr. Davey that we should return, we entirely refused to go ourselves. . . . But as time was passing away, and our consent could not be got, we were compelled to go by being whipped." (Curtin 1997, 314)

In this experience Crowther quickly learned that "liberty" still meant following the rules of Europeans, and punishment would be meted out to any African who challenged British authority in Sierra Leone. Thus, Crowther was free to live on the mission and at liberty to study Christianity, but his liberation from the slave ships came with a price of conformity to a British conception of civility. For liberated Africans (and eventually many other Africans), to be "civilized" in a Western sense was associated with freedom from enslavement and access to material resources and goods.

The ideal missionary story of Samuel Crowther, who took the Christian (European) word into the interior of Africa, was complicated by the end of his life. As noted above, the Niger Mission was begun with an all-African staff that brought Christianity into the interior of Nigeria. However, typical of the racial prejudice (and expanding belief of Social Darwinists of the inferiority of Africans) that accompanied the increasing presence of Europeans in the continent at the end of the nineteenth century, white missionaries began complaining about Crowther and other African missionaries at the Niger Mission. Crowther was forced to retire in 1890 and died a year later. His legacy came to represent the agency and efforts of Africans to adapt Christianity and Western culture to their own needs but also the lack of real liberation for Africans when they engaged with Western societies.

National Liberations

The Conference of Independent African States first met in newly independent Ghana on April 15, 1958, where they declared the founding of African Freedom Day every April 15th. The idea of African Freedom Day was "to mark each year the onward progress of the liberation movement, and to symbolize the determination of the People of Africa to free themselves from foreign domination and exploitation." This meeting crystallized the height of pan-African cooperation across the continent as well as the hope and excitement of independence. Five years later at the first meeting of the Organization of African Unity (OAU) in 1963, the date and name of African Freedom Day was changed to African Liberation Day to be held on May 25th each year, demonstrating the renewed commitment to independence for all African nations on the continent but also the pessimism about when independence would happen. African Liberation Day became an important conduit for global pan-African support for the liberation of African nations from colonization as it was celebrated across the globe and especially in the United States. The name change gives insight into several aspects of the concept of "liberation" in Africa, including the timeline of the usage pre– and post–World War II and the pan-Africanist links between forms of liberation in Africa and in the Americas.

The transition of the name African Freedom Day to African Liberation Day was intentional and reflects the changing mood of African nationalists across the continent. While Western diplomats such as the American Ralph Bunche and officials in the British Colonial Office described 1960 as the Year of Africa, it was a year of many ups and downs. Harold Macmillan, the British prime minister, gave his "Winds of Change" speech in South Africa in early March, offering British recognition that independence was coming to African nations. Macmillan's speech was a warning to the white-minority government that ran South Africa through a system of apartheid ("separation" or segregation of races) that the British government would no longer support the maintenance of an apartheid or segregated system of government that discriminated against the black majority. In 1960, seventeen African nations received their independence, offering a measure of hope to nationalists. However, soon after Macmillan's speech on March 21, 1960, the South African police attacked demonstrators, killing sixty-nine and injuring almost two hundred people in what came to be called the Sharpeville massacre. This ominous event indicated to African leaders and the world that decolonization would not happen in the nonviolent "Ghana model" across the continent. Richard Wright recorded after his 1953 visit to the West African Gold Coast colony (present-day Ghana):

> But here in Africa "freedom" was more than a word; an African had no doubts about the meaning of the word "freedom." It meant the right to public assembly, the right to physical movement, the right to make known his views, the right to elect men of his choice to public office, and the right to recall them if they failed in their promises. At a time when the Western world grew embarrassed at the sound of the word "freedom," these people knew that it meant

> the right to shape their own destiny as they wished. Of that they had no doubt, and no threats could intimidate them about it; they might be cowed by guns and planes, but they'd not change their minds about the concrete nature of the freedom that they wanted and were willing to die for. (1954, 54)

In the 1950s, there was hope across Africa, hope for *uhuru* (Kiswahili for "freedom") as proclaimed across Eastern Africa, but all while the British still maintained a "state of emergency" in Kenya in order to isolate the anti-colonial resistance movement, known as the Mau Mau Uprising. After Sharpeville, Africans still sought freedom as Wright described it, but African leaders such as Kwame Nkrumah of Ghana and Nelson Mandela of South Africa knew that this freedom would come at a price—it would require physical, not simply political resistance. African resistance came to be described as liberation, but the meaning behind this concept of liberation differed from the individualism of Western liberation.

Sharpeville was just the first setback for nationalists in 1960. The tragedy that unfolded in the newly independent nation of Congo where the first prime minister, Patrice Lumumba, was eventually assassinated by Belgian and Katangan officials, left many Europeans and Africans questioning what liberation meant. Could African nations viably be liberated? *Time* magazine offered a cover story in December 1960 on Nigeria entitled "The Other Africa: Independence without Chaos." By the founding of the OAU in 1963, pessimism about the future of African colonies, especially in Southern Africa, found nationalist leaders calling for a stronger language of resistance.

Pan-Africanism before World War II consisted of Western people of African descent meeting in Europe or the US and African nationalist leaders were not central to the proceedings. However, in the 1950s pan-Africanism was redefined as an African movement that encompassed primarily actors from across the continent rather than from the diaspora. It was during the 1960s that African American leaders began calling on African leaders to affirm the linkage between the two groups. In 1964 at the OAU summit, the African American activist Malcolm X warned African leaders: "Your problems will never be fully solved until and unless ours [African Americans] are solved. You will never be fully respected until and unless we are also respected. You will never be recognized as free human beings until and unless we are also recognized and treated as human beings." Stokely Carmichael, another African American activist who lived for many years in Ghana, likewise linked the two regions eight years later when he said, "What we must understand is that until Africa is free, the Black man all over the world is not free." While the two men did not agree whether African liberation or African American equal rights needed to happen first, both pointed to a long-standing connection of racial identity between the two populations. This helps explain why African Liberation Day was celebrated as vigorously in the United States in the 1960s and 1970s as it was in African countries.

Africans were less interested in American politics and in thinking about Western concepts of race as they sought to achieve liberation and build new nations. As Chimamanda Adichie in her 2013 novel, *Americanah*, suggested, Africans do not identify as "black" until they leave the continent of Africa and are confronted with Western perceptions which racialize them. It is in the West that Africans can see the ways in which ideas of liberation are structured with privilege for the few. Many Africans quickly realized that the freedom they believed they had achieved with independence was illusory. Ngũgĩ wa Thiong'o critiqued the freedom achieved in Kenya in his third and fourth books (*Petals of Blood* and *Devil on the Cross*), arguing that the promise of independence was the promise of freedom, as described by Wright above. The notion of freedom understood by most East Africans was a Rousseauian freedom of equality and concern for community. However, newly independent Africans across the continent quickly found their freedom constrained and now had to fight for liberation. Thus, liberation was not just a decolonization effort as found in Southern Africa; it included liberation from corrupt leaders, single party states, and neocolonial economic policies. As many Africans came to see, the OAU fought for decolonization and liberation, but it was remarkably quiet when faced with military coups and African-led dictatorships.

Epistemological Liberation

Ngũgĩ wa Thiong'o, one of the most celebrated novelists of Kenya, quickly became a central voice of postcolonial Kenya's literary scene in the 1960s and 1970s. As a faculty member in the English Department at the University of Nairobi, Ngũgĩ, along with several African colleagues, began to question the Eurocentric approach to teaching literature. In 1969, this group of faculty circulated a proposal, *On the Abolition of the English Department*, to fundamentally change the approach of the department to one that centered on African literature and its engagement with the rest of the world, rather than the preexisting British-centered focus of the English department. In his book *Decolonising the Mind*, Ngũgĩ argued that "African children who encountered literature in colonial schools and universities were thus experiencing the world as defined and reflected in the European experience of history. Their entire way of looking at the world, even the world of the immediate environment, was Eurocentric" (wa Thiong'o 1986, 93). According to Ngũgĩ the key to addressing a true liberation for Africa was through epistemological change. From the moment Europeans stepped onto the continent of Africa as "explorers" they had begun the process of delegitimizing and decentering African knowledge.

European societies defined knowledge as objective, made up of "facts" and "information." However, the construction of knowledge is deeply subjective and, thus as Europeans engaged with the African continent, they began defining what they viewed as valuable knowledge. Many different forms of knowledge exist side by side within any society and it is how those forms of knowledge are valued by different groups that prioritizes their use. Carl Linnaeus, an eighteenth-century Swedish botanist, came up with the classification system still used by Western states for defining the natural world. The Linnaean system was critical to both European exploration and empire building in Africa (and the rest of the world) because it created a system of order that allowed Europeans to organize the "chaos" of newly encountered societies and lands.

Mary Louise Pratt argued that before Linnaeus's classification system, different forms of knowledge coexisted around the world. When Europeans traveled to different parts of the world they would learn about a new culture, society, and environment from their own observations but also from engaging with people from those regions. The value systems of different people were transmitted through the ways in which they communicated knowledge about their societies. Once Europeans began using the Linnaean system of cataloging information, Europeans based all of their knowledge on their observations and classification and engaged less and less with local forms of knowledge. This gave Europeans an epistemological superiority in their approach to other societies and people. Thus, Europeans no longer felt the need to learn local systems of knowledge and they began imposing their own systems wherever they went. This way of approaching societies set a precedent for a Eurocentric approach, where everything in a society is viewed through a comparative lens with the Europeans' home societies. Thus, instead of seeing African societies for the ways in which they did things effectively, a Eurocentric approach only considered how African societies were structured differently from Europe.

This comparative setup meant that Europeans were constantly evaluating spaces, places, and people in relation to their own communities and judging other societies wanting. This epistemological framework allowed Europeans to devalue African forms of knowledge and prioritize their knowledge of Africa as the one true understanding.

Christian missionary education systems became a conduit for the development of European forms of knowledge across the African continent. In places where Islam dominated and Christian missionaries were not allowed, such as Northern Nigeria and parts of Sudan, colonial government systems of education based on European schools were opened. Muslim students in francophone West Africa could attend madrassas, which taught some Arabic and Islamic studies but mostly focused on the superiority of French culture (Brenner 2001). The emphasis of most early Christian missionaries in Africa was to translate the Bible into local languages. While this seemingly was a way of Africanizing European religious ideas, the reality is that missionaries took local religious idioms and co-opted them to fit into Christianity. This work devalued African understandings of belief and faith and recoded these ideas in an epistemological framework that valued only Christian systems. Consequently, as Africans were educated in missionary and European schools, even if they were learning local languages in the elementary years, the course material was still fundamentally framed in European ways. African children were taught from a Western perspective how to categorize and view their lands, families, and societies. This process slowly alienated African children from valuing their own cultures and knowledge systems. In his 1961 novel *Ambiguous Adventure*, Cheikh Hamidou Kane recognized "the foreign school is the new form of the war which those who have come here are waging." By colonizing the minds of Africans, and instilling a sense of intellectual inferiority in Africans through systems of education, Europeans were far more effective colonizers than when they used guns.

Ngũgĩ wa Thiong'o argued that the corruption of the postcolonial African state was a direct reflection of the indoctrination of European epistemological systems that devalued African cultures. In 1977, Ngũgĩ wrote his novel *Petals of Blood* about the corruption of postcolonial Kenya and the need for an epistemological liberation. That year he coauthored a play, *Ngaahika Ndeenda*, in Kikuyu, his indigenous language. This play was performed at the Kamirithu Educational and Cultural Center in Limuru, Kenya. Ngũgĩ continued to publish in Kikuyu, even after his imprisonment by the Kenyan government, because he viewed literature as crucial to creating culture. He argued that Africans who wrote literature in English or other European languages lost aspects of their culture and reinforced the ability of the postcolonial government to devalue African knowledge systems in favor of European systems.

The notion of "liberation" as a term outside of African societies deeply impacts the way in which the scholarship on Africa exists through the twentieth and into the twenty-first centuries. Africans such as Samuel Johnson, the child of "liberated" Africans, became one of the most famous chroniclers of West African history during the nineteenth century. Whether it was through writing down their languages or oral traditions, African scholars in the nineteenth century made an effort to place knowledge by Africans into the lexicon of Western academia. Likewise African American scholars such as W. E. B. Du Bois had set their hands to writing histories and works about Africa. Yet African studies as a discipline did not attain legitimacy in the Western academy until white scholars in the 1940s and 1950s, such as Melville Herskovits, became interested. In 1958 the African Studies Association (ASA) of the US was founded by a group of mostly white men. The growth in white academic interest grew exponentially such that by the time British historian Hugh Trevor-Roper made his famous declaration in 1963 that "at present there is none [African history], or very little; there is only the history of the Europeans in Africa. The rest is largely darkness," hundreds of scholars immediately sought to discount him. Most of these white scholars believed they were working toward a scholarly liberation of Africa by incorporating research about the continent into the academy and the larger body of global scholarship. Thus many felt deeply hurt and confused when the Black caucus of the ASA disrupted the annual meeting in 1969 in order to demonstrate the inequalities pervasive in the leadership of the ASA. The Black Caucus demanded that recognition be given to the links between Africans and Africa-descended populations in the diaspora. As Herschelle Challenor later reflected on the actions of the Caucus, "We maintained that all peoples of African descent are African peoples; we recognized that despite a difference in form and degree we shared a common historical experience of racial oppression that has substantially distorted our history and culture or even denied its validity; we affirmed that Africa's image and political position in the world affect all of us" (1969: 4). Echoing the call by Malcolm X just five years earlier, the Black Caucus argued that until the ASA's leadership was equal in its distribution of resources and positions of power, the organization itself would continue to represent a form of colonization of Africa in the Western academy.

Conclusion

Is there a term better than "liberation" to describe African efforts to shape their relationships with Europeans and between each other during the nineteenth and twentieth centuries? Can "freedom" or "emancipation" carry the weight of meaning more effectively? Each of these terms has a history, a history of when and how it has been deployed by Africans and Westerners and it will continue to carry earlier meanings. These histories continue to shape the reinvention of these ideas by Africans, pan-Africanists, and Western scholars. Knowing the ways in which Africans and Westerners used the concepts allows for a clearer view of the intertwined relationships between ideology and knowledge production over time.

Suggested Readings

Adeleke, Tunde. 1998. *UnAfrican Americans: Nineteenth-Century Black Nationalists and the Civilizing Mission*. Lexington: University Press of Kentucky.

Cooper, Frederick. 2002. *Africa since 1940: The Past of the Present*. Cambridge: Cambridge University Press.

Fanon, Frantz. 1967. *Black Skin, White Masks*. New York: Grove.

Getz, Trevor. 2015. *Abina and the Important Men: A Graphic History*. Oxford: Oxford University Press.

Grubbs, Larry. 2009. *Secular Missionaries: Americans and African Development in the 1960s*. Amherst: University of Massachusetts Press.

Lovejoy, Paul E., and Jan S. Hogendorn. 1993. *Slow Death for Slavery: The Course of Abolition in Northern Nigeria, 1897–1936*. Cambridge: Cambridge University Press.

Meriwether, James H. 2002. *Proudly We Can Be Africans: Black Americans and Africa, 1935–1961*. Chapel Hill: University of North Carolina Press.

Miers, Suzanne, and Richard Roberts. 1988. *The End of Slavery in Africa*. Madison: University of Wisconsin Press.

Ngũgĩ wa Thiong'o. 2004 [1986]. *Decolonizing the Mind: The Politics of Language in African Literature*. Nairobi, Kenya: East African Educational Publishers; London: James Currey Ltd.

Nugent, Paul. 2004. *Africa since Independence*. London: Palgrave Macmillian.

References

Adeleke, Tunde. 1998. *UnAfrican Americans: Nineteenth-Century Black Nationalists and the Civilizing Mission*. Lexington: University Press of Kentucky.

Adichie, Chimamanda Ngozi. 2013. *Americanah*. New York: Knopf.

Brenner, Louis. 2001. *Controlling Knowledge: Religion, Power and Schooling in a West African Muslim Society*. Bloomington: Indiana University Press.

Challenor, Herschelle Sullivan. 1969. "No Longer at Ease: Confrontation at the 12th Annual African Studies Association Meeting at Montreal." *Africa Today* 5/6 (16): 4–7.

Cooper, Frederick. 2014. *Africa in the World: Capitalism, Empire, Nation-State*. Cambridge, MA: Harvard University Press.

Cooper, Frederick, Thomas C. Holt, and Rebecca J. Scott. 2000. *Beyond Slavery: Explorations of Race, Labor, and Citizenship in Postemancipation Societies*. Chapel Hill: University of North Carolina Press.

Cranston, Maurice. 1997. *The Solitary Self: Jean-Jacques Rousseau in Exile and Adversity*. Chicago: University of Chicago Press.

Curtin, Philip D., ed. 1997. *Africa Remembered: Narratives by West Africans from the Era of the Slave Trade*. Long Grove, IL: Waveland Press.

Everill, Bronwen. 2013. *Abolition and Empire in Sierra Leone and Liberia*. London: Palgrave MacMillan.

Kane, Hamidou. 1972. *Ambiguous Adventure*. Oxford: Heinemann.

Miers, Suzanne, and Igor Kopytoff. 1977. *Slavery in Africa: Historical and Anthropological Perspectives*. Madison: University of Wisconsin Press.

Ngũgĩ wa Thiong'o. 1977. *Petals of Blood*. Portsmouth, NH: Heinemann.

———. 1987. *Devil on the Cross*. Portsmouth, NH: Heinemann.

———. 2004 [1986]. *Decolonizing the Mind: The Politics of Language in African Literature*. Nairobi, Kenya: East African Educational Publishers; London: James Currey Ltd.

Pratt, Mary Louise. 1992. *Imperial Eyes: Travel Writing and Transculturation*. London: Routledge.

Wright, Richard. 1954. *Black Power*. New York: Harper.

15 MOBILITY

Patrick Manning

People of the African continent are perpetually in movement. The stereotypical vision of the quiet African village, from which people rarely stray, lives on in the minds of some, but it is hardly relevant to the continent today. A more common and more realistic trope is the vision of the African marketplace. Whether urban or rural, African markets include great numbers of people, dressed in many different ways, exploring goods and interacting with each other. If people are on foot in the heart of the market, many gain access to it by taxi or motorbike. Nearby car parks, jammed with vehicles set to move in any direction, are crowded with passengers impatient to start on their voyage.

Where people are not moving physically, they are in conversation with others, now electronically. Telephones came fifty years too late to Africa. Neither governments nor corporations would invest in the land lines necessary to enable widespread communication, so that Africans were largely cut off from the most updated form of communication. But the rise of mobile technology, which involved small investment in mobile phones and only slightly larger investment in the technology of transmission systems, at last opened up communication for families and businesses all across Africa. Markets in oil-rich Nigeria display great quantities of mobile phones sold at various price points and targeted to a wide demography of consumers. Even in endlessly distressed Congo-Kinshasa, purchasers and users benefit from mobile phones by purchasing and exchanging small numbers of minutes.

Physical or geographical mobility endures, linking Africa's rural and urban regions. Social mobility is complex: one may rise up in social status by moving to the city to complete university studies or by moving from the city to take a community title in the village. Less fortunately, children have been seized by paramilitary groups and turned into soldiers or camp followers in the rebellions of Mozambique, Uganda, and Nigeria. At a more privileged level, government officials are posted to stations throughout the nation or are sent to work in the bureaucracies of the African Union in Addis Ababa.

Mobility also extends to the new African diaspora, succeeding to and interacting with the old African diaspora. The recent stories of desperate migrations across the Mediterranean tell of the impoverished who seek short-term work at all costs; at another extreme are the young students, flying to enroll in universities overseas. In between are the Africans who find work abroad and send remittances to their families, often by using the services of Western Union. Remittances from Africans living abroad now form an important part of African national revenues. African-descended communities in Europe, Asia, and the Americas are sometimes distinct, sometimes mixed communities of the Old and New Diasporas.

Today's patterns of African mobility all depend on the realities of modern-day life, technology, and social organization. Yet today's mobility also relies on the size, shape, and dynamics of patterns inherited from the recent past of the colonial and post-independent years and from the more distant past of precolonial times.

Historical Mobility

Africa, as portrayed in textbooks and scholarly studies, still carries reflections of the era of colonization and the previous era of empires and slave trade. Virtually all of Africa was under European colonial rule from roughly 1900 to 1960. During that time, interpretations of Africa relied on European visitors who wrote their impressions. Brochures inviting tourists to Africa still tend to show animals but not people. Since 1960, African scholars have been able to write about their continent, but they must still contend with the remains of oversimplified interpretations.

Overseas views of African mobility—through colonialism, foreign schools and universities, foreign experts and their ideas—portrayed the continent as a backward region, populated by isolated populations of small families in villages. The old ideas live on. After people of African descent in the Americas began to question where their ancestors might have come from, they were still encouraged to think that they might have ancestors located in a particular village in one country. It did not occur to these

Americans that their African ancestors might have had families stretched over wide areas, or that oral or written communication would enable families to remain in touch over wide areas.

One useful experiment in thinking about African mobility is with music and especially drums. Drums of many sorts, made of different materials with different shapes and tones, have been manufactured and played all over the African continent. But one should not think that each type of drum remained in its own village. Rather, the drums that were popular for their own sound, or for their ties to innovative musical ensembles, were carried far and wide to appreciative audiences. That is, popular culture spread far and wide in precolonial Africa as it does today on every continent.

Yet European rulers of colonial Africa tended to envision Africans as limited in mobility, and commonly preferred to keep them so. Such colonial limitations on African mobility applied especially to women. As cities grew in the early twentieth century, colonial governments and European residents dominated the segregated central cities; African men were enabled to settle in surrounding neighborhoods as long as they were employed, but women were pressured to stay at home in the village.

The city of Léopoldville, capital of the immense Belgian Congo, had a population of just over thirty thousand persons in the 1940s; the great majority of its inhabitants were male. For girls in the city, the Catholic Church declined to allow confirmation or first communion until they had completed three years of primary school; this schooling emphasized domestic training aimed at marriage and domestic life. But after Congo became independent and the city retook its earlier name of Kinshasa, the population shot up, reaching 2.5 million by 1981—migration from the countryside had created a hurriedly built metropolis with a population that had become half female.

Even as the realities of life in Africa changed with many countries earning independence in the 1960s, outside of Africa there still circulated images and narratives of women and family that reinforced the old stereotypes about village life. These approaches, emphasizing submissive and subordinate roles for women, did not account for the active roles of female West African merchants, traveling widely to retrieve and sell their goods, nor did they account for Central African women's leading role in agriculture—planting, weeding, harvesting, and marketing.

Another key area of Africa mobility, today as in earlier times, is pastoralism. The grasslands of East Africa, West Africa, and Southern Africa support large populations that live by tending herds of cattle, sheep, goats, and camels—sometimes on mixed farms, sometimes as pastoral specialists. Families move with their herds on a daily basis and a seasonal basis, then market some of their animals periodically. Now, as before, migrations to the best grasslands lead pastoralists across political borders and into occasional disputes with governments. Differences in the present era are that parents now communicate with mobile phones while children attend religious or secular schools.

The high level of African mobility may be surprising to some readers. History textbooks make little mention of African migration in the nineteenth and twentieth centuries, focusing instead on the worldwide migrations of Europeans and, to a degree, of Asians. These texts make it appear as if Africans migrated in the sixteenth and seventeenth centuries, and not thereafter. Yet Africans in the past two centuries migrated widely within the continent, both on their own and as required by their colonial governments.

In sum, Africans, whether they are farmers or pastoralists, urbanites or rural dwellers, men or women, experience a great deal of mobility. One might think that the many migrations Africans undertake would erase the differences among Africa's regions. Yet every African region has people of diverse origins and who speak diverse languages—so, somehow, mobility reproduces variety while expanding similarities. The remainder of this essay explores African mobility in the past, arguing that Africa's mix of great variety and great mobility has been a common pattern over the centuries.

Large-Scale Migrations and Diversity

Human mobility in Africa has been a factor in the lives of *Homo sapiens* for the past two hundred thousand years and for the preceding hominid species. In the East African homeland, periodic shifts in the intensity of sunlight, brought by shifts in the earth's orbit, led to periods in which, alternately, either Northeast Africa or Southeast Africa was the most humid and productive region. As a result, humans developed a habitual tendency to migrate alternately north or south, building migration into human lifestyle as a slow but beneficial rhythm.

A new reason for migration emerged some seventy thousand years ago, as humans gained fully articulated language. The sharing of a common language brought communities together but the gradual divergence of speech—into separate dialects and then distinct languages—also divided communities into distinct groups. The exchange of ideas and experience among groups brought occasional key innovations and spurred social expansion for those who benefited from them. All of Africa's language groups can trace their roots to Eastern Africa, but successive migrations across the continent have pointed in numerous directions. The Afroasiatic languages, which trace their ancestry to the valley of the Blue Nile, spread in all directions, for instance in the Holocene era over ten thousand years ago as temperatures and humidity rose. To the north, settlers in the Red Sea hills became Beja speakers, settlers in the lower Nile became Egyptian speakers, and groups branching off from the lower Nile became the Berber speakers of the Maghreb and the Semitic speakers of the Fertile Crescent. (It is likely in these cases that settlers from the Nile Valley moved in among local people in each region, but became dominant in language.) At much the same time, migrants from the Afroasiatic homeland moved west to settle and become the Chadic speakers of the Lake Chad region. In another twist, certain speakers of Semitic languages from South Arabia later moved to Ethiopia, and their language became widely adopted through trade: the Amharic language is the most widely spoken language reflecting this pattern.

In a parallel set of migrations, the Niger-Congo-speakers, with ancestors in the Nile Valley, settled in West Africa. The Niger-Congo languages gradually divided into many subgroups in the savanna and forest regions of West Africa. At the southeastern edge of this great language community, at today's Nigeria-Cameroon frontier, the Bantu speakers, a subgroup of Niger-Congo speakers, moved much more recently to the south and east, and became prominent over an immense region in the East African homeland and also in Central and Southern Africa. To a large degree, these were accumulations of small migrations rather than a few great expeditions. Thus the matrilineal system of descent, which encouraged married couples to start new households (rather than live in the father's household as in patrilineal systems), facilitated gradual migration into new territories.

Settlers from abroad have come to Africa in many times and circumstances. Two such settlements stand out. In the first, Austronesian mariners came across the Indian Ocean some two thousand years ago, settling along the East African coast, intermarrying with locals, and moving later to Madagascar. The material remains of their settlement include stilt houses, outrigger canoes, rice, and bananas. Cultural exchange went one or both directions: the discussion continues as to whether xylophones went from Africa to Indonesia or the other way around. In a second and larger immigration, Arab migrants from Arabia launched their political, military, and religious takeover of Northern Africa in the seventh century CE. North Africans initially converted to Islam but kept their Berber languages. Then a still larger Arab migration into the Maghreb, from the eleventh to thirteenth centuries, brought about a social and linguistic conversion making North African society dominantly Arab. Yet it may be remembered that Arabic, a Semitic language, had an ultimately African origin.

In addition to these apparently large-scale movements, probably more important were the many small-scale and local movements, in which merchants, hunters, artisans, and others moved from town to town, exchanging ideas and goods. This continental system of local links can be seen as an African network—not a single great trade route running between major centers but a series of paths leading in all directions. It has brought transmission of material goods and the exchange of culture throughout the continent. The *mbira*, a musical instrument of tuned iron keys amplified by resonation with gourds, came to be played all over the continent though it developed along the Zambezi River. Iron bells, developed for the ceremonies of monarchs along the lower Niger, had spread southeast to Zambia by 1500, in the course of a thousand years. Bananas, introduced to the eastern coast of Africa by mariners from Southeast Asia, soon spread into the highlands of East Africa, the lowlands of the Congo basin, and then to the coastal forests of West Africa. Thanks to the connections facilitated by the African network, Africa is at once the most diverse of continents (in genetics, culture, and social systems)—human societies have differentiated within its boundaries for a very long time—and also a region of remarkable commonality, as key innovations and systems of expression have spread steadily from one group to the next.

Enslavement, Emancipation, and Mobility

In the period from 1500 to 1900, migration was dominated by enslavement. Africa's northern and eastern coastlines, along the Mediterranean and the Indian Ocean, had long maintained regular links to regions across the waters. Slavery, slave trade, and other commerce had existed for two millennia in the Mediterranean and West Asia, and captives from Northeast Africa had been drawn into that enslavement along with captives from the Black Sea and other regions. Then, from about 1500 CE, the opening of maritime connections for West and Central Africa brought change to all of Africa as to every other region.

The development of plantation agriculture, especially the production of sugar on islands of the Atlantic and in the Americas, brought a relentlessly expanding demand for forced labor, and the result was a steadily growing slave trade along Africa's Western Coast. By 1650 the export of captives across the Atlantic had become the majority of all slave trade from Africa, and from 1650 to 1850 Africa had more emigrants than any other continent.

African societies did not easily collect captives for export abroad, but underwent unexpected social change. The readiness of overseas merchants to pay substantial sums immediately provoked brutal decisions within Africa. Rulers, family leaders, and opportunistic individuals seized subordinates who were in any way unwelcome—or prisoners of war who would normally be ransomed—and sold them to slave traders. Especially along the Atlantic coast, the expanding sale of male captives left opportunities to turn females into domestic captives, and a new division of labor began to develop. Many other shifts in the social order emerged: for instance, Kru mariners, took jobs as crew members for ships sailing along the coast from Liberia to Angola, then paddled their canoes back along the coast to Liberia.

Large-scale enslavement began with coastal wars in Senegambia, Angola, and the Bight of Benin. With time, seizures in inland areas grew in what historian Joseph Miller has called a "ring of fire," a zone of heavy enslavement that moved gradually inland. In the early eighteenth century, populations in coastal West and Central Africa declined; by the mid-eighteenth century, the total population of West and Central Africa was in decline. Meanwhile, the numbers of enslaved within Africa grew to be as large as the numbers overseas.

From the late eighteenth century, the number enslaved grew rapidly in Northeast and East Africa—to satisfy growing demand for captives in the Indian Ocean, Egypt, and West Asia and also to feed growing domestic markets for servile labor. A boom in slave exports from Madagascar and Mozambique up to the 1840s led to the long voyage of captives to the Americas; thereafter, East African captives went in even larger numbers to Indian Ocean destinations. As a result, populations in nineteenth-century Africa declined, especially in Southeast Africa.

The remarkable expansion of enslavement throughout Africa—long after the 1807 British abolition of slave trade—is increasingly understood to be part of a phenomenon shared by the tropics globally. In the Americas, enslavement grew in the United States, Brazil, and Cuba. In Asia, enslavement grew throughout Southeast Asia, in India, and in West Asia. In Africa, we can now confirm that enslavement expanded in many regions even as slave exports declined. While some but not all of these slave populations were put to work in market-oriented work, there is a need to explain why the elites throughout the tropics turned so fiercely to enslavement during the nineteenth century. Global commerce had expanded since 1500, leading to enslavement and other forms of labor mobilization from the sixteenth to the eighteenth centuries. In addition, the era of factory production (in New World sugar mills and in North Atlantic textile factories) and the rise of wage labor (mainly in the North Atlantic) appear to be related in some way to the "second slavery" throughout the tropics.

From 1850, steamship-borne migrants from Europe, India, and China joined in migrations that soon outnumbered the movements of Africans. Tens of millions of migrants, some voluntary and some under restrictive labor contracts, moved from continent to continent from the 1850s through the 1930s. Part of this process brought nearly a million migrants from Europe and nearly a million from South Asia into Africa. In light of the magnitude of these European and Asian migrations, a common impression is that African overseas migration simply halted as of 1850. In fact, slave exports from East Africa continued in large numbers to almost 1900. In addition, migration within the African continent continued at an active level—through enslavement, emancipation of those earlier enslaved, and migration of free people.

African mobility since 1900 has consisted mostly of the movement of free people under government constraint. In the years before and just after 1900, the great powers completed their sudden conquest of virtually the whole African continent. In the same era, the European powers and Japan became dominant in Southeast Asia and the Pacific. In territorial terms, this was the high point in imperial rule. Britain, France, Germany, and other powers, with small colonial staffs and armies of local soldiers under European officers, quickly set up systems of taxation and administration. European rule of Africa, established at the peak of racial theory and practices of racial discrimination and segregation, emphasized the cultural denigration of African societies as well as political domination by the imperial order.

The conquering Europeans criticized the extent to which slavery had grown in Africa. Rarely, however, did colonial regimes abolish slavery and emancipate the slaves: Madagascar in 1895 was one such case. Still, the prohibition of slave capture meant that many were able to escape their bondage. Men especially were able to return and see if they could find their home community still in existence. Women, however, many with children, found it difficult to leave without giving up their children, who belonged by law to their owner or the father. Nevertheless, some enslaved women were able to negotiate a semi-free or free status or to escape. Colonial regimes set up "free womb" laws, applied earlier in Asia and the Americas, according to which children born to slave mothers would become free once they reached the age of majority. Even then, violation and neglect of these rules meant that many thousands remained in slavery in the 1930s and perhaps beyond.

As soon as colonial regimes abolished slave raiding, however, communities could emerge from hiding and seek to reoccupy the prime lands they had fled. Thus, at the opening of the twentieth century, the elements of an energetic peasant social order emerged in many parts of Africa. This peasant order combined those previously free, who were now able to rebuild their farms with little fear of attack, and those recently freed, who sought to return home or otherwise find a place to settle. These were now independent families, owning or renting their land, and active in agricultural and artisanal production. (This expansion of African peasantry, mostly in the twentieth century, matched the nineteenth-century pattern of the Americas, where free blacks and newly emancipated slaves combined to build peasant societies.) Families changed, as marriage became more feasible in the era after slavery. (In Africa, however, sorting out lineage and ethnic relations under these circumstances must have been complex.) Just as peasant communities in the Americas adopted Protestant and Catholic Christianity, so also did peasant communities of Africa adopt Protestant and Catholic Christianity and, in even larger numbers, Islam. The post-emancipation peasantries devoted themselves to self-sufficiency and then to commercial agriculture and artisanal work. In another parallel to post-emancipation life elsewhere in the African Diaspora, African communities experienced lively cultural renewal as they built their communities.

Still, the power of the former enslaving aristocracies had not fully faded in these post-emancipation days. Paul Lovejoy and Jan Hogendorn describe how leaders of the Muslim emirates of Northern Nigeria, as late as the 1920s, were able to send deputations to the regions where they had formerly captured slaves, and pressure the family leaders into yielding beautiful young women to be concubines in the emir's court.

Colonial rule changed mobility patterns of Africans. Rising taxation and forced labor for roads and bridges led many families or villages to move across borders and resettle. Labor recruitment for the gold and diamond mines of South Africa relied on specific contracts for workers, especially from Mozambique and Nyasaland (Malawi). For a time in the interwar years, this system infected the male workers with tuberculosis (as they moved from hot mines to cold housing), then sent them home at the end of their term, where they infected their families.

African urbanization proceeded during the colonial era and accelerated rapidly in postcolonial years. Cities grew mainly as a result of small-scale private investment rather than public investment. Ex-slaves were disproportionately numerous in urban populations, and for the same reason post-emancipation culture arose particularly in the music of the cities. Yet colonial regimes preferred to restrict access to the cities to recognized male workers. With independence, women and children were enabled to settle in cities, so that, for instance, the population of Kinshasa rose from fifty thousand in 1958 to two hundred thousand in the early 1960s.

In the 1950s and especially in the 1960s with independence, African social services expanded greatly, notably in public education and public health. Literacy—though normally in a second language—rose steadily in the late twentieth century. In retrospect and especially in demographic terms, one may argue that the 1940s represented a key turning point for African population and society. By this time, it appears that African societies had overcome much of the trauma of enslavement. Most people were free; orderly communities had been able to develop for some years. Death rates declined sharply in the 1940s, and rates of population growth shot up to a high level of 2 percent per year, remaining at those high levels for a full half-century. The steady strengthening of African peasant societies carried on from the 1940s through the 1970s; after the 1970s, the expanding urban sector captured most African growth.

Conclusion

What is the likely future of African mobility? The past several centuries have brought shifting regimes of mobility to Africans. What had been small-scale, community-level mobility patterns were gradually drawn into a global system of private-sector enslavement in which imperial governments, overseas, encouraged enslavement of Africans from the fifteenth century into the twentieth century. The late nineteenth century brought a confusing system of continued enslavement and other restrictions under rapidly changing precolonial African governments. The first half of the twentieth century brought abolition of slave trade (but only slowly of slavery), plus the requirements and restrictions of penurious colonial government. Then came a brief post–World War II period of expansive colonialism followed by the Keynesian programs of public investment by post-independence African socialist governments until the 1970s. Thereafter, African societies have been weakened by domestic strife and by constraints of the world market and of international organizations.

One may argue that these shifting mobility regimes arise from a contrasting pair of underlying pressures for mobility. First is the mobility of people and influences in order to sustain Africa's domestic society and economy—this is the marketplace and the African network. Second is the mobility of Africans in response to overseas pressures: the demands of global empires, the world market for commodities, and, more recently, international financial organizations—this is globalization, and its effects may have been more negative than positive. A third factor, necessarily, is the interaction of African and global demands for mobility.

With time, African needs for mobility are becoming more influential. As African initiatives in mobility develop, one gains a clearer sense of the various dimensions of mobility, beyond the basic focus on labor recruitment that characterized the slave trade. That is, global demands for African mobility have focused on the extraction of labor to meet needs in production. African demands for mobility, in contrast, can be labeled to begin with as social, linguistic, cultural, and verbal mobility. In social mobility, people move up and down the social scale with education, inheritance, or misfortune. In linguistic mobility, Africans move across language barriers, as shown in the impressive book of M. E. Kropp-Dakubu, *Korle Meets the Sea*, which conveys the pleasure and functionality of multilingual exchange in Ghana's metropolis of Accra. Cultural mobility includes such patterns as the musical groups moving back and forth to Europe, performing as they travel. More basic is the mobility of personal communication through voice by mobile phone or text in instant messenger. Does this collection of means of interaction correspond to the emergence of an updated African network?

What should one look for in African mobility? Travel costs are high in Africa, yet people manage to move over short and long distances. Health conditions for Africa are well below average for the world, but have improved sufficiently to expand greatly overall productivity. Communication, too, is behind that of other world regions but it has still greatly advanced. The distortion of family life by slavery, colonialism, and other elite restrictions has declined. It may be that the village is becoming a place to which one escapes, occasionally, from the city.

Suggested Readings

Adeniran, Isaac Adebusuyi. 2014. *Migration and Regional Integration in West Africa: A Borderless ECOWAS*. New York: Palgrave Macmillan.

Asiwaju, A. I. 2003. *Boundaries and African Integration: Essays in Comparative History and Policy Analysis*. Lagos: Panaf Publishers.

Bollig, Michael, Michael Schnegg, and Hans-Peter Wotzka. 2013. *Pastoralism in Africa: Past, Present and Future*. New York: Berghahn.

Cordell, Dennis D., Joel W. Gregory, and Victor Piché. 1996. *Hoe and Wage: A Social History of a Circular Migration System in West Africa*. Boulder, CO: Westview.

Cross, Hannah. 2013. *Migrants, Borders and Global Capitalism: West African Labour Mobility and EU Borders*. London: Routledge.

De Bruijn, Miriam, Rijk Van Dijk, and Dick Foeken, eds. 2001. *Mobile Africa: Changing Patterns of Movement in Africa and Beyond*. Leiden: Brill.

Falola, Toyin. 2013. *The African Diaspora: Slavery, Modernity, and Globalization*. Rochester, NY: University of Rochester Press.

Falola, Toyin, and Bridget Teboh, eds. 2013. *The Power of Gender, the Gender of Power: Women's Labor, Rights and Responsibilities in Africa*. Trenton, NJ: Africa World Press.

Freund, Bill. 1988. *The African Worker*. Cambridge: Cambridge University Press.

Gaibazzi, Paolo. 2015. *Bush Bound: Young Men and Rural Permanence in Migrant West Africa*. New York: Berghahn.

Kropp Dakubu, M. E. 1997. *Korle Meets the Sea: A Sociolinguistic History of Accra*. New York: Oxford University Press.

Manning, Patrick. 1990. *Slavery and African Life: Occidental, Oriental, and African Slave Trades*. Cambridge: Cambridge University Press.

———. 2009. *The African Diaspora: A History through Culture*. New York: Columbia University Press.

Vigneswaran, Darshan, and Joel Quirk. 2015. *Mobility Makes States: Migration and Power in Africa*. Philadelphia: University of Pennsylvania Press.

16 MODERNITY

Simon Gikandi

"Modernity" is both an essential and contested term in reference to Africa and African studies. The term "modernity" is considered essential because it is a significant term for thinking about the transformation of African societies since the consolidation of European colonialism in the nineteenth century. But those scholars who doubt how a category developed in Europe in the age of slavery and colonialism can be applied to subjects considered to be outside the modern experience often contest the term. Not surprisingly, then, the term is often understood in its bifurcated nature. For proponents of the term, modernity is seen as the key explanatory concept in describing the radical changes that took place in Africa during the colonial period. These changes are often presented, in a progressive narrative, as the movement from traditional forms of social life based on the authority of religion and ritual, to a modern world built around rationality, individualism, and modernization. Central to this narrative is the assumption that colonialism in Africa functions as a modernizing process, one involving the reorganization of African spaces within a new political and economic order. Within this order, the argument goes, colonialism creates modern institutions, such as the school and the city, which in turn produce new African subjects oriented away from traditional authority toward a new, modern identity. In the institutions of European modernity in Africa, the argument further goes, a new set of desires, aspirations, and allegiances emerge, irrevocably changing the nature of African life.

The fiercest resistance to the term "modernity" is related to what its opponents see as a singular inefficacy, its privileging of the colonial moment in Africa, and a binarism that seems unable to imagine social processes outside the modern/tradition infrastructure. The argument here is that rather than being the agent of modernization in Africa, colonialism retarded the development of a discourse or economy of modernity on the continent. Far from enabling modernity, critics argue, the colonial state set out to invent the African as an unmodern subject—a figure tied to tribe, custom, ritual, and magic. Evidence of the failure of modernity in Africa, argue its opponents, can be found in the survival and even growth of such unmodern practices as witchcraft on the continent. These practices point to an alternative form of modernity.

These conflicting perspectives already point to the challenges of understanding the meaning of modernity in Africa and the difficulties students have searching for a middle ground in the modernity/tradition dyad. Yet, understanding how modernity is both inscribed and displaced in Africa can go a long way in explaining the history and logic of the term. A valuable starting point here is the recognition of what both sides in the debate have in common: They assume colonialism and modernity in Africa are entwined; they also assume that the problem of the modern matters to African studies, that it cannot simply be dismissed as a hollow European term haunting African histories and experiences. But if modernity is an effect of European colonialism and hence inseparable from it, one of the questions it raises is why and how it is able to have a life in decolonization or, to put it another way, why the nationalist project, which is premised on the radical reversal of colonial rule, comes to appropriate modernity as one of its informing categories. Why is it that many Africans, including those who have doubts about the efficacy of modernity as an imported European project, have found it necessary to adopt the term or some of its key aspects? Why indeed has modernization—a key but only partial aspect of modernity—become the central term of frame of reference in the discussion of African experiences during and after colonialism?

Modernity vs. Modernization

Part of the complexity of thinking about "modernity" as a crucial term in the study of Africa has been the common, and often confusing, conflation of modernity and modernization. If African intellectuals and politicians alike have been suspicious of modernity as a project associated with colonial rule, they have been quick to embrace modernization as a horizon of expectations, of the desire for stronger and modern institutions of governance, thriving economies, and the plentitude of social and cultural goods. Where and when modernization has been seen to be working, especially during the first decades of independence in the 1960s and early 1970s, the conceptual baggage of modernity—its association with Europeanization—has been sublimated to stories of stable governments and the proliferation of social goods. When modernizing projects have collapsed, as happened in the 1980s and 1990s, modernity has come to be perceived as a burden at best and a curse at worst. But this association of modernity and modernization has often masked some foundational problems in the way the terms have been used and discussed in an African context. For one, if modernity is considered to be a project that emerged in Europe in the seventeenth and eighteenth centuries and was then transplanted to Africa under the tutelage of colonialism, then it is not clear how the term can be applied to experiences that seem extraneous to its history. And if modernity has been rationalized by its association with the process of modernization or the politics of development, it is not apparent why the term survives scrutiny in the aftermath of postcolonial failure and crisis. Indeed, for many observers of African life, the appeal of modernity in a situation where its essential categories such as the rights of individuals and democratic governance have been under severe strain remains a puzzle. If its record on the continent is one of abjection and failure, why does modernity sit at the center of African debates in a whole range of fields—from political economy to law to literary criticism?

One further complication to the puzzle of modernity concerns the disciplinary divergence in the field of African studies, a matter of definition, emphasis, and outlook. For many social scientists, especially those working in anthropology, sociology, and politics, modernity is explained by the transitions from one structure of social organization to another and the challenges and expectations of modernization at various levels in an evolutionary scale. Pegged on the idea, if not ideal, of modernization, the social sciences in Africa have been central to debates on economic, social, and political development. Although philosophers working in or on Africa have not had the same kind of visibility as the social scientists, they have foregrounded the fundamental questions that the invocation of modernity raises in relation to rationality and rational thinking in societies that have been described as traditional. The basic assumption in the works of almost all leading philosophers on Africa is that modernity signifies a shift in forms of knowledge from a system defined by a continuous adherence to beliefs and practices that have been accepted as implicitly authoritative, to self-reflection and self-questioning. For scholars in the arts, debates about modernity have inevitably revolved on modernism as an aesthetic project, which, as Chika Okeke-Agulu shows in *Postcolonial Modernism*, combine local artistic traditions with global modernist practices.

In spite of these disciplinary differences, however, the modern/tradition dyad that was once popular in African studies in the 1950s and 1960s has been put under pressure by popular cultures, arts, and everyday practices that seem to point to some of the remarkable ways in which modernity is remade in Africa. Still, the narrative of modernity in Africa boils down to the following set of questions raised by Peter Geschiere, Birgit Meyer, and Peter Pels in *Readings in Modernity in Africa*:

> How can we talk and write about modernity without lapsing into discourses of modernization and their teleological views of world history? How do we avoid losing sight of the diversity of local expressive forms through which modernity is being negotiated or appropriated? Or, conversely: how, in studying such local appropriations, can we avoid sidelining the impact of Western-dominated power structures? Oscillating between, on the one hand, the urge to maintain a critical distance to discourses of modernization and development, and, on the other, the realization that these discourses generate powerful practices that do actually shape African people's lives, scholars still face the classical question: what is modernity? (2008, 1)

The last question on the list—what is modernity?—goes to the heart of the problem: What are we to do about this very European category when it is either appropriated or displaced on the margins of the world system? Or, to put it another way, can we entirely escape from modernity as a European term, one closely aligned to the discourse of the Englightenment?

What Is Modernity?

What does "modernity" mean in Africa? Simple definitions might help answer this question. Let us first consider the meaning of modernity as a category that emerges in Europe in a specific period. Within a space of a hundred and fifty years, beginning with the publication of René Descartes's *Discourse on Method* and *Meditations on First Philosophy* in 1637 and ending with Immanuel Kant's essay "An Answer to the Question: What Is Enlightenment?" (1784), a revolution takes place in European thought. Whereas before the identity of the self and its place in the world depended on religious faith or a set of beliefs built "only upon old foundations" and unexamined principles, Descartes sets out to reconstruct his thoughts on his own (subjective) terms, leading to the canonical formulation—"I think therefore I exist"—that ushers in the idea of the modern individual. Individuals who think for themselves will constitute the cog of modernity. As a matter of fact, within the project of what has come to be known as the European Enlightenment, there is going to be a demand that reason become the central cognitive mechanism of understanding; the public use of reason is a precondition for what Kant calls "enlightenment among men." For Kant, Enlightenment will be pegged on a simple idea: an exit from a self-incurred immaturity, namely "the inability to make use of one's own understanding without the guidance of another" (58). Here Enlightenment is the prelude to a singular vision of modernity. It assumes the liberation of the individual from traditional authority—the church, the monarchy, and the group—and the rejection of forms of knowledge associated with an irrational past.

Above all, the Enlightenment promises a new sense of what it means to be a human subject, emphasizing the freedom of the individual over social bonds built on family and kinship. Now the major actor in the drama of modernity is not going to be the community, but what Jürgen Habermas in *The Philosophical Discourse of Modernity* has described as "the sovereign rational subject," the agent of a process of rationalization in which older forms of social organization, built on collective agency, are dissolved in the process of radical examination (1990, viii). This rational subject, argues Habermas, uses the power of reason to turn all other spheres of social life into the "embodiment of the principle of subjectivity" (18). Thus, in addition to ushering in the age of the individual, the discourse of modernity ushers in a new experience of time, one in which the past is suppressed, or is differentiated, from a preceding, unmodern, era. The newness of modern time is underwritten by an immanent sense of progress: the mark of a modern society is the radical and self-conscious break from a temporality focused on the past to one driven by a future of infinite possibilities. The organization of social life will be justified not by the will of the gods, ancestors, or even past practices, but a teleology, a purpose that will be revealed in time. Out of this teleological sense of time emerge two ideas that are going to be central to the spread of modernity in and outside Europe: the idea of economic modernization and secularization.

It is not hard to see why this version of modernity as Enlightenment has met resistance among students of Africa. For one, Enlightenment has been perceived as a Eurocentric project whose identity and authority have depended on the exclusion of the African from the domain of the modern.

Critics suspicious of the Enlightenment's intentions toward Africa and the African, most notably Emmanuel Eze, can point out how the major architects of the European Enlightenment (Kant, G. W. F. Hegel, and David Hume, for example) have written off the African as a figure without taste or genius, beholden to fetishism, subject to irrational behavior, and outside the narrative of world history. The Enlightenment has not merely been seen as hostile to African and other forms of otherness; at the center of its conceptual schemes, it is argued, lies an inbuilt fear of the black body, which is described as vile and unnatural. Still, the version of modernity as Enlightenment has found strong advocates in African studies. Philosophers such as W. E. Abraham (1962), Kwasi Wiredu (1980), Kwame Gyekye (1997), and Olúfẹ̀mi Táíwò (2014) have argued for the efficacy of modernity even within the traditions and histories of Africa. These scholars have sought to reconcile modernity to African modes of thought and, in the process, to modify its meaning and resources.

But while the version of modernity as Enlightenment has generated many debates in the academy, it has not trickled down to ordinary conversations about African futures, nor has it generated powerful social practices. The idea of modernity that seems to have affected the organization of social life on the continent is the one associated with the culture of capitalism in the nineteenth century. For if in the eighteenth century Enlightenment authorizes itself by promising progress as an inevitable consequence of the liberation of individuals from the past, the development of industrial society and capitalism in the nineteenth century ushers in a new kind of modernity built on material, political, economic, and social development. These developments include the huge concentration of people in urban centers, the sharp division of capital and labor, and what the sociologist Max Weber in *The Protestant Ethic and the Spirit of Capitalism* will famously describe as the rationalization of the world. For Weber, rationalization sits at the center of the contradictions that define modern society: On one side we have advances in technology and bureaucracy that have led to the efficient management of social life; on the other hand, these processes have led to the dissociation of individuals or their loss of meaning and control in the new social structure.

In temporal terms, industrialization and capitalism have created a world in the throes of constant change, a kind of shock that will lead the poet Charles Baudelaire to define modernity as "the transient, the fleeting, and the contingent" (1995, 13). For Baudelaire and the writers of early modernism, modernity is welcomed for opening up new spaces of experience, liberating the conception of time from the past, and locating the individual in an eternal present. But for these writers, modernity has also come to signify the shock of the new and, with it, an acute loss of meaning. As Sigmund Freud will note in *Civilization and Its Discontents* (1929) the progress of civilization, which was supposed to bring happiness to millions of people, has only brought about discontent. Beneath what appears to be the rationalization of the world, however, sociologists and creative writers begin to sense fragmentation and tension between the lived world and its imagination; they embark on the search for a mode of apprehending and representing reality not imprisoned in the dream world of capitalism.

Modernism will be born of the tension between the individuals' experience of time and space as contingent and surreal and an aesthetic that is no longer tied to the demands of the real. Furthermore, in a world where capitalism has established a logic that is built on reification—the objectification of individuals, or, as Georg Lukács imagined it in *History and Class Consciousness*, where the relation between human beings assumes the relationship between things—the central concern of European intellectuals at the end of the nineteenth century is the development of an aesthetics that is capable of reacting against the force of modernity. In the early twentieth century, this reaction against modernity will lead European writers, artists, and intellectuals to Africa in search of what they imagine to be a premodern consciousness and its aesthetic. Ironically, a voyage to Africa in the era of late colonialism confronts one with the shock of the modern as it takes root in societies which had hitherto organized themselves in the very terms that modernity had sought to repress—collective identity, traditional institutions, and magic or ritual. Here, new urban centers such as Johannesburg emerge as black labor and white capital are brought together. In colonial Africa, the city will come to stand out as a symbol of the modern world. But to what extent is this edifice modern? Or, to put it another way, what kind of modernity comes with colonialism?

For most of the nineteenth century, colonialism will be seen, by colonizer and colonized alike, as a modernizing project, but the terms of this modernity are conflicted. To the extent that it is involved in the reorganization of African spaces in European terms, colonialism is driven by a modernizing impulse; but even as it moves to remake the African landscape in the image of Europe, it does so in highly selective ways. For example, colonialism enables the creation of new cities in Africa or transforms old ones; yet these new urban centers, the sites where white capital encounters black labor, are not intended to incorporate Africans into global systems of culture and trade but to facilitate the exploitation of resources (copper in Zambia or gold on the South African Rand) or to rationalize administrative control (Accra and Nairobi are modern cities intended to serve this purpose). Where they don't serve either a commercial or administrative purpose, swaths of African land are left untouched or redefined as labor reserves. The paradox here is that colonialism modernizes African spaces to serve its needs.

A related paradox is that colonialism seeks to modernize African spaces outside the theories and practices of Enlightenment. In fact, doctrines of colonialism in Africa often seize some of the categories that excluded the African from the discourse of modernity (in the Enlightenment) as essential tools in the colonizing project. This explains some of the key anomalies in the colonization of Africa: an administrative celebration of traditional authority (hence the doctrine of indirect rule adopted by Lord Lugard for Northern Nigeria); the valorization of political rituals (both African and European); and the invention of customary law; and, ultimately, the failed attempt to produce Africans as servile bodies (for labor production) or passive agents of the colonial mission (the clerical class). But perhaps the most obvious paradox of colonization as a modernizing project is the adoption of religion as a central category in colonization. While classical modernity may be defined as a secular and secularizing project, Christian missionaries act as the major agents of colonial modernization, building schools, reorganizing domestic spaces, and creating new subjects. The convergence of colonialism, mission, and modernizing institutions has led advocates of modernity (as Enlightenment), most notably V. Y. Mudimbe in *The Invention of Africa* and Táíwò in *How Colonialism Preempted Modernity*, to assert that Christian missions are the major agents of modernity on the continent.

How are the missions able to secure modernity without secularization? A compelling answer to this question can be found in Jean and John Comaroff's *Of Revelation and Revolution*. The Comaroffs aptly describe colonialism as a post-Enlightenment process informed by "two contrapuntal narratives": "One speaks of a specific Christian mission and its consequences; the second of a more general post-Enlightenment process of colonization in which Europe set out to grasp and subdue the forces of savagery, otherness, and unreason" (vol. 1, p. 11). Beneath these narratives, however, is to be found a more subtle process—the simultaneous displacement and affirmation of European theories of modernity dating back to the eighteenth century. On the surface, Nonconformist Churches, unlike their established counterparts, try to separate church and state; but in the end the modernizing projects they undertake will be sanctioned by the colonial state. So, there does not appear to be a contradiction between the religious mission of the church and the secular project of the state. In fact, the colonial state often seems keen to assign the mission the task of modernizing the African in a range of fields from animal husbandry, markets, the nature of dwellings, and even marriage. This process of modernization will lead to the production of Africans as modern subjects, but not exactly in the Enlightenment understanding of the term. The missions set out to produce subjects who are not autonomous individuals. What does this mean? Simply that African subjects produced by the missions are not modern in the Kantian sense—they are not asked to think for themselves or to reflect critically on their condition of existence, the colonial situation. On the contrary, the modernity of the mission subjects depends on their ability to mimic the missionary's version of what the modern African should be in terms of dress, dwellings, and deportment. The missionary hence produces what the Comaroffs aptly call "stylized objects" (vol. 2, p. 219).

In colonial settings, as any reading of African literature will show, modernity is valued for its ornamental or stylistic form. One can identify the modern subjects by their adornments, their square houses with corrugated roofs, their orchards, and their imaginary connection to European ideas of space. The embodiment of this world is the parsonage recalled with nostalgia by Wole Soyinka in *Aké*, his childhood memoir:

> If I lay across the lawn before our house, face upwards to the sky, my head towards BishopsCourt, each spread-out leg would point to the inner compounds of Lower Parsonage. Half of the Anglican Girls' School occupied one of these lower spaces, the other half had taken over BishopsCourt. The lower area contained the school's junior classrooms, a dormitory, a small fruit-garden of pawpaws, guava, some bamboo and wild undergrowth. There were always snails to be found in the rainy season. In the lower compound was the mission bookseller, a shrivelled man with a serene wife on whose ample back we all, at one time or the other, slept or reviewed the world. His compound became a short cut to the road that led to Ibarà, Lafenwà or Igbèin and its Grammar School over which Ransome-Kuti presided and lived with his family. The bookseller's compound contained the only well in the parsonage; in the dry season his place was never empty. And his soil appeared to produce the only coconut trees. (1981, 4)

There is more than mimicry going on in this kind of account. For an important, though not obvious, fact is that although the modernity promoted by the missionaries remains wedded to old European notions about culture and civilization—it assumes that the African exists in a situation of savagery and radical alterity—Africans have found a way of introducing their own style into what seems to be imposed from above. As Soyinka's text vividly shows, there are significant ways in which the foundational doctrines of modernity are displaced in Africa: For one, the old cosmology cannot be wished away and must hence be accommodated into the modern. Furthermore, if one accepts the argument that the Enlightenment had set out to lock the African out of its project, then it could be said that the missionaries unintentionally open the door to this edifice of European culture and civilization. At the leading mission schools where African elites are produced—Mfantisipim and Achimota in Ghana, Alliance High School in Kenya, and Kings College Budo in Uganda, for example—young Africans are taught that they, too, can be enlightened subjects. Even within the inner sanctums of the missions, African subjects like Bishop Ajayi Crowther who might appear to be mimic men will come to function as active agents in the reconstruction of a new order. As the first African Anglican bishop of West Africa, Crowther may appear to some observers to be a mimic man, but the missions he starts at Abeokuta inaugurate a line of inquiry that will lay the ground for nationalism and eventually the radical critique of Europe embodied by Soyinka, a product of that mission.

The identification of Africans as powerful agents of modernity opens up another set of questions: What kind of modernity do these local or native agents have in mind? And do they conceive their modernizing project as the institutionalization of individualism, the rejection of traditional authority, and the adoption of rationality? Do they even perceive any difference between modernity and modernization? One can best respond to these questions by working with a simple maxim—that in the culture of colonialism, modernity is defined by a paradox. The most Westernized Africans, those who have adopted European manners in dress, habits, and even ideas, are also active in the preservation of African traditions. Take the example of Sol Plaatje, the prominent Tswana writer and translator. Although he is surrounded by a rich Southern Tswana culture, Plaatje is born and bred in a European institution, namely the Lutheran mission in South Africa, and is educated in church schools. In both the public and private sphere, Plaatje cuts the image of a modern subject: He dresses like a Victorian gentleman, lives in a European style house, and organizes his household along Western lines. Moreover, like many of his close associates, Plaatje is fully integrated into the modern world: As a literate colonial subject, he acts as a translator in the colonial law courts and serves as a witness to the siege of Mafeking (1899–1900) during the Second Anglo-Boer War, a modern European event playing itself out in the colonial world. In addition, Plaatje is active in the literary culture of Kimberley, involved in translations of Shakespeare and the writing of plays and novels, including *Mhudi*, considered to be one of the earliest African novels in English. Yet, Plaatje assumes that his status as a modern subject has no meaning unless it is founded on a Tswana culture autonomous from colonialism and its institutions. He hence spends considerable time and money working to preserve the traditions of his people. He writes *Mhudi*, not because he is interested in the novel as a genre, but in the hope that sales of the book will help him raise money to finance the publication of his collection of Tswana proverbs.

Here we see an example of an African conceptualization of modernity: it cannot be defined against tradition or traditional authority, nor can it be driven by an impulse to separate individuals from communities. Indeed, the major criticism of colonial modernity in African thought is that by separating individuals from communities, it creates unstable subjects. We find this criticism at the end of Jomo Kenyatta's *Facing Mt. Kenya* (1938), an ethnographic account of the Kikuyu undergoing the process of change. Kenyatta argues that one of the reasons why the Europeans misunderstand the Kikuyu is because of their failure to comprehend the centrality of collective entities such as "the family group and the age-grades, which between them shape the character and determine the outlook of every man, woman, and child in Gikuyu society." For Kenyatta, a modernity premised on individualism is bound to fail:

> According to Gikuyu ways of thinking, nobody is an isolated individual. Or rather, his uniqueness is a secondary fact about him: first and foremost he is several people's relative and several people's contemporary. His life is founded on this fact spiritually and economically, just as much as biologically; the work he does every day is determined by it, and it is the basis of his sense of moral responsibility and social obligation. His personal needs, physical and psychological, are satisfied incidentally while he plays his part as member of a family group, and cannot be fully satisfied in any other way. The fact that in Gikuyu language individualism is associated with black magic, and that

> a man or woman is honoured by being addressed as somebody's parent, or somebody's uncle or aunt, shows how indispensably kinship is at the root of Gikuyu ideas of good and evil. (297)

Kenyatta's rejection of European individualism does not, however, lead him to discard the idea of the modern altogether; on the contrary, redefining the terms of modernity will lead him to embrace it as a condition of an African future outside colonialism. He wants a modernity of political and social goods not values. His dream is that in decolonization, Africans will be left alone to "choose what parts of European culture could be beneficially transplanted, and how they could be adapted" (306). Transportation and adaptation signal a break from colonial versions of modernity popular in the 1930s, which assumed that the African was constantly under the stress of change. There might be a shift in the system of social values, Kenyatta argues, but this does not preclude the African's desire for "a superior way of life" (305). This is how economic modernization informs the process of subject formation. Kenyatta assumes that subjects can undergo the process of modernization and still retain their core identity as traditional subjects.

Modernity vs. Tradition

Now, the persistence of "tradition" as a key term in African debates on modernity could appear, on the surface, to be the proverbial return of the ghosts of modernity—identified by Geschiere, Meyer, and Pels as "fetishism, religion, tradition and charisma" (3). On closer examination, however, the term "tradition" is not the sign of a regressive time; rather, it has been modernized to account for the project of modernization outside its European inheritance. It is not insignificant that when African politicians and intellectuals speak about tradition, they rarely associate it with fetishism, religion, or irrationality; on the contrary, tradition is represented as an alternative order of rationality. For philosophers like Gyekye, "a self-created" African modernity can emerge through the modernization of tradition:

> Modernity, which involves a transition to a new era characterized by advanced forms of knowledge, techniques, economic and political institutions as well as radical departures from some inherited traditions, includes features of a cultural tradition that would be considered symphonic with forms of life

> in the new era. These will include the positive features of a cultural tradition, for these tend to abide on grounds of their considerable normativity and functionality. (1997, 287)

So, if tradition seems to sit at the center of many African debates on modernity and modernization, it is probably because of its association with a normative and functional order. In fact, for African nationalist intellectuals such as Julius Nyerere of Tanzania, tradition functions as a resource for reimagining modernity as an African concept. In his major speeches on the political economy of Tanzania after decolonization and unification, Nyerere rarely uses the word "modernization"; his preference is for the term development or, in Swahili, *maendeleo*. Defined as "going on, progress, advance, success" in the standard Swahili dictionaries, *maendeleo* does not denote a teleology or even a movement from a lower to higher stage of development, but simple movement from where one is to another place or position. In *maendeleo*, the subject does not move from barbarism to civilization nor dissociate itself from one mode of being to another; rather, this kind of development involves continuity between traditional beliefs and a new set of assumptions in a changed social structure and temporality. Although the goal of *maendeleo* is the modernization of the rural economy, Nyerere imagines socialism, or *Ujamaa*, in Tanzania as the return to what he considers to be a core African principle—that of communality. For Nyerere, socialism is the universal term for modernization outside capitalism; but the developments envisaged—mass literacy, better living conditions, and grass roots democracy—will be instituted through a return to *jamaa*, the community or collective body: "Traditionally we lived as families, with individuals supporting each other and helping each other on terms of equality. . . . This attitude is, basically, what we mean by saying that traditionally African society was a socialist society" (1968, 198).

Nyerere is, of course, able to make the case for an alternative path to modernization in Africa because he has had access to the culture of European modernity. Indeed, this access to European modernity has given Africans and Africanists a subtle understanding of the term and its limits; in African contexts, keen distinctions are made between modernity, modernism, and modernization. Consider, for example, how these distinctions work out in Léopold Sédar Senghor's essay "Negritude and Modernity." For Senghor, the ethnographer, negritude is the process by which African ideas are introduced into an already existing narrative of modernity to "build the *Civilization of the Universal*, to which each particular civilization will bring its most creative, because most complementary, values" (2001, 162). For Senghor, the poet, negritude implies the recognition of Africa as an important resource in the idiom of modernism and its aesthetic. He criticizes those who reduce the African aesthetic to "an ethnological document" or confuse it "with a talisman," ignoring its informing notions of beauty (152). He describes black-African art as "a string of signifying catachresis" animated by "the imperious Black rhythm" (154). And for Senghor, the nationalist, negritude represents a new temporality in which new ideas about development and modernization can be instituted within the ideal of a "contemporary Humanism": "The civilization of the twenty-first century . . . will certainly be over-industrial, that is technological. It will be either *Humanism* or *Barbarism*, depending on whether the peoples of the Third World, and among them the Black peoples, will have contributed to it" (162).

Conclusion

Why are the differentiations between modernity, modernism, and modernization important? Primarily because it is through the differentiation of these terms that modernity is made to matter. Located in different spheres of social life, modernity becomes much more than an extroverted European term exported to Africa or imposed through colonial will; it is reimagined as part of a larger conversation on a set of needs and desires that are simultaneously real and imaginary. These needs and desires are real because, as James Ferguson has shown in *Expectations of Modernity*, they are part of an African desire for the goods and privileges of modernity. Indeed, modernity seems to make most sense when it is used as a general description for peoples' aspirations for an improvement in their lives rather than the emergence of new systems of rationality or forms of knowledge. This does not mean that those who advocate for a kind of African Enlightenment are wrong, for there are moments when it seems that the absence of rational or moral choices is what defeats expectations of modernity on the continent. So, both understandings of modernity—improvement and rationality—retain power and appeal. They also point to how the use or invocation of modernity, modernism, or simply a modern experience comes to be defined by the tension between life and thought. It is when we turn to the imagination of modernity, however, that this tension seems to be resolved or to lead us to a set of intriguing antinomies.

The household in which Soyinka, in *Aké*, grows up is defined by the daily encounter between the world of his father, enacting a modern colonial style represented by a "chart pinned to the wall, next to the mirror," doing his best "to imitate the white gymnast who was photographed in a variety of postures and contortions on that chart" (79); and that of his mother reflecting a "profusion of disorder" associated with her continuous engagement with the everydayness of the Yoruba world and its family rituals and obligations (78). We encounter similar contrasts in Isaac Okonkwo's household in Chinua Achebe's *No Longer at Ease*:

> The result of Okonkwo's mystic regard for the written word was that his room was full of old books and papers—from Blackie's Arithmetic which he used in 1908 to Obi's Durrell, from obsolete cockroach-eaten translations of the Bible into the Onitsha dialect to yellowed Scripture Union Cards of 1920 and earlier. Okonkwo never destroyed a piece of paper. He had two boxes full of them. The rest were preserved on top of his enormous cupboard, on tables, on boxes and on one corner of the floor.
>
> Mother's room, on the other hand, was full of mundane things. She had her box of clothes on a stool. On the other side of the room were pots of solid palm-oil with which she made black soap. The palm-oil was separated from the clothes by the whole length of the room, because, as she always said, clothes and oil were not kinsmen, and just as it was the duty of clothes to try and avoid oil it was also the duty of the oil to do everything to avoid clothes. (2008, 115)

The gendered nature of spaces (men are associated with the European modern while women embody the African everyday) needs to be interrogated, but it is an indication of a crucial distinction between the theorization of modernity and its experience. Modernity is associated with an elsewhere—what Soyinka calls "a different, unreal world" (79)—but it also inscribed within another order of things that belongs to the here and now.

Suggested Readings

Achebe, Chinua. 2008. *No Longer at Ease*. London: Heinemann.

Comaroff, Jean, and John L. Comaroff. 1991. *Of Revelation and Revolution: Christianity, Colonialism, and Consciousness*. Vol. 1. Chicago: University of Chicago Press.

Comaroff, John L., and Jean Comaroff. 1997. *Of Revelation and Revolution: The Dialectics of Modernity of a South African Frontier*. Vol. 2. Chicago: University of Chicago Press.

Eze, Emmanuel Chukwudi. 1987. *Race and the Enlightenment: A Reader*. Oxford: Wiley-Blackwell.

Ferguson, James. 1999. *Expectations of Modernity: Myths and Meanings of Urban Life in the Zambian Copperbelt*. Berkeley: University of California Press.

Geschiere, Peter, Birgit Meyer, and Peter Pels, eds. 2008. *Readings in Modernity in Africa*. Bloomington: Indiana University Press.

Kenyatta, Jomo. 1965. *Facing Mt. Kenya*. New York: Vintage.

Mudimbe, V.Y. *The Invention of Africa: Gnosis, Philosophy, and the Order of Knowledge*. Bloomington: Indiana University Press.

Nyerere, Julius. 1968. *Freedom and Socialism/Uhuru na Ujamaa*. Dar es Salaam: Oxford University Press.

Okeke-Agulu, Chika. 1965. *Postcolonial Modernism: Art and Decolonization in Twentieth-Century Nigeria*. Durham, NC: Duke University Press.

Probst, Peter, Jan-Georg Deutsch, and Heike Schmidt, eds. 2002. *African Modernities*. Oxford: James Currey.

Táíwò, Olúfémi. 2010. *How Colonialism Preempted Modernity in Africa*. Bloomington: Indiana University Press.

———. 2014. *Africa Must Be Modern: A Manifesto*. Bloomington: Indiana University Press.

Soyinka, Wole. 1981. *Aké: The Years of Childhood*. New York: Vintage.

Wiredu, Kwasi. 1980. *Philosophy and an African Culture*. Cambridge: Cambridge University Press.

References

Abraham, W. E. 1962. *The Mind of Africa*. Chicago: University of Chicago Press.

Achebe, Chinua. 2008. *No Longer at Ease*. London: Heinemann.

Baudelaire, Charles. 1995. *The Painter of Modern Life and Other Essays*. London: Phaidon.

Comaroff, Jean, and John L. Comaroff. 1991. *Of Revelation and Revolution: Christianity, Colonialism, and Consciousness*. Vol. 1. Chicago: University of Chicago Press.

Comaroff, John L., and Jean Comaroff. 1997. *Of Revelation and Revolution: The Dialectics of Modernity of a South African Frontier*. Vol. 2. Chicago: University of Chicago Press.

Descartes, René. 1985a. "Discourse and Essays." *The Philosophical Writings of Descartes*. Vol. 1. Translated by John Cottingham, Robert Stoothoff, and Douglas Murdoch. Cambridge: Cambridge University Press.

———. 1985b. "Meditations on First Philosophy." *The Philosophical Writings of Descartes*. Vol. 2. Translated by John Cottingham, Robert Stoothoff, and Douglas Murdoch. Cambridge: Cambridge University Press.

Eze, Emmanuel Chukwudi. 1987. *Race and the Enlightenment: A Reader*. Oxford: Wiley-Blackwell.

Ferguson, James. 1999. *Expectations of Modernity: Myths and Meanings of Urban Life in the Zambian Copperbelt*. Berkeley: University of California Press.

Geschiere, Peter, Birgit Meyer, and Peter Pels, eds. 2008. *Readings in Modernity in Africa*. Bloomington: Indiana University Press.

Gyekye, Kwame. 1997. *Tradition and Modernity: Philosophical Reflections on the African Experience*. New York: Oxford.

Habermas, Jürgen. 1990. *The Philosophical Discourse of Modernity*. Translated by Frederick G. Lawrence. Cambridge, MA: MIT Press.

Kant, Immanuel. 1996. "An Answer to the Question: What is Enlightenment?" In *What is Enlightenment: Eighteenth-Century Answers and Twentieth-Century Questions*, edited by James Schmidt. Berkeley: University of California Press.

Kenyatta, Jomo. 1965. *Facing Mt. Kenya*. New York: Vintage.

Lukács, Georg. 1972. *History and Class Consciousness: Studies in Marxist Dialectics*. Cambridge, MA: MIT Press.

Mudimbe, V. Y. *The Invention of Africa: Gnosis, Philosophy, and the Order of Knowledge*. Bloomington: Indiana University Press.

Nyerere, Julius. 1968. *Freedom and Socialism/Uhuru na Ujamaa*. Dar es Salaam: Oxford University Press.

Okeke-Agulu, Chika. 1965. *Postcolonial Modernism: Art and Decolonization in Twentieth-Century Nigeria*. Durham, NC: Duke University Press.

Probst, Peter, Jan-Georg Deutsch, and Heike Schmidt, eds. 2002. *African Modernities*. Oxford: James Currey.

Táíwò, Olúfémi. 2010. *How Colonialism Preempted Modernity in Africa*. Bloomington: Indiana University Press.

———. 2014. *Africa Must Be Modern: A Manifesto*. Bloomington: Indiana University Press.

Senghor, Léopold Sédar. 2001. "Negritude and Modernity, or Negritude as a Humanism for the Twentieth Century." In *Race*, edited by Robert Bernasconi, 143–66. Malden, MA: Blackwell.

Soyinka, Wole. 1981. *Aké: The Years of Childhood*. New York: Vintage.

Weber, Max. 2001. *The Protestant Ethic and the Spirit of Capitalism*. London: Routledge.

Wiredu, Kwasi. 1980. *Philosophy and an African Culture*. Cambridge: Cambridge University Press.

17 NARRATIVE

Stephanie Newell

In the final scene of Chinua Achebe's iconic novel *Things Fall Apart*, a British district commissioner frames the dead protagonist, Okonkwo, by setting his body into a familiar corpus of colonial anthropological discourse. Gazing at the hanging man, the DC muses about the monograph he intends to write, entitled *The Pacification of the Primitive Tribes of the Lower Niger*: "One could almost write a whole chapter on him. Perhaps not a whole chapter but a reasonable paragraph, at any rate" (1986, 147–48). In this frequently quoted scene from the first book to be published in Heinemann's African Writers Series, Achebe shows the capacity of a colonial master—and, through him, a colonial master-narrative—to assemble complex African fragments into a coherent plot under the sign of anthropology as rational, mimetic prose. The fictional village, its characters, its cultural complexities, and Achebe himself as author, are emplotted by colonialism into a "reasonable paragraph" filled with interpretive dead ends for African subjects.

In closing a novel about the reassertion of a dignified precolonial subjectivity with the nonfictional narrative that imperial Britain wrote to itself—that Africans required the civilizing intervention of Europeans in order to learn how to be modern political citizens—Achebe illustrated the necessity of countering such master-narratives with alternative accounts of the African past. *Things Fall Apart* tries to splinter the colonial illusion that its African story was mimetic and reasonable and true. Achebe, like many other nationalist African authors before and after, used the genre of Anglophone literary fiction to tell another story, to assert a narrative of African citizenship that contested the British Empire's self-serving descriptions for the maintenance of its power. In so doing, just as the district officer frames Okonkwo, Achebe is framed by colonial discourse for his reclamatory assertion of African reasonableness.

Things Fall Apart lays bare the textual processes behind what Mahmood Mamdani, in the wake of Edward Said's influential work on orientalist discourse, terms "define and rule," through which each so-called native was fixed permanently to a "tribal" identity by the colonial administration, repeatedly marked as such in the plural texts—newspapers, novels, films, archives, laws, policies, school curricula—generated under the sign of the British right to rule. Out of this institutional history, according to Mamdani, emerged multiculturalist discourse in postcolonial Africa as a form of statecraft that remained marked by colonial categories of race and ethnicity above the recognition of persons.

A general narratological principle drawn from this critique of colonialism would involve a Foucauldian formulation: that power produces narratives, that narratives produce knowledge, and that knowledge produces and sustains power structures, which, in turn, produce further narratives and knowledge (see Said 1979). Situated in the realm of the already-narrated, storytellers and readers are caught up in unevenly distributed global discourses from which nobody can escape. For a person on the peripheries, as the protagonist of Zoë Wicomb's "Another Story" (2003 [1990]) reflects, "she was used to wearing white people's clothes and eating their leftovers, so what difference did it make reading their stories" (423)?

Taken together, the above examples of narrative in situ extend and relativize theories that narrative is a basic cognitive and aesthetic building block to facilitate people's understanding of past, present, and future realities, making possible their interpretations of historical contingency and reality itself (Ricoeur 1984, 41–52). From completely different starting points, Achebe and Mamdani reject any assumption that narrative is universal, operating outside of power structures. Such an assumption risks the creation of hermeneutic dead ends for people at the margins, amply symbolized in *Things Fall Apart* by Okonkwo's end in somebody else's narrative. The subtlety, bias, mobility, speculativeness, and sheer plurality of narrative movement across what Mary Louise Pratt has called international "contact zones" prevent any simple use of narrative as an analytic category in literary and media studies. This is all the more so in contexts with flourishing oral, popular, and performance genres occurring off the printed page, in local languages, and in contexts with lively social media cultures with a capacity for transnational circulation outside of conventional printed archives.

Mimesis, as Simon Gikandi points out, is the sign of realism, and realism both characterizes colonial writing and binds anti-colonial narratives into an intimate relationship with the very representations authors repudiate and wish to displace with other stories. Thus were "colonized writers," as Gikandi terms Achebe's generation, themselves literally—literarily—colonized by nineteenth-century colonial discourse. Given this complex problematic, should postcolonial literary and cultural scholars try to sidestep the consideration of mimesis because of its heritage in colonial claims to reasonableness, and turn instead toward the possibility of other genres, other realisms, other theories of narrative, other stories?

The repeated turn in African literary studies toward non-realist or anti-mimetic narratives—particularly foundational 1950s and 1960s narratives such as Amos Tutuola's *The Palm-Wine Drinkard* and Cheikh Hamidou Kane's *Ambiguous Adventure*—can be understood as a critical bid to step away from the colonizing model of mimesis into unpredictable African narratives and alternative, local theories of representation. Without magically also stepping out of the philosophical frames that contain the disciplines of postcolonial literary and cultural studies, however, we cannot simply access examples of African narratives that are uncolonized or conduct themselves otherwise to realism and mimesis. Such a gesture is hopelessly essentialist, forgetful of the very genres that made it thinkable in the first place.

The effort to rethink the interpretation of mimetic narratives from postcolonial contexts characterizes much postcolonial literary scholarship to date. Authors as well as literary theorists have sought to open up spaces in discourse for the articulation of that which is suppressed by dominant narrative frames. From Said's analysis of orientalism and his later "contrapuntal" readings of canonical English authors to Gayatri Chakravorty Spivak's identification of "subaltern" elements in discourse to the South African author Antjie Krog's interrogation of narrative forms of representation in the Truth and Reconciliation process, postcolonial writers have adopted a recurrent interpretive strategy through which subordinate subjects' capacity for self-articulation is illuminated as palimpsest, as untranslated language, as fragments, as alternative knowledge, and as difference. In so doing, these authors' and theorists' attention to suppressed and emergent discursive spaces highlights the capacity of mimesis and emplotment to make a (post)colonial subject thoroughly wretched in narrative.

Frantz Fanon, Bessie Head, and the (Post)Colonial Subject

In *The Wretched of the Earth*, Frantz Fanon offers an explanation for why anti-colonial armed struggles in the postwar period required coherent narratives of the type created by Achebe in *Things Fall Apart*, through which the national culture's precolonial complexity could be described. For freedom to become an existential reality alongside armed struggle, colonized subjects had to reassert the cultural integrity of their ancestors prior to, outside of, and over and against the truth claims made by European colonial cultures. Only in this way could colonized subjects start to establish an autonomous nationhood, and reject colonial constructions of "native" incoherence and inferiority.

For the colonized intellectual, however, this was a process filled with psychic hurdles. Fanon's powerful term *damnés* describes not only the colonized in relation to European colonial discourse, but also the alienated condition of postcolonial intellectuals who circulate in their newly liberated worlds "without an anchorage, without borders, colorless, stateless, rootless, a body of angels," stranded between the monoliths of European civilization and repeated, failed efforts to identify with and immerse themselves in "national" cultures (2004, 155–58). Wretched, expelled from the time and place of others' narratives, such people—*les damnés*—are the existential embodiment of the philosopher Paul Ricoeur's notion of human experience were it ever possible to be cast out of narrative: in such a space, we would be "confused, unformed, and at the limit, mute" (1984, xi). Fanon's *damnés* lack any representational structure, let alone a mimetic one.

What escapes, if any, do African intellectuals offer from the postcolonial tragedy described by Fanon, where the master-narrative generates reactionary counter-narratives or, failing that, expels its alienated subjects into palimpsestic spaces where the most forceful articulations they can achieve are through mimicry or nonverbal forms of resistance? In his earlier work, *Black Skin, White Masks*, Fanon started to address this double bind, and he did so through a theory of narrative structure and form as much as through attention to the existential and political conditions of people in the colonies. He proposed an alternative to the movement of colonial discourse whereby colonial narratives generate anti-colonial counter-narratives in an uneven return. Outside this structure, Fanon identified "a zone of nonbeing, an extraordinarily sterile and arid region, an utterly naked declivity." This space of absolute negativity, which at first sight seems most undesirable, invokes Ricoeur's hypothetical description of the amorphous confusion of humans located outside discourse, debarred from narrative. Fanon concretizes this space as the place "where an authentic upheaval can be born" (2004, 10). Transcendence, for the colonized subject, comes only from the "descent into a real hell" that entering this space of negativity involves, a journey "the black man" is largely prevented from achieving, not only because of his inescapable immersion in language as a human subject, but also, specifically, because of his perpetual emplotment by colonial discourse as a black man.

Fanon performs resistance to this emplotment in others' narratives by structuring *Black Skin, White Masks* around a series of questions posed in evocative, poeticized language. Through speculation and ellipses, he strives to reintroduce as much ambiguity and complexity to the human condition as possible, in particular to separate off the human subject from the visual economy of race—the rigid body politics of colonial discourse—in order to resist the damage that racist labels inflict upon the subjectivity of the black person. Only then, it seems, can the "black man" enter the hell from which transcendence begins. Fanon's text is thick with open-ended questions about human subjectivity, launched into the time and space of the reader's world, inviting the reader to "rethink Africa," to use Achille Mbembe's resonant phrase for the challenges of finding a resistant language. "My final prayer," Fanon's last line reads: "O my body, make of me always a man who questions!" (2004, 232).

In nonfictional texts such as *Black Skin, White Masks*, the presence of direct, unanswered questions and unfinished sentences interrupts narrative coherence and ruptures the pretense of a coterminous narrator and reader. This disruptive potential is all the more powerful in mimetic fictions, which require temporal completion and spatial coherence for emplotment to succeed. The time lag between narrator and reader must be suspended for the illusion of reality to succeed. This impossibility of direct communication between narrator and reader—let alone between author and reader—is playfully invoked by the first-person narrator of Tutuola's *The Palm-Wine Drinkard*, who suspends the narration of a courtroom scene in order to appeal directly to readers, asking them to send him letters of advice by the next post, about how he should judge the two complicated cases before him at that moment. The space of the appeal (the printed text), the subject of the question (the reader), and the time of any answer (the future) combine comically to expose the folly of taking any mimetic narration at face value, let alone this mimetic moment in Tutuola's fantastic, folkloric text.

Pronouns matter: if Fanon cannot envisage an easy passageway for a black man into the hell from which transcendence can commence, Bessie Head, a black woman, writing a decade after Fanon's death, produced a story that her narrator repeatedly describes as a living death, a journey that takes her into and out of hell. Bessie Head's *A Question of Power*, published as part of the African Writers Series in 1974, features a mother in the depths of a nervous breakdown caused by life in apartheid South Africa. The heroine, Elizabeth, constantly returns to the fact that "in South Africa she had been rigidly classified Coloured. There was no escape from it." The brutal system of racial identification under apartheid leaves no space for complexity and indeterminacy, or "the simple joy of being a human being with a personality" (1979, 44).

From its title onward, Head's complex narrative emphasizes the human capacity for questioning, not for resolving, archaic problems of love, hate, race, and identity. The novel's highly speculative, nonmimetic approach goes a long way toward opening up the "utterly naked declivity" that Fanon calls for as the starting point for a "new humanism," where the colonized body can transcend the marks of colonial discourse. In Head's novel, Elizabeth is tormented by categories of race, sex, and belonging, each one mythically realized, and constantly calls, after Fanon, for an abandonment of labels and discourses that limit and define Africa and Africans in favor of what she repeatedly describes as "the wonderful strangeness of human nature." *A Question of Power* emplots what Fanon called for: narrated directly from "hell," Elizabeth's speculative approach transforms her into a "prophet," posing unresolved questions that push past colonial truth claims into new creative spaces without losing sight of local specificities. Humanist but not mimetic, the narrative provides Africans with a "lever out of hell," making possible "the great leap out of hell" (1974, 198, 188).

A Question of Power is as disruptive of master-discourses as an Anglophone novel can be. On reading the manuscript after it had already received a number of rejections from London literary agents, one of the editors of the African Writers Series, James Currey, sent Head a letter: "*A Question of Power* numbs me," he wrote: "I go back and back to it. We could publish it in [the] African Writers Series though I don't think it is really African. It seems more closely related to the main stream of Anglo-American internal writing, though the whole race thing gets across."

What it means for a narrative to be "really African" has generated considerable debate among literary practitioners and theorists since the African literature conferences of the early 1960s. Most famously, the

African Writers Conference held at Makerere University, Uganda, in June 1962, involved heated disagreements between African intellectuals about the content and definition of "African literature." In his compelling book, *The Postcolonial Exotic: Marketing the Margins*, Graham Huggan insists that the production and marketing of "Africa" by Western publishers frequently involves the imposition of themes, styles, and particular ideas about narrative and identity. Certainly, the editorial response to Head's manuscript begs the question: are there some "not really African" approaches and subjects, and if so, what might these be? Head responded with increasing exasperation to the ambivalence of British literary agents and publishers, whose expectations for African narrative seemed to marginalize her major work for its nonmimetic approach to the representation of time and place. "Chuck the bloody thing out of the bloody window," she wrote furiously to one agent, Hilary Rubenstein of A. P. Watt.

Both Fanon and Head demonstrate that a questioning method can be fraught, anxious, confrontational, broken, polymorphous, speculative, and antagonistic: it can take a narrator into hell. Their approach parallels what the political theorist, Chantal Mouffe, terms "agonistic" discourse: this describes a discourse that occupies a multipolar public space in which questions are not necessarily resolved, resistance is welcomed, and antagonism is articulated rather than suppressed. For Mouffe, agonism is a productive type of conflict in pluralistic democracies, where discourses cease to labor only to reinforce themselves, and where assertions are replaced by questions. The postcolonial theorist Gayatri Chakravorty Spivak also articulates an agonistic approach in her famous essay "Marginality in the Teaching Machine," in which she writes about how teachers in multicultural contexts should question and disrupt what people take for granted as reasonable, and, in so doing, generate a "productive crisis" among those who properly absorb their words.

An agonistic approach to narrative can be found in numerous African novels and short stories since the 1960s, to the extent that a politics of narrative might be identified in large numbers of texts. Again and again, authors interrogate uncritical and homogenizing descriptions—not least labels such as "African"—and they frequently do so through challenges to mimetic narration and strategies aimed at introducing interpretive crises in readers. This includes the genre- and language-busting experiments with form and theme in the so-called new generation of African writers coming out of publishing enterprises such as Kwani? in Kenya and Farafina in Nigeria. It also includes the work of many established authors, not least Ngũgĩ wa Thiong'o, Zoë Wicomb, and Ivan Vladislavić, whose disruptions to conventional notions of mimesis offer a range of different frames from that offered by Gikandi's "colonized writers" for discussions of African fiction.

It is important to note that realist narration in African fiction occupies a position within a broader and historically older body of non-realist writing, including print fiction from the 1880s onward. Novels such as Ngũgĩ wa Thiong'o's *Devil on the Cross*, Zoë Wicomb's *David's Story*, and Ivan Vladislavić's *The Folly* stage acts of narration that break out of the "writing back," counter-narrative model through which *Things Fall Apart* continues to be interpreted. If regarded from the standpoint of literary realism, which is a flawed yardstick by which to judge their works, these authors engage in space-clearing gestures, making room in their narratives for stories that are neither transparent nor mimetic, nor necessarily coherent to all readers. They demonstrate three obvious points: that "narrative" is neither neutral nor universal; that mimesis is culturally specific and must be located in regional as well as global genres and literary cultures; and that diverse forms of representation circulate in global narratives, each one not necessarily translatable into the terms of the other.

Outside the international circuits of print culture dominated by multinational publishing corporations, diverse narrative genres have always existed and found audiences in Africa. In particular, popular literature is a particularly creative area through which non-elite Africans can respond to, and represent, their worlds and worldviews (Barber 1987; Okome 2009). As Uta Reuster-Jahn writes of Swahili language magazines in Tanzania, popular literature "predominantly targets the 'ordinary people' as readership and is unconcerned with the approval of an elitist, let alone Western audience" (email message to author, May 5, 2013). Unconcernedly combining realism and non-realism, fiction and nonfiction, authorship and reading, these creative genres make many of the cardinal categories of literary criticism seem redundant. This is nowhere more evident than in the productive narrative space of the worldwide web.

The Internet and Contemporary Narrative in Africa

To what extent has the rise of the internet in Africa affected the place and time of narrative as articulated by last century's intellectuals? Does worldwide connectivity furnish narrating subjects with new archives, repertoires, identities, genres, discourses, worlds, and audiences? An optimistic answer to these questions is provided by the media scholar Last Moyo, writing about political blogging in Zimbabwe: "Digital technologies like the internet," he states, "have brought about virtual communities or network societies that transcend the limits of time and space" (2011, 747). In Nigeria, Presley Ifukor agrees: "Social media enables freedom of communication," providing "a supplementary avenue for self-expression, a communication medium, and a virtual public sphere" (2010, 407). Countless Africa-oriented sites exist in cyberspace, packed with content generated by "citizen journalists," bloggers, tweeters, and creative writers, supporting Ifukor's suggestion that the internet has opened up a "virtual public sphere." With access to blogs and microblogs, Ifukor argues, "previously faceless and voiceless citizens" can experience empowerment through their involvement in political and social processes.

One of the clearest examples of how cyberspace offers individuals on the margins of global capital opportunities for empowerment is an illegal form of narrative that confers a morally questionable global "citizenship" on its users. A scene in Teju Cole's *Every Day Is for the Thief* describes an internet café in Lagos filled with "419ers," or internet scammers (2014, 24–29). Cole comments on the intense creativity of each scammer as he (the scene refers only to men) labors zealously to perfect a persuasive narrative in his bid "to shake off poverty" (24). Under the nose of a policeman posted in the café to prevent scammers, and under warning signs on the walls with threats of punishment, the young men risk everything for the future their message might deliver in return. Watched covertly by the narrator, the "men work words with the intensity and focus of dowsers, leading their readers down fanciful paths" (28). Just one credulous reader in cyberspace, and the author's future will be transformed.

Scammers' attempts at mimetic narrative show considerable ingenuity: they use internet search engines and websites as research tools, not only to discover names and addresses, but to glean sufficient information about the workings of global finance and its communication genres to persuade their intended readers of their authenticity. Freed from what South African author Ezekiel Mphahlele described, in another time, as "the tyranny of place," cyber-scam space is packed with creative narratives aimed at explaining away the miraculous choice of the email addressee as the lucky recipient of vast deposits of cash.

As Cole observes of Lagos, scammers relish the freedom to ventriloquize with no obligation to be "of" a place or "in" a discourse (see also Beukes 2010; Olukotun 2014). Dislocated at the height of connectivity, scammers perform disruption—of identity and place—in a dream of self-enrichment that cashes in on recipients' reciprocal dreams of miraculous wealth. Paradoxically, these emails say more than their authors could possibly articulate about disparities in global wealth and access to opportunities as well as about how to make money on the periphery of world financial markets. This is a goal-oriented genre filled with forgery, creativity, research, a sense of the future, and, most especially, a careful cross-identification with readers to create trust, all in the space of a single screen. "I have started processing your payment," one scammer writes, personally yet efficiently, continuing with the gravitas of a busy official. "You are required to reconfirm directly to me the above information to enable me use it to process your bill of payment" ("Brian Moynihan" pseud., email message to author, September 26, 2015). Disastrously for most authors, the fabrication fails within the first sentence, hoist by the petard of authors' grammatical inaccuracies or unconvincing turns of phrase: "We are hereby officially notify you . . ." the above email began, before requesting "your address of locations." With this grammatical failure in the adopted voice, the scammer's narrative unravels, and the romance between anonymous author and unknown reader dissolves into farce.

Examples such as these demonstrate how internet connectivity contributes to the decontextualization of narrative and genre by releasing content to potentially unlimited audiences with broad horizons of literary expectation. Cyberspace allows writers the capacity to innovate with identity as well as with narrative forms. At the level of the human experience of time and space, internet access helps to transform peripheral subjects into transnational individuals with the capacity to transcend regimes of time, place, and identity, and to communicate freely across otherwise inaccessible contact zones. The "419ers" may be parasitical borrowers from the narrative of global capital—anything but internet activists—but their appeals demonstrate how access to cyberspace deconstructs, without deleting, postcolonial inequalities.

Scamming aside, as a worldwide medium, the internet allows space for creative collaborations and global forums to the extent that some scholars regard it as part of a "postglobal" moment (de Bruijn and van Dijk 2012, 5–6). Does this mean that African writing is freed from the power-knowledge hierarchies that structured Achebe's discourse back in 1958 and continue to characterize authoritarian states on the continent? Cyberspace is not a singular, universally accessible public sphere any more than its users are, in Fanon's words, "without an anchorage, without borders, colorless, stateless, rootless, a body of angels" (2004, 155). Online as well as offline, neoliberalism is a shaping global force. Money and technology are required for internet access, not to mention stable connectivity, and sustained, substantial contributions to blogs require time and labor as well as self-confidence and education.

Alongside these disparities of access, as Moyo points out, the internet tends to be available for "appropriation by liberal social movements whose configuration is elitist." For these social and economic reasons, therefore, many scholars are skeptical about the existential freedoms claimed for cyberspace by optimistic media scholars. "Do these new and repurposed literary forms and networks really have a pan-African reach?" Stephanie Bosch Santana asks, cautiously, of the burgeoning African online literary culture: "Online literatures have emerged from Nigeria, Kenya, and South Africa, but other countries with less digital infrastructure seem to be approaching the era of Internet literature more warily."

Conclusion

In writing *Things Fall Apart* in the 1950s, Achebe attempted to disrupt and expose the genre of mimetic narration, binding the British story into the structure of his novel in the form of a tragic parable about the decline and fall of one cultural order and its replacement by another. In the decades since its publication, *Things Fall Apart* has sold eight million copies and been translated into fifty world languages. As late as 2006, however, a further death-blow was deemed necessary to Eurocentric claims to the mimetic representation of Africa. In a bitterly sarcastic, and now infamous, essay for Granta entitled "How to Write about Africa," the Kenyan author and controversialist Binyavanga Wainaina wrote a series of instructions to white commentators on Africa: "Always use the word 'Africa' or 'Darkness' or 'Safari' in your title," he wrote. "Note that 'People' means Africans who are not black, while 'The People' means black Africans." "Taboo subjects," he continued, include "ordinary domestic scenes, love between Africans (unless a death is involved), references to African writers or intellectuals, [and] mention of school-going children who are not suffering from yaws or Ebola fever or female genital mutilation." Directly addressing Europeans who write about Africa—as researchers, journalists, NGO workers, educationists—he continued, "You must avoid having the African characters laugh, or struggle to educate their kids, or just make do in mundane circumstances." Wainaina demonstrates how Eurocentric representations of

Africa generate ideas about the continent that are, in turn, often regarded in the Western media as signs of "real" Africa. While he later declared, "I wrote 'How to Write about Africa' as a venting of steam; it was never supposed to see the light of day," the essay went viral for its exposé of Western stereotypes about African authenticity.

This attack on a persistent colonial discourse highlights the necessity for producers and consumers of narratives about Africa to keep the pleasures of close reading at arm's length, and to continue to debate the political apparatus that sustains and rewards particular narratives and genres above others in global settings, including cyberspace. In the decades since the publication of *Things Fall Apart*, African novelists and critical theorists have repeatedly made the point that narrative—whether realist, mythological, oral, epic, biographical, anti-mimetic, romantic, or historical—intersects with broader cultural and political preoccupations, and, as such, is one of the ways through which networks of power and the production of knowledge can be maintained or exposed and critiqued. From this perspective, narrative represents the discursive or linguistic arm (or the persuasive, arm-twisting arguments) of a global political economy that is vested, interested, biased toward maintaining its own interests.

In tension with this hegemonic vision of narrative, however, the diversity of, and the stories within, African literatures show us that no story is singular. No story can be separated from the way it is told, the place and time in which it is narrated, and the other stories that lie within it. If "to write is to perform disruption," as the philosopher and cultural critic Achille Mbembe stated in an interview, in an uneven global economy scholars and readers must remain attuned to the articulation of "truly disruptive" discourses for which, in Mbembe's view, an entirely new language may be required. For scholars and readers whose sources comprise narratives—most especially Anglophone narratives—"rethinking Africa is at once a political, an ethical, an aesthetic and an intellectual project." In the absence of a "descent into a real hell" (Fanon 1986 [1967], 10), the paradigm of agonistic speculation perhaps offers a method that accommodates this combination of specificity, disruption, and surprise, begging further questions about the politics of narrative.

Suggested Readings

Burton, Antoinette, and Isabel Hofmeyr, eds. 2014. *Ten Books that Shaped the British Empire: Creating an Imperial Commons*. Durham, NC: Duke University Press.

Ede, Amatoritsero. 2015. "Narrative Moment and Self-Anthropologizing Discourse." *Research in African Literatures* 46 (3): 112–29.

Gaylard, Gerald. 2006. *After Colonialism: African Postmodernism and Magical Realism*. Johannesburg: Wits University Press.

Gikandi, Simon. 1996. *Maps of Englishness: Writing Identity in the Culture of Colonialism*. New York: Columbia University Press.

Julien, Eileen. 1992. *African Novels and the Question of Orality*. Bloomington: Indiana University Press.

Newell, Stephanie, and Onookome Okome, eds. 2014. *Popular Culture in Africa: The Episteme of the Everyday*. New York: Routledge.

Ogundele, Wole. 2002. "Devices of Evasion: The Mythic versus the Historical Imagination in the Postcolonial African Novel." *Research in African Literatures* 33 (3): 125–39.

Quayson, Ato. 2003. *Calibrations: Reading for the Social*. Minneapolis: University of Minnesota Press.

Wehrs, Donald R. 2008. *Pre-Colonial Africa in Colonial African Narratives: From Ethiopia Unbound to Things Fall Apart, 1911–1958*. Surrey: Ashgate.

Wilson-Tagoe, Nana. 2006. "Re-Thinking Nation and Narrative in a Global Era: Recent African Writing." *African Literature Today* 25: 94–108.

References

Achebe, Chinua. 1986 [1958]. *Things Fall Apart*. Oxford: Heinemann Educational.

Barber, Karin. 1987. "Popular Arts in Africa." *African Studies Review* 30 (3): 1–78.

Beukes, Lauren. 2010. *Zoo City*. Johannesburg: Jacana Media.

Cole, Teju. 2014. *Every Day Is for the Thief*. London: Faber & Faber.

Currey, James. 1972. "Letter to Bessie Head." August 24. In *Correspondence Relating to the Publication of* A Question of Power *by Bessie Head*. HEB 13/03. Reading University, The Archive of British Publishing and Printing.

de Bruijn, Mirjam, and Rijk van Dijk. 2012. "Introduction: Connectivity and the Post-global Moment: (Dis)connections and Social Change in Africa." In *The Social Life of Connectivity in Africa*, edited by Mirjam de Bruijn and Rijk van Dijk, 1–20. New York: Palgrave Macmillan.

Fanon, Frantz. 1986 [1967]. *Black Skin, White Masks*. Translated by Charles Lam Markmann. London: Pluto.

———. 2004 [1963]. *The Wretched of the Earth*. Translated by Richard Philcox. New York: Grove.

Gikandi, Simon. 2012. "Realism, Romance, and the Problem of African Literary History." *Modern Language Quarterly* 73 (3): 309–28.

Head, Bessie. 1972. "Letter to Hilary Rubenstein." June 16. In *Correspondence Relating to the Publication of* A Question of Power *by Bessie Head*. HEB 13/03. Reading University, The Archive of British Publishing and Printing.

———. 1974. *A Question of Power*. Oxford: Heinemann Educational.

Huggan, Graham. 2001. *The Post-Colonial Exotic: Marketing the Margins*. London: Routledge.

Ifukor, Presley. 2010. "'Elections' or 'Selections'? Blogging and Twittering the Nigerian 2007 General Elections." *Bulletin of Science, Technology & Society* 30 (6): 398–414.

Kane, Cheikh Hamidou. 1963. *Ambiguous Adventure*. Translated by Katherine Woods. Oxford: Heinemann Educational.

Krog, Antjie. 1998. *Country of My Skull*. London: Vintage.

Mamdani, Mahmood. 2012. *Define and Rule: Native as Political Identity*. Cambridge, MA: Harvard University Press.

Mouffe, Chantal. 2005. *The Democratic Paradox*. London: Verso.

Moyo, Last. 2011. "Blogging Down a Dictatorship: Human Rights, Citizen Journalists and the Right to Communicate in Zimbabwe." *Journalism* 12 (6): 745–60.

Mphalele, Ezekiel. 1973. "The Tyranny of Place." *New Letters* 40: 69–84.

Newell, Stephanie. 2002. "Introduction." In *Marita: Or the Folly of Love. A Novel by A Native*, edited by Stephanie Newell, 1–37. Leiden: Brill.

Ngũgĩ wa Thiong'o. 1982. *Devil on the Cross*. Translated by Ngũgĩ wa Thiong'o. Oxford: Heinemann Educational.

———. 1986. *Decolonising the Mind*. London: James Currey.

Oboe, Annalisa. No date (ca. 2010). "Africa and the Night of Language: An Interview with Achille Mbembe." *The Salon* 2: 1–6. http://www.academia.edu/7299844/Africa_and_the_Night_of_Language._An_Interview_with_Achille_Mbembe. Accessed October 7, 2015.

Okome, Onookome. 2009. "Reading the Popular: Onitsha Market Literature and the Practice of Everyday Life." In *Teaching the African Novel*, edited by Gaurav Desai, 386–404. Chicago: Modern Language Association of America.

Oliver, Marie Elizabeth. 2013. "Humble Beginnings of Chinua Achebe's *Things Fall Apart*." *Washington Post*, March 22. https://www.washingtonpost.com/news/style-blog/wp/2013/03/22/humble-beginnings-of-chinua-achebes-things-fall-apart. Accessed October 8, 2015.

Olukotun, Deji Bryce. 2014. *Nigerians in Space*. Los Angeles: Unnamed Press.

Pratt, Mary Louise. 1992. *Imperial Eyes: Travel Writing and Transculturation*. London: Routledge.

Ricoeur, Paul. 1984. *Time and Narrative: Volume One*. Translated by Kathleen McLaughlin and David Pellauer. Chicago: University of Chicago Press.

Said, Edward. 1979. *Orientalism*. London: Penguin.

Santana, Stephanie. 2013. "Exorcizing Afropolitanism: Binyavanga Wainaina Explains Why 'I am a Pan-Africanist, Not an Afropolitan' at ASAUK 2012." *Africa in Words*

Blog. February 8. http://africainwords.com/2013/02/08/exorcizing-afropolitanism-binyavanga-wainaina-explains-why-i-am-a-pan-africanist-not-an-afropolitan-at-asauk-2012. Accessed November 20, 2015.

Spivak, Gayatri Chakravorty. 1993. "Marginality in the Teaching Machine." In *Outside in the Teaching Machine*, edited by Gayatri Chakravorty Spivak, 58–85. New York: Routledge.

Tutuola, Amos. 1961 [1952]. *The Palm-Wine Drinkard*. London: Faber & Faber.

Vladislavić, Ivan. 2015 [1993]. *The Folly*. New York: Archipelago.

Wainaina, Binyavanga. 2006. "How to Write about Africa." *Granta* 7. http://www.granta.com/Archive/92/How-to-Write-about-Africa/Page-1. Accessed September 4, 2015.

———. "How to Write about Africa II: The Revenge." http://www.somaliaonline.com/community/topic/how-to-write-about-africa-by-binyavanga-wainaina. Accessed October 9, 2015.

Wicomb, Zoë. 2002. *David's Story*. New York: Feminist Press at CUNY.

———. 2003 [1990]. "Another Story." In *Women Writing Africa: The Southern Region*, edited by M. J. Draymond, Dorothy Driver, Shiela Meintjes, Leloba Molema, Chiedza Musengezi, Margie Orford, and Nobantu Rasebotsa, 419–29. New York: Feminist Press at CUNY.

18 PERFORMANCE

Tsitsi Jaji

Performance in Africa has been as central to its expression of ethnically specific values as to its nation-building projects throughout the twentieth century. At the same time, the live, real-time aspect of performance also makes it an ideal site for contesting officially sanctioned identities and agendas. Few terms encompass as wide a range of objects, practices, and questions as performance. And few cultural forms embody this range as well as arts festivals, as a detailed look at a case study will show: the First World Festival of Black Arts was held in Dakar in 1966 at the instigation of Senegal's president, Léopold Sédar Senghor, who was already a prominent poet when he came to office. As a student in Paris, Senghor had been one of the first and most ardent advocates of negritude, a term first coined by Aimé Césaire of Martinique, and then taken up by other writers from the French-colonized world. Senghor's definition of negritude was "the ensemble of values of the black world," and the festival was intended to perform negritude by making these values manifest. In announcing the festival, Senghor used the performative language of action. Only a decade earlier, linguist J. L. Austin had coined the term *performative utterance* in a lecture at Harvard, deriving it "from 'perform,' the usual verb with the noun 'action': it indicates the issuing of the utterance is the performing of an action" rather than merely describing it (1975, 7). Senghor envisioned the festival as not only a series of performances, but also as a performative act: "An illustration and no longer a theoretical exposition, it [would] constitute a definite action, a positive contribution to the construction of a civilization based on universal values" (Senghor 1963). Dance, theater, and music were heavily represented but so were the visual arts (including painting, tapestry, and sculpture), film, and literature. Art, then, was understood as having the capacity to *perform* the values of negritude through representational structures that did not rely exclusively on staging or liveness so much as on the principle of expression as action. This, then, was the first sense in which the festival itself can be read as performative: it put negritude into action.

Needless to say, turning the festival into a performance of negritude met with some resistance among artists unwilling to be conscripted into an aesthetic and political project they didn't share. Most famously, Wole Soyinka reiterated his quip that a tiger had no need of declaring his tigritude. The negritude agenda also burdened the entire event with a didactic function at odds with many of the most urgent revolutionary political energies of the 1960s. Indeed, the 1969 Pan-African Cultural Festival held in Algiers three years later performed an ideological counterargument. Hosting the festival in a North African nation of primarily Arab and Berber ethnicities challenged the 1966 implication of African culture as quintessentially black. And the 1969 festival projected a more radical political stance by prioritizing the participation of African and African American liberation movements from Guinea Bissau and Cape Verde (PAIGC), Angola (MPLA), Mozambique (FRELIMO), Namibia (SWAPO), South Africa (ANC), and the US (Black Panthers). In both the 1966 World Festival of Negro Arts and the 1969 Pan-African Cultural Festival (and indeed subsequent similar events) staged performance was only part of the work of the gatherings. The public performance of a broadly pan-Africanist cultural politics on a grand scale was just as crucial.

The World Festival of Negro Arts was a discrete event, bounded by the unities of time, place, and action associated with classical Greek theater. It ran for three weeks in April, preceded by a week-long academic colloquium; it took place primarily in the former colonial district of Plateau in downtown Dakar, with satellite events on the island of Gorée and in the working-class neighborhoods of Medina and in stadiums; and its dramatic action told the single story of black artists' contributions to the world. The temporal, spatial, and dramatic elements of the festival thus conformed to the neoclassical unities of drama based on Aristotle's theory of tragedy in his *Poetics*. This is the second sense in which the festival can be read as performance.

Thirdly, and perhaps most obviously, the World Festival of Negro Arts was made up of a plethora of specific performances that have been documented in newspaper and magazine articles, official state records, films, and memoirs. Each performance may be analyzed in relation to the formal criteria of its artistic media or genre, and the national historic context in which it arose. Performance studies often rely on ethnographic work that prioritizes liveness, interviews, and fieldnotes from a trained observer's point of view. However, in order to carry out an analysis of one of the festival performances such as the dance concerts featuring national troupes from Ethiopia, Zambia, Trinidad, the US, and elsewhere, today one would have to take a primarily archival approach. Many large-scale performance events generate documents that present a mediated version of the live event. The ways these documents frame the event encode competing agendas, perspectives, and postures that are themselves performative as they ventriloquize those positions. The version of events conveyed in the independent but generally pro-Senghor daily *Dakar Matin* might well confirm administrative documents held in the state archives, but one might find significant differences in how the US State Department and the Soviet Union covered the festival. The US filmmaker William Greaves gave prominence to visiting elders of the African American arts community by beginning his black-and-white film *First World Festival of Black Arts* with a recitation of Langston Hughes's poem "I've Known Rivers," and footage of Hughes walking along the Dakar coast, and then of Hughes, Duke Ellington, and Brazilian singer Marpessa Dawn viewing the visual art exhibition. The Soviet film *African Rhythmus* was shot in full color, emphasizing the modernity and vibrancy of the event rather than its historic significance, and devoted an extended sequence to Russian poet Yevgeny Yevtushenko's state visit with Senghor, despite the fact that Yevtushenko was asked not to give a reading during the festival itself since he was not black. Employing archival and media sources characterizes a methodological approach to performance common to the fields of history, literature, and cultural studies. Within these disciplines, critical attention to the subtle messages implicit in both the content and omissions of an archive is increasingly essential. In this respect, historian Ann Stoler's work on the colonial archives of the Dutch Indies, *Along the Archival Grain* (2010), holds promise for comparative work.

One other dimension of the festival that reflects the approaches enabled by the term "performance" is the dynamic between the official events and the way that non-elite working-class Dakar residents experienced the festival. The state and ambassadorial receptions and elegant openings at the most prestigious venues in the neighborhoods formerly reserved for colonial French residents were covered extensively in the press; by contrast, the impromptu events in the Medina and the performances held in stadiums for mass audiences are not represented as fully in the official record. Thus interview and oral history become key tools for accessing these dimensions. Attending to the material conditions that performers and audiences encountered informs a crucial school of performance studies grounded in Marxist and materialist approaches.

Definitions of Performance

One might argue that the World Festival of Negro Arts was successful at using performance as an expression of national cultural policy precisely because it built upon widespread core aesthetic and political values. As we have seen, oral history is essential in studying ephemeral live performance events like the World Festival of Negro Arts. But orality is all the more central to formal political speech in diverse indigenous cultural contexts across the continent. Whether in the recitations of family histories presented by *griots* and *griottes* (oral historian-poets) in West Africa or the praising singing traditions of East and Southern Africa, Africans have cultivated multiple ways to "do things with words," as Austin describes it. Austin's notion of how a performative declaration carries out an action through its utterance makes clear how such speech acts not only demonstrate (or state) public status, but also enact it (or make it so). In the Shona cultures of Zimbabwe, greeting individuals with the praise names of their clan ratifies their membership in the group. Such a greeting summons that person to fulfill the qualities referenced in their praise names and activates a network of relationships within and between clans. In a similar fashion, a griot singing familial history to a descendant of Soundiata Keïta, the founder of the Mali empire, may compel the listener to act with the same largesse as his or her ancestor, bestowing gifts of money on the griot and thus proving the noble status of the family to be warranted. Conversely, in many contexts today, the belief in the power of words to bring about material and spiritual changes such as healing or curses drives both the remarkable proliferation of indigenous Pentecostal and other charismatic churches promising "deliverance" and "prosperity" and the summary condemnation and persecution of those purported to practice witchcraft (a phenomenon that has targeted primarily women). So too, a *marabout* (Muslim religious leader) in Senegal may prepare an amulet with a verse from the Koran inscribed and inserted in it. The words of the Koran are believed to grant protection to the wearer. In all these cases, language takes on a performative power.

At the onset I approached the term "performance," vis-à-vis the World Festival of Negro Arts, in its everyday usage, which evokes a scene where artists such as musicians, actors, and dancers present live events on stage before an audience of nonspecialists. However, as the oral performances just described reflect, the arts in Africa are functional (serving a useful rather than a merely aesthetic purpose) and participatory (engaging not only artists with specialized skills but also a broader audience whose responses are integrated into the event or object). Many African societies and scholars conceive of performance as involving all participants—those expressive actors who create an event; those who produce supplies such as instruments, costumes, and masks; and those who respond to the spectacle as live event and social text ripe for interpretation. An Igbo masquerade, for example, is not simply an event presented for the entertainment of passive viewers. As Chinua Achebe points out, the masquerade exemplifies Igbo aesthetics, where the "practical purpose of art is to channel a spiritual force into an aesthetically satisfying physical form that captures the presumed attributes of that force." As an art form that incorporates the plastic arts of masks, as well as music and movement, masquerade requires audiences to participate physically. Achebe cites a proverb that states, "You do not stand in one place to watch a masquerade," to show how the "kinetic energy of the masquerade's art is . . . transmitted to a whole arena of spectators." Biodun Jeyifo traces a similar dynamic in Yoruba traveling musical theater troupes. Improvisation is an essential part of the form because actors win praise by adapting to audience reactions in real time, even going so far as to change the plotline. The conception of performance as a phenomenon where audiences are key actors is not limited to precolonial forms, however. In modern African drama extending this value for collective participation provides fodder for creativity. Ama Ata Aidoo's play, *Dilemma of a Ghost* (first staged in 1964), features a children's song and commentary by two elder women, incorporating voices outside the main action of the play who give voice to community repertoires and opinions.

The concept of performance is critical in African studies, as it facilitates the analysis of live arts and communal happenings that involve multiple modes of expression. During the 1960s and 1970s, the question of how to classify various indigenous performance genres occupied founding figures in the field. The relationship between myth, epic, and African oral poetry, for example, inspired both creative work, such as Ugandan poet Okot p'Bitek's *Song of Lawino*, and scholarly research. Isidore Okpewho and Ruth Finnegan debated whether performed poetry could be considered an epic form while the problem of masquerade's relation to drama was taken up by Michael Echeruo, Emmanuel Obiechina, and others. As the humanities have become increasingly interdisciplinary, the focus on genre has given rise to other questions. As a critical term in African studies today, performance still encompasses form, structure, and aesthetics. But, increasingly, it examines the relationship between those actively engaged in performing and their audience(s); the functions and social efficacy of a given performance or genre; the economic, spatial, and political conditions that provoke, sustain, or condition a performance; and the continuum between the performances and practices of everyday life and the most spectacular and highly curated of secular and religious ritual. It is clear that the complex nodes of expression, reception, and participation discussed thus far demand a highly interdisciplinary approach. In parallel with the development of African studies, performance studies has developed highly useful methodologies for such interdisciplinary work. Emerging from the intersection of anthropology, theater, folklore, and communications, performance studies has broadened the scope of inquiry to include ritual, play, sports, popular entertainment, politics, and practices of everyday life. The history of this discipline is often associated with two schools of thought in the US academy. One is closely associated with Richard Schechner, originally a professor of intercultural theater at New York University, and his collaborations with anthropologist Victor Turner, who developed dramatic and ethnographic approaches to a wide array of embodied practices. The other is associated with Dwight Conquergood at Northwestern University, and emphasizes rhetoric, media studies, and textual analysis. But, despite their differences, these genealogies of performance studies share much in common given their keen attention to a comparable range of cultural practices that have always characterized African studies. As an interdisciplinary field that includes literature and other humanities, social sciences, and health and infrastructural studies, African studies was engaged in performance studies avant la lettre and continues to generate original locally grounded theories that speak to both the continent and a broader field of cultural studies. Whether in indigenous or (post)colonial contexts, the significance that performance studies accords to the participatory dimension of spectacle has turned it into a fruitful approach to African expressive cultures.

Performance studies encompasses a broad spectrum of political, judicial, medical, and other intersubjective scenes. In such scenes, speech acts and self-presentation are bolstered by performative elements such as spatial positioning (staging), role playing (character development), wearing (costuming), and specific postures (stylized embodiment). Indeed, Irving Goffman's sociologically inflected definition of performance brings into view "all the activity of a given participant on a given occasion which serves to influence in any way any of the other participants." The way individual participants influence each other by adopting roles in different situations and before different audiences is one way that social relationships arise, and in charged contexts, such as truth commissions or medical appointments, such relationships may shift profoundly.

The inherent theatricality of judicial processes—whether in hearings before customary leaders such as a council of elders or in court trials—is widely recognized. More recently, scholarship such as Catherine Cole's on transitional justice has highlighted further insights about the specific performative dimensions of truth commissions. Beyond the staged nature of any judicial proceeding, truth commissions inscribe crimes into the public record and display to an (inter)national audience the suppressed events and their historical context. As a political speech act they also perform the reestablishment of the rule of law.

Another sphere in which performance studies is generative is mass spectacles such as sports, cultural festivals, and political rallies. Current scholars attend to all the actors (players, referees, fans, media commentators, and sponsors in the case of a soccer match), and link the use of symbolism, myth, and ritual in approaches consonant with the collaborations of Schechner and Turner. Africanist scholars of stadium sports, for example, may pay as much attention to spectators and the moves they celebrate as to the action on the field, or they might analyze national training structures that impact ordinary athletes as well as the select few who become stars. Peter Alegi's book *African Soccerscapes*, for example, highlights spectator responses to show how local players develop moves adapted to delight their specific fan base: "African players and fans self-consciously [enjoy] the cleverness, beauty and excitement of feinting and dribbling, delightful moves that [elate] fans but also [capture] the cultural importance of creativity, deception, and skill in getting around difficulties and dangerous situations in colonial societies" (2010, 34).

Approaching the performance as a network of actors including artists/players, audience, producers, and sponsors is productive for exploring how vernacular forms are adapted and transformed in contemporary contexts as well as for studying distinctive elements of popular culture. In her influential 1987 essay, "The Popular Arts in Africa," Karin Barber notes that popular music, sports, and political rallies highlight the concept of *publics*, audiences who have limited access to the public sphere given the gap between populist rhetoric and elite political processes in many parts of the continent. Barber suggests that "songs, jokes, and anecdotes may be the principal channel of communication for people who are denied access to the official media" (3). The popular is a distinct category from traditional folk forms (like masquerade), elite postcolonial forms (like scripted theater), and intermediary forms (like Fodéba Keïta's Ballets Africains who transform traditional repertoires for a concert stage). Popular arts are characterized by their unofficial status (unattached to the state or a nationally endorsed canon) and by their syncretic nature, operating as "cultural brokerage" among multiple African and exogenous influences. Barber also distinguishes the popular from the more strategic use of arts (particularly in theater) for conscientization or development (such as in the work of Ngũgĩ wa Thiong'o and Micere Mugo in Kenya, Efua Sutherland in Ghana, or Stephen Chifunyise in Zimbabwe). In these examples performance is a form of activism, mobilizing audiences to recognize and identify more fully with projects of liberation, cultural vindication, and community education.

Popular musicians embody many of Barber's observations and proposals. They garner publics who may well learn and repeat their lyrics as widely disseminated sayings. Perhaps the best-known example of a musician who used his performance to critique the state is Fela Anikulapo Kuti. Kuti's lyrics, musical aesthetic, lifestyle, and permanent performance of defiance at his compound, the Kalakuta Republic, posed such a challenge to the Nigerian state that Kuti and his family suffered violent repression (Olaniyan 2004). And yet his music's popularity spread unabated. On the other hand, because their mode of expression may be indirect or couched in stylized language and musical gestures, popular musicians may have the capacity to voice ambiguous perspectives that only take on a sharp edge when interpreted by their publics. Such multivocal messages cannot easily be censored and, therefore, they have the potential to perform potent political work. Jennifer Kyker has shown how Oliver Mtukudzi's lyrics, for example, articulate a strong indigenous ethic of interdependence and humility, or *hunhu* in Shona. Some listeners interpret this message as an indictment of politicians making prodigious profits at the expense of working and unemployed Zimbabweans, but Mtukudzi's lyrics are dense enough that they have also sometimes been used as endorsements by state officials. Performance is given meaning not only by cultural producers, but also by audiences, consumers, and publics. Senegal's Youssou N'dour is a prime example of a musician responding to a variegated fan base. He has often released multiple versions of his songs simultaneously. He recognizes that local Senegalese fans of *mbalax* music in the dance clubs will value a different tempo and audio effects than the "world music" audience abroad.

Spheres of Performance's Influence

Performance studies is a productively flexible theoretical lens through which to read the multiple roles in cultural production. The ways that such performance arts are archived, documented, and reproduced are also of great interest to African studies. Within the study of "orature" (orally performed poetry, myth, song, story, and other lyric forms), the methods that bards and oral poets use for learning their repertoire and making it their own drives the research agendas of scholars of African vernaculars. And how to record, transcribe, and translate orature remains a core methodological concern, one that musicologists and dance scholars share. Given the importance of oral history in contexts of recent or limited literacy, it is also useful to consider how interviews involve performance on the part of both researcher and informant. Both parties may or may not consciously manipulate their roles; performance theory facilitates self-reflexive analysis and interpretation.

Other scholars may examine how media captures and influences the representation of performance. The film *Keïta! L'héritage du griot*, directed by Dani Kouyaté of Burkina Faso, for example, recounts the story of a griot who visits his nephew's family in the city. Multiple layers of performance are nested within the film. In actuality, the actor playing the role of the visiting griot, Sotigui Kouyaté, is the father of the director. Hence, for the film's production the artists reversed their traditional familial roles, with the son directing the father's performance. As members of the Kouyaté family, they trace their lineage back to the original griot of the founder of the Mandika empire, Soundiata Keïta, so that Sotigui's performance in the film is, in fact, also an enactment of his inherited role. In the film, Sotigui recounts foundational Mandinka narratives to the youngest member of the household, but these stories are narrated rather than performed with music as a griot would present them formally. Thus the film documents the *function* of performing orature, but it also introduces several other frames, including the intergenerational gaps between highly urbanized and Westernized Africans (often committed, as the boy's mother is, to formal secular state education) and indigenous epistemological traditions. Tracking the layers of performance in the film highlights the ways that cultural adaptation is not merely a question of tradition and modernity as stable categories, but a series of mediated scenes of encounter, negotiation, play, and improvisation.

One area in which performance promises to open rich new directions for Africanist scholarship is in gender and sexuality studies. Taking performance as everyday practice elucidates conventions and behavior that ratify gender identity beyond mere biological sex. Thus, approaching gender as performance helps to contextualize histories of flexible indigenous gender roles such as anthropologist Ifi Amadiume's discussion of female husbands in Nnobi, Nigeria, and historian Marc Epprecht's account of male wives in the mining towns of Southern Africa. As with Judith Butler's work on gender as performance, which has focused primarily on the US context, these scholars complicate both African and Western presumptions of heteronormativity. State repression of homosexuality in most African nations overwrites those indigenous traditions predating colonization that authorized various forms of same-sex relationships. Similarly in Austin's foundational work on performative utterances, the main example of a performative utterance (and one he returns to repeatedly in his classic lectures *How to Do Things With Words*) is the marriage vow: saying "I do (take this woman to be my lawful wedded wife)'—as uttered in the course of the marriage ceremony"—effectively counts as the act of getting married. However, performance theory shows us that gender is a role performed iteratively (it has to be repeated constantly), and thus it is a form of performance that may follow alternative scripts under specific conditions. In Amadiume's study of her home culture, the Nnobi people of southeast Nigeria, a financially successful woman of the nineteenth and twentieth centuries, for example, might take an honorific title and, as a demonstration of her status, marry wives with whom to share her wealth and responsibilities. Such titled women enjoy tremendous prestige. Even if the woman already has a husband, her relation to her wives involves a daily performance of gender in which she will act as a husband to her wives by exercising control over their labor and production, providing them with a home, status, and resources, and offering them social recognition within the wider community. Gender may also be deployed in political performance. In her recent scholarship, Naminata Diabaté, for example, has shown how women in multiple sites have deployed nakedness as a form of genital cursing to express protest. Further work at the intersection of gender, sexuality, and African studies holds great potential.

Just as gender is a mutable identity that is constantly and iteratively performed, so many African cultures incorporate performative dimensions in therapeutic and medical practices. Historically, in cultures where indigenous medical knowledge is esoteric and associated with spirituality, divination, or consultation with ancestors, healing events have often incorporated music, formulaic speech and proverbs, dance, and trance. In many contexts, indigenous spirituality and health practices remain important to some degree even where Islam or Christianity holds sway. Medical anthropologists study how subjects navigate simultaneous codes and decipher such scripts alongside the rituals of Western biomedical consultations where the patient role is generally passive, silent, and compliant, and the health-worker role may or may not account for local interpretations of illness and health practices. HIV/AIDS treatment and prevention offer one widely studied instance of the place of performance in medical practice. Visual media like posters and billboards are of restricted use where literacy is limited, but performance modes including songs and theatrical skits (live and in the media) have been used effectively to disseminate information about the disease. However, gaining access to treatment has sometimes required political mobilization and struggle. The Treatment Action Campaign (TAC) in South Africa is a prime example of how multiple forms of organizing, activism, and civil disobedience can be deployed to pressure governments to provide treatment. One of the TAC's earliest tactics to bring visibility to the issue in the late 1990s was for members to don bright red T-shirts emblazoned with "HIV Positive" at a time when official denials of the gravity of the epidemic and its causes imperiled an entire generation. By adopting such costumes, a political uniform worn regardless of one's HIV status, members performed their presence as a constituency and issued their call for the state to take positive action in addressing the need for treatment. Many TAC members were veterans of the anti-apartheid struggle, and images of their campaigns show that embodied protest practices such as the raised fist and *toyi-toyi* street marches—those iconic choreographies of the liberation struggle—were adopted and reinterpreted for this new context where it was now the African National Congress government that was being demonstrated against.

Indeed, such embodied political performances have been crucial modes of intervention for the disenfranchised throughout the twentieth century, first under colonialism and then in confronting the excesses of postcolonial governments. Political philosopher Achille Mbembe has analyzed how the theater of state power and the cunning responses of subjects trying to survive and elude that power represent two sides of a single coin. While he uses Cameroon as a case in point for much of his work, Mbembe's comments address phenomena that occur to varying degrees in a number of autocratically governed nation-states. He describes the "postcolony" as a state characterized not only by "luxuriousness of style" and theatrics of raw power but also by the reliance on simulacrum as a governing device. The state endeavors to define itself as a fetish, "an object that aspires to be made sacred," but it is of course made up of people who are all too worldly in their desire for power and profit. When Mbembe uses terms like *magic*, *spell*, *enchantment*, *applause*, *flattery*, and *lies* to describe the operations and compelled subjectivities of corrupted postcolonial states, he highlights their reliance on performance. And because such power is a simulacrum, a delicate performance that depends on the mutual suspension of disbelief, such power is particularly vulnerable to satire, rumor, and caricature—all forms of irreverent play and mockery. Performance studies offers one lens through which to examine such projections of theatrical state power and how destabilizing skeptical laughter can be for the symbolic systems that undergird power in the postcolony.

Conclusion

What we have seen is that "performance" is a critical term whose multiple meanings and methodologies reflect the rich interdisciplinary range of African studies and allow for divergent sets of scholarly concerns to come into contact and dialogue under its umbrella. Questions over the pertinence of these methodologies animate debates in the field and perform some of the very limits of African studies. Performance studies values the specific, the local, the precise, and the ethnographic, thus highlighting the value of in-depth study of specific sites in their historical moment and with linguistic rigor. As a consequence it puts pressure on the broad comparative gestures sometimes made in a field that purports to account for the dizzying diversity of an entire continent. This challenge to our tendencies to take the coherence of African studies as a single field is one of the most valuable dimensions of the critical work that performance carries out.

Suggested Readings

Alegi, Peter. 2010. *African Soccerscapes: How a Continent Changed the World's Game*. Athens: Ohio University Press.

Barber, Karen. 1987. "Popular Arts in Africa." *African Studies Review* 30 (3): 1–78.

Barz, Gregory, and Frank Gunderson. 2000. *Mashindano! Competitive Music Performance in East Africa*. Dar es Salaam: Mkuki na Nyota.

Chikowero, Mhoze. 2015. *African Music, Power, and Being in Colonial Zimbabwe*. Bloomington: Indiana University Press.

Cole, Catherine. 2000. *Ghana's Concert Party Theater*. Bloomington: Indiana University Press.

Edmondson, Laura. 2007. *Performance and Politics in Tanzania: The Nation on Stage*. Bloomington: Indiana University Press.

Gondola, Ch. Didier. 2016. *Tropical Cowboys: Westerns, Violence, and Masculinity in Kinshasa*. Bloomington: Indiana University Press.

Harding, Francis. 2002. *The Performance Arts in Africa: A Reader*. New York: Routledge.

Jeyifo, Biodun. 1984. *The Yoruba Popular Traveling Theatre of Nigeria*. Department of Culture, Federal Ministry of Social Development, Youth, Sports, and Culture, Nigeria.

Kringelbach, Hélène Neveu. 2015. *Dance Circles: Movement, Morality and Self-Fashioning in Urban Senegal*. New York: Berghahn.

Mbembe, Achille. 2001. *On the Postcolony*. Berkeley: University of California Press.

Murphy, David, ed. 2016. *The First World Festival of Negro Arts, Dakar 1966*. Liverpool: Liverpool University Press.

Olupona, Jacob, and Rowland Abiodun, eds. 2016. *Ifá Divination, Knowledge, Power, Performance*. Bloomington: Indiana University Press.

Peterson, Bhekizizwe. 2000. *Monarchs, Missionaries, and African Intellectuals: African Theatre and the Unmaking of Colonial Marginality*. Trenton, NJ: Africa World Press.

References

Achebe, Chinua. 1989. *Hopes and Impediments: Selected Essays*. New York: Penguin.

Aidoo, Ama Ata. 1995. *Dilemma of a Ghost and Anowa*. New York: Pearson.

Alegi, Peter. 2010. *African Soccerscapes: How a Continent Changed the World's Game*. Athens: Ohio University Press.

Amadiume, Ifi. 1987. *Male Daughters, Female Husbands: Gender and Sex in an African Society*. London: Zed.

Austin, J. L. 1975. *How to Do Things with Words*. 2nd ed. Cambridge, MA: Harvard University Press.

Barber, Karen. 1987. "Popular Arts in Africa." *African Studies Review* 30 (3): 1–78.

Cole, Catherine. 2007. *Performing South Africa's Truth Commission: Stages of Transition*. Bloomington: Indiana University Press.

Diabaté, Naminata. 2011. "Genital Power: Female Sexuality in West African Literature and Film." PhD diss., University of Texas–Austin.

Epprecht, Marc. 2004. *Hungochani: The History of a Dissident Sexuality in Southern Africa*. Quebec: McGill-Queen's University Press.

Goffman, Erving. 1959. *The Presentation of Self in Everyday Life*. New York: Anchor.

Jeyifo, Biodun. 1984. *The Yoruba Popular Traveling Theatre of Nigeria*. Department of Culture, Federal Ministry of Social Development, Youth, Sports, and Culture, Nigeria.

Kyker, Jennifer Wyatt. 2016. *Oliver Mtukuzi: Living Tuku Music in Zimbabwe*. Bloomington: Indiana University Press.

Mbembe, Achille. 2001. *On the Postcolony*. Berkeley: University of California Press.

Olaniyan, Tejumola. 2004. *Arrest the Music! Fela and His Rebel Art and Politics*. Bloomington: Indiana University Press.

Senghor, Léopold Sédar. 1963. "Message from President Senghor to the Senegalese People [First World Festival of Negro Arts]." Bilingual official government publication.

Stoler, Ann Laura. 2010. *Along the Archival Grain: Epistemic Anxieties and Colonial Common Sense*. Princeton, NJ: Princeton University Press.

19 POPULATION

Deborah Durham

When we speak about populations, we may be doing two things, sometimes at the same time. We use the term "population" to refer to an undifferentiated group associated with a place—the population of Tanzania. But a population is something to be broken up, divided, the divisions set against one another, and analyzed. The population of males versus females; of city dwellers versus rural dwellers; of the one percent versus the rest. Populations are evaluated, in the full sense of the term—they are given numerical values, and they are also given moral ones, and both values summon up some kind of response. For populations are not just out there waiting to be seen and counted: they are constituted through these practices. Like Shrödinger's cat, once given form through observation and measurement, they are put into relationships and into action, telling tales, and implying a dynamism behind their measured form.

Social scientists have looked critically at the ways in which evaluating populations by dividing them and counting this and that serve as a form of governance, a means of intervening in, reshaping, and controlling people's lives. Literacy rates by age or gender, pregnancy rates by settlement type or religion, income levels by household structure—all such ways of dividing a population invite interventions to correct or improve conditions measured in ways that do not always please the objects of intervention. But it is worth noting, too, that looking at divisions in populations helps correct for tendencies to homogenize populations: (all) Kenyans seek education, Congolese value high-fashion clothing, Mauritanians are Muslim, Africans have large families. It is worth knowing, perhaps, that school attendance is higher among girls than boys through secondary school but not beyond in a certain locale (as is not uncommon in parts of Africa), that only some percentage of rural people has access to electricity or clean water, that a large proportion of citizens of Botswana are not ethnically Tswana, or that income levels vary statistically according to gender, education, or household composition.

The population of Africa is both unknown and known. By 2013 the continent's population was reported as 1.1 billion—but this number is only an estimate, because while some countries in Africa have highly sophisticated and widely accepted census data, others do not conduct censuses or their counting methods or reports are doubted. Many countries refrain from collecting information on certain things that might be used in politically divisive ways: in Botswana, the postcolonial governments have refused to collect information on "tribal" or ethnic identity, leaving a Tswana ethnic identity for the country hegemonic. Any numbers given about the continent's population, then, are partly guesswork, in spite of the illusions of precise knowledge such numbers give. These numbers, too, often tell us what is *known* independently of any counting: that the population of Africa is growing, that the fertility rates in some countries are among the highest in the world today, that the number of young people on the continent is worrisome, that growing cities host large unemployed and poorly housed populations as well as wealthy enclaves. Whether about the population as a unit or the population as a set of unequal relationships, when we talk about populations we are often talking about things we know, or want to know, or simply assume, in quite different fields than numbers.

Age Demographic: Youth Population in Africa

The population in Africa is growing. Images of Africa going back centuries depict a continent of uncontrolled fertility and growth. An Africa of rank jungles, of rampant evolutionary diversity, of diseases flourishing and spread through unrestrained sexuality or desperate all-consuming diet haunts any discussion of Africa's population as a whole. Africa is imagined as a continent producing populations that overflow it—in the slave trade or, today, in small boats steering north across the Mediterranean. Uncontrolled and uncontrollably proliferating, defying even demographic models. In 2014, the Western media fretted that birth rates on the African continent were not undergoing the "demographic transition," the decline in fertility that is predicted to follow improved health, industrialization, and education of women. As a consequence, women and the children they bear (and usually the "girl child") are often the focus of Western concern about Africa, an invitation to intervention to educate them and protect them from the consequences of sex. With or without an overt goal of intervention, scholars from inside and outside Africa have also been drawn to study the burgeoning youth population. The literature on youth in Africa they have produced has come almost to define early twenty-first-century studies of the continent.

Population figures on youth in Africa sometimes speak in whole numbers, but they are more often reported as percentages (or, as noted above, to point out how divisions in the population relate to one another). These percentages are usually meant to alarm the reader about trends in Africa. In the early 2010s, one might read that 30 percent of the population in Africa is between ten and twenty-four years old; 20 percent between fifteen and twenty-five; or that in fifteen African countries, at least 50 percent of the population is under eighteen. Readers might wonder about choice of age ranges, and the stories each of those tell. But the overarching story is that there is a "youth bulge." Social scientists have statistically associated youth bulges with civil unrest, weakening of liberal democracy, criminality, and war. When the youth measured are very young, they are said to drag down the productive capacity of those who must support them, as the older people cannot invest their labor into those measures of productivity favored by economists and political economists, and children are not expected by social scientists to be undertaking productive labor. When the young dependents get older (yet remain youth), and if the economy cannot absorb them into existing forms of employment, these bulges become sources of discontent and disruption, active in and of themselves, or sometimes harnessed by older power holders as violent enforcers to political movements, a kind of lumpenproletariat. Such an interpretation of youth as an inherently dangerous part of a population focuses on the males, and sometimes implicitly or explicitly refers to Western assumptions of a youth bio-psychological pathology, whereby young males are driven by surging hormones toward violence and unruliness. (A focus on young women, with similar assumptions, might look at their psychobiological character as sexually disruptive and potential mothers.)

While the general trend is to represent youth bulges as dangerous to political stability and the fostering of liberal democracy and to see Africa's youthful population as one source of civil unrest and developmental failure, these same statistics-based studies can also perceive a youth dividend. A youth dividend may accrue if high fertility rates do not persist (the hidden young women of the youth bulge now moderating the uncontained hormonal thrust of the young men). In this view, a bulge cohort moves into (an age-based) period of productivity and consumerism, their energies channeled less into supporting an ever-growing younger cohort of children and more into activities valued in economic and political literature. They start small businesses, augment existing employment positions with their youthful energies and more contemporary insights, and spend the income they get on goods and services which in turn increases productive opportunities for their peers. Less bitter about lack of opportunity, they seek to protect their productive activities in the political arena, pressing for more accountable governments and (neo)liberal freedoms. From this perspective, a large youth population is an asset and not a liability.

These two sides of a youth population have also been noted outside the more statistical social sciences. Two of the important edited collections on youth in Africa to appear in the first decade of the twenty-first century were titled *Vanguard or Vandals* and *Makers and Breakers*. These two collections are anthropological and the chapters within them describe rich cultural and social lives, not statistics and correlations. Yet the titles and the many anthropological articles and books that invoke the same contrasts mirror the two visions of the youth bulge from political demography, and this suggests that there are underlying tropes that surface in a variety of methodologies and disciplinary studies. Juxtaposed with the contrast between youth as dangerous rebels or as creative assets to society are other contrasts found throughout anthropological writing on youth in Africa. Are youth victims of the economic, political, and social configurations of the present? Or should we emphasize their agency in shaping those very configurations? Are they marginalized in the present, disempowered and excluded from political arenas, possibility for employment, and the opportunities for social advancement that political representation and financial stability bring? Or, out of that marginalization, a kind of liminality often associated with youth, do youth emerge as the central actors, core to the future of their countries and continent? Vandals, breakers, marginal, victims . . . makers, agents, vanguard, the future. Contemplating youth in Africa seems to mean contemplating this set of contrasts, contrasts that could as easily be mobilized in discussing the continent as a whole, with reference to its relationship to the rest of the world, in popular discourse.

Such contrasts shape the discussions of urbanization seen across the continent as well as, indeed, around the world. Although Africa is one of the most rapidly urbanizing regions in the world, by 2050 it will still be one of the least urbanized overall, with over 50 percent of its population living in cities. These cities include "megacities" like Kinshasa or Lagos, but also settlements whose changing character has upgraded them from villages, with an agricultural subsistence base, to towns or small cities with not only markets but shopping malls, banks, rental markets, and government services. Africa's cities, especially the larger ones, are sites of economic extremes, with slums and shantytowns surrounding areas of impressive wealth. To many observers, both raise alarms of criminality, as the poor struggle both to survive or to acquire some of the material goods circulating around them and as suspicions of illegitimacy cling to the successful, sometimes in the language of corruption, sometimes in the language of witchcraft. Cities, however, are also where people look for dynamism—economic growth, inventiveness, and new forms of cosmopolitan orientation. Even as we look at African cities as sites of global interactions in world fashion, in music, and in knowledge, we should not ignore the longstanding patterns of movement back and forth between urban and rural areas. Many people in Africa link two homes, one in a city and one in a village, through exchanges of goods and services with kin and through travel to celebrate lifecourse transitions, especially deaths. For decades, anthropologists have puzzled out the tension between a more middle-class pattern of focusing on a nuclear family and its reproduction and an older pattern of developing and maintaining a wide network of kin and fictive kin, between reproduction of wealth and its signs and wealth in people—one associated more with cities and the other with rural life. Exchanges and circulation, however, link Africans not only from village to town but also between those in Africa and kin who have migrated to Europe or the Americas.

Studies of urban populations tend to focus especially on youth, whose economic marginality, creative use of new media in resistance to local patriarchies, and occasional recruitment to violence draw attention. Studies of the elderly often look to villages or to lonely dependents on youthful relatives, suffering urban isolation. Cities are characterized in the literature by their young inhabitants, and those people seen to be active in cities, forging novel ties with the rest of the world, are reciprocally characterized as young.

What many discussions of youth overlook is the problem of establishing who youth are. And when, how, and why. This question extends to other age groups as well, which are today more often reduced to chronological decades of a life span than called elders, or adults. Scholars often use the term "social adulthood" to talk about how different societies recognize achievement of adulthood—although no one uses the term "social youth." Whereas adulthood is understood to be tied to things that change historically, and is today most commonly associated with a set of measurable attainments (independent residence, marriage, children, and career-track employment), youth is typically assumed to be a more "real" demographic category, anchored in a biology that is independent of the social-cultural and historical arena. Population graphs choose age ranges to denote youth, and age ranges are often points of reference for governmentality, for ways of managing, helping, or simply knowing youth. But underlying these age ranges are a variety of assumptions, and it is worthwhile taking time to uncover them. One of the most commonly cited demographics for youth is that unemployment rates for people aged fifteen to twenty-four are very high, across Africa and in many other countries. Why is this age range "youth," and why is it so often quoted in association with unemployment figures?

Botswana's first National Youth Policy, published by the government in 1996, defined "young people" as between the ages of twelve to twenty-nine.* Yet, while conducting research in an urban village in Botswana in the 1990s, I was told by many people in their early twenties that they were not "youth," but still "children." Of course, they said this in response to specific questions or in particular situations, explaining why they did not vote in the national election or why they did not join the local youth association, whose members were nearly all over thirty. The National Youth Policy's age range identified as youth those who might be expected to be in school and those who were unemployed. The policy noted that people as young as ten might be addressed by the policy if they were not in school (and unemployed); at the other end of the age range, the policy focused fairly heavily on creating employment, noting that unemployment can be a cause of other "youth problems," including poverty, health risks (associated especially with sex), and criminality. Within this understanding of youth, people older than twenty-nine would be considered youth, for the policy's intended programs, if they were recently out of school and unemployed. (A revised National Youth Policy in 2010 redefined youth as between the ages of fifteen and thirty-five.) The programs to promote employment, and by the 2010s to foster entrepreneurship, became a key point

*The policy uses terms like "young people" and "youth" without distinguishing between them. It may have been looking at U.N. age ranges for youth, which are from ages 15–24.

of reference by 2014: people often told me that at thirty-six, they were no longer youth, or that at thirty-two they still were youth, and referred to government youth program eligibility.

But government programs are not the only ways in which people come to be youth, or cease to be them, in Botswana and elsewhere. Across Africa, initiation ceremonies both conferred public recognition of new age status, and transformed subjective sensibility through specialized instruction, profound and often frightening emotional experiences, and symbolic enforcement. While sometimes ceremonies were coordinated with biological changes, often they were coordinated with political or other social projects. Among Ehing people in Senegal studied by Marc Schloss, the *Kombutsu* initiation ceremonies transformed young males from children or youth into adults. What was remarkable about the ceremonies was that a five-year-old undergoing them (as occasionally happened) would be considered an adult, while a thirty-five-year-old university student who had missed the ceremony in its twenty-five-year cycle would still be considered a child/youth. What it means to be a child/youth or adult among Ehing, then, is clearly quite different from what it means to be a youth under the Botswana National Youth Policy: whereas Botswana's official youth category is concerned primarily with one's relationship to employment (or education for future employment), the one at work in Ehing Kombutsu ceremonies is concerned with special, very secret and gendered, knowledge which, once obtained in the ceremony, allows adult men (of any age and any relationship to employment) to marry, to eat certain foods, or to see corpses.

In Botswana in the 1990s, when a twenty-five-year-old told me that she was still a child and not yet youth, she was referring to the kind of knowledge and decision-making abilities she possessed, and her comfort presenting those in public settings. She might not yet feel able to speak publicly in the many meetings and conferences held by the youth association, or to take up the responsibilities of its committee work. Yet the same person, or others like her, might also insist on being recognized as an adult during protests at a secondary school or university. Many displayed considerable knowledge and decision making, running households with absent parents or guiding elderly grandparents through modern institutions. Several people said women ceased to be youth when they had babies, even if they were fifteen years old, because at that point they were responsible for someone else—even as the same speakers also dismissed this or that young mother as "just a child" and lacking responsibility. And women in the south of the country told me that you ceased to be youth when you married and "wore a blanket"—a blanket shawl donned at "traditional" ceremonies, such as when blanket-wearers reprimand and instruct a new bride at her wedding.

By contrast with the absolute age ranges used by population studies, then, being youth, child, adult, or "senior" (respected elder) is better seen as flexible and relational. A young woman might become a woman or adult when she has a baby, nursing it and caring for it as an infant, but then return to being just a girl, leaving the child with a mother or aunt to raise and going back to school. Being youth (or child or adult) is also relational, a matter of with whom you are interacting: one might be a deferential youth in a family council discussing plans for a funeral in Botswana, where several elders are present, but a judgmental mature adult in a kitchen council of a group of siblings deciding what to do about a younger sister who has been out late at night. One might also describe youth as situational: someone who is youth in one situation might be adult in another. The young women of southern Botswana who delight in their married adulthood, wearing the checkered blue blankets at weddings and other events, might also demur at wielding the status of adult in many other situations and claim to be youth in yet others, including applying for youth development loans, or even to be just a child when asked to speak authoritatively in a public forum. Insofar as statuses are flexible, relational, and situational, they are also up for contestation and for public negotiation. Young men at funerals in Botswana, or older unemployed men, will don a hat and wool overcoat and carry a stick, clothes associated with maturity, and join the circle of older men sitting around a fire at a house mourning a death. There they may be teased but accepted, or rejected and sent to sit on the logs or overturned buckets outside the inner circle, or ordered to undertake some menial task associated with youth or juniority. When girls are accepted at funerals is also contested and negotiable: when they venture dressing up for the burial, entering the mourning house, or helping (as youth) to serve plates of food. A young woman who, according to her older brother, has been "out too late" might contest her childlike status as the matter is being discussed at the family council of older siblings, and she might then—with resources to do so—move out of his house.

Because youth, among many other social statuses, is relational, situational, flexible, and contestable, I have called it a social shifter, a kind of indexical category put into practice in social action. As a form of symbolic action, an index points to a relationship between an utterance and a context in order to create meaning. Classic indexical terms are "here" or "there" (which depend on situating the place with respect to speaker and the environment), or "we" (which is a variable set of people depending on the situation), or verb tense (the present is present, or past past, with respect to the act of speaking). Indexical terms invoke a kind of metasemantics—or, for the use of statuses like child, youth, or elder, a metasociality—a recognition of the complex ways in which meaning is forged in the intersection of practice and context. When a young man claims to be adult, or a young woman says she is just a child, or the media describes a protesting crowd as a group of "youth" because they are unemployed and protesting, or an older person insists that someone should move from the elders' circle, they are using the term *youth* or *elder* but invoking a range of social values and practices. They are invoking age, but also rights to assert knowledge, the ways that age status is connected with the kind of work one does, the ability to manage or direct emotion appropriately, demonstrated levels of responsibility for others, the expected deference or authority in the presence of specific others, or indeed rebelliousness against authority; all such indexing allows someone to be here or there—youth, child, or elder. To go beyond asking what age ranges comprise youth is to start exposing the very basic principles of social relationship and forms of power that people mobilize to shape and make sense of their social interactions. And because the things that are indexed when someone is called youth are complex, multiple, and connected with historical conjunctures, claims or attributions to youth, adulthood, or old age are always unstable and negotiable in actual social situations. Demographic numbers enter into those attempts to negotiate or make sense of relationships within a population, but they can never, ultimately, define or control them.

Marriage and Family as Factors

Many of the social values indexed by assigning someone to an age status are connected to marriage and to having (in one sense or another) children. Marriage and child-rearing are key measures in any demographic study: marriage rates, average age of marriage, new household formation, numbers of births over a woman's lifetime, and numbers of single-parent (or female-headed) households are standard measures for understanding a population and anticipating its future. They are important to people, too, as they strive to create recognizable social life that extends into future generations—parents want to see children married, have children, and build households that they understand as generative of future security. Yet much as with age status, having children or being married is often the subject of negotiation, is situational, and is flexible. In some parts of Africa, marriage is the sine qua non of having children and being recognized as an adult and full citizen in public affairs. Marriage confers recognized adulthood to Hausa men in Niger, for example, much as the Kombutsu ceremony did for even very young Ehing in Senegal as described by Schloss. Marriage signals that the young Hausa man has the means, both social and material, to start a new household: those who cannot muster those means might be dismissed as idle good-for-nothings, unable to initiate or fulfill social obligations, and feminized as dependents, even as they struggle to find increasingly scarce income.

In other parts of Africa, however, marriage, child-rearing, and heading households have become, or long have been, more loosely articulated and often malleable in practice, even as they remain major points to which people refer to evaluate one another and themselves. Anthropologists all learn about the unusual practices of ghost marriage or woman-woman marriage in classic studies from the mid-twentieth century. When a Nuer male died in Sudan, even as a child, his family might marry a woman to him. She, married to a dead man, was expected to produce children to continue his line within the larger lineage; she might conceive them with his brothers, or with lovers of her own choosing. Among the Igbo in Nigeria, a woman who amassed the means might use her wealth to acquire a wife or wives of her own, even as she was married to a man. Other Igbo found themselves married to a *mami wata* spirit, and unable to sustain other relationships under the spirit's jealous eye. Demographic studies probably do not record such marriages. In Botswana, marriage in the past has been described as a process, not an event, making it difficult to say whether a person is married or not. Series of visits, exchanges, forms of cohabitation, and ceremonies added up to recognized marriage, but because some of these (most notably full and acknowledged bridewealth) might not be accomplished until after the death of one spouse, marriages were always open to dispute about their status. Civil marriage certificates issued by the government, demands that bridewealth be paid in full, and elaborate "white weddings" now mark some people's marriages as events (and events to be seen and admired). Yet the average age of first marriage in Botswana was, in the 2011 census, thirty-six for men and thirty-two for women, and the large numbers of people marrying in their forties suggests that most people take their time in either deciding to, or achieving, the kind of marriage counted by government census. Meanwhile, they live in relationships that may or may not involve co-residence, shared finances or labor in a venture, sexual exclusivity, public recognition of partnership, and shared children. Shared residence by unmarried people is on the rise in Botswana, to the surprise of older citizens; at the same time, it is almost unheard of in Islamic settings like Niger, where men may marry up to four wives and take lovers on the side.

One suspects that "event-marriages," with legal registration and the public recognition of a large wedding party, are accomplished more frequently and at younger average ages by people in the middle or upper classes. It is possible to see marriage itself, as practiced in Botswana today, as a class move. The display of wealth and of organizational capacity at "white weddings" speaks directly to the organizers' power as consumers and to their command of the new and growing service economy, even as such events in fact leave people in considerable debt. One young woman told me that "you can tell a married woman, by the way she walks, the way she carries her handbag." The new ritual passage of weddings may be as much a passage into a role as a particular kind of consumer as into a role as a supporter of dependents or a node in an expanded network of kin relationships, as in the past.

In some societies in Africa, having a child outside marriage is punished severely; in others, it is accepted if frowned upon; in yet others it is commonplace. Yet across Africa, having children is expected of women, and those who do not have children are looked at with pity, suspicion, or unease. Women develop complex identities as women, but the most basic element of being a woman is the ability to have children. In many societies people become known by teknonyms indicating parenthood: MmaBoitumelo, in Botswana, is "mother of Boitumelo." One of Africa's best-known novels, *The Joys of Motherhood*, by Buchi Emecheta, describes one Nigerian woman's hunger for children, and the struggles, unhappiness, and betrayals they bring her in a changing society. If children have always been a screen of hopes for the future, and also a source of disappointment, these hopes and disappointments bear new weight in the context of rapid and radical social and economic change. Demographers fret over the "demographic transition" in Africa, the expected change from patterns of bearing lots of children, consistent with the demands of agricultural economies and the realities of high childhood mortality, to bearing few children as they become expensive in urban and skills-based economies. In some places, such a transition can be witnessed—in Botswana, highly educated women who work have sometimes one or two children, whom they send to private schools; ferry to music, swimming, and language lessons; and socialize with the right friends. They laugh, sitting in elegant coffee shops in town, at the "old women" of their home villages who urge them to have more and more babies. In other places, especially in West Africa, women persist in having large numbers of children, even as mortality rates drop, educational levels increase, and unemployed children become a burden and not extra labor. Clearly, understanding children through the mechanics of economic self-interest tells us little about the value of children anywhere.

In Botswana, many women bear children before marrying (if they ever marry). While parents, peers, and social workers fret about young girls becoming pregnant, about "children bearing children," having children is an important element of personhood. The reasons and ways are multiple, and, as with youth, index different aspects of society and culture, not all of which are brought to bear in any one situation. Women's physical being is understood to be organized around bearing children, and to be childless is to deny it. Women will tell their infants and children, "You are going to buy me a Mercedes," and, while they might not truly expect such a gift, they do anticipate that their children will contribute to their households and support them in their old age. Indeed, old age becomes a recognized and respected experience in part through the actions of children giving aid to physically failing parents. Being recognized as a parent is not straightforward: people might be called "mother/father of Tebogo" in a village neighborhood, but known as Mrs. Kaisara or Elizabeth in the city or at work. And teen parents do not, by and large, merit the teknonymy, suggesting that the ways in which personhood is bestowed through producing offspring are complex. People of all ages in Botswana often leave their children with parents or grandparents to raise, either while the biological parent is working or living elsewhere, or because the grandparent needs help in maintaining his or her household. These children may call their mother *sisi* or *ausi* (sister) and their grandmother "mother." Children may also be raised by childless aunts or other relatives; in other parts of the continent children may be "fostered" by nonrelatives as well, often, though not only, to provide help in fetching water, finding wood for cooking fires, and other household chores. Although this suggests that children are seen as sources of labor, childhood is more often seen as a period of play. Child (and youth) playfulness are important elements to the re-creation of local social and cultural life, as well as sources of complaint. However, in Botswana as in other countries, a growing army of social workers and widespread anxieties about the breakdown of kinship relationships are targeting parenting practices and normalizing child-rearing, pressing them into molds developed in the West. Play itself becomes more structured through organized activities but also through the increasing hold of commodities and consumer culture.

Conclusion

One might describe the population of Africa as shaped through playfulness and creativity in the midst of constrictions, divisions, and often moralistic attempts to reshape it. This is not to suggest that there is an African people characterized by exceptional creativity or play, much as it would be wrong to denote youth as inherently driven to unruly rebellion or older people as self-serving and conservative. Instead, it is to suggest that people in their everyday lives—whether organizing household chores, seeking new opportunities, or pursuing meaning in church or in the face of death—situate themselves in categories they negotiate and rethink. Childhood and youth, marriage and parenthood, categories that seem fixed in so many demographic studies, reveal themselves as flexible, relational, and situated. Yet we must be careful not to suggest that this is the celebrated flexibility of postmodernism, where individuals are free to claim age or identity. Instead, the situational, relational, and flexible nature of age categories is negotiated in the context of social histories and existing relationships, and they only have meaning with reference to the underlying social principles they index.

Suggested Readings

Abbink, Jon, and Ineke van Kessel, eds. 2005. *Vanguard or Vandals: Youth, Politics and Conflict in Africa*. Leiden: Brill.

Alber, Erdmute, Sjaak van der Geest, and Susan Reynolds Whyte, eds. 2008. *Generations in Africa: Connections and Conflicts*. Berlin: Lit Verlag; Piscataway, NJ: Transaction Publishers.

Bledsoe, Caroline, and Gilles Pison, eds. 1994. *Nuptiality in Africa: Contemporary Anthropological and Demographic Perspectives*. Oxford: Oxford University Press.

Bongaarts, John, and John Casterline. 2013. "Fertility Transition: Is Sub-Saharan Africa Different?" *Population and Development Review* 38 (1): 153–68.

Bryceson, Deborah, and Deborah Potts, eds. 2006. *African Urban Economies: Viability, Vitality or Vitiation?* New York: Palgrave MacMillan.

de Boeck, Filip, and Marie Françoise Plissart. 2014. *Kinshasa: Tales of the Invisible City*. Leuven, Belgium: Leuven University Press.

Durham, Deborah. 2000. "Youth and the Social Imagination in Africa." *Anthropological Quarterly* 73 (3): 113–20.

Emecheta, Buchi. 1979. *The Joys of Motherhood*. New York: G. Braziller.

Guyer, Jane. 1995. "Wealth in People, Wealth in Things: Introduction." *Journal of African History* 36 (1): 83–90.

Honwana, Alcinda, and Filip de Boeck, eds. 2005. *Makers or Breakers: Children and Youth in Postcolonial Africa*. London: James Currey.

Johnson-Hanks, Jennifer. 2006. *Uncertain Honor: Modern Motherhood in an African Crisis*. Chicago: University of Chicago Press.

Masquelier, Adeline. 2005. "The Scorpion's Sting: Youth, Marriage, and the Struggle for Social Maturity in Niger." *Journal of the Royal Anthropological Institute* 11 (1): 59–83.

Myers, Garth. 2011. *African Cities: Alternative Visions of Urban Theory and Practice*. London: Zed.

Schloss, Marc. 1988. *The Hatchet's Blood: Separation, Gender, and Power in Ehing Social Life*. Tuscon: Arizona University Press.

Sommers, Marc. 2010. "Urban Youth in Africa." *Environment & Urbanization* 22 (2): 317–32.

Urdal, Henrik. 2005. "A Clash of Generations? Youth Bulges and Political Violence." *International Studies Quarterly* 50 (3): 607–29.

20 SPIRIT

Matthew Engelke

In many African languages the word for "spirit" is closely associated with breath, wind, or air. These in turn index life. From Swahili in the east, to Ewe and Hausa in the west, to Shona in the south, in fact the terms are often exactly the same.

This association is a good reflection on the importance of spirits across the continent; they are as vital as breath itself, as the air we breathe. Within African studies, anthropologists probably acknowledge this most often, given their attention to religion and ritual. But it informs work in some unlikely quarters, too, including history and political science. Imagine a leading figure in American political science, for instance, getting anywhere, other than in figurative fancy, with reference to the invisible world, bewitchment, or political spiritualities. In many African contexts, these are not fanciful references but serious engagements with questions of epistemology and ontology.

Church, Spirit

Africa has long brought spirits to mind. In the early days of European exploration and colonial conquest, this was expressed most arrestingly in the image of Africa as the Dark Continent. A large part of what marked Africa's ostensible darkness—savagery and barbarism—was the commonality of spirit possession, the preponderance of fetishes, the importance of oracles, and talk of witchcraft. Traders, explorers, missionaries, and colonial officials hailed their modernity, marked above all by their own understandings of rationality, superstition, personhood, and semiotic common sense (their ability, in other words, to tell the difference between a symbol and a referent—to recognize that trees, and cowry shells, or BaKongo statuettes are inanimate objects, not agentive forces).

This perceived excess of spirituality did not initially translate into an understanding of Africans as religious. Many of the initial European conclusions were that Africans had no religion. Many early observers in Southern Africa understood religion in fairly rigid Christian terms. Over time this understanding loosened up, while still being characterized by Western, Judeo-Christian concepts and categories: belief, God, the natural/supernatural, and so on. So Africans went from being nonreligious to being irreligious or just getting it all wrong. Part of that had to do with a perceived overabundance of spirits. Again: the Dark Continent, full of shades and fueled by explorers' tales of ecstatic possession or images of *nkisi* figurines banged through with iron nails.

Over time, all of this—as well as less savage things, such as medicinal therapies and divination—came to be known as "African traditional religion." Not everyone likes this term, although it has managed to gain a prominent place both in popular and academic discourse. To add insult to injury, African traditional religion is often presented in its acronymic form, "ATR." Like some smooth object. Even those who employ it, though, often admit to its shortcomings. These are significant because ATR is arguably neither (1) African (you might be able to say Zulu, perhaps, or Akan, but not "African"); nor (2) traditional (at least if you take that to mean ancient and unchanging); nor (3) religion (the colonizer's term, which divides the world into overly discreet categories). Besides, we could just as easily say that Islam and Christianity are African traditional religions. At least they have become so.

Islam, after all, has had a long-standing presence in Africa, including throughout the Sahel and along the Swahili Coast. From northern Nigeria to Zanzibar, Islam has been part of African social fabrics for hundreds of years, often existing alongside of, and blending with, longer standing indigenous traditions. There are many pious Muslims in Africa for whom traditional healing, spirit mediumship, and other indigenous or localized practices are part and parcel of their faith and daily lives. Indeed, the example of Islam, perhaps even more than Christianity, throws into question the very idea that world religions stand separate from local traditions. If Islam is a world religion it is also an African one.

Saint Augustine of Hippo is often used to point to Christianity's deep roots in Africa. In truth, this relies upon an anachronistic understanding of Africa; Augustine inhabited a Mediterranean world. For most of the continent, it makes more sense to trace Christianity in Africa/African Christianity (outside of its Orthodox traditions in Ethiopia and Egypt) to the late seventeenth and early eighteenth century, when a young Kongolese woman, Dona Beatriz, became host to the spirit of Saint Anthony and rose up against the Portuguese Capuchins, claiming to profess a more authentic faith. Even this early example, though, stands somewhat apart. It wasn't until the mid-nineteenth century that Christian missionaries began to make significant headway in sub-Saharan Africa. Conversions were long in the making. The headway did not always go to plan, either. Dona Beatriz's early uprising against the Capuchins marked a more general trend of making Christianity local through acts of appropriation and rearticulation.

Such efforts of appropriation are never wholly successful. In this, the record of colonial Africa confirms what we know about the dynamics of ideology and hegemony. As a wide range of critics has noted, the colonial encounter reshaped the terms of self-understanding throughout much of Africa. Western understandings on a range of matters, from belief to reason, often came to set new terms of debate. Western definitions of civilization have had a significant and lasting impact. Yes, Christianity has often been "Africanized"—but Africa has been "Christianized," too. (There is not space to discuss it here, but the rising influence of China in Africa is recasting dynamics yet again, as a kind of Sinification comes into play).

Nowadays it is often difficult to tell what is indigenous and what is not—what is old and what is new, what is center and what is periphery. The epicenter of Christianity is moving south. A good argument could be made that the Church of Nigeria has more influence within the global Anglican Communion than the Church of England. In any case, the Nigerians are now sending priests to England to help staunch the bleeding away of Anglican congregations—and push back against what some Nigerian bishops (and conservative congregations) see as the errant theological positions of those in the mother church. Meanwhile, a handful of Episcopal congregations in the United States now turn to Nigerian bishops, overlooking the Anglican Communion's tradition of territorial dioceses.

In Nigeria we are also seeing Muslim forms of *dawa* (proselytization) that borrow heavily from the tactics and repertoires of the Pentecostal megachurches. On the highways of Lagos, Pentecostals and Muslims vie for attention. They want buildings with the latest sound systems, high-speed internet connections, and global feel. Nigeria is even home to a movement called "Chrislam," based on a self-conscious, deliberate mixing of Christian and Muslim traditions, practices, and beliefs.

Pentecostal and charismatic churches have really helped shaped the ways in which we understand the boundary blurring and boundary drawing of contemporary religious practice. The rapid growth of Pentecostalism over the past thirty years, not least throughout Africa, has provided a lot of grist for the mills of analysts interested in culture theory, postcolonial theory, and globalization. Pentecostals are best known for their megachurches and loudspeakers, Prosperity-Gospel flash, and strong emphasis on the Holy Spirit. (Although it needs to be said that not all Pentecostal churches are like this.) Many of the churches are explicitly committed to "spiritual battle" or "spiritual warfare;" throughout Africa, pastors rail against demons and ancestors alike, all of whom are thought to inhibit realization of the Kingdom of God. Similar approaches can be found in the African charismatic churches, many of which date from an earlier era (1910s–1930s)—although often to this day without the high-tech trappings of the current wave of Pentecostals. These Pentecostal and charismatic messages have found open ears throughout much of Africa. The idioms they use make sense to local people. In any number of cases, what you will find Pentecostals and charismatics saying is that they are drawn to these traditions because the churches take spirits seriously—that the churches understand "African culture." I myself heard this time and time again in Zimbabwe from people in the charismatic church I studied.

The church I studied is called Masowe weChishanu. (*Chishanu* is the Shona-language term for "Friday," which is the day congregations keep as the Sabbath.) Founded in the early 1930s, by a migrant worker from a place called Makoni, the Friday Masowe Church is one of hundreds of charismatic, or apostolic, churches found throughout Southern Africa. The appeal of apostolic imagery comes in the sense of being close to the origins and source of Christianity: such proximity and connection are a major feature of these groups, and are marked above all by a strong emphasis on the guiding force of the Holy Spirit. It is also marked by styles of worship and organization. African apostolics often worship in white robes, which they associate with the earliest Christians, and they meet out of doors, under open skies. Hierarchies are usually quite flat, at least in principle. And as with Pentecostal groups, the charismatics often take a dim view of "tradition"—what the Masowe apostolics call African culture, by which they mostly mean the attention paid to one's ancestors and other spirits through acts of propitiation, consultation, and care. (For them, African culture also engenders certain dispositions, above all, the negative dispositions of jealousy and envy.)

Within the Masowe Church these Christian commitments are expressed above all in their insistence on a "live and direct" faith. This is a term, borrowed from the radio waves, meant to capture the immediacy of the Holy Spirit—its unalloyed, unmediated presence. For the Masowe apostolics this commitment to immediacy extends to something Johane Masowe, the founder, insisted upon in the early days of his itinerant preaching: casting aside the Bible. Today, Friday Masowe proudly refer to themselves as "the Christians who don't read the Bible." For who needs such a book—such a thing—when one has the Holy Spirit, *live and direct?*

And so we might ask: What does taking spirits "seriously" mean in African contexts?

Generalization is frowned upon in my own discipline of anthropology. We have to consider the particular. And yet while a *tokoloshi* in Johannesburg is not a *jinn* in Malindi; while Hausa speakers are somewhere more Muslim than others; while Roman Catholic and Methodist mission stations affected Manicaland differently; while the Suku tend graves and the Hadza don't; and while Guinea Bissau has "local skeptics" for whom all this spirit-talk is nonsensical, there are, in fact, a range of family resemblances across Africa when it comes to traditional understandings of the spirit world. Because what one finds looking at etymology, as well as the ethnographic record, and novels, and African philosophy, and theology, and even, in some instances, the reports of Victorian explorers, are distinctly different ontological and epistemological framings than what colonialism, evangelism, or *dawa* have often provided. I don't want to label this all "ATR," but neither will I be casting stones at those who might.

Rather, let's chart these family resemblances in relation to three basic points, which I think have to be taken into consideration for anyone interested in understanding the spiritual and spirit-based aspects of African life and lifeworlds.

There Is No Clear Natural/Supernatural Divide

When the Masowe apostolics speak of heaven, the word they use in Shona is *denga* (sky). When they speak of hell, it is *gomba re moto* (pit of fire). There are no words in Shona for heaven or hell. Christian missionaries had to approximate or borrow Biblical terms from the Hebrew and Greek. There is in fact very little indication of some great divide between this world and another world in Shona cosmologies.

The Masowe apostolics *do* accept such a divide. As Christians, it is important to them. They think of heaven and hell as transcendent places. At the same time, spirits are considered rather mundane—certainly the ancestral and other spirits that occupy a good deal of their attention. It is not that spirits aren't different; clearly, they are. Spirits cannot be seen; at least not like you can see a man or a woman. Spirits can do things that humans cannot: inhabit multiple bodies, move in and through objects, and exert powers to affect human dispositions, attitudes, and health. But spirits are part and parcel of everyday life. They have to be dealt with and related to just like other everyday things: cooking the evening meal; commuting to work; tending the garden; or navigating stray dogs in the neighborhood. This is not to say that spirits are unspectacular. Much to do with spirits is very spectacular. But they are not ever really thought of as unusual or out of place.

The emphasis on immanence in Masowe Christian practice is another indication of the extent to which natural/supernatural divides fit poorly for Africa. Having a live and direct faith is a claim about the immediacy and accessibility of the divine. Nothing mattered more to the apostolics than being in the presence of the Holy Spirit, especially when it was speaking to them through a church prophet. This is really why the Bible gets cast aside. Yes, the Bible is associated with the imperial project of subjugation—with colonial and missionary political agendas; but at a theological level, it is seen first and foremost simply as an unnecessary mediation, bridging a distance which need not exist. It frustrates the realization of communion and faith.

The apostolics understand the mundane presence of ancestral and other spirits as part of "African culture." This is a term they use all the time—often, as I have mentioned, for what they are trying to get beyond through Christian practice. When it comes to these spirits, though, it is never a question of whether they are there. The apostolics do not take the view of some nice, liberal Protestant missionary, and politely relegate spirits to the stuff of folktales and myth. This is an important part of what it has meant to take spirits seriously.

In one classic argument, by Igor Kopytoff, such an approach has led to a significant questioning of the terms of analysis and understanding normally employed by social scientists. When we downgrade the kind of natural/supernatural divide structuring the Western-trained mind, the sociology that results can look very different.

When Kopytoff did fieldwork among the Suku, in what is now the Democratic Republic of Congo, he came to realize that such divides simply were not helpful when it came to understanding the nature of authority. On the face of it, the Suku seemed to have what has often been called an "ancestor cult." But this wasn't exactly the case. (It rarely is; this is what outsiders often perceive—this or "ancestor worship"—but in most cases the practice would be recognized within a given community or lineage as a matter of respect, not worship.) Among the Suku, ancestors were not important because they were ancestors—not because they were spirits—but rather because they were elders. The oldest living generation deferred to the ancestors because deference is always due to the preceding generation. The ancestors are dead, yes; and they are spirits. But this is incidental to the structuring of authority within a lineage.

The Suku have no word for "ancestor." They refer to dead relatives in the same way that they refer to older, living relatives: as *bambuta*, which means "big ones" or "old ones." And it is a relative term; old ones are always younger ones, as well. Suku do not revere, or even think much about, lineage members who are several generations gone. The horizon of authority (and interest) extends to those in the age set immediately above one's own. Suku graves thus often quickly fall into disrepair, a fact which is neither surprising nor, for the Suku, especially troubling.

We might use this example to make final point. Inasmuch as religiosity is often connected to an idea of the sacred, and inasmuch as we often understand the sacred as above question—*that which is set apart*, in Emile Durkheim's famous definition—we have yet another term the use of which must be carefully considered. Coupled with the fact that the Suku often berate, scold, and get angry at their (dead) elders, it becomes increasingly difficult to sustain a position that this is uncritical (religious) reverence. What is unfolding among the Suku—as in many, many other cases—are just certain kinds of social relations.

Spirit and Matter Are Not Distinct

I was often struck by the extent to which the Masowe apostolics denigrated the possibility of a material religion. They believe that nothing (no thing) should ever matter in the constitution of a Christian faith. Silk suits, lace dresses, stained glass windows, golden chalices, crucifixes, paintings, and statues—even, of course, the Good Book—were all shunned, because they all only ever detracted from a live and direct faith. Idolatry was a constant danger; iconoclasm, a continual project.

The apostolics have a very pared-down material culture. Their spiritual home is in open fields and abandoned urban lots. (*Masowe* means "wilderness" in Shona.) They wear plain, white robes for worship. They have no altars, buildings, or theological colleges. But no religious community lives free of things, of the world and its trappings, despite the often high value of immateriality. What captures this best for the Masowe is their use of pebbles in healing therapies. Masowe prophets often give blessed pebbles to those who seek their aid; these pebbles can be placed in a glass of water, or a bath, or thrown over the wall of a factory, or simply kept in one's pocket. Doing so (as instructed by the prophet) is a way of keeping the power of the Holy Spirit close, of helping cure an ailment, protect one's job, and so on. What is notable about the choice of pebbles is how unremarkable they are, how mundane and even profane they are—picked up off the ground, worthless and meaningless. Because nothing is more important in this line of thought and practice than the differentiation of spirit and matter. Everything must be in its right place. And in this, pebbles are the perfect symbol of a commitment to immateriality.

For hundreds of years European and American missionaries in Africa scolded and schooled natives about their misguided reverence for powers other than the Christian God. Rivers and trees and mountains have been demystified and done down through sermons and lessons. Wooden figurines, masks, and stone sculptures have been mocked, broken apart, and placed in museums as if to freeze them in time. This has been a spiritual contest, carried out over things, and animated by Western anxiety over fetishes, "those haphazardly chosen material objects believed to be endowed with purpose, intention, and a direct power over the material life of both human beings and the natural world," as William Pietz puts it (1988, 106). This is what the Masowe apostolics are grappling with in their own rendering of Christianity.

After a certain point in time, anthropologists stopped writing about fetishes; the idea was an "embarrassment," as Wyatt MacGaffey remarks, given its primitivizing logic. But there is a loss in this surrender, as he goes on to argue, if it means we neglect the extent to which spirit and matter bleed into one another throughout Africa.

MacGaffey's own exploration of this is situated in relation to a series of early twentieth-century texts on the Kongolese *nkisi* (fetish; sometimes, "charm"). These objects have been marked in the Western imagination by what Pietz calls their "untranscended materiality." But what BaKongo rituals do, MacGaffey tells us, is "override distinctions between spirits (invisible, animate), cult objects (visible, inanimate) and persons (visible, animate), insisting, so to speak, on the community of all three" (1977, 178). Again, then, the matter of transcendence is irrelevant.

It is not only within such classic cases that we find this logic at work. The materiality of spirits and spirits of materiality are not the preserve of "tradition," or found only in missionary accounts from 1905. We can even contrast the apostolics' pebbles, for instance, to a brand new Tommy Hilfiger shirt, sported by a young man in Treichville, the rough-and-tumble neighborhood in Abidjan, Côte d'Ivoire; we can see this as a concern with the spiritual, too.

When anthropologist Sasha Newell began his fieldwork in Abidjan, he was struck by the extent to which the poor young men he knew spent their money on brand-name clothing. They may not have known where the next meal would come from, but *les bluffeurs*, as they are called, would wonder in style, decked out in Hilfiger, Adidas, Dockers, and Sebago. In their world, looking good is not a sign of success; it is success itself, produced through what Newell calls "the magical efficacy of clothing" (2012, 165).

Newell is using this term as more than a run-of-the-mill metaphor. He is not trying to extend some basic Marxian insight about value or cliché after Max Weber about the spirit of capitalism. The *bluffeurs* grew up in a world where spiritual power—all power, really—is understood to derive from that which is foreign and external; *derrière l'eau* (beyond the water), in the local parlance. It is a phrase that many people use to refer to the world of spirits. Inasmuch as the West is understood to be *derrière l'eau*, a strong connection has also developed between the spirit world and the West. (To begin with, this meant France; increasingly it means America.) In many parts of Côte d'Ivoire, in fact, Westerners have long been referred to as spirits. This power extends through association to foreign things, which for the *bluffeurs* means foreign name-brand clothes, shoes, and fashion accessories. Not unlike an *nkisi*, then, or indeed the attitude of some Protestants toward the Bible, on the back of a *bluffeur* a Hilfiger shirt does something; it affects a transformation in status that is deemed, in local cosmological terms, "spiritual."

It has to be a genuine Hilfiger shirt, though; the materiality matters. Authentic brands carry power and value, and here function in much the same way as traditions of masking, which are widespread throughout West

Africa. For Newell, indeed, we should understand this "modernity bluff" as a kind of masking. In such traditions—as often in tightly framed performative registers—the difference between what is fake and what is real doesn't follow everyday lines. The authenticity of the brand—a *real* Hilfiger shirt, *real* Sebago shoes—carries with it a potentiality. Bluffing is a deceptive pretense, yet there is something real about the performance just as in masquerades where the performer, while no longer himself, projects a powerful spiritual presence.

It's Not a Question of Belief

In the Kenyan coastal town of Malindi, the Giriama and Swahili have long lived side by side. In local perspective, though, the Giriama are seen as more indigenous, owing in part to the Swahili's connection to Islam and Indian Ocean trade. The Swahili are Muslim, and they benefit, both culturally and economically, from their connection to this world religion. Some Giriama have converted to Islam (and some fewer still to Christianity), but they often feel, and are made to feel, like second-class Muslims. For most Giriama, moreover, links to one's ancestors and other Giriama spirits are still strong or assumed to be relevant to the constitution of their world.

Despite the proximity and evident mixing that takes places between Muslims and Traditionalists, what we see in Malindi is not syncretism but what the anthropologist Janet McIntosh calls polyontology: it is a form of pluralism that recognizes the ontological reality of several distinct sources of religious powers. For many Giriama, religion is not about truth, but a world of being(s), and it is perfectly possible to think of a "Giriama side" and a "Muslim side," as they put it. Indeed, the boundedness of these sides is made evident and produced in a number of ways, from notably distinct forms of ritual propitiation to more subtle instances of code switching between Kigiriama and Swahili.

Some Giriama have become pious Muslims, dedicated to producing sincere states of submission to God. For most, however, Islam is, like their traditional religion, a source of mystical power. The large majority of Giriama are not committed to a single source of religious authority. This causes real consternation among the Swahili, because it is precisely a sincere belief-based faith that matters to them as modern Muslims, and which is essential to any proper understanding of religion.

The seeming capriciousness of the Giriama, however, is anything but; it is a different approach to "religion" altogether, one in which belief is not a defining element. This is in fact a widespread stance within Africa. (And elsewhere, too.) What McIntosh calls a polyontological view is quite common.

Belief is regularly overemphasized in our understandings of religion. It is not a universal barometer of religiosity. Within the Africanist literature, this point has been well made by Jean Pouillon, who worked among the Dangaleat of Chad. Much like the ill-fitting concept of "ancestral cults" among the Suku, for Pouillon the concept of belief provided very little analytical purchase. When it came to an understanding of spirits, or *margaï*, Pouillon says it would be more appropriate to speak of the Dangaleat's knowledge or experience than belief. Again as for the Suku, such spirits are not thought to occupy a separate world or immaterial plane. So just as one knows that a stone will fall, the Suku know that there are *margaï* in the world. These spirits have what we might call an are/as-if quality; they do not fall into the category of that which is doubted. Here, Pouillon is picking up on a much bigger issue within the human sciences and theology touching on the secular and secularizing aspects of Western modernity. As he quips, "It is the unbeliever who believes that the believer believes"; it is the French anthropologist who draws links between the spiritual and the supernatural, and who feels compelled to bridge the gap between the material and the immaterial through an appeal to belief.

In Zimbabwe, many people came to the Masowe Church for spiritual healing with no intention of "converting" or joining a congregation. They came because Masowe prophets get good results. On other occasions, however, these same people might consult traditional spirit mediums. For committed members of the church, such instrumental approaches were frowned upon, but no one ever really doubted the possible efficacy of the practice, at least in a short-term perspective. (The more pious of my apostolic friends were convinced that, long-term, it would fail—certainly on Judgment Day.) They would never do it themselves. Or at least never admit to it. This made one spirit medium I knew deeply annoyed, for she took the apostolics' position as snobbish and, at core, hypocritical. She insisted to me that she had several apostolic clients—including some prophets who came to her for the powerful *muti* (medicine) she could provide.

Throughout much of colonial and postcolonial Africa, the linking of religion and belief, and the increasing insistence on recognition of one true faith over others, has been the result of Christian and Muslim influences. Such an emphasis on belief has certain effects. As we have seen with the case of the Masowe apostolics, it makes the boundary maintenance between what is Christian and what is African culture quite important. For the more cosmopolitan and international Pentecostal churches, such distinctions are equally crucial, and have been a major focus within African studies. A similar emphasis can be found in Malindi among the Swahili. According to McIntosh, such Swahili views are hardening, in large part as a result of Wahhabist influences from the Middle East.

Conclusion

In conclusion, I return to the point about the close connection we find throughout Africa between the term for *spirit* and terms for *breath*, *wind*, and *air*. The spread of such faiths as Islam and Christianity has led to some revealing renderings of imported ideas. Among the Shona, for instance, one common way of referring to the Holy Spirit is as *Mweya Mutsvene*; this is the term Masowe apostolics usually use. But a literal translation of this phrase would be "clean breath." That's the closest you can get to "Holy Spirit."

And why shouldn't we think of the Holy Spirit as Clean Breath? Throughout Africa, as we can appreciate, this actually makes a certain sense. It brings the spirit down to earth, as it were, an everyday concern. And it acknowledges something that Romance and Germanic languages do not, which is the difficulty of categorizing such a thing, a thing which is in some ways material and in some ways immaterial, there and not there, palpable and impalpable. Indeed, we might take it as a more honest and perceptive approach to what is otherwise the enchanted.

When it comes to clean breath, in fact, the contemporary North Atlantic world is more the exception than the rule. If not universal, the conceptual linkages between spirit and breath/wind/air are certainly very common across the globe. In the inaugural Hocart Lecture, Marshall Sahlins reflected on the extent to which the concept of "spirits" fatally betrays many non-Western worldviews. *Why call them spirits?*, he asks. The Inuit (Arctic regions) don't; neither do the Chewong (Malaysia). Or the Mountain Ok (Papua New Guinea). Or any number of other peoples for whom "spirits" are part of human experience. Indeed when not linked to breath and wind, spirits tend to be known as sorts of people; even "people like us," if you ask the Chewong.

This is just so throughout Africa. Among the Hausa, the lives of spirits parallel the lives of people. For the Beng, death sends you not to an afterlife but, rather, to *wrugbe*, what Alma Gottlieb describes as the "spiritual village." As we have already seen with the Suku, ancestors are "the old ones." Speaking even more generally of what we find in many Bantu languages, David Parkin remarks how healers often refer to spirits as their "people" or their "soldiers" on the basis that they resemble humans. I could include dozens more examples here that reinforce the point. Humans and spirits are part of something the same.

Sahlins has a point; why call them spirits? He argues that it would be more accurate to call them "metaperson others." But one reason to keep calling them spirits is for the humility it ought to engender. "Spirit" can mean many things, but what it almost always seems to signify, if we want to speak of the meta-level, is a certain kind of failure. The failure, really, of many of the divides used to structure academic analysis, certainly when it comes to breath, clean and otherwise: secular/religious; material/immaterial; animate/inanimate; visible/invisible; presence/absence; immanent/transcendent; natural/supernatural; profane/sacred. In all of the cases discussed here, and many more besides, work in African studies provides helpful lessons. Perhaps we could even say, *a breath of fresh air*.

Acknowledgments: I would like to thank Girish Daswani, Naomi Haynes, and Tyler Zoanni for comments on an earlier draft of this chapter.

Suggested Readings

Boddy, Janice. 1989. *Wombs and Alien Spirits: Women, Men, and the Zār Cult in Northern Sudan*. Madison: University of Wisconsin Press.

Evans-Pritchard, E. E. 1956. *Nuer Religion*. Oxford: Oxford University Press.

Johnson, Paul Christopher, ed. 2014. *Spirited Things: The Work of "Possession" in Afro-Atlantic Religions*. Chicago: University of Chicago Press.

Ngũgĩ wa Thiong'o. 1965. *The River Between*. London: Heinemann.

P'Bitek, Okot. 2011. *Decolonizing African Religions: A Short History of African Religions in Western Scholarship*. New York: Diasporic Africa Press.

Peel, J. D. Y. 2016. *Christianity, Islam, and* Orisa *Religion: Three Traditions in Comparison and Interaction*. Berkeley: University of California Press.

Turner, Victor. 1962. *Chihamba, the White Spirit: A Ritual Drama of the Ndembu*. Manchester, UK: Rhodes-Livingstone Institute by the University of Manchester Press.

West, Harry G. 2005. *Kupilikula: Governance and the Invisible Realm in Mozambique*. Chicago: University of Chicago Press.

References

Comaroff, Jean, and John L. Comaroff. 1991. *Of Revelation and Revolution: Christianity, Colonialism, and Consciousness in South Africa*. Volume 1. Chicago: University of Chicago Press.

Ellis, Stephen. 2010. "Development and Invisible Worlds." In *Development and Politics from Below: Exploring Religious Space in the African State*, edited by Barbara Bompani and Maria Frahm-Arp, 23–39. London: Palgrave Macmillan.

Engelke, Matthew. 2007. *A Problem of Presence: Beyond Scripture in an African Church*. Berkeley: University of California Press.

Gable, Eric. 1995. "The Decolonization of Consciousness: Local Skeptics and the 'Will to Be Modern' in a West African Village." *American Ethnologist* 22 (2): 242–57.

Gottlieb, Alma. 1998. "Do Infants Have Religion? The Spiritual Lives of Beng Babies." *American Anthropologist* 100 (1): 122–35.

Hastings, Adrian. 1994. *The Church in Africa: 1450–1950*. Oxford: Oxford University Press.

Janson, Marloes. 2016. "Unity through Diversity: A Case Study of Chrislam in Lagos." *Africa* 86 (4): 646–72.

Kopytoff, Igor. 1971. "Ancestors as Elders in Africa." *Africa* 41 (1): 129–42.

MacGaffey, Wyatt. 1977. "Fetishism Revisited: Kongo *Nkisi* in Sociological Perspective." *Africa* 47 (2): 172–84.

Marshall, Ruth. 2009. *Political Spiritualities: The Pentecostal Revolution in Nigeria*. Chicago: University of Chicago Press.

Masquelier, Adeline. 2001. *Prayer Has Spoiled Everything: Possession, Power, and Identity in an Islamic Town of Niger*. Durham, NC: Duke University Press.

McIntosh, Janet. 2009. *The Edge of Islam: Power, Personhood, and Ethnoreligious Boundaries on the Kenya Coast*. Durham, NC: Duke University Press.

Newell, Sasha. 2012. *The Modernity Bluff: Crime, Consumption, and Citizenship in Côte d'Ivoire*. Chicago: University of Chicago Press.

Parkin, David. 2007. "Wafting on the Wind: Smell and the Cycle of Spirit and Matter." *Journal of the Royal Anthropological Institute* 13 (S1): S39–S53.

Pietz, William. 1985. "The Problem of the Fetish, I." *RES: Anthropology and Aesthetics* 9 (Spring): 5–17.

———. 1988. "The Problem of the Fetish, IIIa: Bosman's Guinea and the Enlightenment Theory of Fetishism." *RES: Anthropology and Aesthetics* 16 (Autumn): 105–24.

Thornton, John. 1998. *The Kongolese Saint Anthony: Dona Beatriz Kimpa Vita and the Antonian Movement, 1684–1706*. Cambridge: Cambridge University Press.

21 THEORY

Joseph Slaughter and Jennifer Wenzel

> They were the fact, they did not pretend to be the idea.
> AIMÉ CÉSAIRE, Discourse on Colonialism

In *Our Sister Killjoy; or, Reflections from a Black-eyed Squint*, Ama Ata Aidoo's novel about the postcolonial "brain-drain" from Africa, the young Ghanaian protagonist Sissie has won an award to spend the summer with other Third World youth on an exchange program in Germany. An unidentified communal voice, which is as cynical about colonial promises as Sissie herself, narrates the scene of her departure from Africa by airplane:

> The hours of the flight had been organised in such a way that they passed over the bit of Africa left in their way in the dead hours of the night.
>
> So that it was nearly dawn when they crossed the Mediterranean Sea. And as they left Africa, there was this other continent, lighted up with the first streaks of glorious summer sunshine.
>
> Good night Africa. Good morning Europe. (Aidoo 1977, 10–11)

Sissie and the narrators of her story are inveterate theorists; that is, everywhere they look, they see systems and the principles that undergird them. In this early scene from the novel, the timetables and routings of international flights have been scrutinized to discover an internal logic that both denigrates Africa (quite literally relegating it to darkness) and presents Europe in its best, dawning light. Perhaps that logic, at least as it manifests in flight timings, is merely economic: international airline schedules have long been organized to serve the financial interests of Europe, by delivering thousands of passengers to European capitals in time for a full business day. However, the narrators' insight reveals other epistemological resonances in Sissie's itinerary.

Sissie's journey from the "dark continent" to the continent of "light" (a long-standing image for European Enlightenment) not only underscores the continued imperial ordering of the world, the enduring traffic lines of power, goods, people, and ideas that have long disadvantaged Africa. It also repeats the introductory dismissal of Africa with which G. W. F. Hegel (in)famously introduced his *Lectures on the Philosophy of History* (1830). For Hegel, as for Sissie aboard the aircraft, Africa remains "enveloped in the dark mantle of Night" (Hegel 1900, 91). Africans, according to Hegel, lack "the principle which naturally accompanies all *our* ideas—the category of Universality": among Africans, "consciousness has not yet attained to the realization of any substantial objective existence—as, for example, God, or Law—in which the interest of man's volition is involved and in which he realizes his own being" (93). With this gesture, Hegel dispenses with the continent altogether: "We leave Africa, not to mention it again. For it is no historical part of the World" (99). Hegel's *Philosophy of History* writes Africa out of history and philosophy in one fell swoop. In this seminal negation, Africa is seen not to have—indeed, to be the very antithesis of—the qualities that make Europe Europe. In Hegel's opinion, Africans had not yet entered history and were incapable of making history because, he posited, they were unable to reflect upon their concrete circumstances. They were, in other words, unable to theorize.

Sissie's journey is inverted when she returns to her native land in the full light of day. A small novel written by a Ghanaian woman in the 1970s and a big book of philosophy penned by a German giant in the 1820s might seem an unlikely pair to begin an essay on theory in the context of African studies. But Aidoo's sly invocation of Hegel, and her artful overturning of his canonized philosophical prejudices, should force us to ask, What is theory? Where is it found? Who theorizes? What does theory do? Indeed, *theory* is a word that does not sit easily alone, particularly with regard to Africa and African studies. So much depends on the preposition: the syntactic hinge that joins *theory* and *Africa*. Theory of or about Africa? Theory in Africa? (Or Africa in theory?) Theory from Africa? Theory for Africa? Or theory *without* Africa, which is what Hegel's dismissal amounts to, given his sense that Africa is *without* theory. We could rewrite that negative relationship as theory *vs.* Africa, to denote both European intellectual and philosophical inventions deployed against Africa and Africans that justified imperialism, colonialism, and slavery, as well as the structure of a binary opposition in which theory is Africa's privileged other, the shining light of philosophical awareness to its epistemological darkness.

The Meaning and Impact of Theory

The word "theory" itself can strike terror in those seeking to make sense of an academic discipline or body of thought. The term is sometimes invoked to differentiate and discriminate between those in the know and those who are not. Thus, it is helpful to begin with general parlance, everyday speech and everyday practices (like Sissie's reading of flight schedules), where theory refers to a particular kind of knowledge, knowledge-production, and orientation toward knowledge. General rather than specific. Abstract rather than empirical. "Universal," in the European Enlightenment philosophical tradition, rather than concrete. Contemplative rather than practical. From the perspective of the sciences, hypothesis rather than data. In general, theory is understood as conceptual or interpretive frameworks, often extrapolated from specific examples, which can be generalized for "application" to other particular cases.

Theory should be seen as a relative and contested term. Not only is one person's theory another person's fact (in the ordinary sense of a difference in definition, perspective, or valuation), but one person's fact is often the occasion for another person's theory. Different academic disciplines and schools of thought have different notions of what constitutes theory and where one can find it, but any discussion of theory (especially in a book like this) should take into account the history of the dominant academic disciplines that now define and are the custodians of contemporary theory. Many of the disciplines that now organize knowledge in the modern university—from anthropology, archaeology, biology, and botany to medicine; and from philosophy and psychology to political science and sociology, as well as even English literary studies—emerged in their modern form from European encounters with Africa and peoples in other colonized spaces around the world.

Europeans needed theories to explain to themselves—and to manipulate—the cultural, social, political, religious, and economic practices of those foreign peoples they were colonizing. Even the Belgian missionary, Father Placide Tempels, who "elevated" native African beliefs to the level of complex systems of reason and thought in *Bantu Philosophy*, wrote his famous study as a handbook "addressed to colonials of goodwill" to better pursue the "real mission" of implanting Christianity and "civilization" on the continent. From such amateur theorizing (often with absurd ideas and devastating practical results) arose some of the central approaches now formalized in major fields of intellectual inquiry, which could be said to have been developed to take account of peoples ostensibly incapable of taking account of themselves—explaining people who couldn't explain themselves to Europeans. "Theory" in this sense, as Christopher Miller has written, "stands as a figure for the role that Westerners have assigned themselves in relation to Africa—detached, objective, universal, synthesizing, and, most of all, powerful" (1990, 7). And yet, ironically, when Senegalese Egyptologist Cheikh Anta Diop presented his argument in *Nations nègres et culture* that pre-pharaonic Egypt was a black African society, which would imply that classical Greece (and, therefore, modern Europe) was an inheritor of ancient African civilization, it was often cursorily dismissed as so much theory. Hegel's negation of Africans' capacity for and relevance to theory is perhaps better described as a dead end rather than as seminal, but we begin there in order to acknowledge the historical fact that for many people, including many important thinkers whose work has become "theory" in the academic definition above, *Africa* has been understood as the opposite of *theory*, and theory has been yet another vector for the marginalization of Africa, Africans, and African thought.

Against the Negation Model

When Hegel speaks of universality and slavery in the same breath, telling us that European enslavement was "the occasion of the increase in human feeling" (1900, 98) among Africans, we hardly need a Michel Foucault or Edward Said to tell us about the imbrication of knowledge and power. Indeed, Aidoo herself makes this point about the murderous exclusions that accompanied Eurocentric universalisms; the novel opens with a polemical denunciation of the postcolonial African "academic-pseudo-intellectual . . . who in the face of reality that is more tangible than the massive walls of the slave forts standing along our beaches, still talks of universal truth, universal art, universal literature and the Gross National Product" (1977, 6). One could wish that Hegel had said nothing about Africa—that he had committed a gross, continental oversight in leaving Africa out of his philosophy of history altogether—rather than inscribing such a pernicious theory of Africans that could be put to venal purposes in justifications for slavery and rapacious dispossession and extraction in the imperial conquest that would follow.

"By dialectically *negating* Africa," as the Nigerian philosopher Emmanuel Chukwudi Eze observes, "Europe was able to posit and represent itself and its contingent historicity as the ideal culture, the ideal humanity, and ideal history" (1997, 13). Another problem with this antagonistic negation model (theory vs. Africa; theory ≠ Africa) that identifies knowledge production solely with Europe is that it obscures the actual role of Africa and Africans in producing knowledge systems that now pass as "European" or "Western." Africa (along with other colonized spaces around the world) has played a significant and largely unrecognized role as a living "colonial laboratory" for formulating and testing a range of theories—from scientific, medical, military, environmental, and agricultural to anthropological, economic, political, and racial hypotheses. In this sense, colonies in Africa and elsewhere became "an immense storage place for new scientific facts," writes Beninese philosopher Paulin J. Hountondji; such facts were "gathered in their crude state in order to be communicated to the urban laboratories and centers [in Europe and the US], who took it upon themselves . . . to treat them theoretically, to interpret them, to integrate them in their proper place in the system of the totality of the facts" (1992, 240). This extractive model of epistemological relation, which sees "'theory' as exclusively Western and 'information' as all that Africa can provide" (Miller 1990, 3), is not only analogous to economic extractivism, where Europe appropriated raw materials from its colonies for manufacture in imperial centers, but also complicit with it, as Hountondji has written forcefully, since knowledge production under colonialism was oriented primarily to facilitate economic exploitation (1992, 240–42).

This kind of argument—which we would call theory, for its generalized claims about a history of relation—is significant for a number of reasons. Firstly, it radically defamiliarizes what we talk about when we talk about "Western knowledge": what it is, who produces it, and where it comes from. In insisting upon the indispensability of the colony to metropolitan knowledge production—"what European science owes to the Third World" as a "precious source of new information" that drove scientific and social experimentation, knowledge production, and the formation of academic disciplines—Hountondji and scholars like him helpfully identify what we might understand as European epistemological debts to Africa. This knowledge debt is the intellectual complement to the economic and ecological debt that Europe owes to its colonies, as the Martinican psychiatrist and theorist of Algerian liberation Frantz Fanon enumerates in his great analytical treatise on decolonization, *The Wretched of the Earth*: given the material riches, natural resources, and slave labor that flowed (not of their own volition) for centuries out of Africa and other colonial territories toward European capitals, Fanon insists, "Europe is literally the creation of the Third World."

One consequence of Africa having been construed as *a laboratory* for European colonial knowledge production is that it could also be described as a place *without laboratories* of its own, whether in the literal sense of the paucity of scientific infrastructure or the broader sense of discursive spaces of contestation out of which knowledge systems can emerge. Indeed, lack of laboratory facilities in Africa is the rationale that many of Sissie's compatriots who are studying medicine abroad in Europe cite as the reason for not returning to the home continent in Aidoo's 1977 novel. Writing in 1992 from an explicitly theorizing stance—considering the systems, structures, and habits of mind that shape individual career trajectories—Hountondji identified a continuing relation of "dependency" and "extraversion" in science in Africa, which he found "ruled by and subordinate to outside needs instead of being self-centered and destined, first of all, to answer the questions posed by the African society itself, whether directly or indirectly." Thus, Hountondji sees the *persistence* of colonial relations of knowledge production into the postcolonial period, and he arrives at a startling and subtle conclusion: in as much as research in peripheral spaces like Africa "bears most frequently on the immediate environment, it remains riveted to the local context, enclosed in the specific, incapable of and not very eager to rise to the universal." It remains, in a word, *untheoretical*. Although the turn to local concerns might be seen as a liberation from an extroverted relation of Africans producing knowledge on European terms, Hountondji warns that a narrow investment in immediate, local concerns—particularly given all of the other persistent modes of inequality that disfavor the continent—can mean that Africans end up continuing in the role of "knowledgeable informer," serving up local facts for the systematizing North. This predicament, however, is not, as it was for Hegel, an essential aspect of the "African character." Instead, it is the historical product of a contradictory knowledge relation where Europe simultaneously "data-mined" Africa and disavowed Africa's relevance to knowledge.

The philosophical negation model presents the problem of theory and Africa as an either/or proposition according to what V. Y. Mudimbe deems an ethnocentric "dichotomizing system" that colonialism itself produced and upon which neocolonial relations persist. More recent approaches to thinking about knowledge production and theory in Africa have stressed the involvement of both Europeans and Africans in a coproduction of knowledge, even of theoretical knowledge created primarily to serve the needs of colonialism—what Mudimbe has called the "colonial library." Gaurav Desai has observed that "the colonial library must include those African subjects who took it on themselves to engage with the discourses of the colonizers and to produce their own inventions of Africa" (2001, 7); as such, "construction of the library and of the colonial process itself" can be understood "as a complex series of interactions between the colonizers and the colonized," who both participated in the production of knowledge. Indeed, the feminist Nigerian/British scholar Amina Mama argues that African women have "always been" coproducers of so-called Western feminism, "even if not properly acknowledged as such," noting, among other examples, that the colonial office sent women anthropologists to try to make sense of the "Women's War of the [19]20s" in British Nigeria (2001, 60). Although the actual working relationships between Africans and Europeans in this coproduction of knowledge would have varied widely, the generalized designation of Africans as mere *informants* in these processes belies the ideological assumptions underlying such divisions of intellectual labor that transformed "raw facts into verified knowledge" (Hountondji 1992, 240).

Indeed, as the Zimbabwean science and technology studies (STS) historian Clapperton Chakanetsa Mahvunga writes powerfully, "What masquerades as a colonial library . . . turns out to be also European confessions of African ideas. . . . I see African knowledge as the bridge . . . that enabled Europeans to cross, occupy, partition, settle, exploit, and make home out of Africa" (2014, 3). African knowledge that was deemed less useful to the colonial project, or even hostile to it—say, systems of healing or hunting or languages—was often suppressed: delegitimized, policed, and sometimes explicitly criminalized. For example, the Kenyan novelist, playwright, critic, and theorist Ngũgĩ wa Thiong'o writes movingly of the humiliating punishments meted out at English-medium colonial schools when a child was caught speaking a native language. Worse than the corporal punishment, for Ngũgĩ, was "the domination of the mental universe of the colonized" (1986, 16). The imposition of colonial languages created a particular kind of mental alienation with important implications for questions of theory: for the colonized African child, according to Ngũgĩ, "the language of his conceptualisation was foreign. Thought, in him, took the visible form of a foreign language" (1986, 17).

This line of analysis invites us to rethink the problem of "brain drain," which generally refers to the migration of educated professionals and intellectuals away from peripheral spaces like Africa, such as Sissie's acquaintances in *Our Sister Killjoy* who are lured by superior salaries and funded laboratory facilities in Europe. But *brain drain* might also refer to processes of colonial education that first "empty [. . .] the native's brain of all form and content," as Fanon wrote in *The Wretched of the Earth*, and then partially fill them again with Eurocentric forms of knowledge and values. The result, in Hountondji's striking image, is a pervasive form of brain drain among both those who leave and those who stay: "The brains of the Third World, all the intellectually and scientifically competent, are rigorously carried by the whole flow of worldwide scientific knowledge toward the center of the system"—even if their bodies never leave Africa or other sites in the Third World.

Ngũgĩ's poignant account of colonial education as a process of alienation and externalization ("seeing oneself from outside oneself as if one was another self") demonstrates how the processes and relations we have described as negation, extraction, and extraversion pertain not merely to the natural and social sciences but to the arts and humanities as well. Pablo Picasso's generative fascination with masks has become the quintessential example of Western culture's too-often unacknowledged debt to African artists and aesthetics. But in the postcolonial period, note the echo of Hountondji's analysis in literary critic Eileen Julien's diagnosis of "extroverted African novels," which "speak outward and represent locality to nonlocal others" (2006, 684), or in the broader critique of an extractive division of labor in literary studies, in which celebrated African novelists, poets, and dramatists produced primary texts whose interpretation was channeled through frameworks provided by European critics and theorists. A signal text in this line of critique, *Towards the Decolonization of African Literature*, decried what its Nigerian authors Chinweizu, Onwuchekwa Jemie, and Ihechukwu Madubuike saw as the Eurocentrism pervading both the composition and criticism of African literature. Promoting a brand of cultural nativism, these self-identified *Bolekaja* critics (in Yoruba, "come down, let's fight!") argued forcefully for reorienting poetry and literary theory toward traditional African cultural forms and endogenous logics, particularly precolonial and persisting popular traditions of orature.

Note the parallels with the "colonial laboratory" idea in the natural and social sciences: here African literature and other arts have been seen to occupy the structural position of raw data, grist for the mill of interpretation and theorizing along Eurocentric lines. But more specifically and more insidiously, African cultural producers have often quite literally been posited as native informants, their works as sources of so much ethnographic "information" or "sociological datum," as Ghanaian/British/American philosopher Kwame Anthony Appiah has observed, that do not seem to "require a literary reading" (1988, 165). Without careful attention to aesthetic concerns and complexities—how genre, form, rhetorical address, point of view, tone and irony, and other aspects of literary and artistic mediation shape a reader's understanding of the world rendered in the text—Chinua Achebe's seminal novel *Things Fall Apart* is too often perceived by our students (and even our colleagues in other disciplines!) as a transparent window on "Nigerian" or "African" culture writ large, rather than as a highly ironic narrative of conflict, critique, and change within a fictionalized Igbo village in the late nineteenth century.

This reduction of an artwork to a data set is particularly ironic and unfortunate with regard to a novel like *Things Fall Apart*, which is so deeply interested in colonialism as a collision of multiple forms of knowledge and ignorance that ultimately generates profound epistemic and physical violence. It is not merely that Achebe's project of cultural recovery and affirmation offers a powerful rejoinder to Hegel's negation: "I would be quite satisfied if my novels . . . did no more than teach my readers that their past—with all its imperfections—was not one long night of savagery from which the first Europeans acting on God's behalf delivered them," Achebe wrote in his 1965 essay "The Novelist as Teacher." Rather, his manipulation of irony, traditional and anthropological modes of storytelling, and multiple narrative points of view achieves a stunning epistemological reversal which lays bare the prejudices and power imbalances that underwrote colonialism and the creation of the colonial library—anticipating by several decades the critiques of Mudimbe, Said, and Foucault. We are suggesting (with critics like Barbara Harlow and the Cameroonian writer-scholar Juliana Nfah-Abbenyi) that, far from being mere inert ethnographic, historical, or literary data awaiting interpretation or theorization within European frameworks, the forms of narrative intelligence at work in *Things Fall Apart*, *Our Sister Killjoy*, and countless other texts are themselves forms of theory.

Theory Is Connected to Praxis, in Africa as Elsewhere

Assertions of Africans as autonomous theory-makers explicitly "write back" against the negation model that posits Africa as the opposite of theory. It is no accident that both the *Bolekaja* critics, in *Towards the Decolonization of African Literature*, and Ngũgĩ wa Thiong'o, in *Decolonising the Mind*, equate theory with an ongoing struggle for true decolonization: in terms of the range of prepositions we outlined at the beginning of this chapter, theory *from* Africa is closely associated with theory *for* Africa. These arguments from the 1980s for the cultural and linguistic decolonization of postcolonial African literature carry forward the theories of national liberation that shaped mid-twentieth-century struggles for independence from European colonial rule. In his many speeches, Amílcar Cabral, a leader of the national liberation struggle in Guinea-Bissau and Cape Verde, argued that "imperialist colonial domination" depended upon "theories [such as apartheid or assimilation] which, in fact, are only gross formulations of racism." As a counter to such "so-called theories," Cabral extrapolates from "the study of the history of national liberation struggles" a general observation: that the cultural realm is where the "first seed of opposition" to imperialism emerges. Since "imperialist domination . . . requires cultural oppression," Cabral theorizes, "national liberation is necessarily an act of culture" (1974, 43). In "The Weapon of Theory," a speech at the first Tricontinental Conference of the Peoples of Asia, Africa, and Latin America held in Havana in 1966, Cabral suggests an additional formulation, that national liberation is also necessarily an act of theory: "Every practice produces a theory, and that if it is true that a revolution can fail even though it be based on perfectly conceived theories, nobody has yet made a successful revolution without a revolutionary theory" (1970, 93).

Cabral's revolutionary theory echoes that of Fanon, whose *The Wretched of the Earth* famously insists upon the importance of anti-colonial violence in the decolonization struggle to counter the violence of colonialism. Violence, for Fanon, is what makes the difference between "the farce of national independence" (1963, 67) and the more profound economic, political, and psychological transformations entailed in national liberation. Yet Fanon means something quite specific by anti-colonial violence: not only that it is dialectical, in the sense of an opposing force to counter colonialism's founding acts of violence. As the Eritrean philosopher, Tsenay Serequeberhan, glosses it, with echoes of Aimé Césaire,

"The counter-violence of the colonized is a *de-thingifying*, life-enhancing project of human liberation" (1994, 78). Anti-colonial violence represents a total commitment to mass struggle by a populace that is conscientized, able to recognize the contradictions in the "old colonial truths" and to resist "all attempts at mystification" by self-interested native elites or colonial masters (Fanon 1963, 147). In other words, decolonization is (among other things) a knowledge project that demands from the masses the cognitive labor of coming to understand one's situation in systemic terms: the people's capacity to *theorize* their situation.

This association between liberation and theory offers important answers to the questions of who theorizes, what theory is, and what it is for. Here theory is decidedly not an elite form of knowledge, nor is it contemplative and abstract. Theory is understood to be necessarily connected to practice. One name for this interconnection of "reflection and action directed at the structures to be transformed" is "praxis," as the Brazilian philosopher-activist Paulo Freire writes in *Pedagogy of the Oppressed*; Freire was influenced by Fanon and, in turn, was himself influential for thinkers in Africa, especially in Lusophone locations. Praxis is an important concept in the Marxian tradition; Freire, like Fanon, Cabral, and Ngũgĩ, drew upon Marx's analysis of the workings of capital, modes of production, class formation, and the possibilities of revolution. Cabral's "The Weapon of Theory" speech argues that anti-colonial liberation struggles reveal some of the limitations of classical Marxian analysis; as Fanon writes, "Marxist analysis should always be slightly stretched every time we have to do with the colonial problem." This "stretching" represents another important category of relation to theory: the critical and strategic *adaptation* of bodies of thought (like Marxism) that might originate outside of Africa, in this case for the express purpose of freeing Africa from (neo)imperialist domination. This adaptation is not the same thing as passive adoption of external theories.

Nevertheless, the problem with using "conceptual frameworks based on Foucault, Marx, Kant, and other Westerners," according to Mahvunga, is that it is "expanding and universalizing Western thought while also purporting to postulate a Southern view." Mahvunga offers an alternative model of liberation-as-theory/theory-as-liberation that is striking for both its similarities to and its differences from the versions of decolonizing the mind described above. His "epistemic chimurenga" invokes the century-long history of organized mass struggles against colonialism in

Zimbabwe, in which ancestors and spirit mediums played a central role in mobilizing armed struggle against British invaders and the white settler regime. A scholar of science and technology studies, Mahvunga urges "taking ancestral knowledge and practice seriously enough to turn it into a solid theoretical standpoint from which to understand the South's realities and engage with the world" (2014, 6). Such knowledge survives, despite the indignities of colonialism and the difficulties of contemporary Zimbabwe's imploded economy, Mahvunga maintains, in the everyday practices of people as forms of improvisation, risk-taking, and knowledge production—"innovation as the art of survival." Considering the ways that ordinary people have theorized their experiences of, and relations to, power in order to resist and reshape it helps us to recognize that survival itself demands theory. Although derived from a radically different genealogy than the Marxian notion of praxis described above, Mahvunga's "chimurenga of the mind" insists on a dynamic, close connection between theory and practice ("practiced knowledge") forged throughout a community rather than restricted to a privileged elite.

One of the most influential philosophical discourses from Africa in the mid-twentieth century that claimed to take up ancestral African culture and its worldview was Senegalese poet, philosopher, and politician Léopold Sédar Senghor's negritude. However, as Kenyan literary critic and cultural theorist Simon Gikandi explains, Senghorian negritude "involved the translation of extroverted European theories on the African into introverted theories of African identity" (2001, 7)—"the African mask for Eurocentric ideas." In other words, negritude was itself (at least in part) a strategic adaptation and inversion of European discourses about Africans. Indeed, some thinkers would reject the distinction between adaptation and adoption of external theories altogether and insist that in the colonial and postcolonial African contexts, ideas have nonlinear transcultural histories that "overlay one another, interpenetrate one another, and envelop one another: an *entanglement*" (2001, 14), as French Cameroonian philosopher and political scientist Achille Mbembe theorizes the term. Thus, any search for a pristine African (or European, for that matter) idea, theory, or point of view that hasn't already been constituted within the (unequal) structures of power, comparison, deflection, diffusion, and difference that colonial contact entails will eventually discover that such things are not "the simple continuation of an indigenous tradition nor . . . a mere intrusion from the metropole" (Appiah 1988, 172).

Conclusion

Mbembe's idea of entanglement and Mahvunga's references to "the South's realities" point toward recent conversations regarding "theory from the South," which look to the Global South as a site and source of theory, where the effects of globalization, speculative capitalism, and environmental crisis are manifest first in places like Africa. Mbembe is interested in the entwined roots of ideas while Mahvunga finds the persistence of past practices and theoretical approaches in the present, but both are looking for theoretical resources "to interrogate the workings of the contemporary world order—to lay bare its certainties and uncertainties, its continuities and contingencies, its possibilities and impossibilities, its inclusions and exclusions" (Comaroff and Comaroff 2012, 48). South African anthropologists Jean and John Comaroff have recently described this orientation toward knowledge as "grounded theory"—"the historically contextualized, problem-driven effort to account for the production of social and cultural 'facts' by recourse to an imaginative methodological counterpoint between . . . the concrete and the concept" (48). Not to theorize "is not an option": "the courage to criticize, the courage to theorize, is indispensible to any effort at making the history of the future different from the history of the present" (48). Such grounded, historicized theory that does not begin with a pretense to the universal is certainly not a new development in Africa, even if it takes on a certain urgency in our contemporary era of globalization. Most of the approaches to theory that we have discussed throughout this chapter could be described as grounded, including Sissie's squint-eyed perspective in Aidoo's novel, whether she is theorizing from the concrete reality of slave forts that still dot the beaches of West Africa or from thirty thousand feet as she wings her way home across a sunlit continent.

Suggested Readings

Appiah, Kwame Anthony. 1992. *In My Father's House: Africa in the Philosophy of Culture*. New York: Oxford University Press.

Diagne, Souleymane Bachir, Amina Mama, Henning Melber, and Francis B. Nyamnjoh. 2001. *Identity and Beyond: Rethinking Africanity*. Uppsala: Nordiska Afrikainstitutet.

Ekotto, Frieda, and Kenneth W. Harrow, eds. 2015. *Rethinking African Cultural Production*. Bloomington: Indiana University Press.

Gikandi, Simon. 2001. "Globalization and the Claims of Postcoloniality." *South Atlantic Quarterly* 100 (3): 627–58.

Mazrui, Ali. A., and Alamin M. Mazrui. 1998. *The Power of Babel: Language and Governance in the African Experience*. Oxford: James Currey.

Mbembe, Achille, ed. 2012. *The Johannesburg Salon*. Volume 5. Johannesburg: Johannesburg Workshop in Theory and Criticism. http://jwtc.org.za/resources/docs/salon-volume-5/JWTC_V015_FINAL.pdf Accessed November 15, 2015.

Ngũgĩ wa Thiong'o. 2012. *Globalectics: Theory and the Politics of Knowing*. New York: Columbia University Press.

Ogundipe-Leslie, Molara. 1994. *Re-creating Ourselves: African Woman and Critical Transformations*. Trenton, NJ: Africa World Press.

Olaniyan, Tejumola, and Ato Quayson, eds. 2007. *African Literature: An Anthology of Criticism and Theory*. Oxford: Blackwell.

Osseo-Asare, Abena Dove. 2014. *Bitter Roots: The Search for Healing Plants in Africa*. Chicago: University of Chicago Press.

Tilley, Helen. 2011. *Africa as a Living Laboratory: Empire, Development, and the Problem of Scientific Knowledge, 1870–1950*. Chicago: University of Chicago Press.

Wiredu, Kwasi, ed. 2004. *A Companion to African Philosophy*. Oxford: Blackwell.

Wynne-Jones, Stephanie, and Jeffrey B. Fleisher, eds. 2015. *Theory in Africa, Africa in Theory: Locating Meaning in Archaeology*. New York: Routledge.

References

Achebe, Chinua. 1989. "The Novelist as Teacher." In *Hopes and Impediments: Selected Essays*. 40–46. New York: Anchor.

Aidoo, Ama Ata. 1977. *Our Sister Killjoy; Or, Reflections from a Black-eyed Squint*. London: Longman.

Appiah, Kwame Anthony. 1988. "Out of Africa: Topologies of Nativism." *Yale Journal of Criticism* 2 (1): 153–78.

Cabral, Amílcar. 1970. *Revolution in Guinea: Selected Texts*. New York: Monthly Review Press.

———. 1974. *Return to the Source: Selected Speeches*. New York: Monthly Review Press.

Chinweizu, Onwuchekwa Jemie, and Ihechukwu Madubuike. 1985. *Toward the Decolonization of African Literature*. London: KPI.

Comaroff, Jean, and John L. Comaroff. 2012. *Theory from the South: Or, How Euro-America Is Evolving Toward Africa*. Boulder, CO: Paradigm.

Desai, Gaurav. 2001. *Subject to Colonialism: African Self-Fashioning and the Colonial Library*. Durham, NC: Duke University Press.

Eze, Emmanuel Chukwudi. 1997. "Introduction: Philosophy and the (Post)colonial." In

Postcolonial African Philosophy: A Critical Reader, edited by Emmanuel Chukwudi Eze, 1–20. Cambridge, MA: Blackwell.

Fanon, Frantz. 1963. *The Wretched of the Earth. Translated by Constance Farrington.* New York: Grove.

Freire, Paulo. 2000 [1970]. *Pedagogy of the Oppressed: 30th Anniversary Edition.* Translated by Maya Bergman Ramos. New York: Bloosmbury.

Gikandi, Simon. 2001. "Theory, Literature, and Moral Considerations." *Research in African Literatures* 32 (4): 1–18.

Harlow, Barbara. 1987. *Resistance Literature*. London: Methuen.

Hegel, G. W. F. 1900 [1830]. *The Philosophy of History*. Translated by J. Sibree. New York: Colonial Press.

Hountondji, Paulin J. 1992. "Recapturing." In *The Surreptitious Speech: Présence Africaine and the Politics of Otherness*, edited by V. Y. Mudimbe, 238–48. Chicago: University of Chicago Press.

Julien, Eileen. 2006. "The Extroverted African Novel." In *The Novel, Volume 1: History, Geography, and Culture*, edited by Franco Moretti, 667–700. Princeton, NJ: Princeton University Press.

Mahvunga, Clapperton Chakanetsa. 2014. "Writing Chimurenga: Towards an African Discourse of Self-Rehumanization." Paper presented at Centre for Indian Studies in Africa, Wits University, Johannesburg, South Africa, August 21. https://www.academia.edu/8040129/Writing_Chimurenga_Towards_an_African_Discourse_of_Self-Rehumanization. Accessed March 26, 2015.

Mama, Amina, and Elaine Salo. 2001. "Talking about Feminism in Africa." *Agenda* 50: 58–63.

Mbembe, Achille. 2001. *On the Postcolony*. Berkeley: University of California Press.

Miller, Christopher. 1990. *Theories of Africans: Francophone Literature and Anthropology in Africa*. Chicago: University of Chicago Press.

Mudimbe, V. Y. 1988. *The Invention of Africa: Gnosis, Philosophy, and the Order of Knowledge*. Bloomington: Indiana University Press.

Nfah-Abbenyi, Juliana Makuchi. 1997. *Gender in African Women's Writing: Identity, Sexuality, and Difference*. Bloomington: Indiana University Press.

Ngũgĩ wa Thiong'o. 1986. *Decolonising the Mind: The Politics of Language in African Literature*. Portsmouth, NH: Heinemann Educational.

Serequeberhan, Tsenay. 1994. *The Hermeneutics of African Philosophy*. New York: Routledge.

Tempels, Father Placide. 1959 [1945]. *Bantu Philosophy*. Translated by A. Rubbens. Paris: Présence Africaine. http://www.congoforum.be/upldocs/Tempels%20BantuPhil%20English%201959.pdf. Accessed May 29, 2016.

22 VALUE

Leonard Wantchekon and Paul-Aarons Ngomo

Since its messy insertion into the asymmetric economy of the Atlantic world, Africa has struggled to establish itself as a locus of value, and self-assertion has remained at the heart of that struggle. The stakes are pretty clear, as are their implications. Insofar as the wealth of nations determines their standing in the global sphere, value creation emerges as the medium through which nations strive to consolidate their sovereignty. Moreover, value creation generates surpluses that are subsequently translated into valuable public goods to create the material conditions of prosperity. As such, value makes might since honor accrues to countries based on their status in the competitive world of self-valuation.

Patterns of value creation range from extractive activities such as those that typify the economy of resource-abundant countries to the forms of transactions though which goods are generated and exchanged in the tertiary economy or in the complex value generating world of credit markets. In its quest for self-assertion, Africa has sought to shed its persistent Conradian image as a place of disvalue only worthy of attention because of its raw materials. The independence era brought the promise of self-assertion to the fore as newly independent countries sought to consolidate political agency by enhancing state capacity to create value. "Seek ye first the political kingdom, and all things shall be added unto you," Kwame Nkrumah trumpeted (1957, 164). While the sobering inefficiencies of post-independence mismanagement vividly remind us that the political kingdom has yet to realize hopes of agency and prosperity, it would be a mistake to disregard the phenomenal economy of signs that defined idioms of self-valuation in the postcolonial era. Value creation began with processes of self-branding to appropriate national spaces. Accordingly, national currencies and a variety of tools of sovereignty reshaped the sense of belonging to consolidate nationhood. As states took control of the economy, important debates spurred by the clash between contrasting approaches to setting priorities and valuing the world shaped patterns of value generation and distribution that threw into sharp relief deep economic disagreements. The central divide was between those who favored capitalism as the best way to generate value and those who stressed the importance of a communal economic ethos dubbed African socialism as the most appropriate route to human flourishing.

Representations of Value in Africa

Arguably, representations of value and disvalue feature prominently in Africa's economic and political history. The episodes of this odyssey are well known. Slave trades commodified persons by turning them into objects of value that could be forcibly appropriated, bought, and sold to generate profit; then came the scramble for Africa and the age of colonization. The colonial project ushered in a new era of value extraction with its many trading posts, concessionary companies, and large-scale mining ventures set up to tap into abundant natural resources. For much of the postcolonial era, economic extraversion has continued unabated albeit with a new variant, as exemplified by the growing importance of market-driven foreign direct investment.

Paradoxically, though Africa generates value, it is hardly translated into valuable capabilities than can enhance human capital and the quality of life. On aggregate, standard indicators such as the annual *human development index* that gauge levels of human flourishing display results that document the extent of Africa's dire economic predicament. But caution is certainly in order if we are to escape the trap of hollow generalizations. To be sure, talk of Africa as a whole can be misleading; it says little about divergent trends within the continent and the contrasting circumstances of a variety of states as regards their resources and their levels of human capital. In many respects, resource-abundant countries like Nigeria, the Democratic Republic of Congo or Angola certainly differ from Malawi or Burkina Faso. However, converging trends reveal a common denominator: across the continent, the experience of disempowerment remains prevalent while economies struggle to generate value consistently enough to sustain human flourishing, leaving the continent oscillating precariously between promises and disappointments, shifting from chaos to glimmers of hope. In the early years of independence, the continent seemed primed for economic takeoff. Yet after what seemed like a promising start, economic growth came to a halt. By the early 1980s, tales of inefficient governance translating into low economic performance painted the grim picture of what William Easterly and Ross Levine described as "Africa's growth tragedy."

As the grips of recession tightened, many states soon found themselves under the stern financial custody of the International Monetary Fund and the World Bank whose policy prescriptions imposed tightly binding market-oriented conditionalities on countries seeking loans. The era came to be known as the apex of what critics dubbed neoliberalism to characterize policies that significantly curtailed the economic role of the state. At best, results are mixed as years of macroeconomic stabilization have done little to halt the descent into poverty. Though many African economies are once more growing steadily, a gap persists between patterns of value creation and their transformation into agency to spur and sustain a virtuous cycle of prosperity. Indeed, whether one takes economic growth or human development as yardsticks to gauge progress, Africa lags behind other regions in key indicators of prosperity. As a case in point, we need look no further than the wealth of information on display in the human development index. From its inception in 1990 to the latest installment (2015), the majority of African countries have remained clustered in the lower rung of the classification with a consistently low human development score. While a few outliers like South Africa and Botswana—and recently Gabon, Namibia, and Zambia—feature in the "medium human development" cluster, the broader picture of human flourishing remains appreciably underwhelming not least since low human development scores translate into low standards of living and limited human capital that lead to short life spans. Two contrasting pictures emerge from the preceding characterization of the combined effects of economic distress and low levels of human development on the generation of value in Africa.

On the one hand, Africa remains a coveted site of value extraction owing to its abundant raw materials. Though conditions are certainly heterogeneous across countries given the uneven spatial distribution of mineral deposits, including oil, diamonds, and other commodities, there are few cases of sustained value generation and transformation to retain a bigger share of the natural wealth. Botswana largely remains an outlier since its success in avoiding the debilitating trap created by the paradoxical combination of resource-abundance and persistent poverty has not been replicated in other resource-rich African countries. Compounding this issue is the fact that resource extraction is a capital-intensive activity that creates comparatively fewer jobs than labor-intensive ventures. Likewise, the structural dependence of African economies on primary commodity exports often vulnerable to price volatility means that endogenous value creation remains appreciably weak.

On the other hand, low human development scores testify to the difficulty of spurring collective flourishing by enabling "people to lead," in the words of Indian economist and philosopher Amartya Sen, "the kind of lives they have reason to value." Worryingly, despite the remarkable growth rates of the past decade averaging about 5 percent that helped twenty-one African countries achieve middle-income status, the much-heralded increases in the size of African middle classes obscure unsettling patterns of growth without development. In varying degrees, all societies are confronted with this issue. To be sure, enabling an environment that channels social cooperation toward wealth generation is a matter of utmost urgency insofar as failure to achieve this goal usually leaves many people vulnerable to material destitution. Indeed in a sense, national economies are systems of value creation writ large.

Much like companies whose purpose is to generate value for their stakeholders, societies must create value to enhance the quality of life of their members; typically, they are deemed successful when they generate and sustain affluence to improve the life chances of their members. However, unlike companies, they cannot enhance value primarily through straightforward self-seeking profit maximizing behavior since social welfare is not derivatively enhanced merely when economic actors pursue their own ends. As the pioneering human development theorist Mahbub ul Haq aptly reminds us, "income may be unevenly distributed within a society. People who have no access to income, or enjoy only limited access, will see their choices fairly constrained." Admittedly, while value generation without socially desirable ends typically favors savvy economic actors, it might leave society worst off by undermining the broader goal of facilitating human flourishing that underwrites, as John Rawls puts it, the vision of "society as a fair system of cooperation over time, from one generation to the next."

Value is understood here in a narrow economic sense, with an emphasis on the transformation of social surplus. As such, the standard vision of value as a measure of preference that undergirds subjective assessments of worth falls outside the purview of the ongoing discussion, as are aesthetic and philosophical theories of value that generally focus on elucidating the nature of ascriptions of worth entailed in judgments of value that describe objects or practices as intrinsically valuable. In contrast, the notion of value is used here to describe the social surplus generated by social cooperation. In general, societies skim off social surplus from cooperative transactions to provide for public goods such as education, infrastructure or healthcare. In this light, the generation of value in a society is simply the process through which social surplus is extracted from transactions and exchanges to sustain the institutional structures that enable social cooperation. In a market economy, societies optimally accrue value by designing fiscal mechanisms that facilitate value generation without undercutting the incentives to produce for those who contribute most to the productive process.

Difficulties often arise when a society has to determine how to allocate goods, that is, how to distribute value. Value transformation unavoidably raises normative issues when competing political interests and ways of valuing the world collide because of persistent disagreements over the distribution of the social surplus. Though the connection is rarely made, similar concerns underlie the challenge of generating and transforming value that lies at the core of Africa's quest for agency. For African states, generating and transforming value remains as important today as it was over fifty years ago when new states emerged from imperial subjugation. Then and now, development—that is, value creation to meet demands for infrastructure, education, public health, and jobs—features centrally in the political agenda of governments.

Modern Statecraft and Value Creation

It is easy to forget that the challenge of value creation began with the constitution of nations as objects of value in order to forge national identities. In practice, the task required amalgamating groups that had little in common beyond their shared experience of colonial domination. As Kwame Anthony Appiah reminds us, "Europe left Africa at independence with states looking for nations" (1992, 162). To address this issue, independence-era leaders imagined nations using a repertoire of performative signs to generate a powerful unifying iconography. The tools of modern statecraft soon became the focal point of symbolic value creation. In this economy of signs, flags, anthems, postage stamps, and other emblems of national identity displaced the symbolic structures of domination to set the stage for a new framework of valuation. With the notable exception of the majority of francophone countries that maintained close financial ties with France, Africa's monetary landscape drastically changed once national currencies replaced colonial monetary arrangements.

National currencies played a central role in the process of self-branding to assert national sovereignty in two ways. First, by disestablishing colonial monetary boards such as those that implemented common colonial currencies in West and East Africa, newly independent states engaged in a deconstructive process to undo the material foundations of financial colonial identities consolidated through currencies extolling the virtues of the imperial order. Second, by establishing national currencies, the new states astutely performed national identities by designing the monetary scripts of nationhood that subsequently came to typify the constitution of the national community as an object of value. It was all the more important since the production of national signs was an important step in the consolidation of an overarching political, economic, and cultural identity. As such, the politics of currency production and banknote iconography was part and parcel of a broader economy of signs whose aim was to consolidate an emerging national identity. Nations could all the more be perceived as objects of value insofar as their currencies consolidated stories of peoplehood that strengthened the lived experience of membership in sovereign communities. In Ghana, Kwame Nkrumah proved particularly adept at understanding and harnessing the symbolic power of signs when, upon gaining independence from the United Kingdom, he pompously declared himself "*Civitatis Ghaniensis Conditor*—Founder of the State of Ghana" (Fuller 2008).

There was certainly more than a hint of self-aggrandizing hubris in Nkrumah's decision to have his image minted on the cedi, the newly established national currency; but he struck a chord with his fellow compatriots by recognizing the performative impact of an iconography of self-valuation. In an op-ed piece aptly titled "Why the Queen's Head Is Coming Off Our Coins" that appeared in a local gazette, he argued that the decision to have his "head on the coinage" was motivated by the fact "many of my people cannot read or write. They've got to be *shown* that they are now really independent. And they can only be shown by *signs*" (1957, 12). As we suggest below, the economy of signs found greater resonance in the debates between African socialists and advocates of capitalism in the early years of independence when discussions arose as to which economic system could steer Africa toward prosperity.

It is certainly not controversial to argue that economic systems are predicated on value choices. African leaders who rose to prominence in the years leading to independence sparred over the respective merits of socialism and capitalism as the economic value systems most suitable for the challenging task of generating and transforming value. Choosing socialism meant taking a road to modernity that required economic centralization, a tight control over the acquisition of private property, and economic decision making as well. By contrast, the capitalist road promised prosperity as the assured reward for those who would embrace free enterprise. At the heart of these debates was the central question of value creation. With little human capital available amid widespread scarcity, finding efficient ways to enhance the welfare of the citizenry quickly became a matter of pressing concern for independence-era African leaders once they assumed power.

Those who, like the Senegalese Léopold Sédar Senghor, Nkrumah, or the Tanzanian Julius Nyerere, had a penchant for philosophical musings set out to articulate theories of human flourishing predicated on native socioethical frameworks. Underlying this vision was the idea that policy choices and the structure of the economy should be consonant with an African traditional communal ethos. Proponents of this worldview argued that traditional African communities were essentially classless societies that could not foster the kind of self-seeking proclivities that motivate individuals in a Smithian capitalist world of profit maximizers. Hence, for Nkrumah and his fellow travelers, the generation and transformation of value necessitated an economic system "in tune with the traditional African egalitarian view of man and society" (Nkrumah 1970, 70). In sum, as Nkrumah hastened to conclude, "the restitution of Africa's humanist and egalitarian principles of society requires socialism" (77). A similar stance can be found in Nyerere's claim that "we, in Africa, have no more need of being 'converted' to socialism than we have of being 'taught' democracy. Both are rooted in our past—in the traditional society which produced us" (1968, 12). Echoing this view, Senghor went so far as to suggest that Africans "had achieved socialism before the coming of the European" (1964, 49).

Unlike Afro-socialists, those who embraced capitalism as the best way to generate and transform value were not staunch doctrinaires interested in grand theorizing. Nor did they envision value creation as something that required fervent cultural commitments to restore somewhat romanticized representations of life as it might have been before its disruption under colonialism. For these advocates of capitalism, production had to come first, not redistribution as dictated by the egalitarian commitments of the Afro-socialists who viewed private ownership of the means of production with suspicion. The Ivorian president Félix Houphouët-Boigny was arguably one of the most important flagbearers of capitalism in Africa. As a successful and wealthy planter, his "class interests" in a prosperous cash crop economy tilted his ideological allegiance toward capitalism. He often proclaimed that wealth creation was more important than wealth distribution, that what needed emphasis was the human aspect of growth and that the best way ahead was a policy of state capitalism. Despite the overbearing presence of the state in the economy, this variant of capitalism was a far cry from the kind of public control of the means of production Julius Nyerere implemented in Tanzania. A brief contrasting discussion will help shed light on the respective fortunes of Afro-socialists and Afro-capitalists in the discharge of their duties.

Tanzania under Nyerere epitomizes the ambition and the pitfalls of African socialism. While many other leaders of his generation verbally committed to socialism without decisive action, he stood out for his determination to embark on a large-scale socialist experiment by restructuring the economy to achieve his ultimate ambition: establishing an egalitarian society. However, above all else, his ambitious project also required the creation of a strong centralized state by amalgamating ethnic groups in order to forge a national identity. Thus, nation building took center stage in the process of value creation because only an efficient state could build economies of scale by linking local communities through networks of reciprocity and collective agency. In the farewell address to the Tanzanian people delivered shortly before his voluntary resignation, Nyerere reemphasized the importance of nation building as a foundational value and a springboard to other pursuits in the larger project of building a self-reliant country. Without a functioning state, it might have been impossible to turn the produce of social labor into a collective good subsequently reallocated to citizens based on the socialist metric of justice that governed the generation of value in Tanzania.

Though an assessment of Nyerere's socialist policies is beyond the purview of this discussion, we might still get a glimpse into how value choices mapped onto actual policies by focusing on the strides made toward the implementation of key social goals despite the severity of Tanzania's economic decline between the mid-1960s and the mid-1980s. Value creation was particularly noticeable in the voluntaristic pursuit of egalitarian policies. Crucially, a freely accessible educational system allowed a generation of Tanzanians to achieve social mobility. When Britain left Tanzania, 85 percent of its adult population was illiterate. Strikingly, when Nyerere stepped down, Tanzania had achieved significant milestones in the cultivation of human capital. The country had the highest primary school enrolment in sub-Saharan Africa (96 percent). Furthermore, important strides were made to reduce gender inequality as girls made up 50 percent of all enrolled pupils. In the area of health, life expectancy for women jumped from a paltry forty-one years in the baseline year 1960 to 50.7 in 1985. Likewise, maternal mortality decreased from 453/100,000 births in 1961 to under 252 in 1972. By 1985, the corresponding figure was 167/100,000 (Mandara and Kaisi 1991; TDHS 2005 and 2010). Such bright spots are often discounted or barely noticed in critical assessments of African socialism. Typically, such assessments paint a grim picture that magnifies failures, highlighting the fact that states that embraced the socialist road to development eventually abandoned their experiments to seek assistance from the International Monetary Fund.

A similar fate also befell those who embraced capitalism to create value. Like their socialist counterparts, they did achieve important milestones in the provision of public goods. In Zambia, Nigeria, Kenya, the Democratic Republic of Congo formerly known as Zaire, and Côte d'Ivoire, urban middle classes achieved some prosperity as wage earners in the public and the private sectors. But patterns of value generation remained lopsided because of the persistence of an urban vs. rural divide. While copper in Zambia, tea and coffee in Kenya, oil in Nigeria, or cocoa in Côte d'Ivoire subsidized comparatively well-off urban workers, rural areas bore the costs of their relative prosperity through extractive transfers that deprived rural dwellers of the surplus generated from cash crops. By and large, capitalism took extractive forms, generating value from natural resources while also diverting funds extracted from agricultural surplus to subsidize urban industries. Virtually everywhere state marketing boards turned into channels of wealth transfer through which surpluses were routinely shifted from rural agricultural areas to urban centers that were pivotal to industry and manufacturing. Originally established under colonial rule, such marketing was useful in stabilizing prices as it used cash reserves set aside to protect farmers from the fluctuation of commodity costs. In practice, however, state marketing boards used their monopoly on agricultural exports to buy goods at prices set by the government while often selling them at much higher prices in global commodity markets. Although a fraction of the resources taken from rural agricultural areas were reinjected there in the form of public goods provision, a sizable portion went to the state and urban areas. In Kenya, Zambia, and Côte d'Ivoire, economies grew steadily during the first decade following independence depending on the fluctuations of commodity prices before slowing down by the mid-1970s. But gains in primary and secondary school education were not matched elsewhere. Exemplifying broader African trends, economic growth did not contribute significantly to poverty reduction. As a result, the relative prosperity of the early years of independence exhibited the familiar picture of growth without development that entrenched inequalities.

It is undoubtedly unwarranted to join the chorus of those who indict African states as historical anomalies unable to facilitate human flourishing. Despite their many failings and the chaos occasioned by war and disease, people nonetheless strived to forge ahead. Recounting the circumstances of life in native Ghana as the state worryingly proved unable to deliver basic services, Appiah notes that "Ghanaian life was not a brutish war of all against all. Life went on . . . people made deals, bought and sold goods, owned houses, married, raised families" (1992, 168). We should pause to recognize the historical resilience of African states and their people in the face of crippling circumstances. Despots came and went; democracy arose in many parts of the continent and occasionally stuttered; but it has remained vibrant, a sign of things come. In a sense, what is often derided under the umbrella term *neoliberalism* is just another proof that salvation will not come from those who act as though they could just wave the magic wand to materialize the prosperity Nkrumah and many of his contemporary had hoped the political kingdom would swiftly deliver.

The failure of the aggressive liberalization of the structural adjustment era to enhance value creation significantly suggests that dismantling the state to accommodate theologians of the market and their one size fits all policy prescriptions is not the solution to Africa's developmental woes. The fact that global financial institutions now recognize that poverty reduction is not a redistributive fallacy signals that prioritizing the creation of social value is not an impediment to development, but its very condition of possibility. The choice is not between economic growth and social welfare since human development requires synergistic action that combines value creation in the economy and the cultivation of human capital. Thus, priorities must be set based on valuational constraints that prescribe valued ends. In short, a "system of value creation" (Munn 1986, 6) must shape patterns of value generation and transformation.

Conclusion

To reiterate: three key moments have defined processes of value generation and transformation since the early days of independence in Africa. Postcolonial states set out to accomplish what colonialism would not do: using the facilitating power of the state to promote human flourishing. But as the harsh realities of misgovernance coupled with the structural dependency of African economies to the vagaries of commodity prices in market beyond their control set in, it became clear that distressed economies could not efficiently sustain value creation. Barely two decades after the exhilarating years of independence, virtually all African states went to Washington. There, they found some relief albeit with heavy strings attached to it in the form of policy prescriptions to liberalize, scale back social welfare spending, and usher in the era of privatizations. Yet economies hardly flourished; they added little value despite implementing structural adjustment programs.

There was no trickle-down effect; it soon became clear that macroeconomic stabilization does not necessarily maximize social value because economic growth does not automatically translate into significant poverty alleviation. Coming to terms with the reality of growth without development has prompted a policy shift. In the new dispensation, economic growth alone is no longer the metric of development. Growth must translate into effective agency to spur human development. Otherwise, merely focusing on macroeconomic performance could undermine societal ends and entrench poverty. As Denis Goulet, a development ethicist, suggests, "We must peel away, in phenomenological fashion, the value assumptions and sacrifices entailed in proposals advanced by political and technical experts" (2006, 64). This claim conveys a critical ethical view: we require valuational constraints to determine what the end of development should be.

The increasing importance of the annual index of human development in Africa signals the rise of political morality of human flourishing. Ranking states based on the extent to which they facilitate human development means that the constitution of agency is now increasingly recognized as the cornerstone of the theory and practice of development. This is not merely a welfarist egalitarian argument for redistribution; the point here is that it is intrinsically in the general interest of a society to promote an economic mode of value creation that enhances agency by expanding the set of opportunities available to people. There are at least two reasons to take valuational constraints seriously. First, focusing on human flourishing as the end-term of value creation highlights the social and political import of a vision of economic progress consonant with social expectations of evenhandedness. Policy adjustments are required to reverse socially inefficient outcomes that entrench inequalities. As the persistent gender gap in wages and opportunities reminds us too well, a market left to its own devices does not necessarily generate value in a socially optimal way. Second, valuational constraints on the mechanisms that facilitate the expansion of economic output ensure that processes of value generation are adequately structured to engineer a more equitable and sustainable society. It goes without saying that the argument thus expounded is value-laden; it is predicated on a normative theory of value that posits the importance of ascribing normative ends to the generation of value. In turn, these ends are valuable only insofar as they promote self- and collective empowerment, that is, the acquisition and consolidation of agency. Similar concerns shaped Nyerere's vision of equitable development and its focus on two core values: political participation and agency in the determination of ends and means. Even without endorsing his socialist leanings, it is easy to see why his framework of valuation remains important today, decades after the political and economic demise of African socialism. Admittedly, these core values are consonant with what Amartya Sen refers to as a "freedom-centered understanding of economics and of the process of development" that focuses on expanding agency. At a time when poverty reduction has become the focus of development policies on par with growth and economic diversification, it bears emphasizing the importance of valuational constraints in setting the end-term of value generation and transformation to facilitate human flourishing.

Suggested Readings

Appiah, Kwame Anthony. 1992. *In My Father's House: Africa in the Philosophy of Culture*. New York: Oxford University Press.

Easterly, William, and Ross Levine. 1997. "Africa's Growth Tragedy: Policies and Ethnic Divisions." *Quarterly Journal of Economics* 112 (4): 1203–50.

Nkrumah, Kwame. 1957. *Ghana: The Autobiography of Kwame Nkrumah*. Edinburgh: Thomas Nelson and Sons Ltd.

———. 1964. *Consciencism: Philosophy and Ideology for Decolonization and Development with Particular Reference to the African Revolution*. London: Heinemann.

Nyerere, Julius K. 1968. *Ujamaa: Essays on Socialism*. Dar es Salaam: Oxford University Press.

Sen, Amartya. 1999. *Development as Freedom*. New York: Knopf.

Senghor, Léopold Sédar. 1964. *On African Socialism*. New York: Praeger.

References

Appiah, Kwame Anthony. 1992. *In My Father's House: Africa in the Philosophy of Culture*. New York: Oxford University Press.

Easterly, William, and Ross Levine. 1997. "Africa's Growth Tragedy: Policies and Ethnic Divisions." *Quarterly Journal of Economics* 112 (4): 1203–50.

Fuller, Harcourt. 2008. "Civitatis Ghaniensis Conditor: Kwame Nkrumah, Symbolic Nationalism and the Iconography of Ghanaian Money 1957—the Golden Jubilee." *Nations and Nationalism* 14 (3): 520–41.

Goulet, Denis. 2006. *Development Ethics at Work Explorations, 1960–2002*. New York: Routledge.

Mandara, M. P., and M. Kaisi. 1991. "Maternal Mortality." In *Health and Disease in Tanzania*, edited by G. M. P. Mwaluko, W. L. Kilama, M. P. Mandara, M. Murru, and C. N. L. Macpherson, 273–78. London: Harper Collins Academic.

Munn, Nancy. *The Fame of Gawa: A Symbolic Study of Value Transformation in a Massim (Papua New Guinea) Society*. New York, Cambridge University Press, 1986.

Nkrumah, Kwame. 1957. *Ghana: The Autobiography of Kwame Nkrumah*. Edinburgh: Thomas Nelson and Sons Ltd.

———. 1964. *Consciencism: Philosophy and Ideology for Decolonization and Development with Particular Reference to the African Revolution*. London: Heinemann.

———. 1970. *Consciencism: Philosophy and Ideology for De-colonization*. New York: Monthly Review Press.

Nugent, Paul. 2004. *Africa since Independence: A Comparative History*. New York: Palgrave Macmillan.

Nyerere, Julius K. 1968. *Ujamaa: Essays on Socialism*. Dar es Salaam: Oxford University Press.

Rawls, John. 2005. *Political Liberalism: Expanded Edition*. New York: Columbia University Press.

Sen, Amartya. 1999. *Development as Freedom*. New York: Knopf.

Senghor, Léopold Sédar. 1964. *On African Socialism*. New York: Praeger.

Tanzania Demographic and Health Survey (TDHS) 2005/2010. National Bureau of Statistics, Dar es Salaam, Tanzania and ORC Macro.

Ul Haq, Mahbub. 1996. *Reflections on Human Development*. New York: Oxford University Press.

23 VERNACULAR

Derek R. Peterson

The literary history of Africa occurred quickly. Since the mid-nineteenth century books in hundreds of hitherto unwritten languages have been published. Never before have a people's languages been so wholly subject to outsiders' management and control. As textual systems, African languages came of age at the convergence of three historical conjunctures: the colonization of the African continent; the rise of the evangelical missionary movement; and the maturation of comparative linguistics. For every language there were committees—the Interterritorial Swahili Language Committee, the Yoruba Orthography Committee, the Shona Language Committee—in which experts set the standards that writers were obliged to observe. They authorized orthographies, composed dictionaries, launched essay competitions, sponsored translations, and funded the publication of approved books. In this way Africa's languages were dragooned into service as vehicles for evangelization and as instruments for colonial rule.

But there was space within the vernacular library for experimentation, creativity, and imagination, as well. The standardization of Africa's languages and their widespread dissemination in books and newspapers gave literate men and women a tremendous sense of empowerment. In their newly defined vernaculars they found a means by which to talk to their people, all at once. Language standardization entailed the amalgamation of hitherto regionalized vocabularies, the erasure of secret and specialized forms of knowledge, and the creation of a homogenous vocabulary. Standardized vernaculars were integrated. They were addressed to audiences that saw themselves as a coherent people. Literate men and women found in them a tremendously powerful means of hailing their people. Writing in the vernacular was an experimental undertaking: it required new modes of address, provoked new audiences, and constituted new communities. The history of vernacular-language writing in Africa is an aspect of the continent's political history, for it was in the vernacular that new solidarities were conjured into being.

Standardizing Languages

The project of language standardization went hand in hand with European efforts to understand and govern the extra-European world. There was a proliferation of orthographies in the late eighteenth and nineteenth centuries, as European linguists cast about for alphabets that could be used to write exotic Oriental and African languages. The most influential orthography was composed by Egyptologist Richard Lepsius, who in 1855 published a *Standard Alphabet for Reducing Unwritten Languages and Foreign Graphic Systems to a Uniform Orthography in European Letters*. His aim was to "bring [foreign] languages with their literature more completely within our reach, and to increase our knowledge of the nations to which they belong" (Lepsius 1855, 23). Decrying the "intolerable confusion of orthographic systems and signs," Lepsius conceived an alphabet that would allow Christian missionaries to "furnish destitute nations, first of all, with that most important, most indispensable means of intellectual, moral, and religious culture, a *written language*" (26). The alphabet consisted of Roman letters to which were added diacritical marks to identify sounds that were not ordinarily pronounced in European languages. The Lepsius alphabet was endorsed by a number of missionary organizations, including the Church Missionary Society, the Basel Mission, and the White Fathers. Within five years of its publication the alphabet had been employed in the writing of fourteen African languages, among them Ewe, Hausa, Maasai, and Zulu, and seven Asian languages, including Korean and Kurdish. Over the ensuing decades Lepsius's script became the dominant orthography for African languages.

The Lepsius alphabet made African languages legible to a European readership. There was already a written literature in several African languages: in Yoruba, Wolof, and several Sudanic languages there were *ajami* manuscripts (in which the writing was in Arabic script); and in Swahili and Malagasy there was a considerable poetic and historical literature in Arabic letters. Missionary linguists wanted nothing to do with Arabic script.

Lepsius himself thought it essential that Roman letters should replace other writing systems, since Chinese, Arabic, and other letters "constitute a natural and almost impassable barrier between foreign and European civilization" (1855, 29). All over Africa linguists used the Roman alphabet to transform intractable scripts and languages into vehicles for evangelization. The first studies in Yoruba language were composed by Samuel Ajayi Crowther, the great missionary bishop of West Africa. His 1843 *Vocabulary of the Yoruba Language* utilized the Roman alphabet to spell the language, replacing the Arabic letters in which earlier writers of Yoruba had composed (Ogunbiyi 2003). By 1852, when Crowther published a longer and more extensive vocabulary, he had adopted two modified vowels, ẹ and ọ, to signal vowel sounds that lay between the vowels of the English language. Crowther's spelling system established the alphabetic framework for the later fluorescence of Yoruba language literature. The Swahili language was likewise transformed in missionary linguists' hands. Ludwig Krapf, whose *Outline of the Elements of the Kisuáheli Language* (1850) was the language's first published grammar book, worried that using Arabic letters would facilitate the spread of Islam. For Krapf, it was the "Japhetic race which will and must give the impulse to the improvement of the Nilotic tribes." Arabic would be an "encumbrance on the Europeans who are, or will be engaged in the work of civilizing and Christianizing these tribes" (Krapf 1850, 16–17). Krapf contemplated using the Amharic letters of highland Ethiopia to write Swahili, but settled instead upon a system based on the Roman alphabet.

Africa's vernacular languages were thereby dragooned to serve as adjuncts to the European languages of colonial government. They were easy for translators to work with, for their orthographies bore a close resemblance to English, French, German, and Portuguese. Books like A. C. Madan's *Outline Dictionary Intended as an Aid in the Study of the Languages of the Bantu and Other Uncivilized Races* (1905) furnished amateur linguists with a list of essential English-language words, arranged alphabetically in columns. Beside each word there was a space where the vernacular-language equivalent could be written. With Madan's book in hand, it was possible for missionaries and other language workers to think about translation as a simple matter of finding the right words. In central Tanganyika, the earliest missionaries were convinced that local people lacked a religious vocabulary. But in 1881 J. T. Last began to compose a dictionary for the Gogo language. He ruled a notebook in parallel columns, with English at the left and Gogo at the right, then he "wrote down what I thought were the most suitable [English] words from A to Z in their proper places, and . . . put [native words] in the places allotted to them." This definitional work made the Gogo language accessible and useful. By 1894 missionaries had translated the Gospels into Chigogo, and by 1900 they had a Gogo grammar book ready for printing.

In fact Chigogo—like many other African languages—was polyglot. The orality of African languages did not automatically make them intelligible, even to competent speakers. There was esoteric vocabulary; elocution was specialized and tailored to specific audiences. There was circumlocution, especially when speaking of controversial matters (Yankah 1995). In Rwanda poetry performed before the king was often incomprehensible to its listeners and, indeed, to its performers. In Yoruba performers of *oriki* (praise epithets) compressed the complicated and winding biographies of their subjects into condensed syllables and allusive references (Barber 2007). Speakers and listeners had to develop competences. And there was regional variety, too, especially in places where there had not hitherto been a large state to consolidate languages and cultures. Many translators must have shared the frustrations of the missionary Miss Davis, in southern Uganda, who struggled to compose a vocabulary book in the Chiga language. "It is an endless task," she wrote. "The variation in the dialects spoken in the different parts of [the region] are so many that one may greedily light on a new word only to find it contradicted the next minute by someone who says he has never heard of it" (Davis 1927).

The work of standardization involved the leveling of secret vocabulary, the creation of hierarchies between different spoken languages, and the elevation of one variant as the standard form (Errington 2001). In this way language standardization was necessarily partisan. It involved discrimination. Some people—who linguists called the majority—found themselves in a privileged position in relation to the committees that were organizing African languages. Other people, who were marginal to language committees' work, found their ways of speaking made into variants from the norm. The standard for Xhosa vocabulary and grammar was set by the Ngqika people living in the vicinity of the Glasgow Missionary Society station at Lovedale. The standard for Ewe vocabulary was set by the coastal Anlo-speaking people, whose particular idiom was taken up by German missionaries (Meyer 2002). Once the dictionaries and grammar books were in place, all of these contingencies were rendered invisible, and the standard became the ruler against which other uses of the language were measured. When in 1904 the missionary T. O. Westgate sat an examination in

Gogo language—it was the first-ever written examination in Chigogo—he failed spectacularly, earning only six marks out of one hundred. Westgate excoriated his examiners, arguing that the standard Gogo dictionary was full of mistakes. But in the end he had to submit himself to the established form. His examiners determined that the language he had learned had been adulterated, since the "natives from whom he had learned were not pure Wagogo" (Briggs and Rees 1906). After two years of study with different teachers, Westgate passed the exam. He would go on to translate several books of the Old Testament into the Gogo vernacular.

Rev. Westgate failed his Chigogo examination because Chigogo—like most African languages—was not already a coherent and integrated system. Seen from the point of view of the examiner, the standard seemed readily available: it was there in the dictionary and the grammar book. But outside the pages of the book things were more complicated. There were many people who, like Rev. Westgate, found themselves unwittingly rendered incompetent by the process of standardization (Irvine 2015). Language standardization was productive of ethnic and cultural differentiation. Even as it produced a lingua franca, it also produced dialects.

It was the experience of becoming an outsider that inspired excluded groups to campaign for recognition: for their own languages, their own dictionaries, their own grammar books, their own Bibles. The dictionary was a passport to recognition. That is why the process of language standardization—which was meant to consolidate languages—always seemed to occasion demands for more dictionaries, more committees, more grammar books. In western Kenya, linguists working to define a standard vocabulary for the heterodox Bantu languages of the region formed the "Luhya Language Committee" in 1940. By the mid-1950s the committee had published a book about Luhya customs and traditions, a collection of proverbs, and several books of the Bible in the Luhya vernacular. From the start, all of this was the subject of a great amount of controversy. A "Maragoli Society" was created among southerners in 1943. Its leader argued that the Committee's Luhya publications were composed in a specific idiom that his people did not comprehend. In the north there was a "Bukusu Language Committee," whose members sought to defend their people's distinctive manner of speaking. "The words in most Luhya readers are outside the child's vocabulary," they argued. "Luhya words are only found in the classroom's cupboard." The Bukusu Committee asked for a government-funded language committee of its own, and for the publication of a book on Bukusu grammar and vocabulary.

Marginalized Languages: Endangerment and Creativity

A great number of languages were, as in the Bukusu case, constituted as acts of resistance to the enfolding cultural power of the majority. They were creations of a people who, finding themselves marginalized by the standard language, sought to access the machinery of standardization in order to define and defend their ways of speaking. The most vociferous campaigns to defend linguistic and cultural locality were occasioned by government efforts to promote a Swahili lingua franca in Eastern Africa. When after the First World War the British government took on Tanganyika as a League of Nations Trust Territory, they adopted Swahili as the language of government administration. Missionaries thought Swahili to be a divine provision. "To some of us it appears to be a miracle that this language has developed throughout the centuries," one of them wrote (Williamson 1942). African advocates for Swahili were confident about the language's integrative powers. Swahili "is the only language capable of bringing all peoples, white and colored, of different districts, provinces and territories in touch in East Africa," argued the president of the "Society for the Study of Swahili." "This is a great linguistic blessing that nature has bestowed upon the inhabitants of the East African territories" (Kihere 1954). But for many East Africans Swahili was a vehicle of cultural and linguistic dispossession, not a blessing. In Uganda there was a great furor when, in 1927, the British government proposed to make Swahili the language of instruction in schools. British officials hoped to use the language to promote integration among their three East African territories. Uganda's people thought integration would bring their country under the thumb of Kenya's powerful white settlers. They insisted that Luganda, or English, not Swahili, should be the language of education and government. "Swahili is, in my opinion, a bulldozer language," argued a Ganda memoirist. "Hear any European army officer addressing an African—the language would be Swahili. But it is not the language for friendly talk. Who would drink pepper if there is sugared tea?" (Peterson 2012, 83).

What animated all of these defensive projects was a pressing feeling of endangerment. Virtually from the very time they were codified African languages were said to be under threat, needing protection from the bulldozer power of a cultural hegemon, endangered by the amnesia and delinquency of the young. This feeling of fragility arose from the particular social position that the first African writers of the vernacular occupied. They were Christian converts, schooled in mission stations. They knew themselves to be dislocated from native ways of life, and they felt it was their duty to preserve the old customs against loss. The first African-run newspaper in Kenya was the Kikuyu-language journal *Mwigwithania*, the "Reconciler." Its contributors sought to reconcile the old regime with the new, modern era. "Rinse out your mouths with water, you people of today, rinse them and recall how we were accustomed to speak formerly," wrote an editorialist in 1928. "Unless you think about it quickly, your ways of speaking will become changed and you will become Swahilis." Another enjoined readers to recall the names of their ancestors, for "if we of the present generation fail to honor the names of our fathers and mothers . . . it appears to me that in the year 1999 we shall ourselves be like foreigners." For these men the prospect of linguistic loss conjured upon a nightmarish future. "Unless we put [our country] right now and establish firmly our own ways of life, I tell you that later on we shall be like the little appendages on a goat's neck—pertaining neither to flesh nor to the skin," wrote the newspaper's editor, Jomo Kenyatta.

In Kenya and elsewhere in colonial Africa the first literate people felt themselves to be at the edge of a radically different epoch. That is why, in very many African languages, the first books to be published by African authors were collections of proverbs, folktales, or transpositions of praise poems. Texts like these were created by people who used the medium of print to record ways of life that were in danger of dying out. Among newly literate men there was an urgent effort to capture oral wisdom, put it on the page, and make it available for future generations. From the beginning African writers saw writing as a vehicle for preservation. Buganda's parliament resolved in 1917 that Prime Minister Apolo Kagwa should create a written description of "all native customs that he considered should be maintained," so that government officers could recognize and protect them. The resolution was the legal impetus for Kagwa's long-running career as Buganda's first auto-ethnographer. The first book composed in Xhosa by an African author was an 1876 collection of folktales. The earliest written literature in the Sotho language was *Mekhoa le Maele a Basotho*, the "Customs and Proverbs of the Sotho," authored in 1893 by Azarieli Sekese.

Men like Azarieli Sekese and Apolo Kagwa represented themselves as preservationists. But the literary genres they created were, in fact, quite new. Oral knowledge was not common knowledge. Oral discourse had been specialized, tailored to the specific audiences to which speakers addressed themselves. In Yorubaland the possession of historical knowledge was differentiated by gender and status. Women generally performed *oriki*, praise epithets that were allusive, compact, and addressed to a specific recipient and his household. Men performed *itan*, narrative history, which set out explanations for obscure *oriki* and offered a context. In central Kenya, oral performers relied on audiences' specific knowledge of ecology and environment. *Ndaĩ* were pithy riddles that Kikuyu men and women competed to interpret. The relationship between the riddle and its answer was never transparent: riddlers played on double meanings and took advantage of metaphors. The answer to the riddle "In your place there is a lily and a castor oil plant," for example, was "Boy and girl." The lily—a deep-rooted plant—was like a boy, who stayed close to home upon his marriage; the girl, by contrast, was like a castor-oil plant, a cash crop whose produce was to be traded away. Kikuyu *ndaĩ* were addressed to people who had specific knowledge about agronomic economies, who had closely observed the qualities of plants and people, and who knew how things grew and how they were harvested.

The preservationists of the late nineteenth and early twentieth centuries took these obscure puzzles and put them on the page, where they could be enumerated, standardized, and circulated to a wide and integrated audience. The first collection of Kikuyu proverbs, published in 1939, was composed by a cadre of Catholic schoolteachers. In this and in other collections the obscure Kikuyu *ndaĩ* were stripped of their demanding specificity and recast as moral wisdom, available for the whole of Kikuyu people to learn from. In a similar way the earliest Yoruba-language historians used their texts to integrate and explain hitherto segmented forms of oral knowledge. Historical works like I. B. Akinyele's *Iwe Itan Ibadan* put the obscure *oriki* poems alongside the narrative histories, using the technique of contextualization to explain the oddities and profundities of the poetry (Barber 2009). Akinyele's book was written for a readership that was homogeneous and integrated, not divided by gender, a readership that regarded its past as shared property, belonging to the collective totality. Composed in the homogenized idiom that Bishop Crowther had defined, Akinyele's work was addressed to—and helped to conjure up—an audience that saw itself as a coherent Yoruba people (Peel 2003).

The creation of printable vernaculars gave literate people a political community to address. Writers of newly defined vernaculars could regard themselves as engaging with an internally integrated, biddable audience. They had at their disposal textual media with which to hail their people, all at once. The mission stations where they learned to read and write were also the incubators for the first African newspapers. The first African-run newspaper in Uganda, *Sekanyolya*, was edited by Sefanio Sentongo, who had learned the business while working on the missionary newspaper *Ebifa* (Scotton 1973). South Africa's first African-run newspaper, *Imvo Zabantusundu*, was published from 1884 by John Tengo Jabavu. He had begun his career as editor for the Presbyterian missionary newspaper *Isigidimi sama Xosa*. For literate men and women there was a palpable sense of excitement about the possibilities that this new mode of communication could offer. "There is no joy equal to this of having a little book in Kikuyu," wrote a contributor to the journal *Mwigwithania*, for in the newspaper "the Kikuyu will be able to give advice to each other, so that the people of our country may agree together."

Their social position allowed literate men and women to dictate to their unlettered contemporaries. They were skilled in the vernacular lingua franca of their people, and they had access to a medium—the newspaper—that seemed to give them a ready-made audience. Their command over the new infrastructure of communication endowed Africa's literate men and women with the proprietorship of their people's culture. They saw themselves as editors. By putting the customs and traditions of their people on the page, literate men could see what needed to be amended. In 1944 the newspaperman Eridadi Mulira had an early-morning dream about the reorganization of Buganda's government. The ideas, he said, "came as if someone was dictating from an unseen source." Shortly thereafter Mulira formed the "African Cultural Society." The aim, he said, was to "take all culture by the horn and in the end try to produce a synthesis of culture which would be our own." For Mulira as for other editors, the work of cultural reform arose from the prior labor of entextualization. That is why the newspaper was essential. It was the venue wherein the generality of a people could be remonstrated with. The linguist Benaiah Ohanga thought *Ramogi*, the newspaper of the Luo Union, ought to encourage the "elimination of the conditions which make for the persistence of superstitious and diabolic beliefs, particularly witchcraft in all its forms" (Peterson 2012, 121). On *Ramogi*'s pages contributors chronicled a range of social ills and debated techniques by which to bring about reform. In September 1949, for instance, a contributor asked Luo people to "abolish the shameful habits of Luo women: smoking the burning side of cigarettes; wearing short dresses; putting too many pins in their hair; buying fish bones in foreign hotels and being employed as *ayahs* [nursemaids]." He also complained over men who played guitars in brothels and talked to each other in the Kikuyu language, instead of Luo.

Here was the machinery for the production of African culture. In most African languages "culture" was a novel word. It was defined as part of the same process by which literate men came to see themselves as spokesmen for a people, an aspect of literate men's effort to consolidate, assess, and reform their people's habits. When in the 1930s the first Kikuyu autoethnographer, Stanley Kiama Gathigira, came to write about the "culture" of the Kikuyu people, he had to invent the term *mĩikarĩre*. It is derived from the verb *ikara*, to "sit" or to "stay," a term that referred to a place where people dwelt. *Mĩikarĩre* are "ways of staying." There were other words available—*mĩtugo*, for example, were "customs" or "manners," derived from the verb *tuga*, "be generous, kind, hospitable, treat well." Gathigira thought *mĩtugo*, with its behavioral connotations, was insufficiently abstract. His book *Mĩikarĩre ya Agĩkũyũ*, published in 1933 under the auspices of the Church of Scotland Mission, was a winding summary of Kikuyu social order. It deployed a new word to assess a whole people's way of life. "Culture" was likewise a late arrival in the Yoruba language. Neither Crowther's 1843 vocabulary nor his 1852 dictionary offered a definition for the word. The terms that did refer to "customs" or "habits" were associated with an individual's preferences. Thus *iṣe* referred to "character, action, custom, fashion," an individual's habits, not a collective set of characteristics. It was not until 1913 that "culture" surfaced in the Yoruba vernacular. In that year a dictionary published by the Church Missionary Society offered *riroko* and *oju lilà* for "culture." The same dictionary offered *iṣe*—hitherto an individual's disposition—for "custom." Here we can see evidence of Yoruba writers' efforts to develop a vocabulary with which to amend their people's ways of life. In Yoruba and other African languages, "culture" was constituted out of literate men's earnest efforts to address an audience that was extensive and integrated, an audience that shared a language and a heritage, an audience that needed instruction.

There was an overlap, infrastructurally and demographically, between the audiences that Africa's moral reformers addressed in the vernacular and the tribes that the colonial government thought Africans belonged to. The policy of indirect rule elevated chiefs as the authorities within the localities that they governed and made vernacular languages into the idiom of local government. Colonial officials were convinced that "a man's native speech is almost like his shadow, inseparable from his personality" (Advisory Committee on Education in the Colonies 1943). Bilingual people were liable to become unhinged, since "the psychological effect of the repeated change over from one medium of expression to another" would lead to "moral disintegration and psychological disruption." British education policy therefore emphasized vernacular-language teaching during the first six years of school; only advanced students were exposed to English. The Bantu Education Act in South Africa was the fullest articulation of this policy of linguistic enclosure. After its adoption in 1953 the readership for vernacular-language texts expanded dramatically. South Africa's racial regime created an impressive architecture for the study of African languages: there were lectureships in phonetics and in Bantu languages in all the major universities. In 1977 the South African state established autonomous language boards that worked within each of the ethnically defined "homelands." The boards' task was to standardize vocabularies, prescribe books for schools, and clarify the orthographies of their languages.

In fact vernaculars were always more than languages of specific and distinct people groups. The audiences for African-language literature was larger, more variegated, and less biddable than colonial officials and apartheid planners could recognize. Africa's languages were constituted as textual systems at the very edge of a new era, and they were the media for shockingly ambitious intellectual and political experiments. New constituencies came suddenly into view. New genres emerged, were developed and transformed. Some genres became part of the library; others were dropped. African writers were always working to expand the range—in vocabulary and in geographic space—of their languages. Some had breathtaking visions. When in 1946 the Kenyan schoolmaster Benaiah Ohanga visited Kampala, he read through an assortment of newspapers and was surprised to discover that his own language, DhoLuo, was "akin to the Lango dialect" of eastern Uganda. Ohanga made a tour through Uganda, meeting with members of the Alur Language Committee and with the leadership of the Acholi Association. In his report he set out a table comparing the vocabularies of the languages of eastern Uganda and western Kenya and concluded by recommending that an interterritorial Luo language committee should be established. Ohanga foresaw a future in which Luo would rank with Swahili and Hausa as one of the preeminent lingua francas of Africa. His career was dedicated to the promotion of a cultural bloc—the Luo—whose borders did not cohere around the embankments of indirect rule. In his language work he was marshalling a people who could be East Africans, not natives of a particular place; whose vernacular language crossed borders and made alliances possible; whose vocabulary welded cosmopolitans together. Here was a language of the world.

Africa's vernaculars were never the languages of localities. Colonial officials thought they were, and they sought to box Africans into ethnic containers. But African entrepreneurs were always expanding what was sayable in their native tongues. They were folding in new words, melding languages together. Vernacular languages were never frozen in place. The Kikuyu language, for example, is a composite; in the distant past its speakers borrowed the most elemental of their words from the Maasai pastoralists alongside whom they lived. In the twentieth century the architects of the Kikuyu political community avidly borrowed from English, transposing the vocabulary and procedures of British bureaucracy into vernacular terminology and creating trustworthy political institutions with these new instruments. In the Lagosian press of the 1920s newspapermen searching for ways to expand their readerships created entirely new literary genres. Among them was the editor I. B. Thomas, whose *Life Story of Me, Sẹgilọla* was published in serial form in the newspaper *Akede Eko*. The narrator, a dying ex-prostitute, took delight in remembering and recounting the songs that Lagos people had sung, the events they had witnessed, the personalities they had known. Here was a text that Lagosians could, regardless of class or education, take pleasure in. In its evocation of a whole people's historical experience, it helped to constitute Lagos as an integrated cultural and political field. It was the first novel in the Yoruba language.

Conclusion

The most exciting experiments in colonial Africa's intellectual history happened in African languages. Shona, Yoruba, Luganda, Kikuyu, isiZulu, and many other African vernaculars were lingua francas, created out of the machinery of language standardization. For the African men and women who learned to read and write in them, vernacular languages were powerful tools with which to do politics. They opened up new means of addressing a people. It was this vertiginous sense of possibility that animated creative people to compose new genres and cultivate new forms of authority. It was from these possibilities that the vocation of the moral reformer and the literary genius came together.

Suggested Readings

Barber, Karin. 2007. *The Anthropology of Texts, Persons and Publics: Oral and Written Culture in Africa and Beyond*. Cambridge: Cambridge University Press.

———. 2009. "I. B. Akinyele and Early Yoruba Print Culture." In *Recasting the Past:*

History Writing and Political Work in Modern Africa, edited by Derek R. Peterson and Giacomo Macola, 31–49. Athens: Ohio University Press.

———, ed. 2012. *Print Culture and the First Yoruba Novel: I. B. Thomas's 'Life Story of Me, Sẹgilọla' and Other Texts*. Leiden: Brill.

Barber, Karin, and Graham Furniss. 2006. "African-Language Writing." *Research in African Literatures* 37 (3): 1–14.

Hofmeyr, Isabel. 2003. *The Portable Bunyan: A Transnational History of The Pilgrim's Progress*. Princeton, NJ: Princeton University Press.

Lonsdale, John. 2005. "'Listen While I Read': Patriotic Christianity Among the Young Kikuyu." In *Christianity and Social Change in Africa: Essays in Honor of J. D. Y. Peel*, edited by Toyin Falola, 563–94. Durham, NC: Carolina Academic Press.

Opland, Jeff. 2004. "Nineteenth Century Xhosa Literature." *Kronos* 30: 22–46.

Peel, J. D. Y. 2003. *Religious Encounter and the Making of the Yoruba*. Bloomington: Indiana University Press.

Peterson, Derek R. 2004. *Creative Writing: Translation, Bookkeeping, and the Work of Imagination in Colonial Kenya*. Portsmouth, NH: Heinemann.

———. 2012. *Ethnic Patriotism and the East African Revival: A History of Dissent*. Cambridge: Cambridge University Press.

References

Advisory Committee on Education in the Colonies. 1943. "Memorandum on Language in African Schools." Tanzania National Archives, file S.1/19191.

Barber, Karin. 2007. *The Anthropology of Texts, Persons and Publics: Oral and Written Culture in Africa and Beyond*. Cambridge: Cambridge University Press.

———. 2009. "I. B. Akinyele and Early Yoruba Print Culture." In *Recasting the Past: History Writing and Political Work in Modern Africa*, edited by Derek R. Peterson and Giacomo Macola, 31–49. Athens: Ohio University Press.

———, ed. 2012. *Print Culture and the First Yoruba Novel: I. B. Thomas's 'Life Story of Me, Sẹgilọla' and Other Texts*. Leiden: Brill.

Barber, Karin, and Graham Furniss. 2006. "African-Language Writing." *Research in African Literatures* 37 (3): 1–14.

Barra, G. 1994 [1939]. *1,000 Kikuyu Proverbs*. Nairobi: Kenya Literature Bureau.

Briggs, John H., and D. Rees. 1906. "Report, First Exam." Church Missionary Society Archive, file G3 A8 O.

Buganda Provincial Commissioner to Chief Secretary. February 26, 1917. Uganda National Archives, file A46/1517.

Church Missionary Society. 1913. *Dictionary of the Yoruba Language*. London: Church Missionary Society.

Crowther, Samuel Ajayi. 1843. *Vocabulary of the Yoruba Language, to Which Are Pre-*

fixed the Grammatical Elements to the Language. London: Church Missionary Society.

———. 1852. *Vocabulary of the Yoruba Language*. London: Seeley's.

Davis, Miss. 1927. "Dispensing under Difficulties." *Ruanda Notes* 21.

Errington, Joseph. 2001. "Colonial Linguistics." *Annual Review of Anthropology* 30: 19–39.

Gathigira, Stanley Kiama. 1986. *Mĩikarĩre ya Agĩkũyũ*. Nairobi: Scholars Publications.

Hofmeyr, Isabel. 2003. *The Portable Bunyan: A Transnational History of* The Pilgrím's Progress. Princeton, NJ: Princeton University Press.

Irvine, Judith. 2015. "Language as Cultural 'Heritage': Visions of Ethnicity in Nineteenth-Century African Linguistics." In *The Politics of Heritage in Africa*, edited by Derek R. Peterson, Kodzo Gavua, and Ciraj Rassool, 191–208. Cambridge: Cambridge University Press.

Kihere, M. 1954. "Memorandum from the Society for the Study of Swahili." September 1. Tanzania National Archives Acc. 602, file ARN/3.

Krapf, Ludwig. 1850. *Outline of the Elements of the Kisuáheli Language*. Tubingen, Germany: L. F. Fues.

Last, J. T., to J. B. Whiting. 1881. August 8. Church Missionary Society archive, file G3 A5 O.

Lepsius, Richard. 1855. *Standard Alphabet for Reducing Unwritten Languages and Foreign Graphic Systems to a Uniform Orthography in European Letters*. London: Williams and Northgate.

Lonsdale, John. 2005. "'Listen While I Read': Patriotic Christianity Among the Young Kikuyu." In *Christianity and Social Change in Africa: Essays in Honor of J. D. Y. Peel*, edited by Toyin Falola, 563–94. Durham, NC: Carolina Academic Press.

Maake, Nhlanhla P. 1992. "A Survey of the Trends in the Development of African Literatures in South Africa." *African Languages and Cultures* 5: 157–88.

Madan, A.C. 1905. *Outline Dictionary Intended as an Aid in the Study of the Languages of the Bantu and Other Uncivilized Races*. London: Henry Frowde.

Mamdani, Mahmood. 1996. *Citizen and Subject: Contemporary Africa and the Legacy of Late Colonialism*. Princeton, NJ: Princeton University Press.

Meyer, Birgit. 2002. "Christianity and the Ewe Nation: German Pietist Missionaries, Ewe Converts and the Politics of Culture." *Journal of Religion in Africa* 32 (2): 167–99.

Mulira, Eridadi. "Autobiography." Cambridge University, Centre of African Studies, Mulira papers, Gen. 1/2.

Ogunbiyi, Isaac Adejoju. 2003. "The Search for a Yoruba Orthography since the 1840s: Obstacles to the Choice of Arabic Script." *Sudanic Africa* 14: 77–102.

Ohanga, B. 1 May 1946. "The Nilotic Peoples of Central Africa." Kenya National Archives, file PC/Nyanza/3/6/129.

"One from Karura." 1929. Editorial letter, *Mwigwithania* 1 (4). Kenya National Archives, file DC/Machakos 10B/13/1.

Opland, Jeff. 2004. "Nineteenth Century Xhosa Literature." *Kronos* 30: 22–46.

Peel, J. D. Y. 2003. *Religious Encounter and the Making of the Yoruba*. Bloomington: Indiana University Press.

Peterson, Derek R. 2004. *Creative Writing: Translation, Bookkeeping, and the Work of Imagination in Colonial Kenya*. Portsmouth, NH: Heinemann.

———. 2012. *Ethnic Patriotism and the East African Revival: A History of Dissent*. Cambridge: Cambridge University Press.

Scotton, James F. 1973. "The First African Press in East Africa: Protest and Nationalism in Uganda in the 1920s." *International Journal of African Historical Studies* 6 (2): 211–28.

Williamson, Jack to Leonard Beecher. 1942. November 4. Anglican Church of Kenya archives, "Language" box, file "Languages Board."

Yankah, Kwesi. 1995. *Speaking for the Chief: Okyeame and the Politics of Akan Royal Oratory*. Bloomington: Indiana University Press.

24 VIOLENCE

Kamari M. Clarke

Perhaps no idea has enjoyed more success or has so fundamentally defined the sociopolitical and ethical terms of our era than violence. Yet, violence, usually understood as the deliberate attempt to inflict injury to a being's physical or psychological integrity, is also among the most controversial concepts of our time. Today, the concept of violence is bandied about in the context of social debates on victimhood and how to recognize and protect victims, especially those from Africa, the Caribbean, and Latin America. With the increasingly spectacular mediatization of judicial trials as a modality for addressing issues of responsibility, accountability, and liability, conceptions of violence have captured the global imagination. Africa has long been a staging ground for the deployment of violence. However, scholars are less inclined to include equally a notion of violence that involves the ways that colonial extraction and experimentation have been constituted through violence. The unmasking of various tropes depicting Africa as a place and an object of violence allows us to see that violence is not easily separable from the broader social and political processes that often structure it.

In the past three decades, the social scientific scholarship on violence has tended to focus on the effects of violence and its moral quandaries as well as questions of justice and restoration. Out of this literature a general consensus prevails that violence is nothing more than the "most flagrant manifestation of power." Defining violence as the power some people exert over others on the basis of supposedly legitimate authority, Max Weber (1921) sought to explain what was at the heart of violence. Disagreeing with Weber's focus on legitimacy, scholars such as Hannah Arendt expanded the conceptualization of violence to speak to its collective nature and to address the fact that violence was not simply about the illegitimacy of extreme forms of action but also about the ultimate kinds of power—that is, the institutionalized manifestation of power that "corresponds to the human ability not just to act but to act in concert" (1969, 44). By introducing key distinctions between power, strength, force, authority, and violence, Arendt defined violence as both a tool and a process.

What Is Violence?

At the heart of these attempts to make sense of violence are also questions about the power to classify what constitutes violence. This power is tied to what political scientist Mahmood Mamdani referred to as the "power to name"—a function central to contests over the legitimacy of modern state formation. The modern nation-state emerged in tandem with the development of regulatory mechanisms to monitor the deployment of state violence: central to the legitimacy of the modern state was the distinction between sanctioned and unsanctioned violence. These entanglements of violence and governance formed the basis upon which questions of sovereignty, individual rights, and entitlements were negotiated alongside modern constitutionalism. And nowhere are these social mechanisms better manifested than in the making of the modern world in which European expansionism involved the deployment of laws and legislative acts to justify various forms of conquest and subordination in the name of colonial or imperial rule. The management of Africa's violence within a new sphere in pursuit of international justice is directly connected to the management of postcolonial African resources and to Europe's and America's new transnational economies.

The creation of new governance zones through the imposition of colonial rule radically transformed people's social worlds. From the imperial colonies in Africa to Latin America, from the Caribbean to Asia, and Australia to North America—these projects contributed to structural and explicit transformations that went well beyond physical violence against the body. In Africa, like elsewhere, colonial rule led to the transformation of whole lifeworlds. It spanned the dispossession of land and livelihoods, the reconfiguration of cultural values and languages, the production of unequal domains of public recourses, the re-hierarchization of human value, and the instantiation of new modes of governance and legal forms.

Various approaches to violence, especially what is referred to as political violence, tend to reinforce explicit forms of extraordinary harm as the baseline for its definition (Chenoweth, Lawrence, and Kalyvas 2010). They presume a form of physical and political harm that can be measured and whose effects can be rendered tangible and demonstrable. However, it has become clear that violence encompasses a wide spectrum of violations as well as the processes by which the "normal" functioning of institutions and policies may result in forms of exclusion and violations. From explicit forms of physical brutality to witchcraft accusations to female and male rituals involving genital cutting to poverty, violence is about the structure, processes, modes of consciousness, and material sites that enable and disable it. For, in the end, violence is a process of injury as much as it is about the manifestation of injury. It is connected to ongoing intimacies that live on beyond the materiality of violation.

Violence is largely assumed to have an easily discernable cause (or culprit) and is understood to have been inflicted by one or several perpetrators who can be readily identified and held accountable for their "crime." Not all forms of suffering are directly observable, however. The more diffuse processes of victimization that originate in conditions of economic, psychological, or political inequality and marginalization are generally relegated to invisibility. They kill people slowly by preventing them from satisfying their basic needs. As a result, they are often dismissed as insignificant, despite the tangible injuries they inflict. The damaging impact that diverse forms of social and institutional failings have on individuals or populations is what scholars refer to as "structural violence." If identifying structural violence is challenging, assigning culpability is even more so as it cannot accurately, or exclusively, be ascribed to community or society, nor to an offending individual. Tracing the mechanisms by which large-scale social forces come to translate into injury requires attending to both the personal experience of suffering and the larger social matrix in which it is enmeshed.

Rather than being subjected to physical violence, the majority of the world's populations is at risk of being victimized by forms of structural violence such as poverty, economic inequality, and ethnic bias. Significantly, structural violence often occurs in conditions that are also accompanied by forms of political violence by the state against targeted populations. These conditions have also been known to provide the breeding grounds for the emergence of some of the most flagrant forms of violence committed by collectivities. For example, the case of Sierra Leone points to a history in which people indigenous to the region, freed slaves from the Americas who had settled there in the early 1800s and become known as Creoles, European settlers and sex workers, and even British imperial government officials converged to establish a new colony. In 1896, the British declared itself as a protectorate of the region (that eventually became Sierra Leone) and they set up a legislative council to which various local Creoles were elected. This move not only established a sphere of priviledge and access that made possible the imperial plunder of economic resources but it also displaced the preexisting chieftaincies of the nonsettler communities, rendering them peripheral within a rapidly changing political landscape. By 1951 Sierra Leone created an internal self-government that led the country toward independence. However, this new democracy came together with disparately connected groups of interests without shared language and history and quickly descended into repressive rule, resulting in military coups and violent attacks as vying parties—the Creoles and those who see themselves as members of the indigenous populations—fought for control of government and resources (such as diamonds). The material violence the Revolutionary United Front rebel forces engaged in resulted in various forms of bodily mutilation, like amputations of limbs; this was a way to terrorize populations and make visible the consequences of protest.

In the wake of this extraordinary violent conflict, a Truth and Reconciliation Commission (TRC) was established, followed by public hearings and criminal trials. In Sierra Leone and elsewhere, these institutions quickly became instruments for the management of mass-atrocity violence. TRCs were critical tools of national reconciliation and post-conflict development. They provided a space for victims to narrativize their suffering as well as an opening for peaceful transitions in post-violence contexts. Under the purview of the TRC in South Africa, Rwanda, Sierra Leone, and Morocco, a range of persons claiming "victim" status developed discourses through which they articulated their losses and channeled their anger within these national domains. This was the human rights path for recourse against violence in the 1990s in Africa.

By the turn of the new century, however, the exponential growth of international courts surpassed that of TRCs. The International Criminal Court (ICC) was established in 2002 as an independent judicial body to bring to justice the most heinous criminal offenses. Rather than aiming for "forgiveness and transition" as was the case for earlier TRCs, the ICC was largely concerned with the arrest and punishment of individuals responsible for enabling the mass murder of significant numbers of people or for committing extreme forms of harm, such as bodily mutilation or sexual violence in times of war. Today the individualization of criminal responsibility through international adjudication provides the language for avenging victims and for articulating justice, writ large.

In fact, the adjudication of individual responsibility as way to address the problem of violence through juridical solutions has proven so symbolically popular that it has now become difficult for many people to imagine other ways of making sense of violence in the contemporary period. From this perspective, it is by blaming a specific set of social actors for wrongs suffered by the poor and the disenfranchised that justice is best served. Aside from the fact that some crimes but not others are scrutinized, the ICC has been unable to examine the larger context of power relations and how it creates the conditions that facilitate the perpetration of violence. By focusing on assigning individual criminal responsibility to a few higher ranking agents, the ICC has ignored how the sale and export of arms to wartorn areas has aided and abetted violent exactions on people there.

Violence as Banal, Violence as Extraordinary

With violence as both extraordinary and ordinary, one of the greatest challenges for students and scholars of contemporary Africa is to figure out how to define violence outside of constructs that presume its exceptionalism. By characterizing violence as a process through which senses of certainty and ambivalence are at play and forms of precarity are at large, we can discern how its manifestations might structure ongoing practices that come to be seen as normal. Nowhere is this more vivid than in Africa, where structural violence prevails in everyday life (Mamdani 2002) and the only ways of addressing such forms of violence is through its classification as a crisis or emergency. We see this point made eloquently in Nancy Scheper-Hughes and Philippe Bourgois's *Violence in War and Peace: An Anthology*, in which Scheper-Hughes demonstrates how banal forms of violence are inflicted upon people through the institutionalization of social inequalities. Through the reinforcement of particular tropes of poverty as a function of individual failure, structural inequality is decoupled from other forms of violence and resides in the domain of individual choice and/or responsibility.

In examining violence as a critical term for the study of Africa, it is useful to consider how colonialism produced a critical stage for the development of a scholarly literature on violence as a site of engagement in African contexts. Violence is about the relationship between the intersubjective management of the body and our sociopolitical classificatory mechanisms that shape ontological determinations about what is acceptable and normal. It is connected to our ethical and philosophical principles and is rooted in the distinction between practices that are seen as unacceptable and in contradiction with the social order and those that are deemed normal and in keeping with liberalist cultural values.

A starting point for exploring the complexities of violence is therefore the distinction between extraordinary violence as visible, as an aberration of daily life, and other forms of structural inequalities that are part of the social order and are rendered "normal." Africa has long provided the zone of engagement through which a radical reorganization of global power and rights has taken place around the management of violence. Today this new reorganization is engaged in the fundamental redefinition of political rights of citizens of democratic sovereign states and is framed as new forms of internationalisms and globalisms. Under these frameworks, new developments are complicating older forms of sovereignty and state legitimacy and are calling into question the way that violence has been managed by the nation-state as an extension of the democratic project. In keeping with increasing definitions of violence through legality and attempts to reclassify rights and responsibility, new judicial arenas, like international criminal law, have emerged as key domains for addressing what the former South African president, Thabo Mbeki, and Mahmood Mamdani have separately referred to as deeply political questions. What this means, Mbeki and Mamdani argue, is that international courts cannot solve African violence. For the root causes of manifestations of violence that occurred in Sierra Leone, Rwanda, and elsewhere are political and require political solutions. Political inequalities produce structural violence which allow social inequalities to fester. But, as we shall see, political inequalities cannot be solved through adjudication or counter-violence or through resorting to culture and tradition as a defense.

Violence and Its Underside

Derived from the Latin *violentia*, meaning "vehemence," violence emerged into contemporary consciousness as a passionate and uncontrolled force that exceeds normal force. Punishment in Europe up until the eighteenth century was presented as a spectacle through which the use of excessive force on the prisoner's body was a public manifestation of the state's control over citizens. Acts of punishment frequently resulted in the violation of norms, rights, or rules. The nineteenth century witnessed a shift from the use of physical and spectacularized violence to the pursuit of judicial trials and punishment through "suspended rights" such as imprisonment (Foucault 1975, 11). Punishment ceased to be a spectacle that served as a deterrent against crime. Instead, the focus was on repairing the soul of the prisoner. This represented a conceptual shift in how violence came to be managed. By the twentieth century the popular Euro-Western meaning of violence in the Global North came to be conflated with the notion of extraordinary "violation" tied to expectations of recompense. As such, the development of modern conceptions of violence was eventually understood through the relation between physical violence and whether that violence was deemed *normal* and *acceptable* or *abnormal* and *intolerable*. Such distinctions have been proven to be problematic, however.

In *The Wretched of the Earth*, Frantz Fanon, describing the Algerian War of Independence, detailed the way that the violence of subordination through the colonial state perpetuated violence between those colonized. Violence, he argued, is fundamental to the process of colonization and the condition of being colonized. Repression and control as exerted by the colonial state and its officials as well as the related negation of personhood must be understood as forms of violence. For Fanon, colonialism was a manifestation of violence in its natural state and the only way to eradicate it was to confront it with greater violence. Only by transgressing the limits imposed by the colonial order and claiming violence as a tool of liberation would colonial subjects control their destinies, Fanon claimed. By describing the inscriptions of colonial violence, Fanon pointed to the ways that regimes of subjugation are deployed and reproduced. However, for Fanon, violence can also be used as a restorative means of rebalancing the scales of power insofar as freedom, for the colonized, must be achieved through violence. For the native, "life can only spring up again out of the rotting corpse of the settler" (Fanon 1963, 93).

Violence, in Fanon's argument, could restore the self-respect of the "native" and make him or her fearless. By addressing the social imbalance manifested in "the scandalous opulence of Europe vis-à-vis the colony," the counterviolence of decolonization was a source of unification and a means of overcoming colonial inequalities (Fanon 1963, 94).

Ethnic and Political Violence

British colonialism contributed to the production of deep structural inequalities that shaped the changing forms of political power in various African polities (Mamdani 2002). Though it lasted only sixty years, colonial rule in Nigeria contributed to rapid change, ranging from the development of extraction economies, the expansion of agricultural products and consumption patterns, and the production of particular cultural and moral orders, which grew alongside new educational formats aligned with modern forms of sociality and productivity. The creation of new territorial boundaries, the development of roads, laws, and new forms of political order that reinforced British colonial interests led to the emergence of deep regional inequalities within the colony. People in the South and the East within closer proximity to extractable resources, in particular oil, developed greater intimacies with British rule and benefited from its ideologies of progress. After independence in 1960, minimal attention was given to developing state institutions and equalizing them between the North and the South. A highly centralized federal body with little to no accountability formed to replace the colonial administration, further reinforcing existing networks of structural violence. Over the years the Nigerian South has benefited from local resources, infrastructure, and general economic development. To this day the North lacks the type of economic resources, the infrastructure, and the administrative and social institutions enjoyed by the South. This is a pattern repeated across the continent.

It is these structural inequalities between the Nigerian North and South that have produced the conditions in which the radical Boko Haram "freedom fighters" emerged. As an Islamic militant group based in West Africa, Boko Haram ("Western education is sinful/forbidden") has led violent attacks against both the state and ordinary people as part of what its members believe to be a divinely guided war for Islam. Since 2009 military attacks by Boko Haram in Borno State and military incursions in neighboring Niger, Chad, and Cameroon have contributed to the uprooting of more than 2.5 million people in the Lake Chad region. Boko Haram's tactics of plunder and pillage have inflicted widespread suffering and reduced large swaths of population to utter poverty. Visible as they are, the atrocities perpetrated by Boko Haram forces on local populations have become the object of widespread condemnation in popular and academic discourses. On the other hand, the systematic ways in which ordinary Nigerians are harmed or otherwise disadvantaged by social and political arrangements that are rooted in the country's history of long-standing disparity between the North and the South are far less visible. Though it works in subtle fashion, structural violence is no less effective in the way it puts individuals and, in some cases, entire populations in harm's way.

The postcolonial Africanist literature has detailed how the imposition of Western education has been articulated through discourses of civility vs. backwardness by those engaged in the formation of colonial education. Colonial education was meant to craft citizens able to reproduce colonial governance. To that end, it produced discourses of "primitivity" and "backwardness," eventually fueling the epistemic violence that became characteristic of Islamic militancy in contemporary Nigeria. These narratives made their mark publicly in the early formation of the Nigerian nation-state through early missionary writing and colonial arguments about the "native savages." And their impact continues to be felt in the contemporary public sphere where representations of Islam as backward, anti-rights, and anti-feminist are circulated through electronic technologies, videos, talk shows, nightly news captions, senate congressional hearings; through the invocation of legality these representations are further concretized in a world deemed secular and without religious bias. Yet, as Weber and Talal Asad have documented, even the most ostensibly secular European society is a deeply Christian manifestation in its forms of legality, moral sensibilities, and modern temporality. Insofar as the secular is an implicitly Christian rather than neutral arrangement, it can only consider Islam as "other." By pointing to the limits of the secular project, these scholars have shown that current understandings of Islam as a "problem" requiring intervention are the product of a particular history of knowledge and power.

Among other influences, Boko Haram as a social movement came into being as a response to structural inequalities that laid the foundation for ongoing underdevelopment, unemployment, and social unrest. A range of actors emerged, who, under the leadership of charismatic leaders, were willing to exercise violence (kidnapping, rape, torture, and pillage) against the perceived encroachment of Western knowledge, politics, and religion. At its core Boko Haram rejected an African alliance with a socio-moral Christian order that encouraged Western observers to construct the people of the northern region as ideologically backward—especially when it comes to their treatment of women and girls. Despite the fact that most people in northern Nigeria widely believe Boko Haram to be un-Islamic,

Western observers tend to portray the Islamic insurgency as representative of the kind of violence that radical Islam typically engenders.

It is not surprising that the race for political control in many African countries has led to extreme forms of violence, military coups, or rebel groups vying for political influence to control various extraction industries. The ultimate erosion of state capacities to build viable economies for citizens, regulate access to resources in the domestic economy, and build innovative mechanisms capable of incorporating indigenous cultural traditions to direct future action has given rise to visible forms of abuse and suffering that mask the actual violence of social inequality. These expressions of political instability point to the ways that violence can be identified as operative or not operative. Making certain types of violence, notably structural violence, invisible and keeping them outside the purview of the law (rather than seeing them as produced by it) enables other forms of violence, such as the violence perpetrated by Boko Haram, to become legible and recognizable. Obfuscating the conditions (structural inequality, systems of colonialism, imperialism, racism, and ethnocentrism) that led to the emergence of Boko Haram has enabled important social inequalities between Christian southerners and Muslim northerners to be ignored. This, in turn, makes the claims by Islamic fundamentalists that Western education is detrimental seem misplaced or inconceivable—despite the fact that Western education, like Islamic education, has its own agendas. Countries, such as Nigeria, that have been constituted through violence are productive sites for elaborating and testing social theories about violence.

The commonly evoked image of Africa as a place fueled by violence is instructive. For not only do such constructs miss the fact that contests over democratic governance have provided minimal options for economic and social power for those who see themselves as subordinate, but they also gloss over how colonial powers fueled the regional conflicts that are so often characterized as religious and ethnic clashes. In Rwanda, a country colonized by Germany in the late 1880s that later fell under the control of Belgium during World War I, ethnic distinctions between the Hutu and Tutsi intensified, fueled by a mixture of myth and "racial science." Tutsis were said to be a "Caucasoid" tribe from Ethiopia and were seen as more European, thus superior. The Hutu, on the other hand, were dismissed as inferior since they belonged to what was seen as a more "primitive" racial typology. These racial classifications extended into preferential governance mechanisms by which land reform and compensation privileged Tutsis and led to the disenfranchisement of Hutus through the early twentieth-century implementation of wide-scale forced labor regimes.

At independence in 1962, when Tutsi chiefs were deposed and replaced by a Hutu leadership, the racial and ethnic typologies that had emerged during the colonial period were fully articulated: Hutus and Tutsis were separate "races." In the early 1990s the dissemination of national ID cards by Hutu state officials provided Hutus with ways of systematically distinguishing between Hutus and Tutsis. This led to the violence against card-carrying Tutsis and those seen as moderate Hutu sympathizers that resulted in the death of hundreds of thousands of people in 1994.

In reflecting on the histories of Sierra Leone, Nigeria, and Rwanda, one cannot ignore the realities of structural violence that contributed to what Deborah Thomas (2011) has referred to as "exceptional violence," the recognition that if the end of imperial control in the colonies was cause for celebration, at independence the new elites in power shared their former colonial masters' basic beliefs about the forms that nation and citizenship should take. Political, social, and economic structures (including modes of control) established during colonial times thus often remained unchallenged in the new nation-states. As Thomas indicates, nationalist leaders triumphantly appropriated "the master's tools," as they took charge of government, only to find that these tools were designed in ways that perpetuated the very problems independence was expected to solve. Here, analyzing the structural links between colonialism and the postcolonial state opens up new avenues for making sense of the types of extreme violence that have plagued postcolonial Africa in past decades.

Pondering the way that global markets and institutions continue to shape Africa as a place of extraordinary violence requiring external interventions can be useful for detailing the ways that inequality, racism, and colonialism remain enduring problems in the postcolonies. From the sale of firearms to African nations to the paramilitary presence in some regions of Africa to the emergence of a slate of hybrid institutions aimed at promoting both "security" and "nation building" to the recent juridification of violence through the activities of the ICC, the continent is awash in demonstrations of violence, arbitration, and peace-keeping efforts.

Political science approaches to violence on the continent have constituted Africa through their articulations of violence (Ahluwalia, Bethlehem, and Gino 2007). This has had implications for social, political, and economic practices. Political predicaments long identified, often exclusively, with postcolonial African states—their diminished capacity to regulate their own economies, the constraining dictates of international financial institutions—have now played out more visibly across the globe in Syria, Afghanistan, Palestine, and Sri Lanka. State contraction; the erosion of social safety nets; the demands for flexibility in forms of work and sociability; the large-scale privatizations of, on one hand, social goods and utilities, and enterprises and security operations on the other; the diminished capacity of states to discipline their citizens by means of consent—these widespread transformations witnessed in political systems of various kinds have made Africa's "exceptional" crises seem suddenly mainstream. Continent-specific poverty and correlations between individuals and communities, as well as the realities of the international market, have led to the obfuscation of older forms of sociality. But on the subject of rethinking citizenship and indigeneity, it has been the absence of sufficient settlements on land, water, and boundary disputes, coupled with the African majority's limited access to adequate resources, that have led to resultant postcolonial hostilities. Such realities of violence raise more questions than answers. For it is clear that attempts to invoke notions of violence are widespread but the definitional problem of "what is violence?" remains long-standing. It remains this way not because its working assumptions do not appear "real" to those involved. The definitions are competing and at times contradictory as perceptions of what constitutes "normal" or acceptable are politically charged; acknowledging the banality of the everyday as fundamentally violent carries consequences along with it.

Physical Harm and the Judicialization of Violence in Africa

In 2002, the World Health Organization (WHO) published *The World Report on Violence and Health*, which reviews violence on a global scale. The WHO defines violence as "the intentional use of physical force or power, threatened or actual, against oneself, another person, or against a group or community, which either results in or has a high likelihood of resulting in injury, death, psychological harm, maldevelopment, or deprivation" (WHO 2002, 5). This definition aligns closely with understandings of violence in criminal law, where intent is central to determining liability for harm caused. The WHO offers a typology of violence that divides violence into three broad categories, which can each be divided further into more specific forms of violence: self-directed violence, interpersonal violence, and collective violence. Self-directed violence is subdivided into suicidal behavior and self-abuse. Interpersonal violence is divided into family and intimate partner violence, and community violence—which, for the WHO, includes "youth violence, random acts of violence, rape or sexual assault by strangers and violence in institutional settings such as schools, workplaces, prisons and nursing homes" (WHO 2002, 6). Collective violence is divided into social, political, and economic violence, where social violence is committed to advance a particular social agenda—that is, terrorism or hate crime. Political violence, following the WHO, includes war and violent conflict perpetrated by states or similarly large and organized groups. Economic violence (as per the WHO) is motivated by economic gain: it includes attacks aimed at disrupting economic activity, preventing access to essential services, and producing economic dysfunction.

The WHO has also articulated four different natures of violent acts: physical, sexual, and psychological acts, as well as violent acts involving deprivation and neglect—any or all of which may be present within the types of violence set out above. While the WHO accepts that its typology may be flawed and not universally accepted, it argues that the typology provides a

> useful framework for understanding the complex patterns of violence taking place around the world, as well as violence in the everyday lives of individuals, families and communities. It also overcomes many of the limitations of other typologies by capturing the nature of violent acts, the relevance of the setting, the relationship between the perpetrator and the victim, and—in the case of collective violence—possible motivations for the violence. However, in both research and practice, the dividing lines between the different types of violence are not always so clear (WHO 2002, 7).

We can recognize here an attempt to bridge the divide between the wide and restrictive approaches, with the WHO including physical harm as well as psychological harm, and economic forms of harm such as underdevelopment and deprivation. Yet, violence remains fundamentally tied to intention here, pointing to the necessity that there be a clear, recognizable movement of force from perpetrator to victim. There is something about the visibility or traceability of this connection and the proximal distance between the perpetrator and the victim that has become central to popular understandings of violence—and how observers judge the violence witnessed. When the existence of violence depends on particular evidentiary standards and visible signs of pain and harm, how do we trace less visible forms of alienation, misery, or repression?

In recent years, a small but growing group of scholars critical of the "tribunalization of African violence" (Clarke 2009) has explored the *underneath* of violence and its conceptual, structural, and practical genealogies. By exploring the political content of violence that has become the subject of increasing judicialization, they have begun to question the popular twentieth-century trend on the right to punish. This right, often popularized as the right to criminal accountability, is deemed central to the democratic project. However, as a dimension of internationalist discourse, its logic was borne out of the Nuremburg model of post–World War II criminal accountability for war crimes. Though applied in very different contexts—in which postcolonial violence was propelled by earlier manifestations of colonial violence—the Nuremberg model has had a particularly strong impact in Africa, resulting from the growing focus of the ICC. However, the most acute observers have shown that the weakness and limits of domestic criminal justice similarly hamper international courts.

The Judicialization of Violence and What Recedes to the Margins

To adopt the terms of the newly emergent interdisciplinary academic field of transitional justice, how did the ICC become such a successful institution for addressing African violence? To fully understand the popularity of the concept of international criminal justice, one must remember that the emergence of the ICC took place at a time when *domestic* criminal justice—both as an ideal type and in practice—was in a period of fundamental crisis in a number of countries in the Global South. Critical attacks on various alternatives to criminal justice, such as historical and reparatory justice, had proved effective. Domestic courts premised on retributive justice, self-selecting juries, and get-tough prosecutors, coupled with the increasing push toward police security and the expansion of the prison industrial complex, provided corollaries propelled by the need for solutions to economic crises. This trend led to the standardization of statist modern law which large numbers of scholars, politicians, and activists have come to see as fully compatible with the proliferation of progressive, pluralist ideals about law, norms, and social movements produced by post–Cold War globalization (de Sousa Santos 1995).

What developed was an increasingly pro-judicial accountability movement whose manifestation was extended through the construction of new forms of executive orders that could exceed the modern sovereign state. Their reach was nevertheless limited; it only extended to sites of violence deemed illegitimate and under the preexisting treaty system. It did not include those states that did not fall under the court's jurisdiction and whose acts of violence were deemed legitimate according to existing rules of war and imminent threats (that justified violence as a form of self defense). Although some violence went unaccounted for, a number of African leaders were prosecuted by the ICC. As of August 2015, the ICC had pursued twenty-two cases in nine conflicts across several African states: the Central African Republic (CAR), the Democratic Republic of the Congo (DRC), Côte d'Ivoire, Sudan, Uganda, Kenya, Mali, and Libya. From the cases of alleged African warlords to the indictments of African leaders—ranging from President Uhuru Kenyatta and Deputy President William Ruto to Presidents Omar al-Bashir and Laurent Gbagbo—the focus of the ICC has been on African violence, a trend for which the ICC has come under fire.

Alongside attention to African violence was a new formulation of responsibility through a shift to the individual as a new constitutional category. With individual criminal responsibility at the core of international criminal law, the focus of the international management of violence went beyond the proximate actor convicted of a direct criminal act. Now an individual commander, a leader, or a high-ranking official could be found responsible for violent crimes (Clarke 2015). As resolutions about ending impunity and its mantra that "no one should be above the law" spread, a global internationalism emerged, fueled by a new generation of lawyers, prosecutors, and civil society actors determined to punish those responsible for inflicting extraordinary violence on innocent victims. So successful has been this move toward the individualization of criminal responsibility as a measure for how we understand and reattribute harm that it has now become almost impossible for people to even conceive of alternatives.

The lessons learned from the experience of the International Criminal Tribunal for the former Yugoslavia (ICTY) have implications for the subsequent development of international law and the way that contemporary Africanist scholars are speaking back to such conceptual erasures. At the time that the United Nations Security Council (UNSC) was created in 1993, no precedent existed for this form of international criminal law. As a result, the UNSC decision to base the new international criminal law jurisdiction on its Chapter VII powers has meant that the new regime must be understood as the product of the *emergency* and *executive* powers of the UN system. A careful analysis of its first Tadić Decision of 1995, which provided the legal precedent on which contemporary international criminal law is now based, suggests that a properly cosmopolitan criminal law regime created a transnational system of *sovereign law*. And though we remain—after two decades—with no name yet for this institution, it represents the corpus of modern statist systems of criminal justice and comprehends itself as a properly unitary, top-down, and subjecting system incapable of coexisting with a system of state sovereignty. In its wake—and filling the void where sovereignty, treaties, and a broader international system recognized no powers of compulsion as normative—emerged a new modality based on international judges extrapolating a modern statist criminal justice system. As a result, what we had with the ICTY was a top-down and unitary criminal law system that divided the world into those with UNSC power or big military or economic might, those with guarantors, and those without—which, of course, included African states.

Initially, it was difficult to find non-polemical accounts of just what is at stake in the new domain of international criminal justice and its management of African violence. However, in recent years a small but growing group of critically engaged Africanist legal scholars has begun to concern themselves with making sense of the conceptual, structural, and practical terms and the logic of the criminalization and individualization of justice and its implications for how we understand violence. Not surprisingly, given Africa's role as the object of this new system of law and order, it is scholars concerned with the turn to international judicial solutions in Africa who have been at the forefront of this rethinking (Mamdani 2000 and 2002; Kendall and Nouwen 2014). Through their examinations of the histories of colonial violence that have continued to shape contemporary violence in its various forms, these observers have shown what is rendered visible through particular manifestations of violence and what recedes to the margins. Yet again, despite these revelations, the juridicalization, tribunalization, and individualization of violence has flourished and as such it has become difficult for scholars to see other alternatives outside of legality. This inability to recognize that judicial solutions to violence cannot address past violence is at the heart of the problem. The contemporary pathologies that shape the conditions by which inequalities are produced and sustained highlight the fiction of justice—the idea that law can rectify the violence of structural inequalities without addressing the way that structural inequalities are embedded in our social order. But when we recognize the ways that everyday violence is propelled through power, then we can see how it is that the relationship between our social order and social inequalities is central to contemporary constellations of violence. In keeping with this sense of the endemic nature of violence, we now move beyond formal law and point to the place of "culture" and "tradition" in hiding social violence through political inequality. Hidden discourses concerning female rituals and the existence of witchcraft in various African contexts highlight the deeply embedded aspects of violence and how it is manifest in discourses concerning the "culture" and "traditions" of a people.

The Violence of the Everyday: The Modernity of the Occult

In the midst of protracted political and economic struggles, the African continent has witnessed the rise of Pentecostal-Charismatic crusades to eradicate witchcraft as well as the turn to violent exorcism rituals and accusations against socially marginalized populations. Coupled with the ritualization of female genital cutting in a range of areas where girls are subjected to the removal of some or all of the external female genitalia, children and the socially vulnerable have been subjected to violent practices in the name of "cultural traditions."

Until recently scholarly efforts to broaden approaches to structural violence have largely been dismissed for stretching the concepts of violence and human rights until they are no longer useful. Johan Galtung, a sociologist and a prominent scholar in the field of peace studies, insisted that while peace is taken to be the absence of violence, violence is present whenever human beings are somehow denied the opportunity to realize their full potential. He offered this definition to replace what he felt was an inadequate concept narrowly focused on the intentional somatic incapacitation or denial of health (potentially leading to death). In offering this critique, he argued that if violence was only about explicit killing and peace was its negation, "then too little is rejected when peace is held up as the ideal" (Galtung 1969, 169). For Galtung, violence encompassed the entire conceptual territory between personal violence and structural violence. To work toward peace was to limit both personal and structural violence. This includes limiting cultural practices with the power to violate.

From witchcraft accusations to female genital mutilation (FGM), a number of practices are rooted in forms of inequality that promulgate the control and incapacitation of women, children, and other minorities. Other forms of controlling vulnerable populations have emerged in the midst of rapid social changes that range from pain infliction to incarceration to starvation, and, in some cases, death, and have led to the perpetuation of cultural logics that attribute misfortune, disease, and the death of others to the psychic powers of witches. While addressing the social and cultural logics that shape witchcraft accusations is key to addressing the nature of mundane forms of daily violence in Africa, addressing the underlying socioeconomic and political problems of poverty and disenfranchisement is also part of the solution. For, in the end, it is critical to highlight the workings of structural violence as it is manifest not only in persistent wounds on the corporal body but also in conditions of inequality that are perceived as "traditional" or "normal" but are nevertheless deeply violent.

Suggested Readings

Ahluwalia, Pal, Louise Bethlehem, and Ruth Gino, eds. 2007. *Violence and Non-Violence in Africa*. New York: Routledge.

Arendt, Hannah. 1969. *On Violence*. New York: Harcourt, Brace & World, Inc.

Asad, Talal. 2015. "Reflections on Violence, Law and Humanitarianism." *Critical Inquiry* 41 (2): 390–427.

Bufacchi, Vittorio. 2005. "Two Concepts of Violence." *Political Studies Review* 3: 193–204.

Das, Veena. 2006. *Life and Words: Violence and the Descent in the Ordinary*. Los Angeles: University of California Press.

Fanon, Frantz. 1963. *The Wretched of the Earth*. New York: Grove Weidenfeld.

Mamdani, Mahmood. 2002. *When Victims Become Killers: Colonialism, Nativism, and the Genocide in Rwanda*. Princeton, NJ: Princeton University Press.

Thomas, Deborah Zoll. *Exceptional Violence: Embodied Citizenship in Transnational Jamaica*. Durham, NC: Duke University Press.

References

Ahluwalia, Pal, Louise Bethlehem, and Ruth Gino, eds. 2007. *Violence and Non-Violence in Africa*. New York: Routledge.

Arendt, Hannah. 1969. *On Violence*. New York: Harcourt, Brace & World, Inc.

Chenoweth, Erica, Adria Lawrence, and Stathis Kalyvas, eds. 2010. *Rethinking Violence: States and Non-State Actors in Conflict*. Cambridge, MA: MIT Press.

Clarke, Kamari M. 2009. *Fictions of Justice: The International Criminal Court and the*

Challenge of Legal Pluralism in Sub-Saharan Africa. New York: Cambridge University Press.

———. 2015. "Refiguring the Perpetrator: Culpability, History and International Criminal Law's Impunity Gap." *International Journal of Human Rights* 19 (5): 592–614.

de Sousa Santos, Boaventura. 1995. *Toward a New Legal Common Sense: Law, Science and Politics in the Paradigmatic Transition*. New York: Routledge.

Fanon, Frantz. 1963. *The Wretched of the Earth*. New York: Grove Weidenfeld.

Foucault, Michel. 1975. *Discipline and Punish: The Birth of the Prison*. New York: Vintage.

Galtung, Johan. 1969. "Violence, Peace and Peace Research." *Journal of Peace Research* 6 (3): 167–91.

Kendall, Sara, and Sarah Nouwen. 2014. "Representational Practices at the International Criminal Court: The Gap between Juridified and Abstract Victimhood." *Law and Contemporary Politics* 76 (3–4): 235–62.

Mamdani, Mahmood. 2000. "A Diminished Truth." In *After the TRC: Reflections on Truth and Reconciliation in South Africa*, edited by Wilmot James and Linda Van De Vijver, 51–57. Athens: Ohio University Press.

———. 2002. *When Victims Become Killers: Colonialism, Nativism, and the Genocide in Rwanda*. Princeton, NJ: Princeton University Press.

Scheper-Hughes, Nancy, and Philippe I. Bourgois, eds. 2004. *Violence in War and Peace*. Malden, MA: Blackwell.

Thomas, Deborah. 2011. *Exceptional Violence: Embodied Citizenship in Transnational Jamaica*. Durham, NC: Duke University Press.

Weber, Max. 1921. "Politics as a Vocation." In *Max Weber: Essays in Sociology*. Translated and edited by H. H. Gerth and C. Wright Mills, 77–128. New York: Routledge.

World Health Organization. 2002. *The World Health Report*. http://www.who.int/violence_injury_prevention/violence/world_report/en/. Accessed November 15, 2015.

25 WITCHCRAFT

Adam Ashforth

Witchcraft, along with equivalent indigenous terms, describes forms of interpersonal violence. These are distinct from but equivalent to physical violence in their effects. Perpetrated in secret by invisible means and evident primarily in manifestations of misfortune (which can take virtually any form), witchcraft—which can also be described as occult assault—is nonetheless considered to be every bit as real as any other form of violence. Serious illness and untimely deaths, particularly, provoke speculation about witchcraft. Witchcraft, it should be noted, is but one of many ways in which invisible evil forces are said to cause harm.

The matters to which the term "witchcraft" refers are dynamic; the ideas, discourses, idioms, and narratives used to account for them are constantly in flux. When approaching these issues, therefore, it is most important not to presume that we are searching for some sort of stable, static, "system of belief" applicable to "Africans," or some particular subset thereof, which can be compared with other putative systems or for which a history can be described. Indeed, for reasons explained by Rodney Needham several decades ago, we should be extremely careful when deploying the term "belief" in regard to these issues, for when people speak of witchcraft, they are primarily telling stories not outlining propositions, and stories have very different conditions of believability from propositions.

The history of scholarship on witchcraft in Africa has been shaped by a combination of Western fascination with the fact that people still believe in witches, when such superstition was thought long dead in the West, and the need to counter Western prejudice about Africans. Early European travelers and missionaries in Africa tended to write or talk about witchcraft, along with rituals and procedures for its control, as yet more evidence for the prevailing prejudice that Africans were primitive people marked by savagery, awaiting only the "civilizing mission" of colonialism and Christianity. Missionaries tended to treat witchcraft as part of a general pattern of paganism that would surely retreat in the face of the Gospel, thus underlining the imperative of evangelization. Colonial authorities and settlers frequently cited African talk of witchcraft in justifying the need for white rule. Despite more than a century of scholarly research showing otherwise, the presumption that "belief in witchcraft" indicates some sort of premodern backwardness remains firmly entrenched among outsiders encountering African preoccupations with witchcraft. Nonetheless, students of Africa, whatever their focus, can hardly avoid consideration of witchcraft—since the sense of insecurity the term indicates permeates virtually every aspect of life. Given the history of Western prejudice and racism, however, students of Africa must be circumspect, careful, and respectful when conducting research and discussing these issues.

Historical Treatment of Witchcraft

The first extended scholarly study of the subject was by E. E. Evans-Pritchard, in the south of Anglo-Egyptian Sudan in the late 1920s and early 1930s. In *Witchcraft, Oracles and Magic among the Azande*, a book which remains the keystone for all studies of the subject, Evans-Pritchard set out to show how, while witches, as the Azande conceived them, cannot exist, their ideas about witches and witchcraft were by no means absurd. Rather than a failure to understand the basic realities of the empirical world, Evans-Pritchard argued that Azande talk about witchcraft was, in its own terms, an entirely reasonable way of making sense of fundamental existential questions about the meaning of misfortune. In what was to become his signature exemplum, he showed how the Azande he worked with were well aware that termites eating out the supports of a granary could cause the structure to fail and collapse on people resting in its shade. Such knowledge, however, failed to answer the questions, *Why me? Why now?* For these questions, suppositions about chance were quite unsatisfactory whereas witchcraft supplied a viable hypothesis: *someone* has caused it to fall on me; the question is, *Who?* Evans-Pritchard strove to show how the Azande worldview was internally consistent and reasonable, given their circumstances. The Zande philosophical system, he suggested, largely implicit though it was, could be described and translated by the anthropologist into terms understandable by outsiders. The conviction, pioneered by

Evans-Pritchard, that African talk of witchcraft should not be treated as a form of "primitive mentality" indicative of "prelogical thought," as argued by Lucien Lévy-Bruhl, has remained the foundation of all serious studies of the subject since. (Indeed, Evans-Pritchard's work spurred a long-running debate about the nature of rationality and scientific explanation.)

In the middle decades of the twentieth century discussions of witchcraft became a staple of Africanist anthropology, dominated as it was by British social anthropologists. While some earlier anthropologists, notably Audrey Richards in the 1930s, and, some would argue, those associated with the Rhodes-Livingston Institute in the 1940s and 1950s, had attended to the impact of social change attendant on colonialism and urbanization, for the most part anthropologists were disinclined to study colonial power relations in favor of reconstructing putative "belief systems" of "Native tribes." A number of colonial administrators, however, such as Frank Melland in Northern Rhodesia and C. Clifton Roberts in the Nyasaland Protectorate grappled with the difficult question of how to align "modern" colonial law and administration with the fact that Africans feared, and felt a strong need to deal with, witchcraft.

Two broad approaches to witchcraft dominated the field of African studies in the mid-twentieth century. The first, emphasizing the sociology of knowledge, attempted to catalogue for other groups what Evans-Pritchard had done for the Azande, while seeking, further, to trace connections between the "social structure" of African societies and patterns of witchcraft "beliefs." Monica Wilson, for example, famously argued that witchcraft beliefs represented the "standardized nightmare" of a society, equivalent to the "reds under the bed" fantasies of McCarthyite investigators in the United States at the time. Among the Nyakyusa, where people lived not with kin but cattle-owning neighbors from whose wealth they were excluded, other than to dine occasionally on a beast at a feast, Wilson argued that witchcraft stories tended to involve accounts of prodigious feasting on that most illicit resource: human flesh. Among the Pondo, on the other hand, where complicated kinship rules prohibiting marriage between even quite distant relatives—any member of your mother's or grandmother's clans, possibly numbering in the thousands, most of whom are strangers—kept people in a state of anxiety about incest, witchcraft stories primarily conjured scenes of erotic transgression.

The second preoccupation of midcentury modernist anthropologists involved tracing the micro-politics of witchcraft accusations in particular societies—figuring out who accuses whom, when, where, how, and why—so as to ascertain the functions such accusations performed in maintaining social order or facilitating social change. Witchcraft accusations could then be read as, in the words of Max Marwick, a sort of "social strain gauge" to identify the real underlying conflicts, typically within kinship groups, that marked a particular kind of society. As Victor Turner first pointed out, however, most of these studies were predicated on a static image of their subjects when in reality the societies in question were highly dynamic, changing in ways that could only be understood by studying them closely over time, rendering pointless any efforts to generalize from patterns of accusation in particular places at particular times.

By the late 1960s, as the wave of Independence swept through colonial Africa, anthropological interest in witchcraft declined. The new states of Africa were embarking on ambitious modernizing schemes, with political elites recycling the great twentieth-century modernist narratives of capitalism, socialism, and nationalism. Attention by outsiders to the implicit backwardness inherent in talk of witchcraft came to seem not only impolite, but also irrelevant. African scholars were also disinclined to waste time on such matters. Africanists in other disciplines, while occasionally recognizing the salience of matters such as witchcraft, were able to ignore such issues because they fell under the purview of anthropology. African talk of witchcraft was generally presumed to be a steadily disappearing trace of a tradition-bound past. Urbanization, moreover, meant that presumptions about stable "belief systems" identifying bounded "cultures" such as informed earlier anthropology became increasingly harder to sustain.

In the late 1980s, however, Africanist anthropologists began to realize they could no longer ignore the persistent talk of witchcraft they were encountering in their fieldwork. Nor could they ignore the legacy of colonialism in the contexts within which they worked. At the same time, dynamic religious movements were sweeping the continent, particularly robust forms of global Pentecostalism, which were, and remain, preoccupied with countering evil forces such as witchcraft. Witchcraft came to be understood not as a remnant of the belief systems of past cultures but as part of the complex ways Africans were creating modern societies as well as ways of understanding "modern" changes in their social worlds, connected as these were to the rest of the world. The seminal texts in this field were Peter Geschiere's *The Modernity of Witchcraft* and the collection edited by Jean and John Comaroff, *Modernity and Its Malcontents*. These and other authors have worked to show, among other things, how witchcraft discourses circulate among the global flows of ideas, people, commodities, and capital in the worlds of late capitalism.

Since the 1990s, African studies has seen a proliferation of writing on witchcraft in Africa covering a wide range of topics and approaches. The issue is no longer considered the sole province of anthropology but has become rather a central concern of students of economics and development, law and human rights, public health (particularly in the wake of the HIV/AIDS epidemic), religion, politics, and violence—to name but a few.

Some critics have argued that this renewed scholarly interest in witchcraft has led to an overemphasis on the occult, contributing, yet again, to a sense that Africa is rife with ignorance and superstition. Some African scholars, from both religious (Bongmba 2001; Ngong 2012) and secular perspectives (Igwe 2004), have also been critical of this work as impeding the proper modernization of African societies. Nonetheless, the impact of recent scholarship has meant that students of Africa now have to take into account dimensions of social life that are not ordinarily, or easily, accounted for in the social scientific disciplines as they have emerged in the Global North.

The Nature and Implications of Witchcraft

Invoking witchcraft in accounting for misfortune is a way of interpreting suffering as a form of harm deliberately inflicted on a victim by another person, usually someone in an intimate relationship with the victim, such as a relative, friend, or neighbor. Witchcraft is also said to be an illicit means for accumulating wealth and power at the expense of others, just as physical violence serves similar purposes in robbery and domination. Virtually every community knows someone named, usually quietly in circuits of gossip, as a "witch."

While anyone with a sufficient grudge might be capable of witchcraft, some people are deemed so addicted to evil, so hungry for death and misfortune, that they seem like a different kind of being: a Witch. In most African languages a distinction can be found between witchcraft as a form of action and the witch as a distinct kind of being—at once human, though with superhuman powers, and subhuman in having forfeited membership in the human community through their unspeakably evil desires. The distinction is analogous to the distinction we make when speaking of physical violence: that everyone is capable of acts of violence, while only a few are innately violent or habitual killers.

In his classic work on Azande notions of witchcraft, Evans-Pritchard introduced a distinction he claimed the Azande made between what he translated as "witchcraft," being an inherent capacity of certain persons, and "sorcery," meaning the manipulation of substances to cause harm, which in principle was open to anyone. For decades, the investigation of this distinction preoccupied anthropologists of Africa as they sought to determine whether or not the people they studied applied a similar distinction. While the distinction between witch and sorcerer can at times be useful, I would argue it is less useful than the simpler distinction, outlined above, between the witch as a kind of being and witchcraft as a form of doing. Most of what anthropologists have documented in terms of the witch/sorcerer distinction can be better understood by reference to being and doing.

At the heart of stories about witchcraft in Africa are accounts of how one otherwise ordinary person acquires the power to cause harm to another by extraordinary means. There are four basic answers to the question of where the power of witchcraft comes from. These include the following: innate capacity, usually inherited, sometimes, though not necessarily, with physical manifestations; special knowledge of substances and rituals learned from others (often, but not necessarily, kin); secret relations with invisible beings bestowing power (these days, as in early modern Europe, most usually the devil); and magical substances purchased or otherwise acquired from experts (which traditional healers and herbalists are often, despite protestations to the contrary, presumed to possess). When speaking of witchcraft, people frequently disagree over the source of the invisible evil power. The occult dimensions of any particular event or misfortune are always open for debate. The general possibility of such acts occurring, however, is rarely disputed. The existence of witches, similarly, is generally taken for granted.

Witchcraft signifies a disruption of relations among human persons. As mentioned at the outset, however, the term, with all its vernacular equivalents, refers to but one subset of interactions involving invisible forces shaping human life. When encountering African stories of witchcraft, then, outsiders should realize that such talk refers to relations among persons and invisible entities of a much more complex and dynamic nature than is typically presumed by Western modernist discourses, such as those underpinning the social sciences. These interactions involve relations as follows: among persons (including some with mysterious supernatural capacities); between persons and invisible beings resembling persons in possessing agency and intention (such as ancestors, spirits, deities, and demons—to name but a few); between persons and invisible agencies inherent in certain substances, images, objects, and texts (which can sometimes be aids in healing as well as harming); between persons and invisible entities resembling animals (including both real and imaginary creatures); and among all of the above. Life, for most people, is dependent on the successful management of all these relations, and more, in such a way as to create harmony and security. For most people, human life depends upon the good favor of invisible beings—ultimately, these days, the one known as God. It is not merely a matter of relations among humans, as social science would have it.

As with physical violence, certain categories of people are widely presumed more likely than others to use witchcraft to perpetrate malicious acts, either from necessity, due to an inability to use other means of causing harm, or from a desire—born usually from impotence—to keep one's malfeasance secret in order to avoid retaliation. Older women, for example, who tend to use physical violence infrequently, are commonly said to be more prone to the use of witchcraft; young men, on the other hand, are generally thought to incline more toward using physical rather than occult violence. Thus when communities punish accused witches, the pattern is generally one of young men beating older women. When confronted with such events, it is important for outsiders to realize that the people who see themselves as meting out justice perceive the targets of anti-witchcraft violence as immensely powerful and dangerous, not the innocent, vulnerable, and marginalized little old ladies that outsiders imagine them to be.

Jealousy, envy, hatred, anger, and the desire for revenge are the main emotions said to motivate the use of witchcraft; the same motives are said to apply to the use of physical violence. Just as anyone can perpetrate physical violence, anyone so motivated, and with the motive to acquire the means, can perpetrate witchcraft. In this sense, anyone can do witchcraft, though that does not automatically make him or her a "witch." Just as physical violence can at times be deemed legitimate, so can the use of occult force. Generally speaking, however, the term "witchcraft" and its cognates is reserved for the illicit uses of such power.

Living in a World with Witchcraft

Stories about witches, in the sense of a distinct kind of being devoted to evil, vary in their particulars from place to place and change over time. Some witches, for example, are said to be addicted to the consumption of human flesh; others are devoted to perverted forms of sex. Some are born; others are made. Despite the diversity of detail, however, such stories share certain common narrative patterns and their plausibility derives from common presuppositions about the nature of human experience, particularly in relation to possibilities of action in the realm of dreams. People who worry about witches tend not to draw a firm line between the realities of the waking world and terrors of the night. Events experienced in dreams are often thought to have real, physical, consequences on events unfolding in the light of day. That certain dreams can presage the future is largely taken for granted. And few deny the possibility of communication with invisible beings through the medium of dreams. When listening to stories of witches, then, it is important to investigate understandings of the ontological status of dreams.

Living in a world with witchcraft creates distinct problems of security and justice additional to those created by ordinary physical violence. These arise from the problem of knowing who is doing witchcraft and of what they are capable. Jealousy, the primary motive of witchcraft, is, by definition, an emotion predicated on secrecy—for once jealousy is openly acknowledged its power is diminished. The resulting emotion is something other than jealousy. Witchcraft, similarly, is action perpetrated in secret; were it performed in the open it would lose its power and be readily countermanded. The witch, moreover, will generally deny his or her true nature unless forced to confess. Furthermore, witchcraft is said to involve the deployment of invisible forces that are imperceptible to ordinary people.

People living in a world with witches, then, face an epistemological double bind: they can never know who does *not* have a motive, since jealousy will be hidden, nor do they know who has the means, or indeed, what those means are, since only the witch knows that. Furthermore, no one can say what a witch is *not* capable of. Social life in such contexts, therefore, must be premised upon a presumption of malice, which complicates the building of trust in social relations. Despite evident appearances of amity and comity in a community, the danger of witchcraft is always present and must be guarded against. Protection, then, is imperative. A great deal of time, energy, and money is devoted to the protection of individuals, families, and communities from occult assault. When protection fails, when harm is experienced, questions of who is to blame and what is to be done, in other words questions of justice, inevitably arise.

Protection against the dangers of witchcraft takes two basic forms: social and spiritual.

Since jealousy, resentment, and hatred can lead to illness, injury, death, or other misfortunes caused by witchcraft, efforts must be taken to manage interpersonal relations so as to minimize the potential for those feelings arising. Social conflicts, since they can spin out of control into multiple forms of metaphysical as well as physical violence, must be carefully managed and harmony sought at all costs. Managing such conflicts, then, places particular imperatives before authorities within families, kinship networks, communities, and nations.

However, since the means deployed in witchcraft are invisible, protection for human persons at risk ultimately depends on similarly invisible forces, particularly in the form of spiritual beings. Human security in a world of witches, then, depends on relations with invisible beings. Legions of spiritual entrepreneurs across the continent, of every variety of tradition and faith, promise mediation with invisible beings in pursuit of human security in a world of witches, making Africa the most dynamic continent for religious enthusiasm and nonmedical healing. Managing relations with invisible beings was historically, and continues to be for many people, a major role of social and political authorities. The ability of these authorities to perform these roles, however, has been compromised in many cases, if not completely undermined, by the histories of slavery, colonialism, capitalism, urbanization, and religious proselytizing on the continent.

Given the essential premise of stories of witchcraft, that misfortune is *harm* deliberately inflicted, remedying such misfortune requires identifying and neutralizing the powers of perpetrators. This sometimes involves open accusation, occasionally resulting in trials and punishment of accused witches. Persons so accused have sometimes been subjected to physical violence, even killed—mostly in eruptions of mob violence, typically in the absence of authorities capable of adjudicating accusations. It is important to stress, however, that anti-witchcraft violence is rare, an exception to the norm. By far the majority of cases in which people worry about witchcraft are resolved privately by means of healing and prayer, without open accusation. In tightly knit communities, gossip is frequently deployed against suspected witches, again without open accusations being made, in order to put suspects on notice that their activities are being monitored.

As with ordinary physical violence, not all uses of invisible force are necessarily deemed illegitimate. As it is used in African contexts, however, the word "witchcraft" is generally reserved exclusively to describe illegitimate uses of such force. While there is no ambiguity about witchcraft, the distinction between what constitutes the legitimate or illegitimate use of occult power is open to debate in relation to particular cases. Many women, for example, see love magic as a legitimate, if regrettable, means by which men might be constrained to ignore the blandishments of other women and perform their duties as husbands and fathers. Men, on the other hand, tend to view it as an illegitimate assault on their free will and agency, a pernicious form of witchcraft.

Specialists in the arts of countermanding witchcraft, generically referred to in English as "traditional healers," while generally recognized as capable of possessing extraordinary powers in the service of the good, must constantly struggle to distinguish themselves from their nefarious alter egos. All healing traditions enshrine rituals designed to accord their members an aura of legitimacy. Nonetheless, the suspicion that a healer might also have access to the powers of witchcraft remains widespread. For this reason, most healers are extremely sensitive about being labeled with the colonial-era denomination "witchdoctor." From the healer's standpoint, this term implies the doctor is a witch—a highly offensive suggestion to one who considers himself a doctor who works against witchcraft.

The most dynamic religious movements in Africa over the past century or so have devoted considerable attention to the imperatives of combatting the evils of witchcraft and promoting the health and well-being that is undermined by evil invisible forces. Pentecostalism, for example, offers the faithful the prospect of enlisting the power of the Holy Spirit in combatting the evil forces besetting everyday life, not the least of which is witchcraft. As with traditional healers, however, successful preachers also have to reckon with the fact that many attribute their healing powers to invisible evil forces; a claim to heal by channeling the power of the Holy Spirit, for example, might just as well be evidence of a diabolic pact with Satan.

For many people in contemporary Africa, the fear of witchcraft is compounded by a sense of spiritual insecurity, a feeling of danger, doubt, and fear arising from awareness of the need to manage relations with powerful invisible forces shaping life coupled with uncertainty over how to do so. The proliferation of interpretive authorities, such as healers and preachers, often compounds this sense of spiritual insecurity.

When protective measures fail, when harm is suffered and when the evil forces cannot be repelled by means of rituals or prayers, and especially when a putative victim of witchcraft dies, questions of justice inevitably arise. Given the amount of misfortune people suspect might be caused by witchcraft, the numbers of people openly accused, let alone punished, is small. When a person, or more usually a family, believes someone they care about has been killed by witchcraft a variety of avenues are available for seeking justice. Most commonly, justice is sought through the intercession of healers. Healers, typically, will claim to be able to determine the identity of the wrongdoer but will refuse to identify him or her, promising instead to use mystical means to right the wrong.

When anger boils over in a family or community over suspected witchcraft, the perpetrator might be named and perhaps directly confronted, shamed, or even punished. In the past, most African communities had established procedures for handling such accusations and resolving conflicts in ways designed to restore harmony to social relations. Sometimes these involved trials in which accused and accusers brought their stories before community assemblies. Sometimes poison ordeals were also involved, whereby invisible beings were called on to act through substances to identify and punish the witch. When they are made, accusations of witchcraft are extremely difficult to defuse, since proving the negative is necessary: *I am not a witch*. Accused witches, therefore, often find that their best hope is to confess while at the same time renouncing witchcraft, undergoing ritual purification, and begging forgiveness.

Witchcraft cases are heard in a wide variety of forums throughout the continent, sometimes within the formal legal system, often within so-called "traditional" or "customary" forums, and frequently within other nonlegal, or extralegal, forums such as a manager's office or a community leader's home. Where such forums are not available, the anger aroused by suspected witchcraft can lead to mob violence or acts of revenge punishing the putative perpetrators. Generally, however, people are wary of openly accusing others of witchcraft, not the least for the reason that witches are considered to be extremely dangerous and powerful people. Perhaps the most common form of revenge is the story surreptitiously shared of a particular person's perfidy. Within virtually every community, if you listen long enough, you will hear gossip about the people known to be witches. Usually, however, the fact that someone is known as a "witch" is not particular cause for concern—unless, and until, acts of witchcraft are suspected or detected.

During colonial times, authorities enacted laws preventing Africans from taking steps to control witchcraft. Most British colonies, for example, enacted ordinances modeled after the Witchcraft Act in force in England since 1736. In England, this law took issues of witchcraft away from consideration by courts. In the colonies, law forbade holding trials of witches (which had been a central part of chiefly authority in much of the continent), prevented subjecting them to ordeals, outlawed the making of accusations, prohibited the raising of money to cleanse communities of witchcraft, and outlawed divination in quest of knowledge about witchcraft (a central feature of all traditional healing).

Such laws, needless to say, were incompletely and unevenly applied. Nonetheless, they offered colonial authorities a convenient mechanism, when needed, for limiting the powers of chiefs and other rulers to exercise capital punishment (a right monopolized, of course, by the colonial governor) or banishment (which created problems of vagrancy). They also offered the authorities an instrument to use when popular leaders created social movements in the name of healing and cleansing witchcraft that might become a challenge to the colonial order.

The fact that colonial law, at least on paper, prevented Africans from addressing what they considered the most heinous of crimes compromised respect for that law, and not just in respect of witchcraft. In postcolonial times, most African states have grappled with reforming law to take cognizance of the fact that most of their citizens consider witchcraft a real and present danger, a serious crime. Reformers have argued that colonial era laws be changed to recognize the reality of witchcraft and serve in distinguishing true from false accusations. The record of legislative reform in this regard, however, is mixed. Even where statutes provide no basis for legal action, formal and informal courts still regularly deal with issues of witchcraft accusations, mostly resolving them without resort to violence.

In recent years, human rights activists and international organizations have become concerned about witchcraft accusations and anti-witchcraft activities in Africa. Since most of the people who find themselves accused of witchcraft are older and female, the humanitarian interest in accusations dovetails with concerns about gender equality and violence against women. While laudable in their desire to protect people from hardship and violence, interventions to protect accused witches in the name of human rights share the colonial-era attitude of foreigners, convinced that witchcraft is imaginary, seeking to undermine local judicial processes while offering no solutions to the problems of security and justice that communities worried about witchcraft see themselves as facing.

Conclusion

Most Africans, when asked about witchcraft, will profess some degree of ignorance. The standard answer to the question "what is witchcraft?" takes the form: witchcraft is real, but I don't know how it works. Even people who claim expertise in the subject, such as healers, will aver that only the witch really knows witchcraft. Judging from the tentative responses reported in the ethnographic literature over the past century or so, this state of "not-knowing" is not new.

Given this fact, it is somewhat surprising that the vast majority of outsiders writing about witchcraft in Africa have sought to delineate "systems of belief," sets of logically interrelated propositions—usually implied but not stated—to which members of specific cultural groups are said to accord credence, or which they presumably would were they to see the need to articulate them. Catalogues of such "beliefs" can be found for virtually every part of the continent.

Underpinning this effort has been a conviction that all human cultures possess coherent systems of belief, more or less reminiscent of the archetypal model in Western Christendom of the Nicene Creed, and that the work of the ethnographer is to uncover, document, and report on the key propositions of each particular system of belief. In recent decades, as the old ethnological project of documenting the cultures of the family of man fell out of fashion, the old impetus to document "beliefs" has lived on, most recently in the urge to discover indigenous notions that might assist (or, more usually, hinder in the form of "myths and misconceptions") the spread of AIDS awareness.

While definitive statements about the nature of witchcraft are scarce in Africa, stories about witches and witchcraft are plentiful. Rather than mine these stories for propositional "beliefs" constitutive of some putative philosophical system, I would urge students of witchcraft to examine the predicates that make such narratives plausible and the processes through which particular stories, in particular times and places, are adjudged true. From there, we must explore how the telling and retelling of such stories serve in the ordering of social relations, not only among the denizens of the world as we know it, but also within the complex dimensions of African power relations with entities both visible and invisible.

Suggested Readings

Ashforth, Adam. 2000. *Madumo, A Man Bewitched*. Chicago: University of Chicago Press.

Bongmba, Elias K. 2001. *African Witchcraft and Otherness: A Philosophical and Theological Critique of Intersubjective Relations*. Albany: State University of New York Press.

Comaroff, Jean, and John L. Comaroff. 1993. *Modernity and Its Malcontents: Ritual and Power in Postcolonial Africa*. Chicago: University of Chicago Press.

Douglas, Mary. 1970. *Witchcraft Confessions and Accusations*. London: Tavistock.

Evans-Pritchard, E. E. 1937. *Witchcraft Oracles and Magic among the Azande*. Oxford: Clarendon.

Geschiere, Peter. 1997. *The Modernity of Witchcraft: Politics and the Occult in Postcolonial Africa*. Translated by Janet Roitman and Peter Geschiere. Charlottesville: University of Virginia Press.

Marwick, M. G. 1965. *Sorcery in Its Social Setting: A Study of the Northern Rhodesian Cewa*. Manchester, UK: Manchester University Press.

Needham, Rodney. 1972. *Belief, Language, and Experience*. Chicago: University of Chicago Press.

Niehaus, Isak. A. 2001. *Witchcraft, Power, and Politics: Exploring the Occult in the South African Lowveld*. Cape Town: David Philip.

Ranger, Terence. 2007. "Scotland Yard in the Bush: Medicine Murders, Child Witches and the Construction of the Occult: A Literature Review." *Africa* 77 (2): 272–83.

Richards, Audrey I. 1935. "A Modern Movement of Witch-Finders." *Africa: Journal of the International African Institute* 8 (4): 448–61.

ter Haar, Gerry. 2009. "The Occult Does Not Exist: A Response to Terence Ranger/Response to Ter Haar and Ellis." *Africa* 79 (3): 399–415.

Turner, Victor W. 1964. "Witchcraft and Sorcery: Taxonomy versus Dynamics." *Africa: Journal of the International African Institute* 34 (4): 314–25.

West, Harry G. 2005. "Kupilikula: Governance and the Invisible Realm in Mozambique." Chicago: University of Chicago Press.

Wilson, Monica. 1951. "Witch Beliefs and Social Structure." *American Journal of Sociology* 56 (4): 307–13.

Yamba, C. Bawa. 1997. "Cosmologies in Turmoil: Witchfinding and the Aids in Ciawa, Zambia." *Africa* 67 (2): 201–23.

References

Ashforth, Adam. 2002. "An Epidemic of Witchcraft? The Implications of AIDS for the Post-Apartheid State." *African Studies* 61 (1): 121–42.

———. 2005. *Witchcraft, Violence, and Democracy in South Africa*. Chicago: University of Chicago Press.

Beere, Jonathan. 2009. *Doing and Being: An Interpretation of Aristotle's Metaphysics Theta*. Oxford: Oxford University Press.

Bongmba, Elias K. 2001. *African Witchcraft and Otherness: A Philosophical and Theological Critique of Intersubjective Relations*. Albany: State University of New York Press.

Bruner, Jerome. 1986. *Actual Minds, Possible Worlds*. Cambridge, MA: Harvard University Press.

Evans-Pritchard, E. E. 1937. *Witchcraft Oracles and Magic among the Azande*. Oxford: Clarendon.

Fields, Karen E. 1982. "Political Contingencies of Witchcraft in Colonial Central Africa: Culture and the State in Marxist Theory." *Canadian Journal of African Studies / Revue canadienne des études africaines* 16 (3): 567–93.

Geschiere, Peter. 1997. *The Modernity of Witchcraft: Politics and the Occult in Postcolonial Africa*. Translated by Janet Roitman and Peter Geschiere. Charlottesville: University Press of Virginia.

———. 2013. *Witchcraft, Intimacy, and Trust: Africa in Comparison*. Chicago: University of Chicago Press.

Igwe, L. 2004. "A Skeptical Look at African Witchcraft and Religion." *Skeptic* 11 (1): 72–75.

Kalu, Ogbu. 2008. *African Pentecostalism: An Introduction*. Oxford: Oxford University Press.

Lévy-Bruhl, Lucien. 1923. *Primitive Mentality*. Translated by L. A. Claire. London: George Allen and Unwin.

Marwick, M. G. 1982 [1964]. "Witchcraft as Social Strain Gauge." In *Witchcraft and Sorcery, Selected Readings: Second Edition*, edited by M. G. Marwick, 300–313. Harmondworth, UK: Penguin.

Meyer, Birgit. 1992. "'If You Are a Devil, You Are a Witch and, If You Are a Witch, You Are a Devil.' The Integration of 'Pagan' Ideas into the Conceptual Universe of Ewe Christians in Southeastern Ghana." *Journal of Religion in Africa* 22 (2): 98–132.

Ngong, David T. 2012. "Stifling the Imagination: A Critique of Anthropological and Religious Normalization of Witchcraft in Africa." *African and Asian Studies* 11 (1–2): 144–81.

Niehaus, Isak. A. 2001. *Witchcraft, Power, and Politics: Exploring the Occult in the South African Lowveld*. Cape Town: David Philip.

Contributors

ROGAIA MUSTAFA ABUSHARAF is professor of anthropology at Georgetown University's School of Foreign Service in Qatar. She is the author of *Wanderings: Sudanese Migrants and Exiles in North America* (2002) and *Transforming Displaced Women in Sudan: Politics and the Body in a Squatter Settlement* (2009), and the editor of *Female Circumcision: Multicultural Perspectives* (2006).

OMOLADE ADUNBI is associate professor of Afroamerican and American studies at the University of Michigan. His most recent book is *Oil Wealth and Insurgency in Nigeria* (2015). He is also the editor of *Behind the Mask: An Insight into Informal Repression in Nigeria* (2002).

ADAM ASHFORTH is professor of Afroamerican and American studies at the University of Michigan. His most recent book is *The Trials of Mrs. K.: Seeking Justice in a World with Witches* (2018). He is also the author of *Madumo: A Man Bewitched* (2000) and *Witchcraft, Violence, and Democracy in South Africa* (2005), among others.

SUZANNE PRESTON BLIER is the Allen Whitehill Clowes Chair of Fine Arts and of African and African American Studies at Harvard University. She is the author or editor of several books, including, most recently, *Art and Risk in Ancient Yoruba: Ife History, Power, and Identity, c. 1300* (2015) and *The Image of the Black in African and Asian Art*, with David Bindman and Henry Louis Gates, Jr. (2017).

GWYN CAMPBELL is Canada Research Chair in Indian Ocean World History at McGill University. He is the author of *An Economic History of Imperial*

Madagascar, 1750–1895: The Rise and Fall of an Island Empire (2005) and the editor of several volumes, including, most recently, *Early Exchange between Africa and the Wider Indian Ocean World* (2016).

BRENDA CHALFIN is professor of anthropology and director of the Center for African Studies at the University of Florida. She is the author of *Shea Butter Republic: State Power, Global Markets, and the Making of an Indigenous Commodity* (2004) and *Neoliberal Frontiers: An Ethnography of Sovereignty in West Africa* (2010).

KAMARI M. CLARKE is professor of anthropology at the University of California, Los Angeles. She is the author of *Mapping Yorùbá Networks: Power and Agency in the Making of Transnational Communities* (2004) and *Fictions of Justice: The International Criminal Court and the Challenge of Legal Pluralism in Sub-Saharan Africa* (2009). She is also the editor of several books, including *Transforming Ethnographic Knowledge* (2012), with Rebecca Hardin.

JEAN COMAROFF is the Alfred North Whitehead Professor of African and African American Studies and of Anthropology at Harvard University. She is the author or editor of several books, including, most recently, *The Truth about Crime: Sovereignty, Knowledge, Social Order* (2016) and the edited volume *The Politics of Custom: Chiefship, Capital, and the State in Contemporary Africa* (2018), both with John L. Comaroff.

JOHN L. COMAROFF is the Hugh K. Foster Professor of African and African American Studies and of Anthropology at Harvard University. He is the author or editor of several books, including, most recently, *The Truth about Crime: Sovereignty, Knowledge, Social Order* (2016) and the edited volume *The Politics of Custom: Chiefship, Capital, and the State in Contemporary Africa* (2018), both with Jean Comaroff.

GAURAV DESAI is professor of English at the University of Michigan. He is the author of *Subject to Colonialism: African Self-Fashioning and the Colonial Library* (2001) and *Commerce with the Universe: Africa, India, and the Afrasian Imagination* (2013). He is also the editor of *Postcolonialisms: An Anthology of Cultural Theory and Criticism* (2005), with Supriya Nair, and *The Virtual Transformation of the Public Sphere* (2013), among other works.

DEBORAH DURHAM is a deputy editor of *HAU: Journal of Ethnographic Theory*. She is the editor of several books, including *Generations and Globalization: Youth, Age, and Family in the New World Economy* (2006) and *Figuring the Future: Globalization and the Temporalities of Children and Youth*

(2008), both with Jennifer Cole, and *Elusive Adulthoods: The Anthropology of New Maturities* (2017), with Jacqueline Solway.

MATTHEW ENGELKE is professor of religion at Columbia University. He is the author of *A Problem of Presence: Beyond Scripture in an African Church* (2007), *God's Agents: Biblical Publicity in Contemporary England* (2013), and *How to Think Like an Anthropologist* (2018). He is also the editor of *The Limits of Meaning: Case Studies in the Anthropology of Christianity* (2006), with Matt Tomlinson.

MARC EPPRECHT is professor of Global Development Studies at Queen's University. Among his recent publications are *Heterosexual Africa? The History of an Idea from the Age of Exploration to the Age of AIDS* (2008), *Sexuality and Social Justice in Africa: Rethinking Homophobia and Forging Resistance* (2013), and *Welcome to Greater Edendale: Histories of Environment, Health, and Gender in an African City* (2016).

PETER GESCHIERE is professor emeritus of anthropology at the University of Amsterdam. He is the author of *The Modernity of Witchcraft: Politics and the Occult in Postcolonial Africa* (1997), *The Perils of Belonging: Autochthony, Citizenship, and Exclusion in Africa and Europe* (2009), and *Witchcraft, Intimacy, and Trust* (2013), among other works. He is also the editor of *Globalization and Modernity: Dialectics of Flow and Closure* (1999), with Birgit Meyer, and *Readings in Modernity in Africa* (2010), with Birgit Meyer and Peter Pels.

SIMON GIKANDI is the Robert Schirmer Professor of English at Princeton University. His books include *Maps of Englishness: Writing Identity in the Culture of Colonialism* (1996), *Ngũgĩ wa Thiong'o* (2009), and *Slavery and the Culture of Taste* (2011), as well as the edited collections *The Columbia Guide to East African Literature in English Since 1945* (2007), with Evan Mwangi, and *The Novel in Africa and the Caribbean Since 1950* (2016).

JANE I. GUYER is professor emerita of anthropology at the Johns Hopkins University. She is the coeditor of *Money Struggles and City Life: Devaluation in Ibadan and Other Urban Centers in Southern Nigeria, 1986–1996* (2002), and the author of *Marginal Gains: Monetary Transactions in Atlantic Africa* (2004) and *Legacies, Logics, Logistics: Essays in the Anthropology of the Platform Economy* (2016).

TSITSI JAJI is associate professor of English at Duke University. She is the author of *Africa in Stereo: Modernism, Music, and Pan-African Solidar-*

ity (2014). She has also published a poetry collection entitled *Beating the Graves* (2016) and a chapbook entitled *Carnaval* (2014).

PATRICK MANNING is the Andrew W. Mellon Professor of World History, Emeritus, at the University of Pittsburgh, where he founded the World History Center. Among his many publications, see, recently, *The African Diaspora: A History through Culture* (2009), *Big Data in History* (2013), and *Social Movements and World-System Transformations* (2016), coedited with Jackie Smith, Michael Goodhart, and John Markoff.

ADELINE MASQUELIER is professor of anthropology at Tulane University. She is the author of *Prayer Has Spoiled Everything: Possession, Power, and Identity in an Islamic Town of Niger* (2001), *Women and Islamic Revival in a West African Town* (2009), and *Fada: Boredom and Belonging in Niger* (forthcoming). She is also the editor of *Dirt, Undress, and Difference: Critical Perspectives on the Body's Surface* (2005) and *Muslim Youth and the 9/11 Generation* (2016), with Benjamin F. Soares.

ELISABETH MCMAHON is associate professor of history at Tulane University. She is the author of *Slavery and Emancipation in Islamic East Africa: From Honor to Respectability* (2013).

STEPHANIE NEWELL is professor of English at Yale University and professor extraordinaire in the English Department at Stellenbosch University. She is the author of *Literary Culture in Colonial Ghana* (2002), *West African Literatures: Ways of Reading* (2006), and *The Power to Name: A History of Anonymity in Colonial West Africa* (2013), among other books.

PAUL-AARONS NGOMO is lecturer of politics at New York University. He is the author of *La Théorie politique de Frantz Fanon* (2018).

FRANCIS B. NYAMNJOH is professor of anthropology at the University of Cape Town. His most recent publications are *Modernising Traditions and Traditionalising Modernity in Africa: Chieftaincy and Democracy in Cameroon and Botswana* (2015), *#Rhodes Must Fall: Nibbling at Resilient Colonialism in South Africa* (2016), and *Drinking from the Cosmic Gourd: How Amos Tutuola Can Change Our Minds* (2017). He is also the author of several works of fiction.

DEREK R. PETERSON is professor of history and African studies at the University of Michigan. He is the author of *Creative Writing: Translation,*

Bookkeeping, and the Work of Imagination in Colonial Kenya (2004) and *Ethnic Patriotism and the East African Revival: A History of Dissent* (2012), and editor of *Abolitionism and Imperialism in Britain, Africa, and the Atlantic* (2011).

JEMIMA PIERRE is associate professor of African American studies and anthropology at the University of California, Los Angeles. She is the author of *The Predicament of Blackness: Postcolonial Ghana and the Politics of Race* (2012) and the coeditor of the journal *African Diaspora*.

MAANO RAMUTSINDELA is professor of environmental and geographical science at the University of Cape Town. He is the author of *Transfrontier Conservation in Africa: At the Confluence of Capital, Politics, and Nature* (2007), *Sponsoring Nature: Environmental Philanthropy for Conservation* (2011), with Marja Spierenburg and Harry Wels, and *Land Reform in South Africa: Uneven Transformation* with Brent McCusker and William G. Moseley (2016). He is also the editor of *Cartographies of Nature: How Nature Conservation Animates Borders* (2014).

JOSEPH SLAUGHTER is associate professor of English and comparative literature at Columbia University. He is the author of *Human Rights, Inc.: The World Novel, Narrative Form, and International Law* (2007) and the editor of *The Global South Atlantic* (2017), with Kerry Bystrom.

LEONARD WANTCHEKON is professor of politics at Princeton University. He is the author of *Rêver à Contre-Courant: Autobiographie* (2012) and the editor of *New Advances in Experimental Research on Corruption* (2012), with Danila Serra.

JENNIFER WENZEL is associate professor of English and comparative literature and Middle Eastern, South Asian, and African studies at Columbia University. She is the author of *Bulletproof: Afterlives of Anticolonial Prophecy in South Africa and Beyond* (2009) and the editor of *Fueling Culture: 101 Words for Energy and Environment* (2017), with Imre Szeman and Patricia Yaeger.

LUISE WHITE is professor of history at the University of Florida. She is the author of *Speaking with Vampires: Rumor and History in Colonial Africa* (2000), *The Assassination of Herbert Chitepo: Texts and Politics in Zimbabwe* (2003), and *Unpopular Sovereignty: Rhodesian Independence and African Decolonization* (2015), and editor of *The State of Sovereignty: Territories, Laws, Populations* (2008), with Douglas Howland, among other works.

SUSAN REYNOLDS WHYTE is professor of anthropology at the University of Copenhagen. She is the author of *Questioning Misfortune: The Pragmatics of Uncertainty in Eastern Uganda* (1997) and *Social Lives of Medicines* (2002), with Sjaak van der Geest and Anita Hardon, and the editor of *Disability in Local and Global Worlds* (2007), with Benedicte Ingstad, and *Second Chances: Surviving AIDS in Uganda* (2014).

Acknowledgments

The idea of this book first emerged almost three decades ago when one of us (Gaurav Desai) was in graduate school at Duke University working on his doctoral dissertation under the supervision of Valentin Mudimbe. The University of Chicago Press had recently published *Critical Terms for Literary Study* edited by Frank Lentricchia and Thomas McLaughlin, a book that was rapidly gaining deserved attention and praise. It was time to try something similar for the study of Africa, we thought, and yet there was a dissertation to be written and other books and projects to attend to. Discussing the possibility and desirability of such a project over the years, neither Valentin nor Gaurav could give it the time and attention that it deserved. Until around 2015. Valentin was getting ready to retire and Gaurav had finished working on his second monograph. This seemed like an opportune time. In the meantime, over the years, as a faculty member at Tulane University, Gaurav had also collaborated on a number of projects related to Africa with Adeline Masquelier and had very much enjoyed those collaborations. We invited Adeline to join our editorial team and to lend her expertise and critical acumen to our project.

The volume has taken several years to develop. After his retirement, with a need to attend to personal matters, Valentin had to withdraw from the project. We thank him, nevertheless, for his early support and for the many years of consultation on it. We are particularly grateful as well to Priya Nelson, our editor at the press, and to Ellen Kladky, Dylan Montanari, Susan Karani, and Kristen Raddatz for shepherding the process through. We thank as well our contributors for their generosity and for the patience and good humor with which they have handled the many challenges of an edited volume with multiple authors. Thanks are due as well to the many students at Tulane University who gave us feedback on the manuscript at various stages. Finally, thanks to David Robertson for his help in preparing the index and to the College of Literature, Science, and the Arts at the University of Michigan for research funds dedicated to the project.

Index

AFRICAN STUDIES

For far too long, the Western world viewed Africa as unmappable terrain—a repository for outsiders' wildest imaginings. This problematic notion has had lingering effects not only on popular impressions of the region but also on the development of the academic study of Africa. *Critical Terms for the Study of Africa* considers the legacies that have shaped our understanding of the continent and its place within the conceptual grammar of contemporary world affairs.

Written by a distinguished group of scholars, the essays compiled in this volume take stock of African studies today and look toward a future beyond its fraught intellectual and political past. Each essay discusses one of our most critical terms for talking about Africa, exploring the trajectory of its development while pushing its boundaries. Editors Gaurav Desai and Adeline Masquelier balance the choice of twenty-five terms between the expected and the unexpected, calling for nothing short of a new mapping of the scholarly field. The result is an essential reference that will challenge assumptions, stimulate lively debate, and make the past, present, and future of African studies accessible to students and teachers alike.

CONTRIBUTORS: ROGAIA MUSTAFA ABUSHARAF, OMOLADE ADUNBI, ADAM ASHFORTH, SUZANNE PRESTON BLIER, GWYN CAMPBELL, BRENDA CHALFIN, KAMARI M. CLARKE, JEAN COMAROFF, JOHN L. COMAROFF, DEBORAH DURHAM, MATTHEW ENGELKE, MARC EPPRECHT, PETER GESCHIERE, SIMON GIKANDI, JANE GUYER, TSITSI JAJI, ELISABETH MCMAHON, PATRICK MANNING, STEPHANIE NEWELL, PAUL-AARONS NGOMO, FRANCIS B. NYAMNJOH, DEREK R. PETERSON, JEMIMA PIERRE, MAANO RAMUTSINDELA, JOSEPH SLAUGHTER, LEONARD WANTCHEKON, JENNIFER WENZEL, LUISE WHITE, SUSAN REYNOLDS WHYTE

"*Critical Terms for African Studies* will serve as a sourcebook for connecting contemporary African studies not only to the classical canon but also to the specific regional, global, and colonial history that forged the concept of Africa. This book will be both a crucial teaching tool in undergraduate and graduate classes and as required reading for Africanist scholars. The essays it contains deftly master a readable tone that makes a complex history and set of theoretical ideas accessible without dumbing down the material or making it redundant to those who are already well versed in the field. Perhaps most remarkable is that despite the great diversity of authors, perspectives, and disciplines present in this book, there remains an underlying unity of vision connecting the threads—a vision with the capacity to breathe new life into the domain of Africanist scholarship."

SASHA NEWELL, UNIVERSITÉ LIBRE DE BRUXELLES

GAURAV DESAI is professor of English at the University of Michigan.
ADELINE MASQUELIER is professor of anthropology at Tulane University.

ISBN-13: 978-0-226-54897-5
ISBN-10: 0-226-54897-X

CRITICAL TERMS

THE UNIVERSITY OF CHICAGO PRESS
www.press.uchicago.edu